Storm Warning

How to photograph the Colorado
Rocky Mountain Winter

Steven W. Krull

ISBN-13: 979-8-9860766-2-1

Cover design by: Steven W. Krull
Printed in the United States of America

Introduction

Warm summer months are a beautiful time for photography in the Colorado Rocky Mountains with cool mornings, warm days and long pleasant evenings perfect for long days of shooting. The columbine and mountain bluebell are blooming and trees are filled with the joyful sound of bird song. Lakes, rivers and reservoirs are alive with activity and vibrant colors with which to test the limits of our camera sensors.

However the Rocky Mountain summer is as short as it is beautiful and soon the nights are getting colder and aspen trees take on their mantle of autumn gold. Photographers flock to the mountains to capture images of the beautiful colors before the first snows of winter blow in to wipe the slate clean.

There was once a time when the bitter cold of winter marked the end of my outdoor activities and my camera went into it's bag for the winter, along with my hiking boots and camping equipment. The trails I so love lay frozen under the snow while the treadmill and stair machine occupied my days until the warm rays of sunshine returned in the spring.

But there was a change afoot, almost imperceptible at first as I slowly became intrigued with the quiet and solitude of the long cold Rocky Mountain winter. My photography began to evolve from favoring the colorful action of summer to an appreciation of a more bleak minimalist winter style. I became drawn to leafless aspen tree stands, drifting snow, angry skies and the beauty and despair of winter wildlife.

This book is about appreciating the stark beauty of the mountain landscape and desperate survival of wildlife in the unforgiving cold and snow of the Rocky Mountain landscape. In this book you will learn how to embrace the cold as you learn techniques for enduring and capturing such unforgiving beauty.

Contents

About the Author

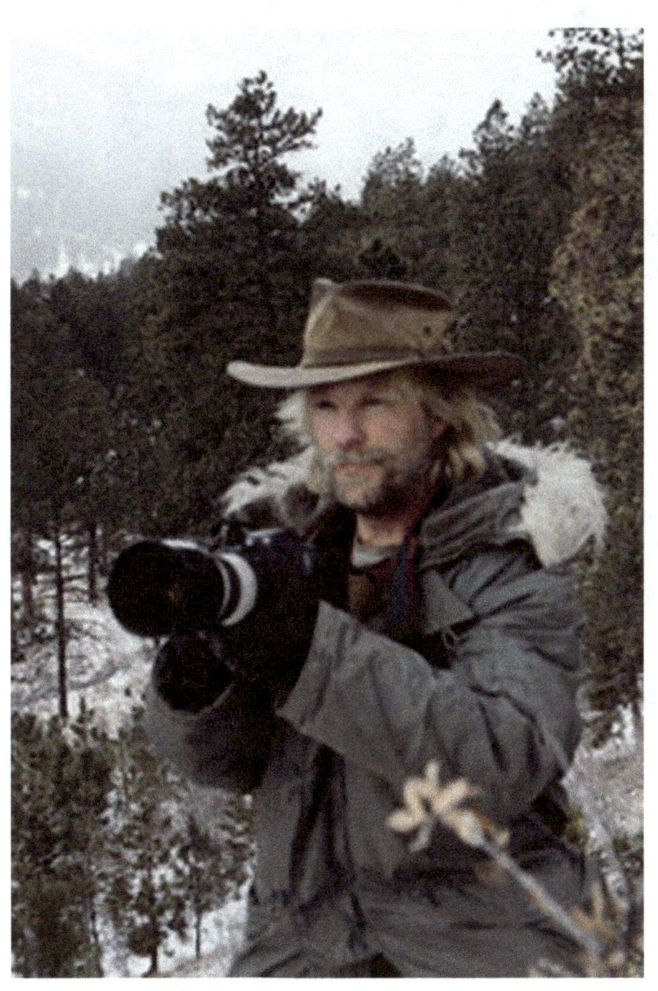

Mr. Krull is a widely published sports and wildlife photographer specializing in imagery captured in the rugged Rocky Mountains of Colorado.

More of his work can be found on his official website at:

www.swkrullimaging.com

Steven W. Krull

A Change in Perspective

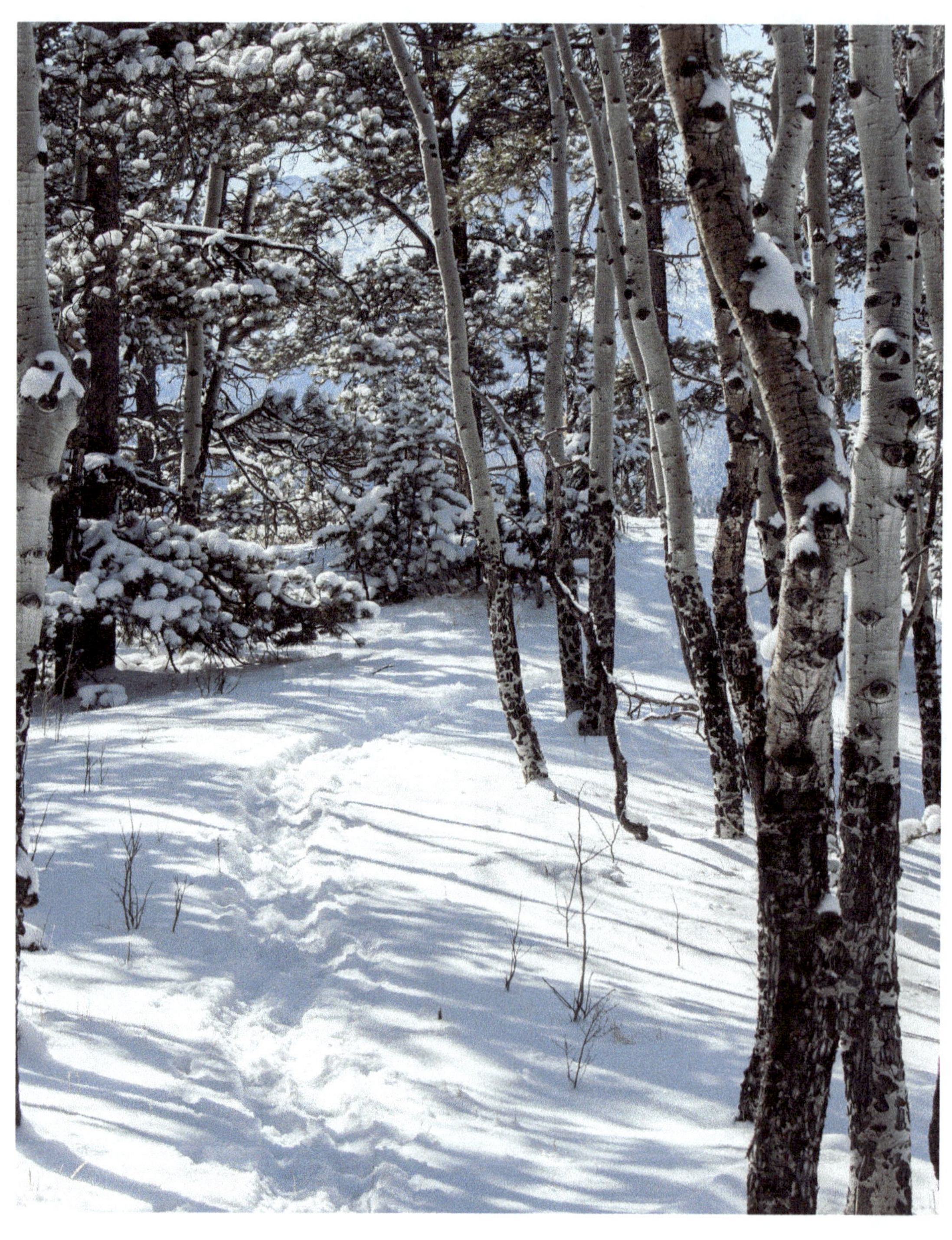

This saga actually begins in Arizona at the first inaugural Bill Rogers Phoenix Marathon, which was also my own personal first marathon. Months of grueling road running had gone into this effort for my two friends and I who were not at all confident that we could complete such a daunting physical challenge. Despite our misgivings, we made the long drive from Denver to Arizona to run the January race in the pleasant snow free climate of the desert southwest.

Our race strategy was simple, start out slow and push the wall back as far as possible. Much to my surprise the wall never reared it's ugly head and we finished the marathon with relatively little pain. In fact the race went so well that on the return trip through the Grand Canyon and Utah's most magnificent scenic locations including Canyonlands and Natural Bridges, a preposterous plan was hatched. Instead of taking the rest of the winter off from running, the training would continue unabated and one of America's most famous trail races would be our next conquest. The **Leadville 100 Race Across the Sky** is a one hundred mile trail run over three mountain passes at an average elevation over 10,000 feet.

However a winter of treadmill and stair machine workouts with an occasional road run stood before the spring melt, and access to Colorado's rugged mountain trails would once again become possible. And so it continued for the next half a decade, glorious summers of trail running followed by long cold boring winters on the machines of gyms and health clubs, intermixed with long weekend runs on the hard frozen pavement of city streets.

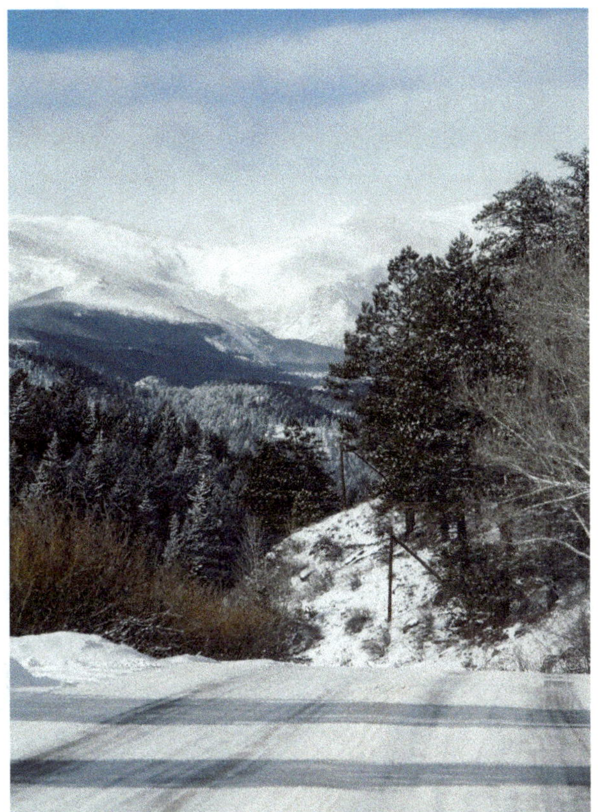

Occasionally when the weather cooperated, long weekend runs could be accomplished in the beautiful scenery of a Front Range scenic byway. This magnificent vista (left) is visible just down from Evergreen Lake as Upper Bear Creek Road winds it's way toward 14,265 foot Mount Evans, perhaps soon to be renamed Mount Blue Sky..

On this particular day there was a tremendous wind blowing over the mountain from the west, creating this stunning scene including snow blowing over the top of the mountain.

I was fortunate to live near some trails that remained mostly snow free during one particular fateful winter, in an open space park in Douglas County that I was using for a training course. That is until the famous Thanksgiving blizzard buried the entire Denver area under feet of snow. The snow began falling on Thanksgiving Day as the biggest snowflakes I had ever seen began drifting lazily down from the sky. As darkness closed in the beautiful flakes became tiny wind driven pellets that buried streets under a foot of white powder by bedtime. In the morning I awoke to at least two feet of snow with drifts much deeper than that in places.

My training course was buried and would remain so for at least a couple of weeks before the warm Colorado sun could once again clear the trails. My workouts were grudgingly moved to local streets for a few weeks while I eagerly waited for the snow to melt and the mud to dry. November passed and December came before I was able to return to the dirt. And then it happened again, a massive winter storm once again buried the Denver area under several more feet of snow. I was fully aware that the days were now too cold for any significant melting, and with a bitter feeling inside I had to accept that my trails weren't going to be accessible until spring.

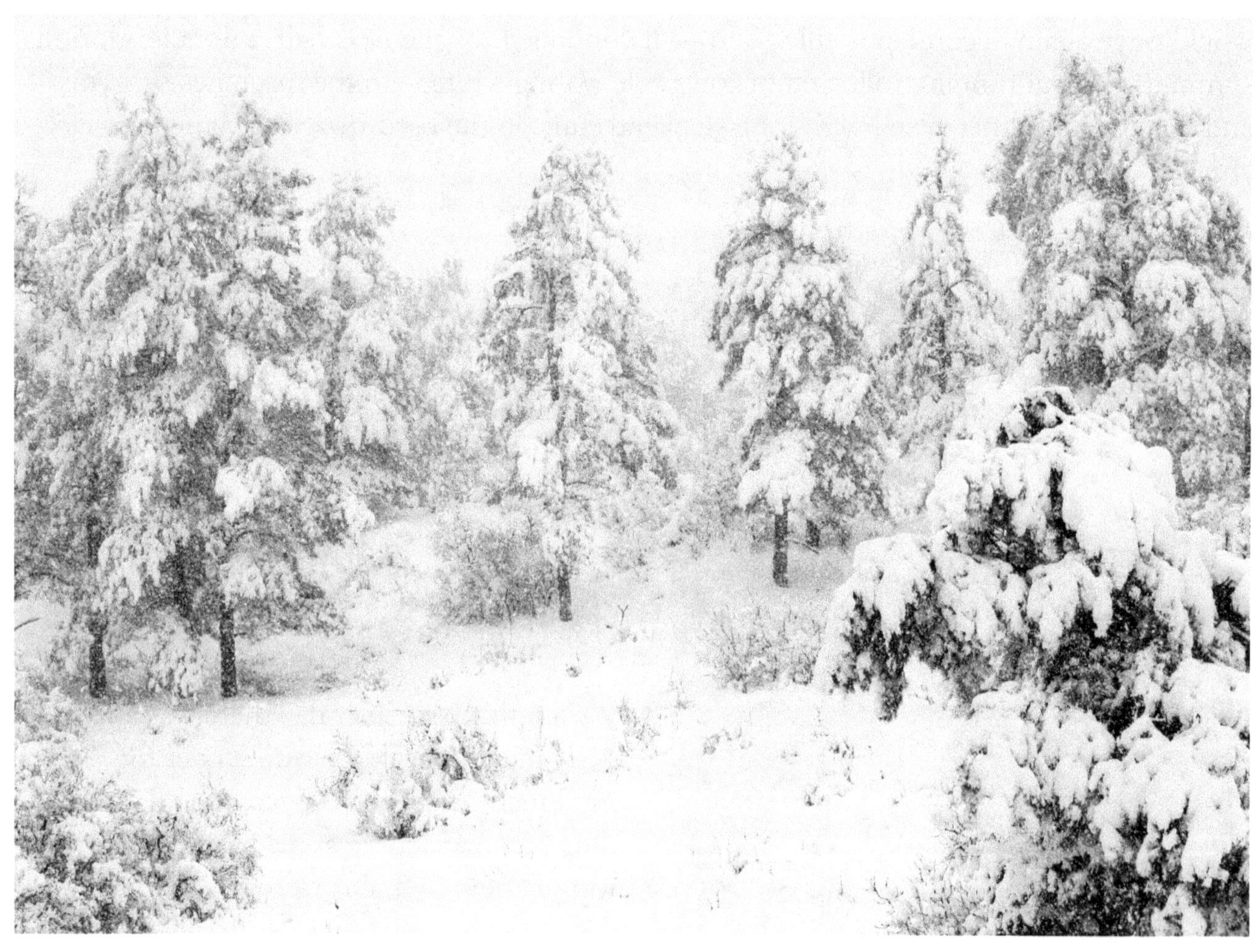

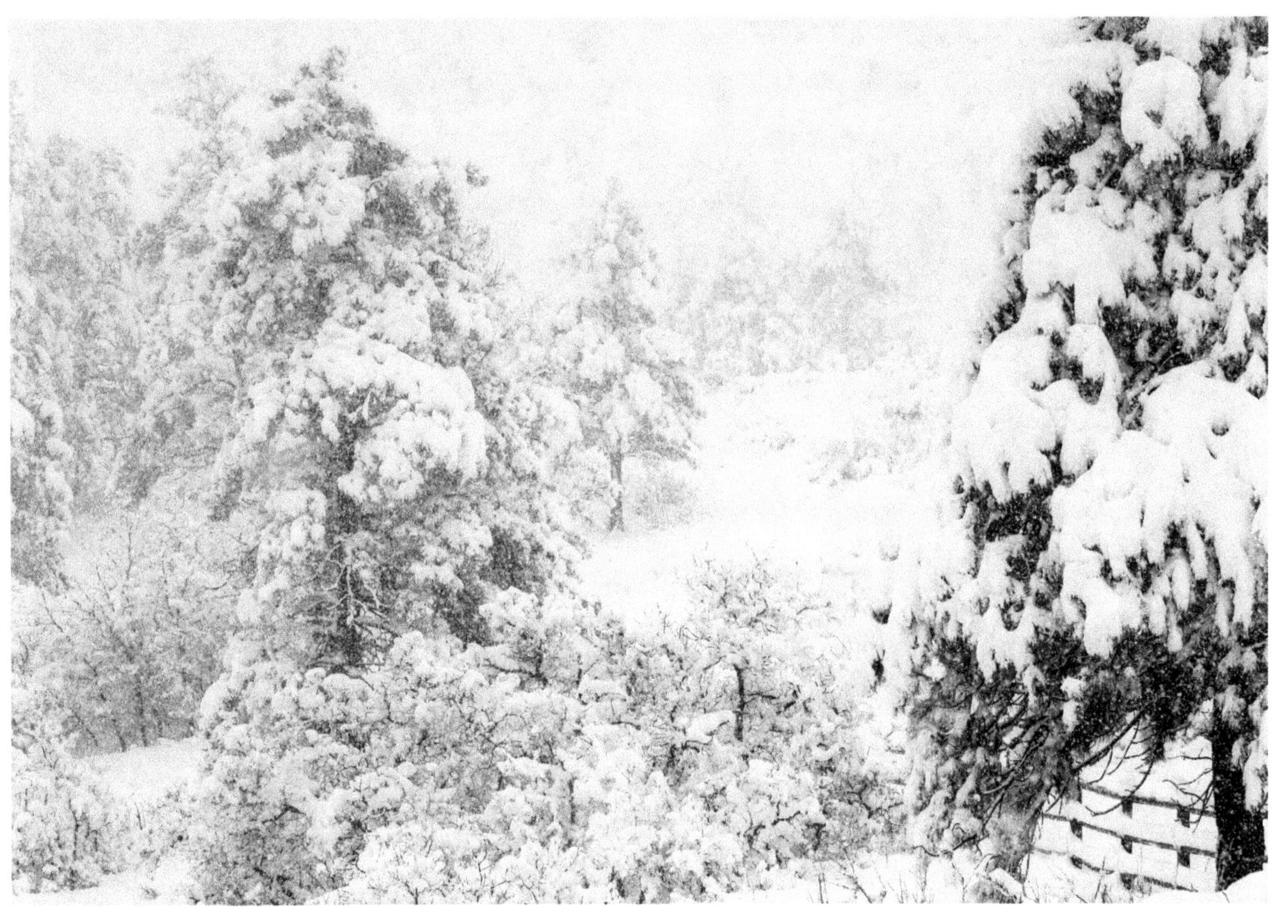

However I had been hearing about a new trend in trail running circles, especially among those fortunate enough to dwell in or near the mountains. Snowshoeing was growing in popularity and I saw an ad that Christy's Sports even had some available to rent. So the wife and I got in the truck and headed to the store to see if we could get our hands on some shoes for a few days, especially while the powder was still fresh. After a short bit of practice we were both off and running. I could not believe how much fun it was to swoosh through the deep snow in the solitude of the cold winter air.

Eventually the rental shoes had to be returned but I was hooked. Following a little online research I decided upon a pair of Red Feather Blackhawk back country shoes, manufactured by a Colorado company based in Leadville. The Blackhawks were a fairly large model equipped with both front and rear claws, perfect for deep snow on mountain trails. Soon though, my training course was hard packed and the big shoes had become unwieldy and slow. Now I understood the reason for the much smaller racing shoe models and I was soon the proud owner of a pair of Red Feather Osprey racing shoes which carried me over the snow for the rest of the winter until March, when the remnants of that massive December blizzard were finally vanquished by the warm rays of the Colorado springtime sun.

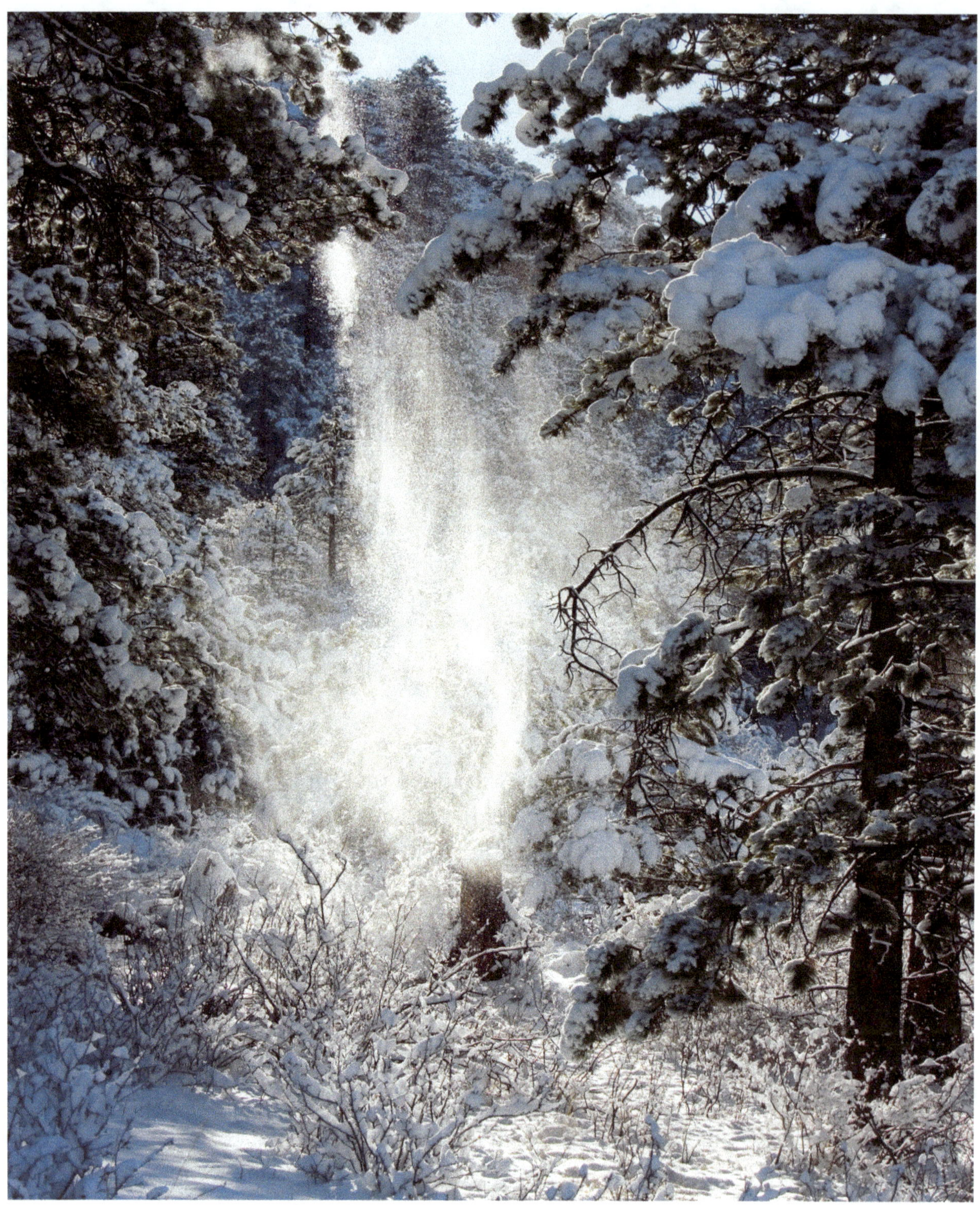

That year for the first time in my life, the advent of spring and the melting snow was met with sadness. My perspective on the seasons had made a complete 180, winter had become my friend and the heat and crowds of summer had become a time of year to be endured rather than reveled.

Accompanying me on my nascent snowy incursions into the mountain winter landscape was an old film camera, a Minolta X-700 which I had purchased in 1984 when I first arrived in Colorado. The X-700 was a wonderful manual focus 35mm film camera with some of the very first auto exposure capabilities, sporting full auto program mode, aperture priority, shutter priority and of course manual mode for advanced users. The mountains were so beautiful in the winter that I knew it was imperative to have a record of my treks, and my X-700 with it's f/1.4 nifty fifty became a regular staple in my pack. Regrettably however, I only snapped a few pictures in those days and the prints are now buried in the archives in my basement. Locating them would be a massive project requiring weeks of digging, which I am far too lazy to undertake.

Mostly though, I was content to awake early in the morning to arrive at my trailhead with my dog for a run before work on the packed trails of the wildlife reserve a few blocks from my home. My dog Bear loved the morning excursions and I did my best to make sure he was comfortable on the trails. At first we had a lot of trouble with ice building up in his foot pads and I worried that the bright sun reflecting off the snow would damage his eyes. Just as with a human, the solution was of course sunglasses and boots.

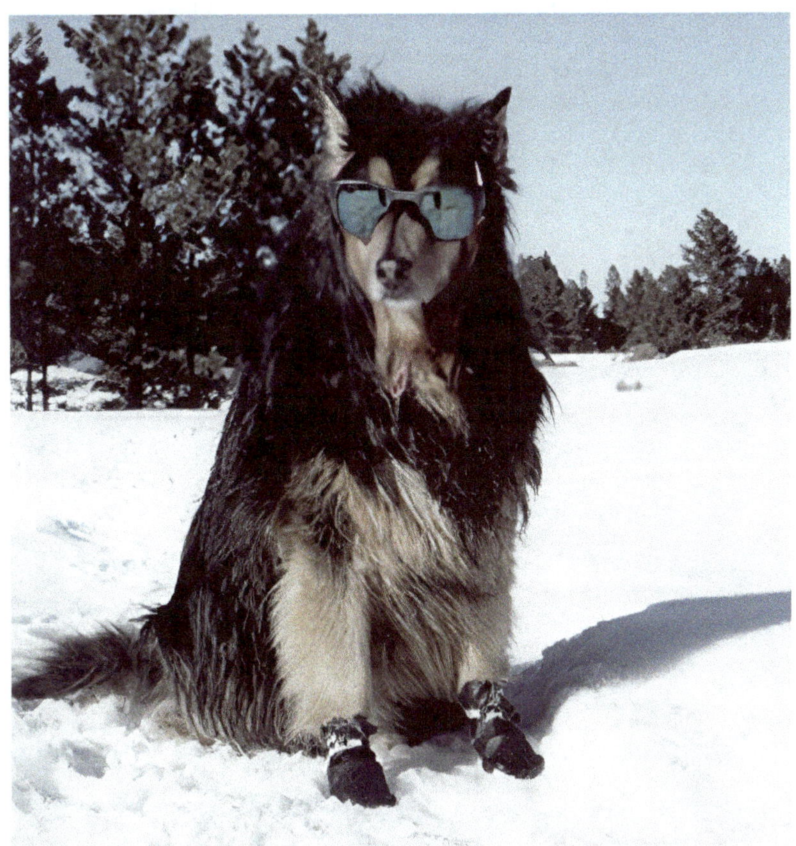

He wasn't too sure what to think of his new equipment the first time we tried it, but once he understood the obvious benefits he was all in. Here he is sporting his snow boots and special doggy sunglasses.

All I needed for myself on the packed trails was a pair of gators and a waterproof suit to keep the fresh powder out of my running shoes and off the back of my neck. It didn't take long to figure out that running in snowshoes will flip snow all the way over the top of your head. Without a good suit a runner will soon find himself quite soaked and very cold!

I loved photographing my treks but film and processing was time consuming and expensive, shooting a bunch of pictures everyday was just not feasible in those days. However with the first digital cameras starting to hit the market, the age of film photography was rapidly coming to an end. Digital technology of course completely sidesteps the film and processing obstacle to everyday shooting. These days it costs nothing to shoot hundreds of images in a session, and the dark room consists of a desk and a computer with all kinds of amazing software available to process and edit images.

In 2002 Canon brought out their first professional digital camera, the EOS-1D. It was a 4.5 megapixel Digital Single Lens Reflex (DSLR) model capable of meeting the performance needs of professional sports and nature photographers, and I had to have one. A quick trip to the photo store and I had joined the digital photography revolution.

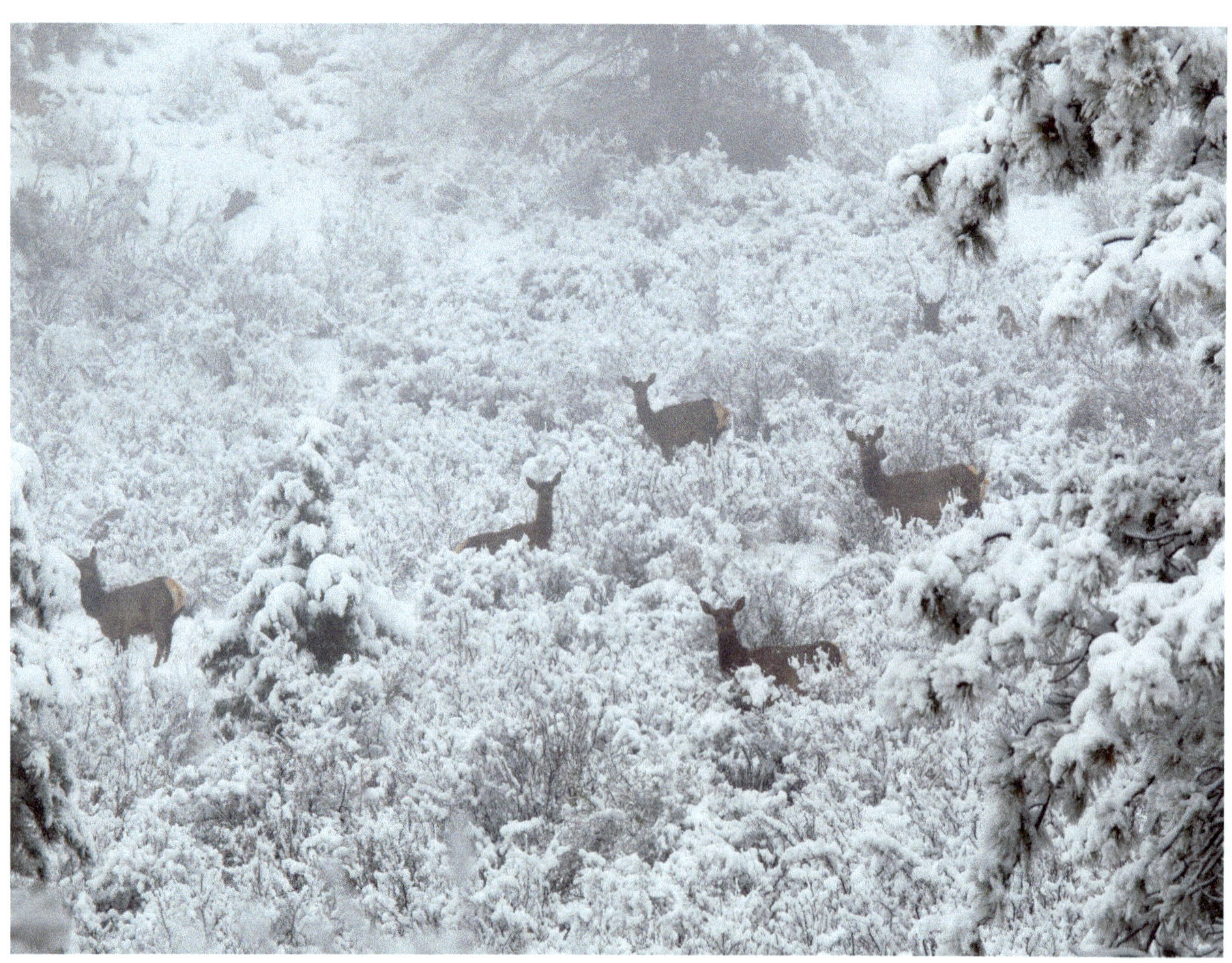

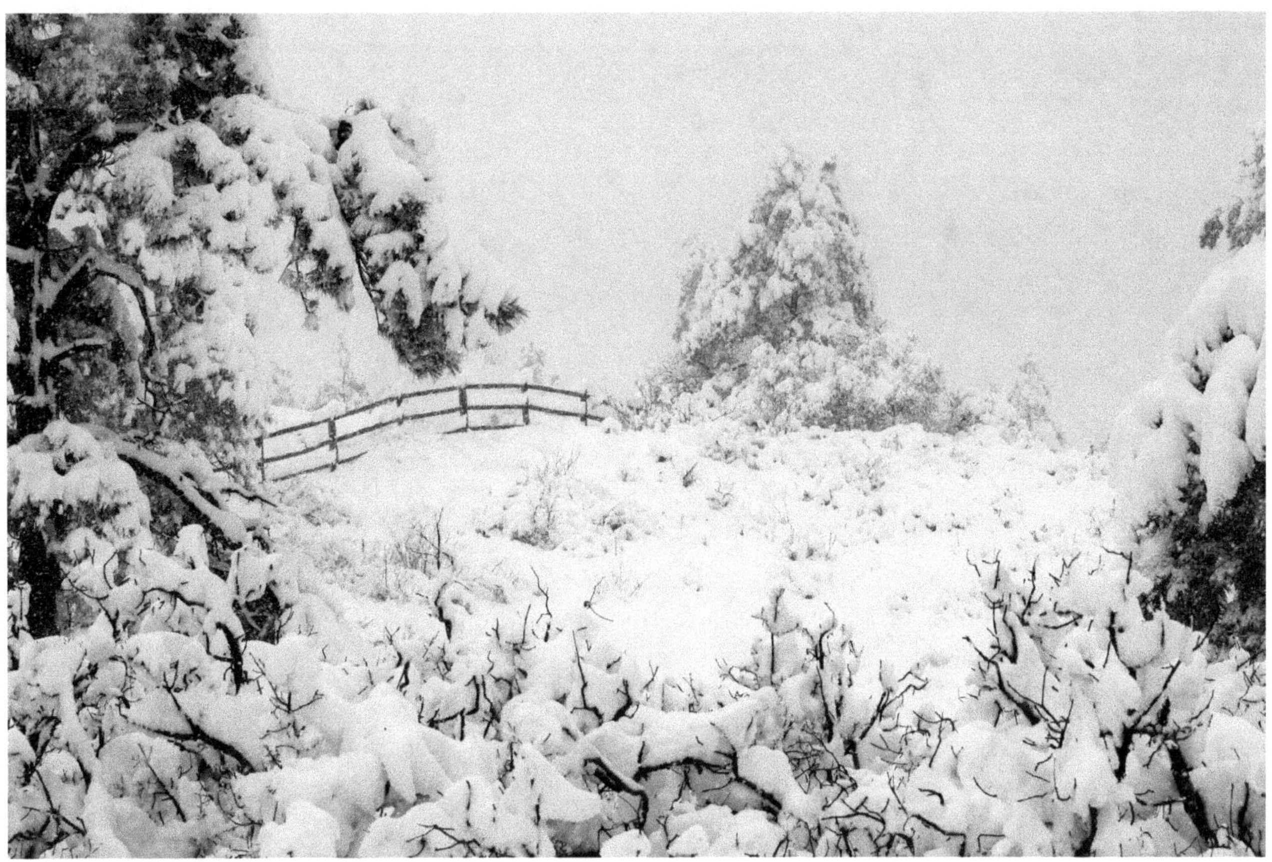

The expense issue for film and processing was resolved by the new digital paradigm but carrying a camera everyday on long hikes in winter conditions brought with it a whole new set of problems. Wet snow soaking my shiny new camera didn't seem like a good idea, so on the best days for dramatic captures I was forced to leave the camera at home. My particular camera was supposed to be weather sealed but I wasn't confident enough to risk my investment on snowy days. I was soon in the market for a camera rain cover and settled on a professional grade Aquatech Rain Shield. The cover came with a special eyepiece designed to provide an impenetrable seal against the weather while keeping the cover in place for unobstructed use of the viewfinder. A neoprene strap in the front provided a tight cover over a professional lens hood and a clear window in the back allowed viewing of the LCD playback screen after each shot.

Extensive weather gear was required when cameras were more vulnerable to moisture, often limiting access to buttons and dials. Now of course, modern weather sealing on professional digital cameras makes weather less of an issue. With greater confidence I can now just throw on a simple cover that can be moved out of the way while I'm shooting and quickly pulled back over the body when I'm done. I always carry an inexpensive Ruggard brand rain cover that I just throw on when I encounter heavy snow. This uncomplicated model can quickly be pulled over camera and lens without the requirement of special eyepieces and elaborate fasteners.

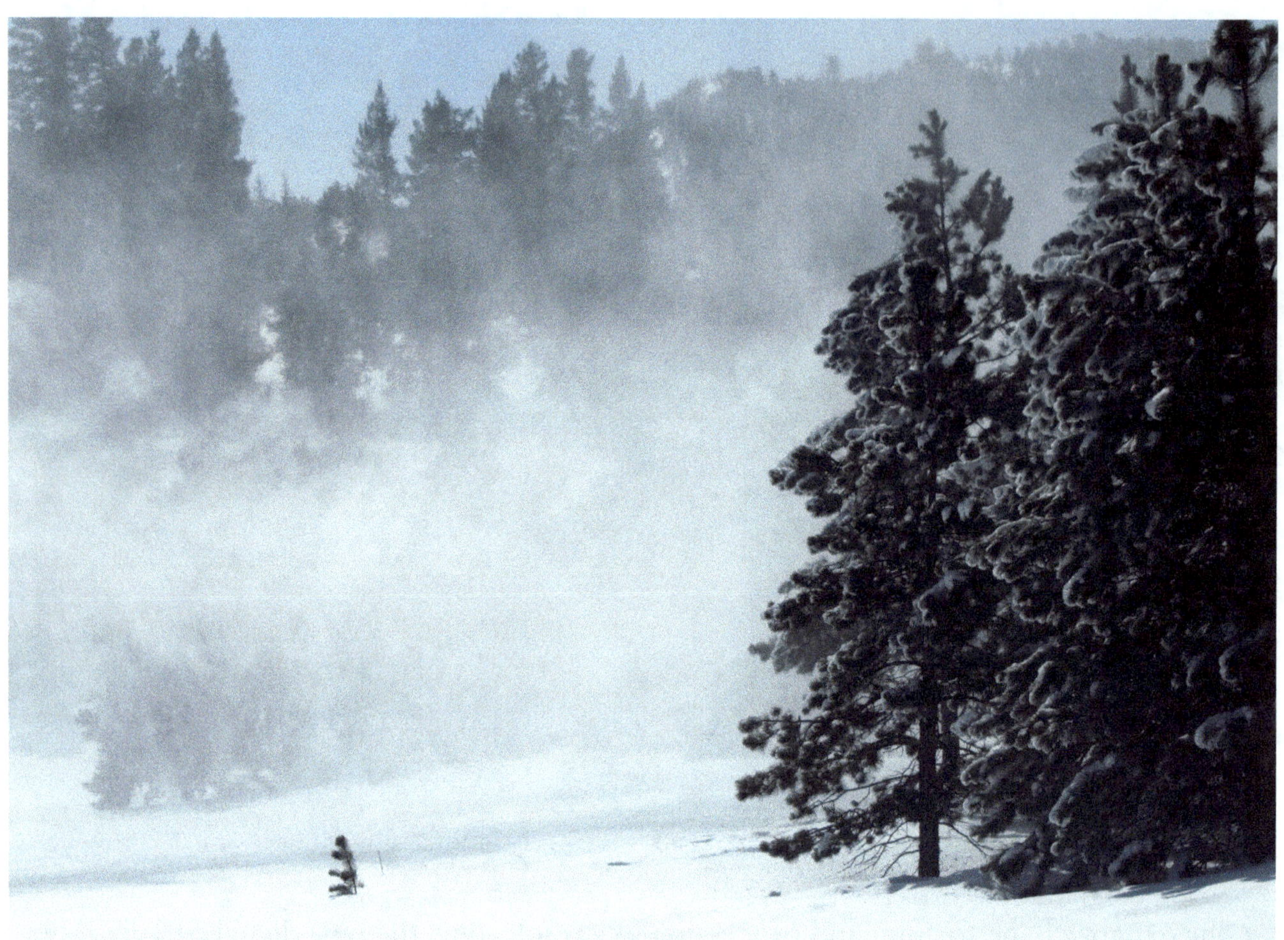

Photographing scenes covered in a mantle of white is not an easy task. Bright white snow is extremely unfriendly to camera meters, and fiddling with exposure settings in a blinding snowstorm is nearly impossible. My approach is to analyze weather and lighting conditions before venturing out into the snow so as to make an educated guess at the proper exposure prior to putting the weather cover on the camera. Camera controls are harder to access once the cover is properly fastened and cold weather gloves don't help either.

Raw format tolerates fairly large exposure adjustments in post processing so I rarely switch the camera to anything but the raw quality mode setting. In stormy weather I can then shoot the entire session without uncovering the camera for exposure adjustments that can easily be accomplished in post processing.

The Deer Herd

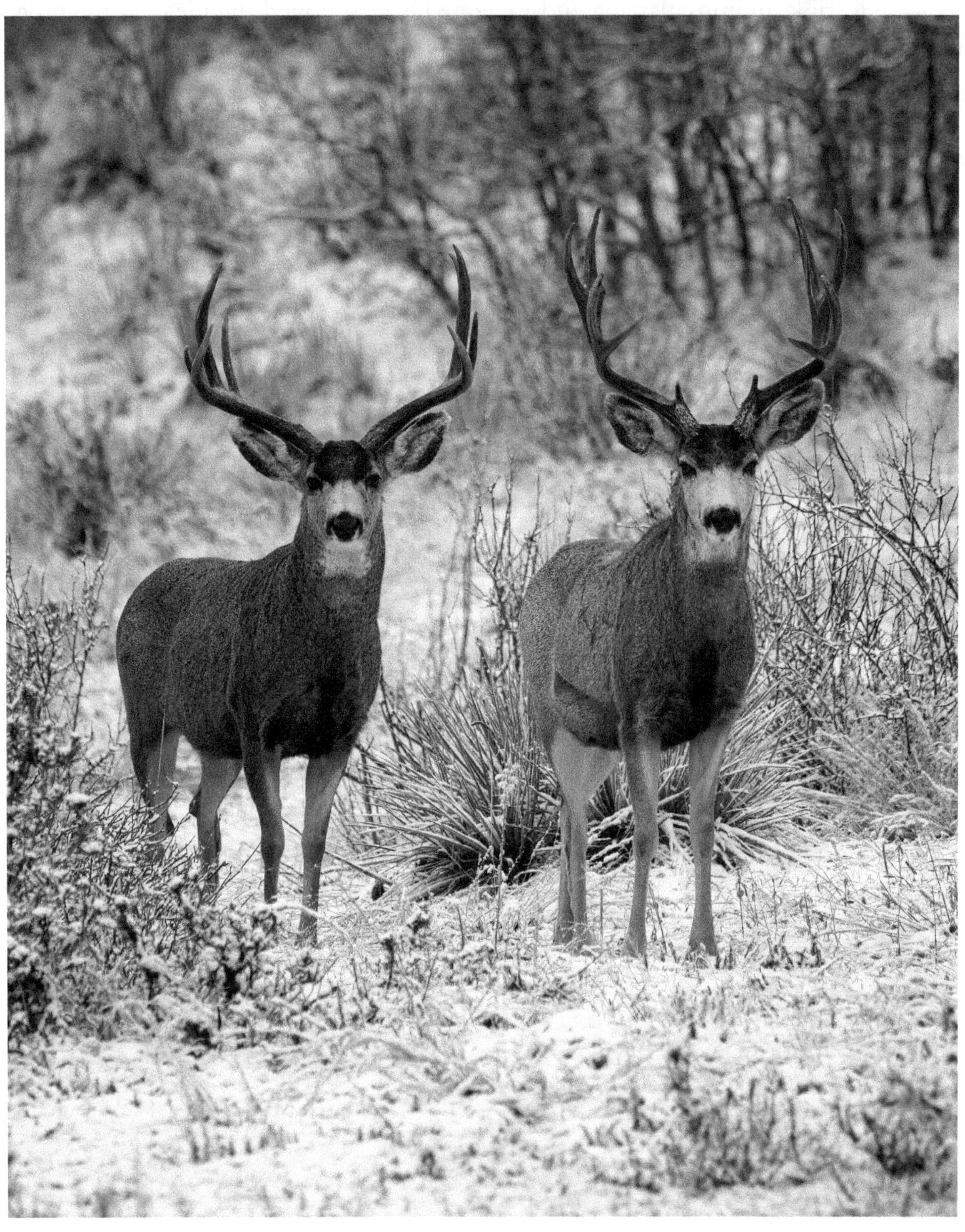

I often saw deer in the refuge as I drove by on the road and occasionally toyed with the idea of photographing them. A couple of times I even went home to get the camera and my 135mm portrait lens to try and capture an image. With only about 3x magnification to work with I had to get really close for a decent capture. The animals weren't used to me and were naturally quite distrustful. By the time I was in position to take a picture they were already well on their way into the safety of dense brush and out of the range of my puny lens. The pictures were terrible and unsatisfying and I eventually abandoned the idea. At the time I had little interest in wildlife photography and it seemed to be just a waste of film and time.

It wasn't until I transitioned to digital with its freedom to experiment that it ever occurred to me to venture deep into the forest to actually seek out the deer. I'll never forget the first time I captured a good image of our giant resident buck, the leader of our local band. It was a beautiful late autumn morning after a light dusting of snow and I was exploring a new trail near the back of the refuge. As I strode along I noticed the big fellow peering out at me from the depths of a scrub oak thicket. It was the closest I had ever been to a deer in the wild and I could barely contain my excitement as I raised the camera and pointed my newly acquired 75-300mm lens in his direction. The massive beast stared warily as I carefully snapped the picture. From that point in time on I was hooked on wildlife photography and spent as much time as possible in the refuge.

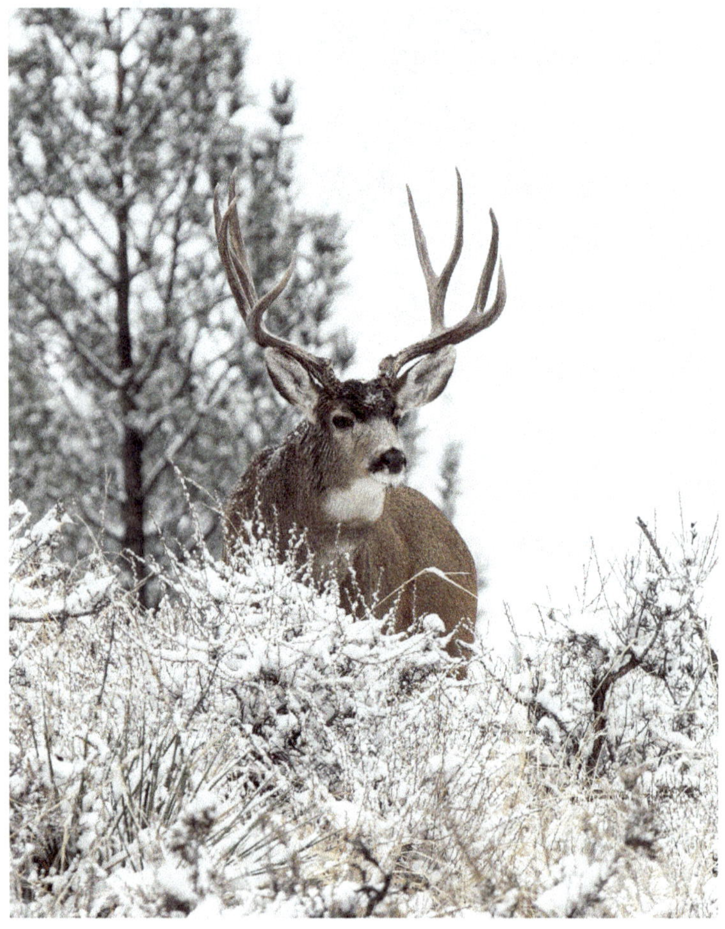

Autumn soon turned to winter and I quickly discovered how beneficial the snow and cold could be for my new passion. Most importantly, wildlife is much easier to locate and capture without the dense canopy of leaves to hide them, and animals in the foreground are more clearly visible with clean white snow as a backdrop. It seems the more snow the better when it comes to photographing deer. Deep snow and daily familiarity allowed me to get closer to the herd without disturbing them than I ever had before.

Over time I've learned that early morning is the best time to photograph wildlife in the snow, before the forest floor is filled with mottled light as the rising sun shines through the pine canopy overhead. Dawn is also the time when wildlife is the most active so I make sure to be ready by first light to hit the forest for the best images. There is plenty of time for sitting at the computer processing images and making social media posts later in the day when the overhead light is too harsh for pictures.

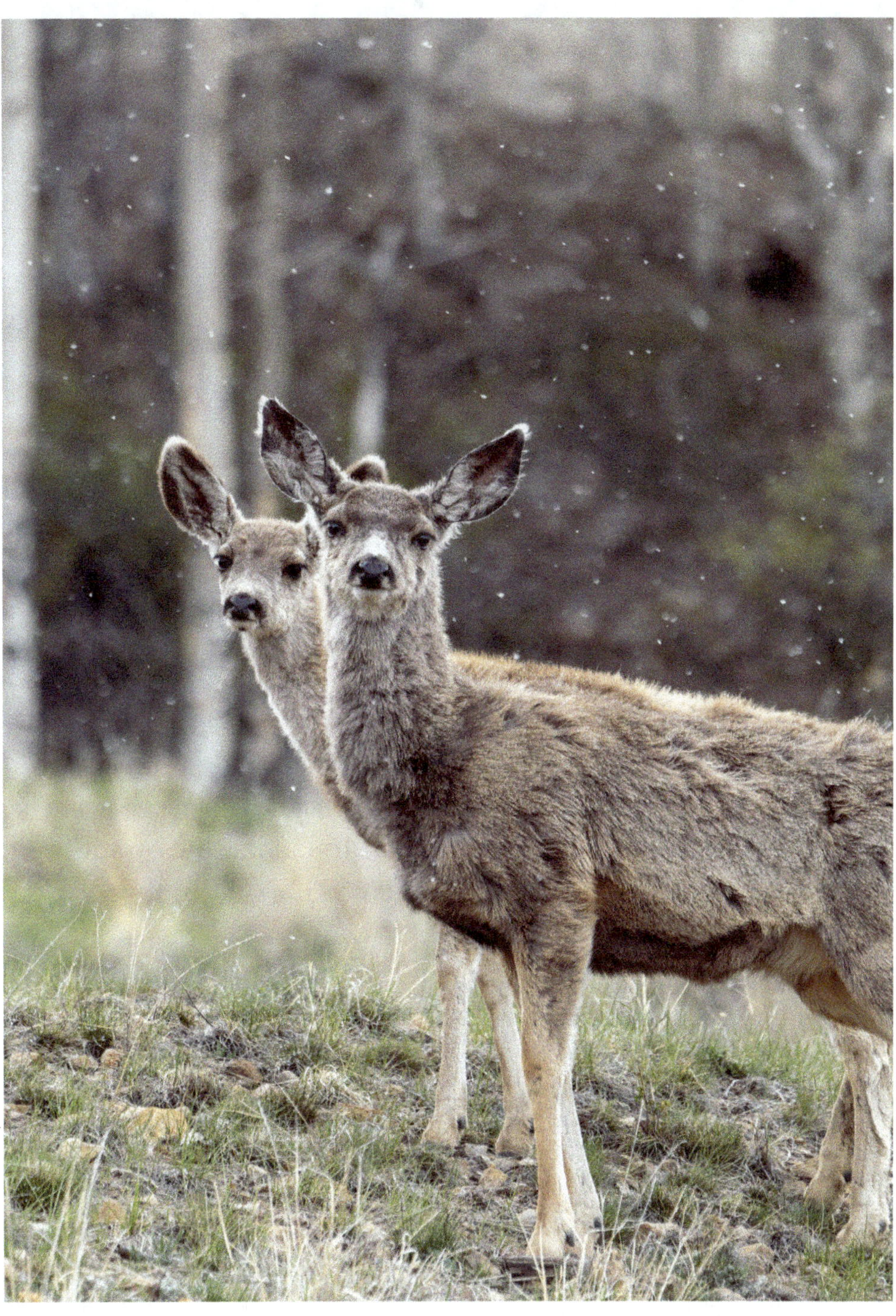

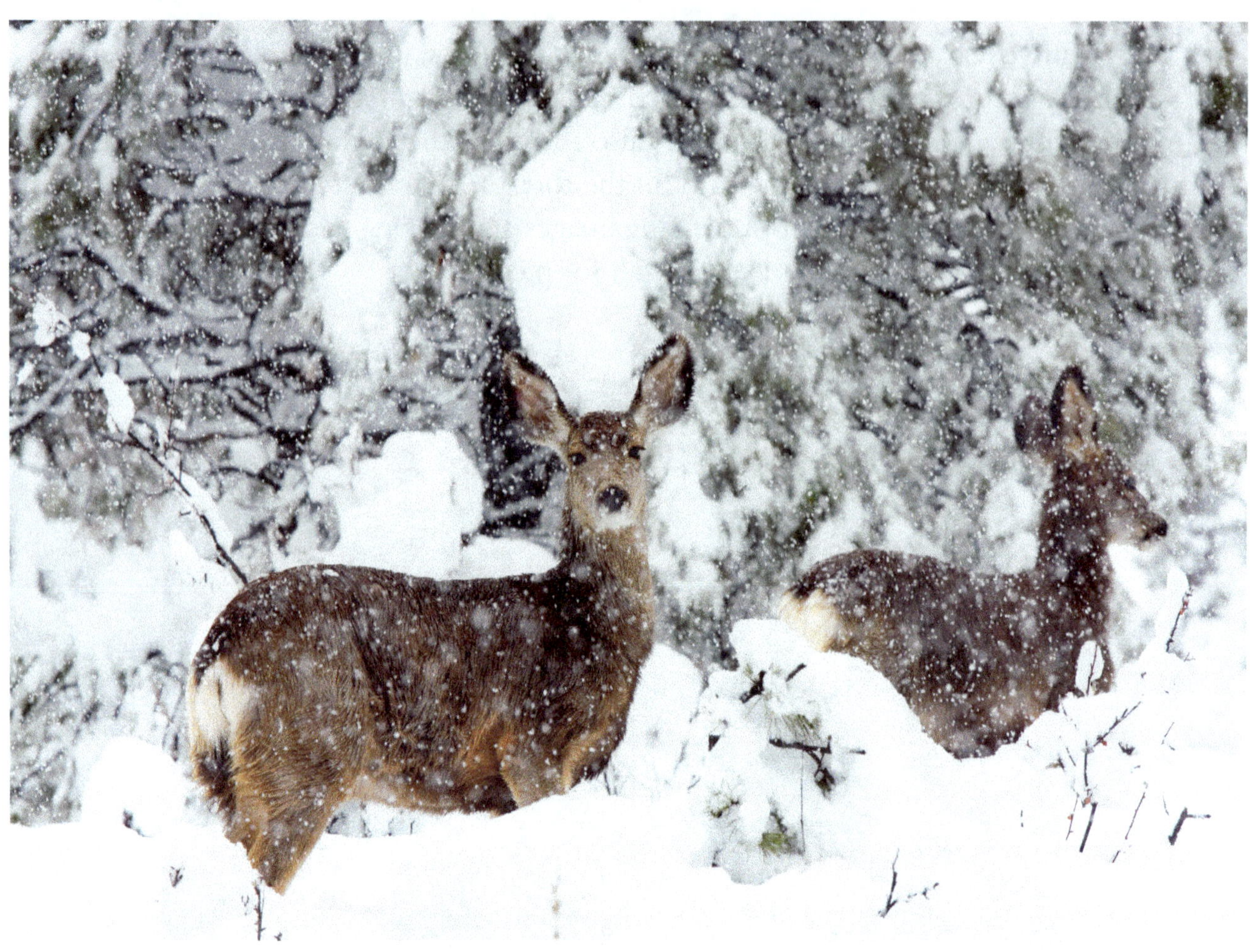

Mixed results on my early excursions revealed a hard truth. My initial lens selection was simply not up to the task of low light action photography. The cheap 75-300mm zoom lacked image stabilization and the glass wasn't producing sharp images even in the best of conditions. I was soon out shopping for better glass and eventually decided upon a professional Canon 70-200 f/4 L series model with image stabilization. The lens maintained an even f/4 all through the zoom range and I found it to be of sufficient speed and focal length for the conditions in my little five acre refuge.

With my Aquatech cover and weather sealed lens I was able to fearlessly shoot in any weather conditions, and experienced some of the most memorable photo opportunities of my entire career in that little patch of wilderness. The animals grew to trust me, eventually viewing me as only a mild curiosity while they went about their business of foraging for food. The harder it was snowing the less attention they paid me, and on one occasion in a particularly horrendous storm they were passing by my so closely that I could have reached out and touched them. Of course I didn't, they are wild animals and you never know how one is going to react to brash and unwise human interaction. A 150 pound deer can make a mess of a photographer in a hurry, so even the most docile wild beasts must always be treated with respect.

One morning after a light dusting of snow I encountered this pair of magnificent buck mule deer. I could not believe my eyes when I crested a hill and the beauty of this scene filled my eyes. As always, without delay I slowly but smoothly raised the camera and snapped a few shots to assure a capture. I was amazed when the animals were still standing there after the initial activity, giving me time to check my exposures and focus points.

I start out with the camera set to shutter priority (Tv mode) with a relatively fast shutter speed so as to be ready for most situations. From there it's easy to quickly examine the histogram to determine the best exposure compensation (EC) and shutter speed for the situation. A snowy backdrop often deceives the camera meter into underexposing the scene, requiring a significant positive EC to overcome. For this particular image I dialed in +2/3 of a stop EC to correct for the snow. The animals were standing still, so an ISO value of 400 and an aperture of f/4 and relatively slow shutter speed of 1/125th of a second along with four stops of image stabilization rendered the best capture possible. With a longer focal length or animals in motion, a faster shutter speed of an 850th or 1000th of a second might have been a better choice. In uncertain conditions it may be wise to select auto ISO to assure the camera can create a proper exposure in all conditions. In a more predictable setting, manual mode with a fixed ISO will guarantee that you have full creative control over the capture, shutter speed, aperture and digital noise from ISO gain.

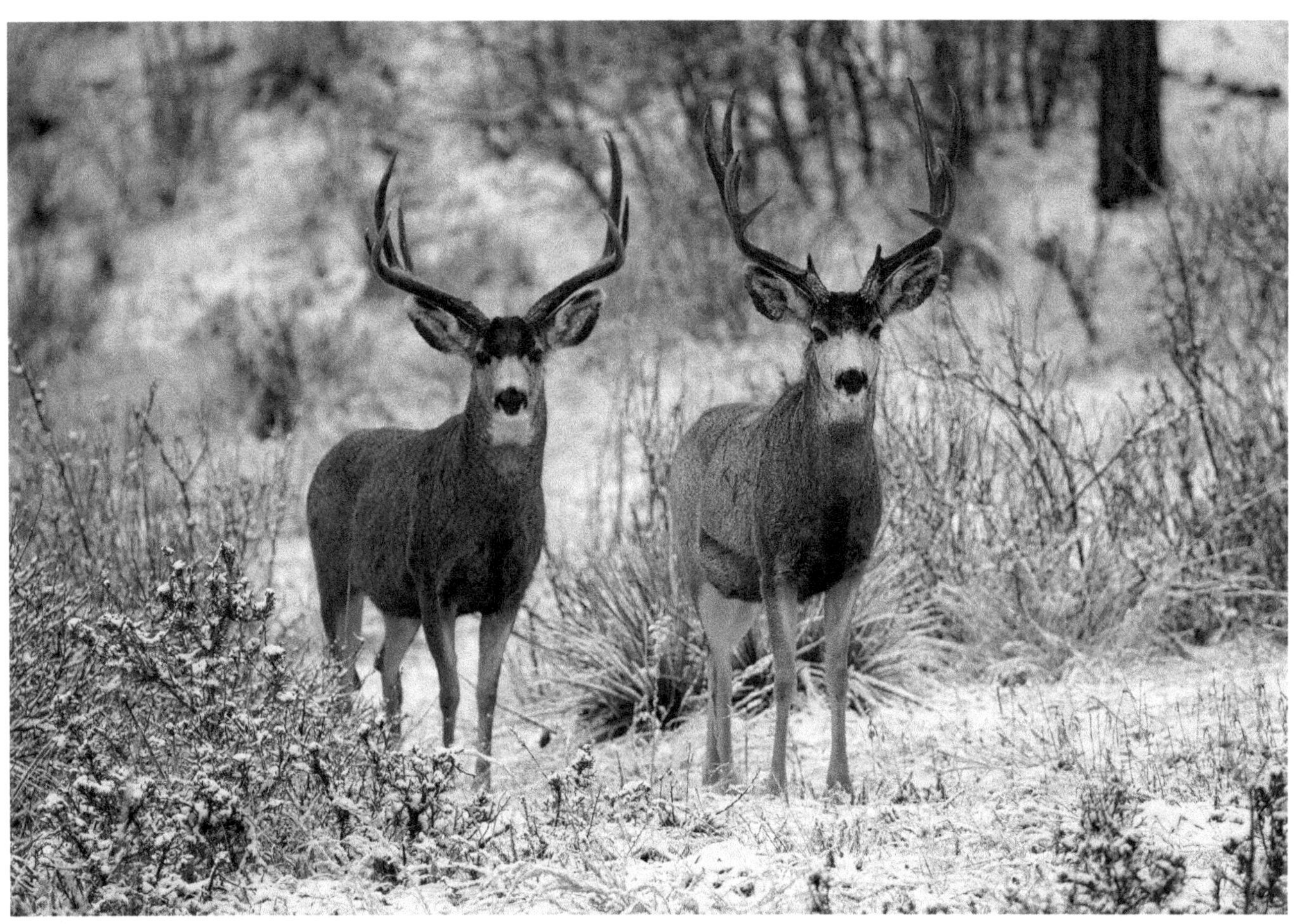

Mornings following a light dusting of snow are always beautiful, but I also enjoy strapping on the snowshoes and heading out into a total blizzard. I always felt sorry for the deer when the snow was so deep, their spindly legs and sharp hooves sinking deep into the drifts. After dozens of treks through their habitat over the years I was cognizant of their favorite paths, and with my snowshoes it was no trouble to pack down a trail for them. Even though it was against the rules, other kind souls would toss in a few bales of hay to sustain them until they could once again get to the grass and leaves for sustenance.

It was on one of these snowy mornings that I came face to face with my favorite buck as I was trudging through this magical white winter setting (below). We stared into each other's eyes for a few moments as if to gauge the other's intentions. I slowly raised the camera, watching carefully to make sure I didn't startle him. He stood still, intently watching as I moved the camera up to my eye. Undisturbed, he held his ground as I snapped away until I was confident I had the capture. Eventually I slowly moved away in the opposite direction as he went back to chewing on branches of snow covered scrub oak.

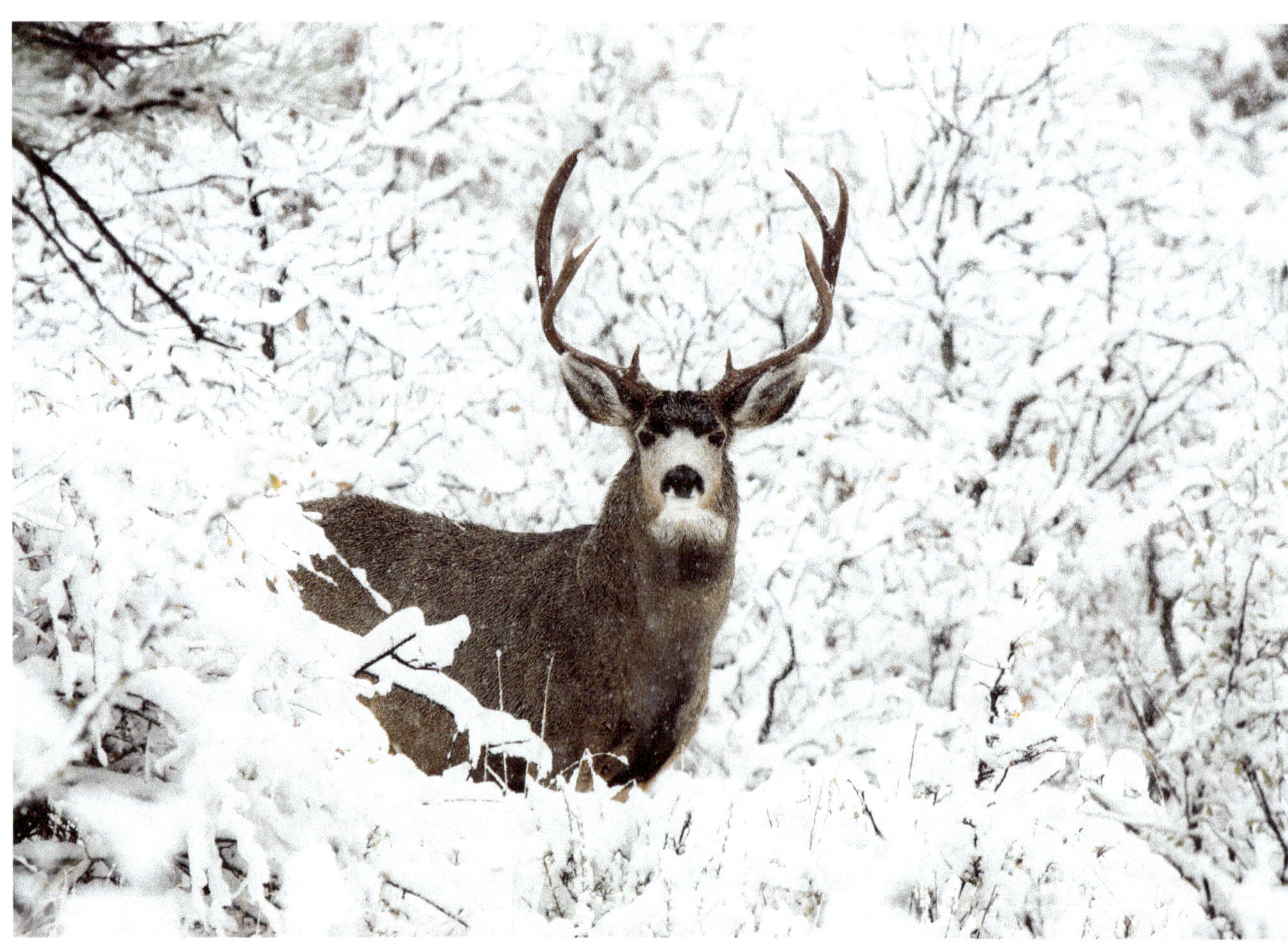

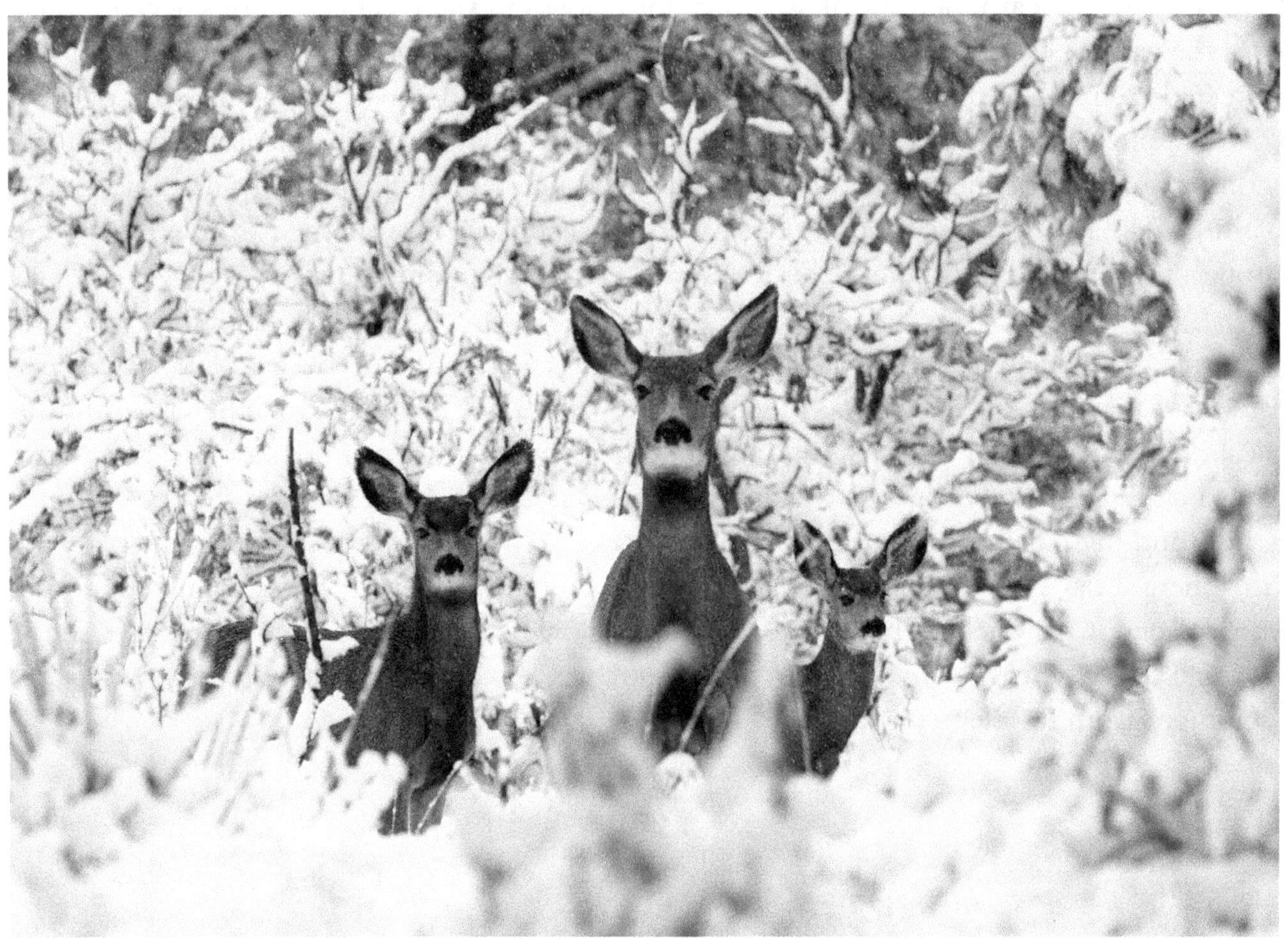

The snow and wind were abating and the sky brightening just as I was nearing completion of my path making project. I was cold and wet by then but decided I would make use of my own trails to make one more pass through the forest in hopes of making some images in better light. I passed through a thicket of scrub oak and as I burst through the snow covered leaves on the other side I looked up, and much to my surprise found myself staring into the eyes of three beautiful young does standing not ten feet from me. They looked as surprised as I was, their eyes seeming to ask the question, "Who are you, and what are you doing in our forest?"! I pulled my camera up as stealthily as possible, hoping upon hope that the trio would not flee before I could get a shot off!

The little group stood fast enjoying the leaves, seemingly unbothered by my presence. I aimed at the closest doe, training one of the more left oriented focus points right on her eye. I captured a few images that way and then adjusted the focus point to the center animal. Once I was sure I had an acceptable capture of the scene, I started making adjustments to the shutter speed and aperture in hopes of the perfect image. Surprisingly the trio waited patiently while I made sure I was getting the shot of a lifetime! Eventually I was confident with my session and I backed away out of their sight and exited the forest using an alternate path.

Now I would learn the folly of wearing cloth gloves in such wet conditions. Even though the camera came was equipped with a certain amount of weather sealing and remained protected from the elements by the rain cover, there was no defense against my soaking wet glove gripping the camera. I soon began to notice odd behavior on the display and eventually a complete failure of the shutter button. I hustled home fearing the precious memory chip might be damaged from condensation, or worse that the camera was fried from water leaking through the shutter button into delicate internal electronic components.

I quickly opened all the accessory doors, removed the lens and batteries and left the camera to dry for awhile. Later on I was quite relieved when I put it all back together and found the shutter and all other buttons to be functioning properly once again. Lesson learned, don't allow a cloth glove to become so soaking wet that water runs down into the shutter button. If I do find myself in a wet storm I make sure to keep my hand dry inside the rain cover with the camera. I have also purchased a pair of relatively thin waterproof cross country ski gloves which I keep in my pack in the winter. When the snow becomes too heavy I can swap out my usual fleece gloves for the warmer waterproof winter version, protecting both hands and equipment from the elements.

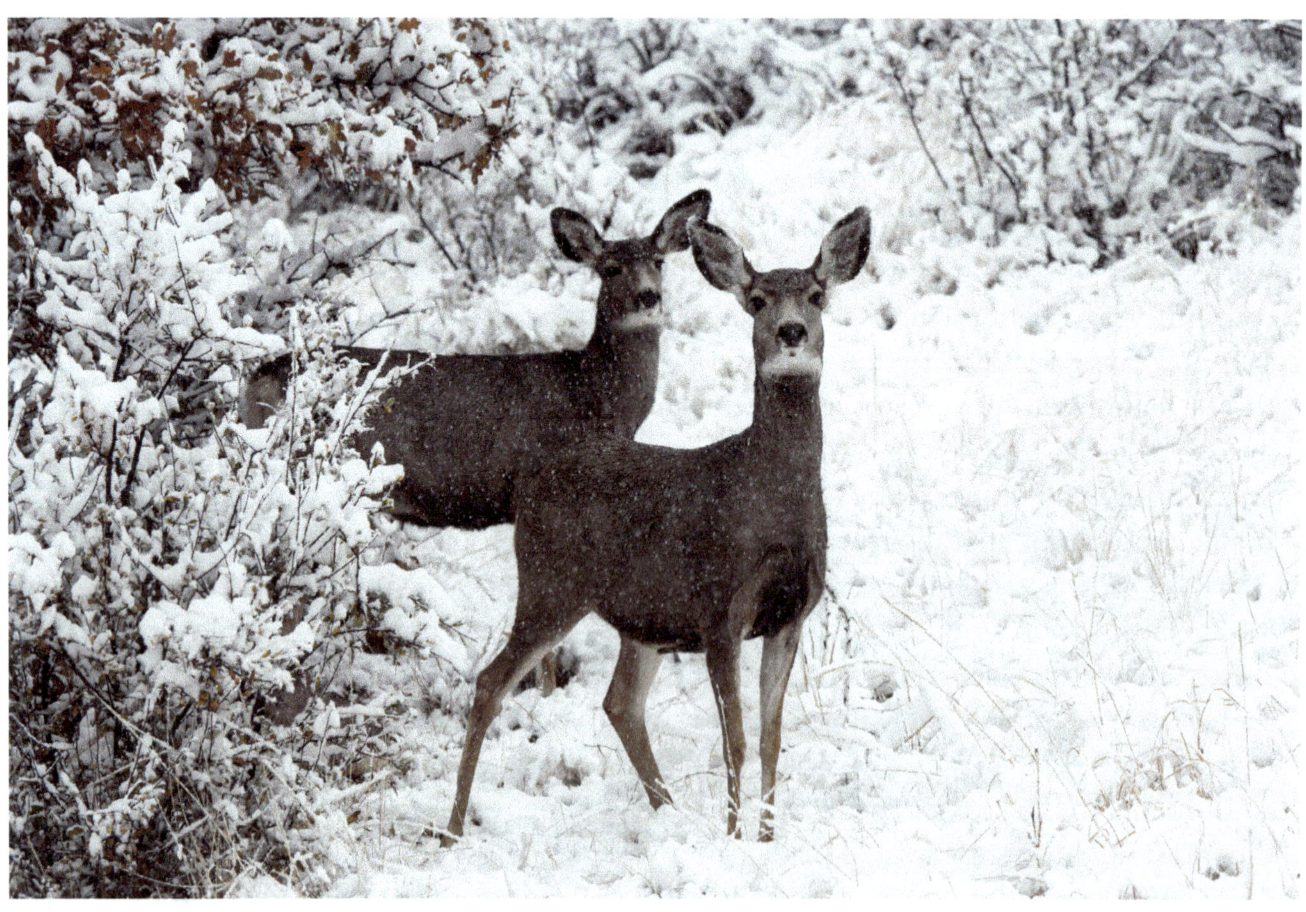

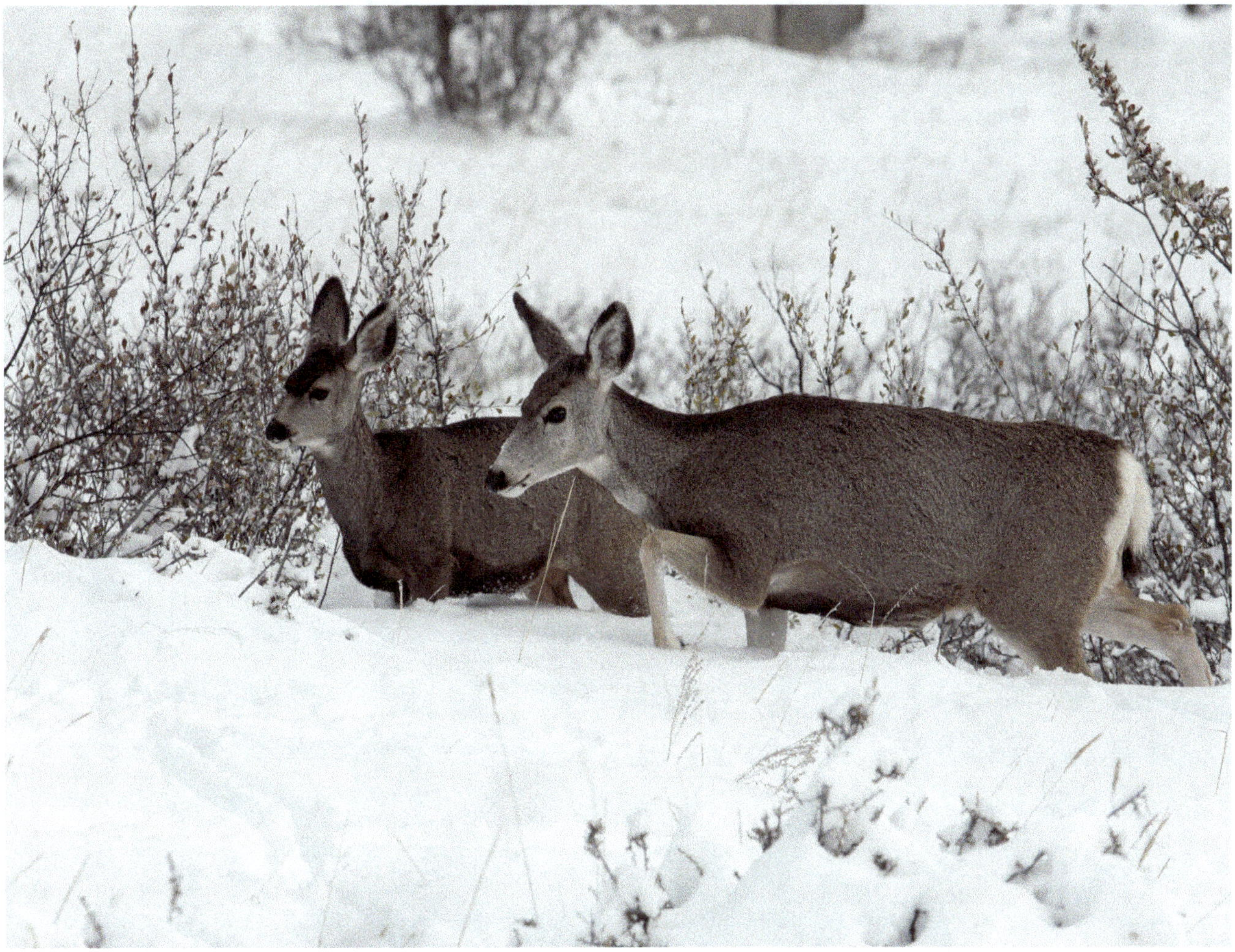

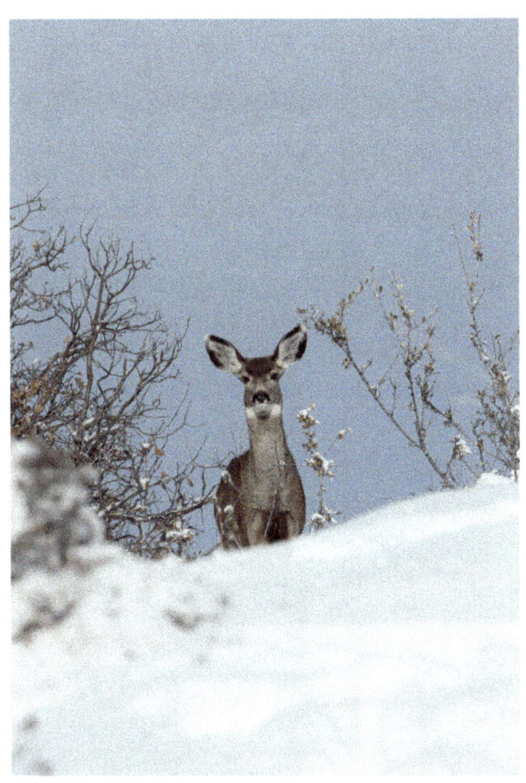

Here is a great example of the difficult conditions faced by a couple of mule deer does (above) as they fight their way through deep snow after a fierce blizzard. Soon my packed snowshoe trails would assist these two with their search for leaves and tree bark. Here they pay no attention to me at all as their minds are one hundred percent focused on their fight for survival.

A young mule deer doe (left) rests for a moment to assess possible threats before continuing through the drifts in search of food.

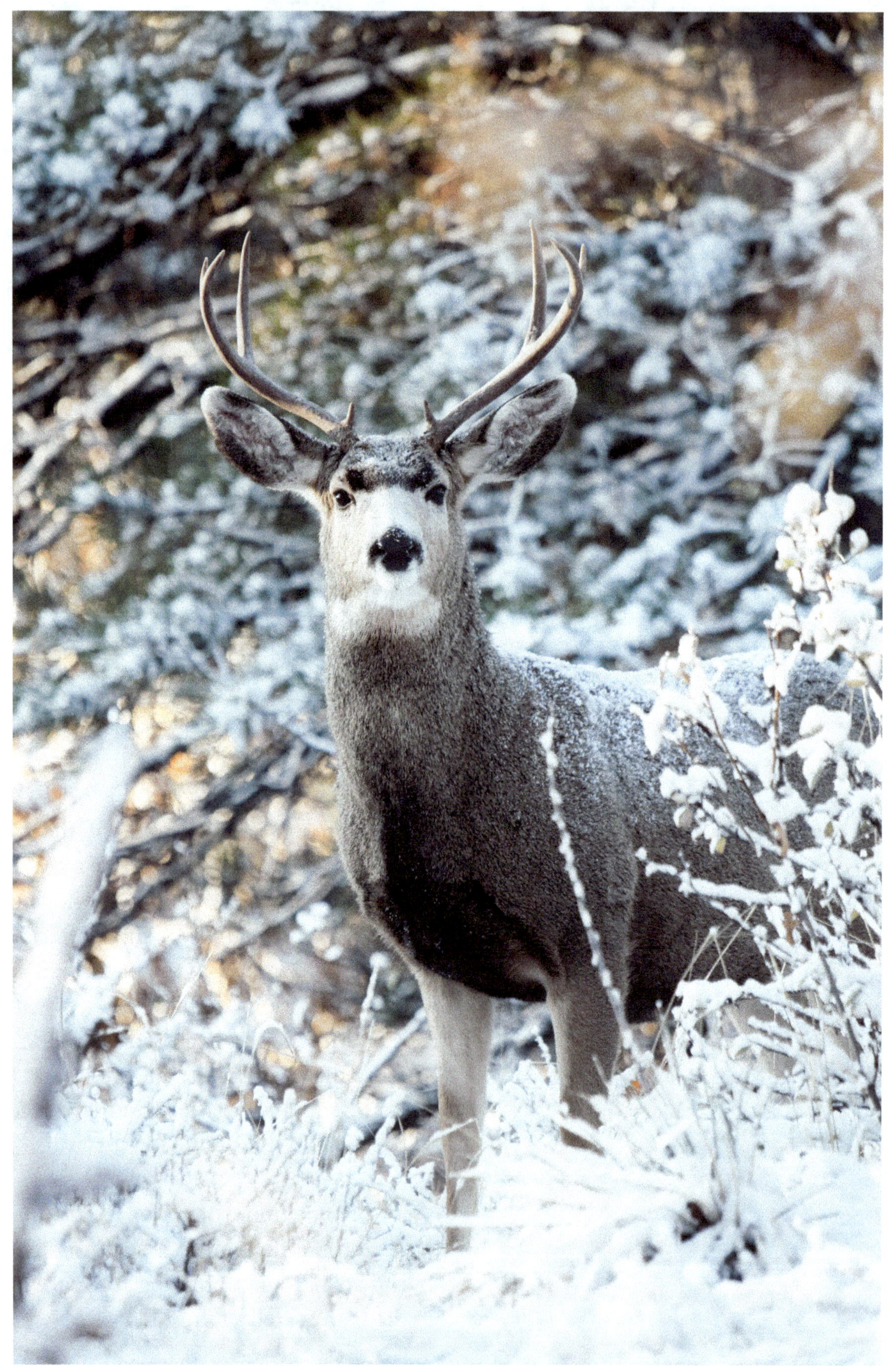

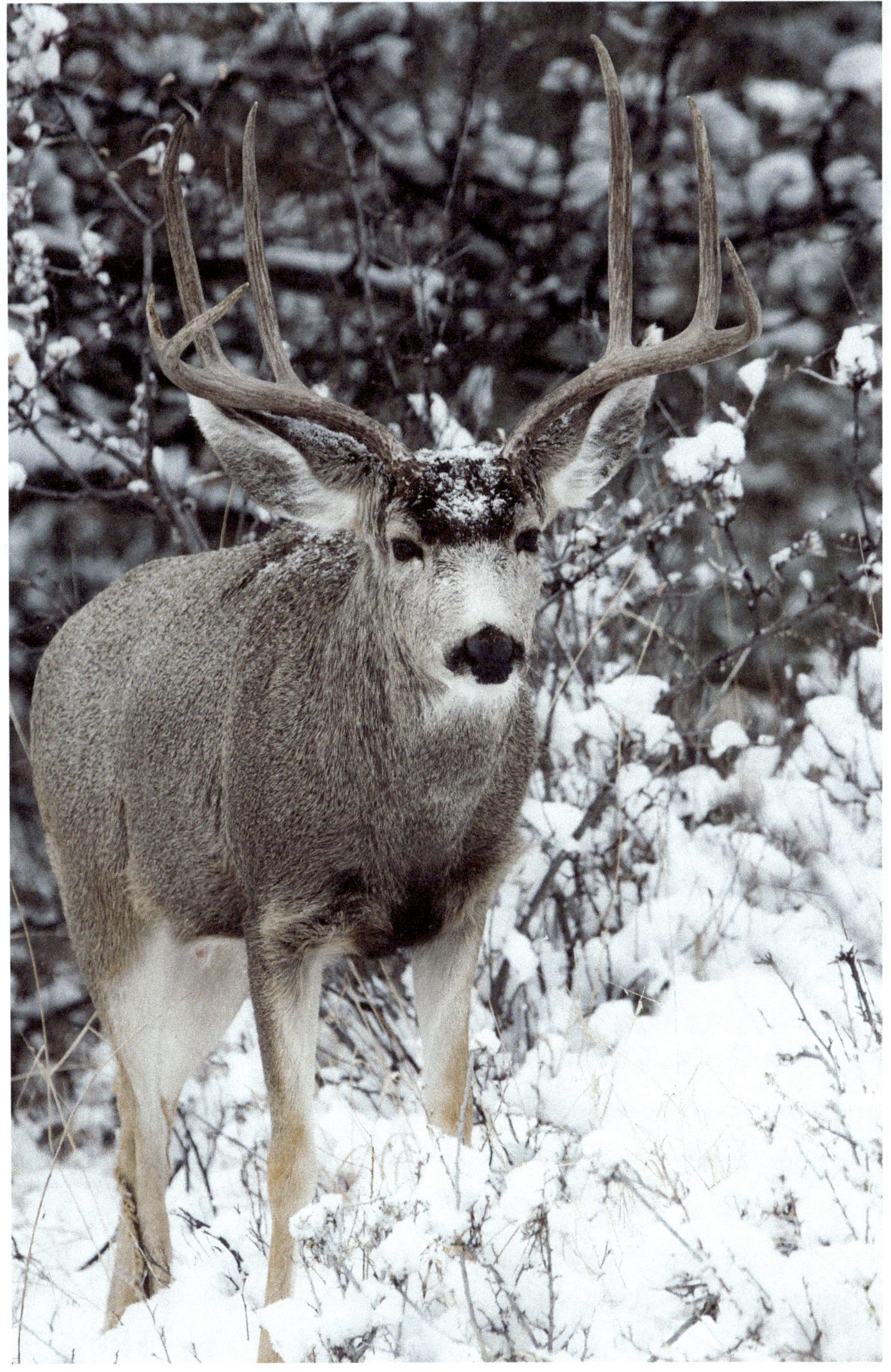

Fox and coyote are also frequent visitors to this winter paradise. I used only a 60th of a second shutter speed to blur the background and highlight the speed of this little fellow, all four feet off the ground as he sailed past.

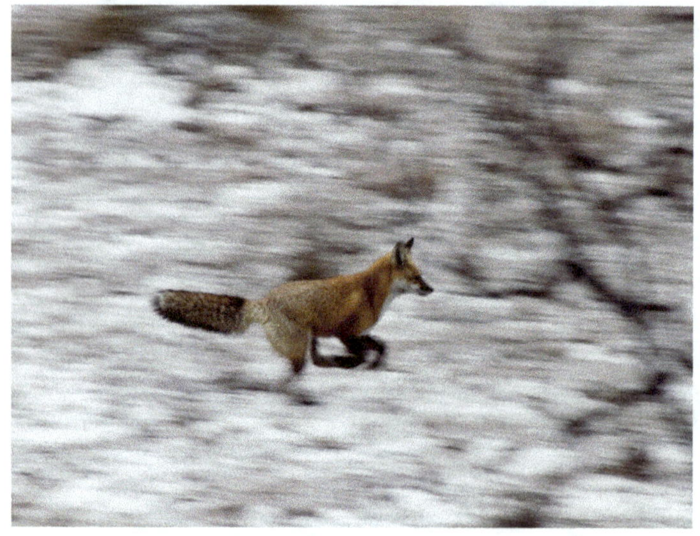

The coyote (below) and his little feathered magpie friends were busy feeding on a deer carcass when I came upon the scene. The wild canine was a bit suspicious of me at first but eventually allowed me to set up a 500mm Sigma on a tripod to capture this rare moment. I was fortunate to encounter the scene in winter, tall green mountain grass would have obscured the animals during warmer seasons.

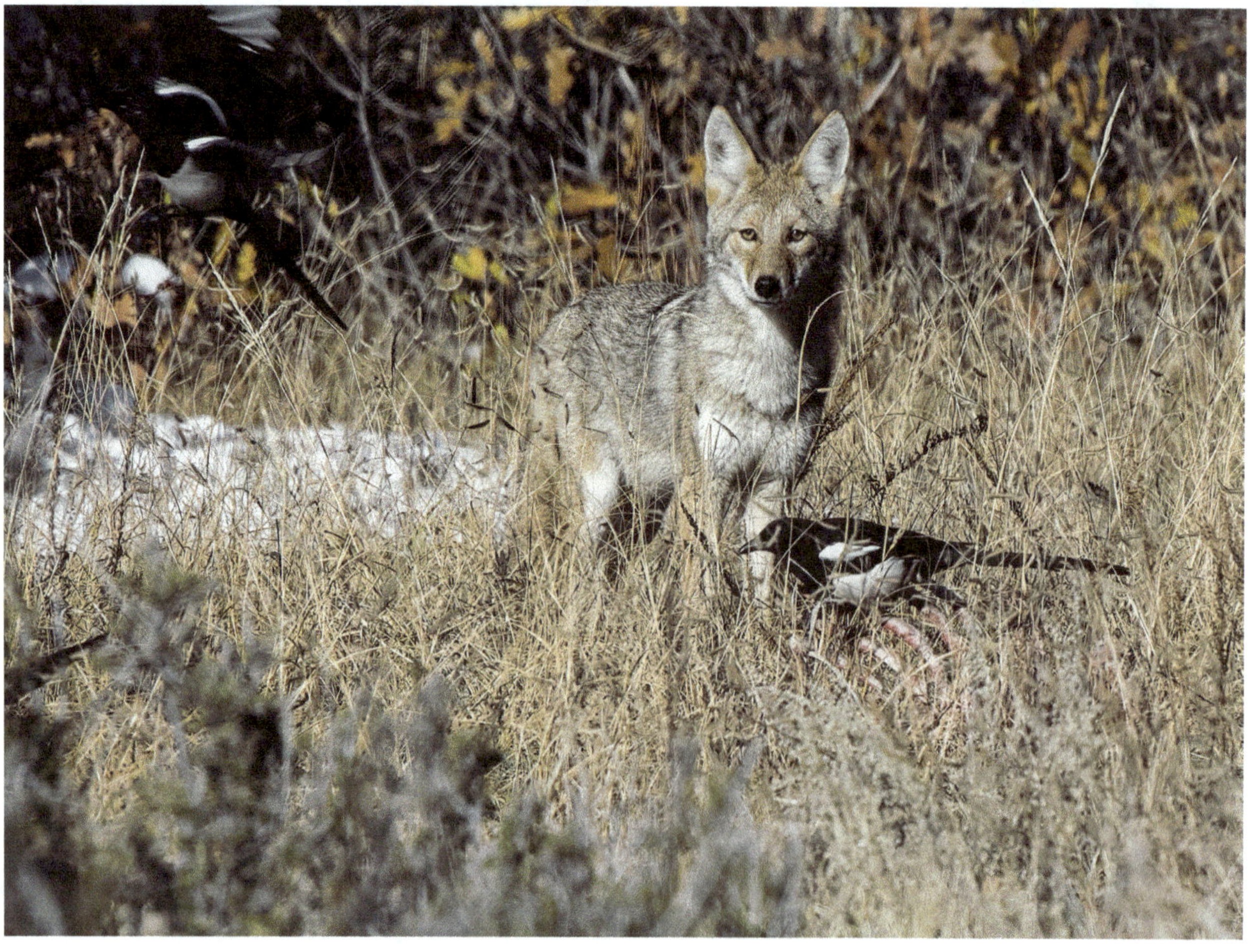

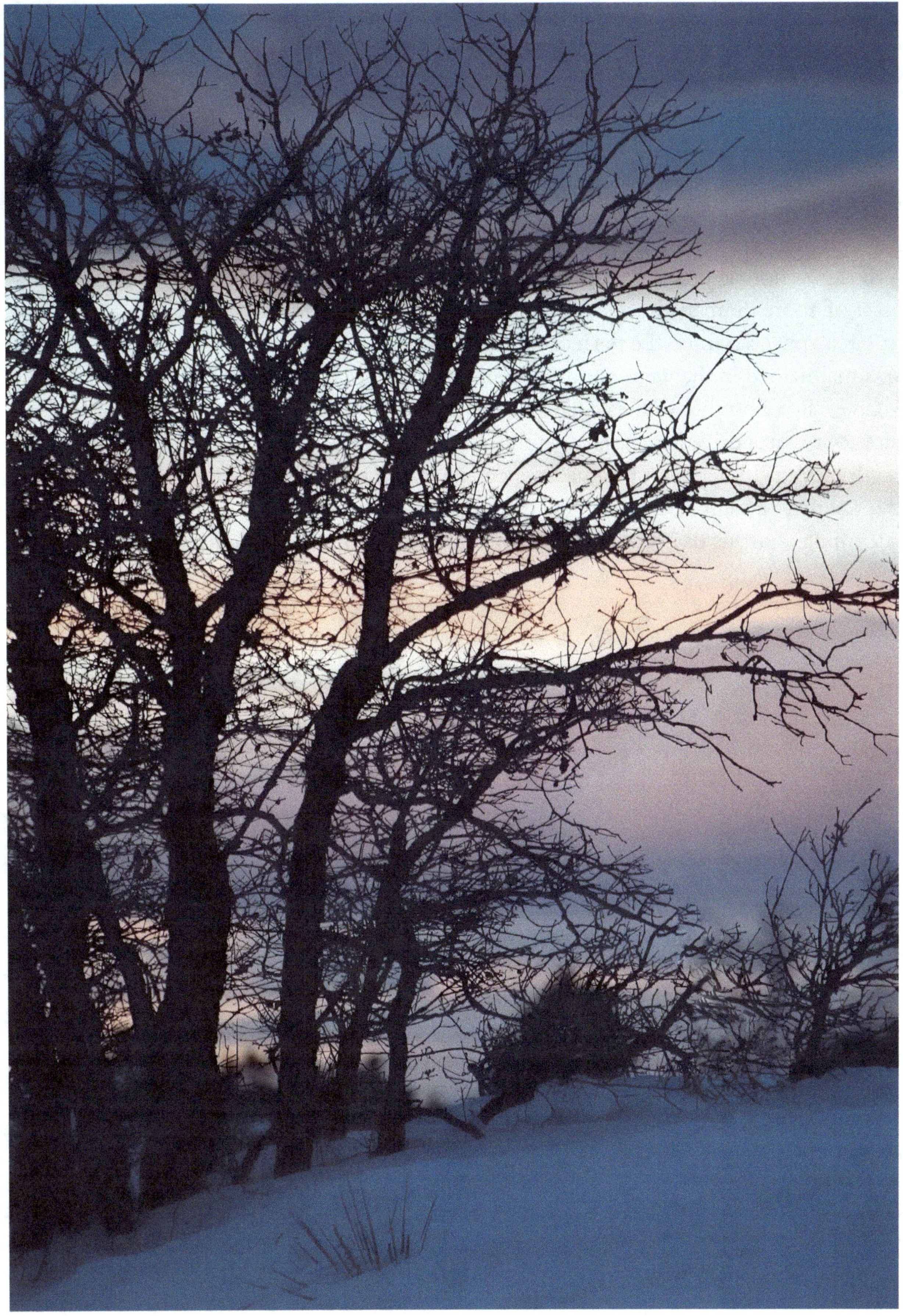

Winter on the Front Range

The winter wildlife and heavy snows of the Front Range are awesome, but nothing can match the stark beauty of winter's harshness in the alpine region. With a couple seasons of snowshoeing under my belt I was ready to venture into the mountain backcountry in quest of more dramatic images. **Mount Evans** just a few miles to the west of the Denver metro area appeared to be the perfect the place to level up my game. Highway 103 to Echo Lake is maintained in the winter and the trail system there is perfect for winter hiking. Upper Bear Creek Road on the southeast side of the peak sports an excellent trail system but may require four wheel drive to access in winter months. The road isn't particularly rough but two wheel drive vehicles tend to struggle on steep snow packed hills. Be sure to keep a close eye on the weather though, heavy snowfall can explode over the peak in a matter of moments, transforming a joyous day on the trails into a life threatening struggle for survival.

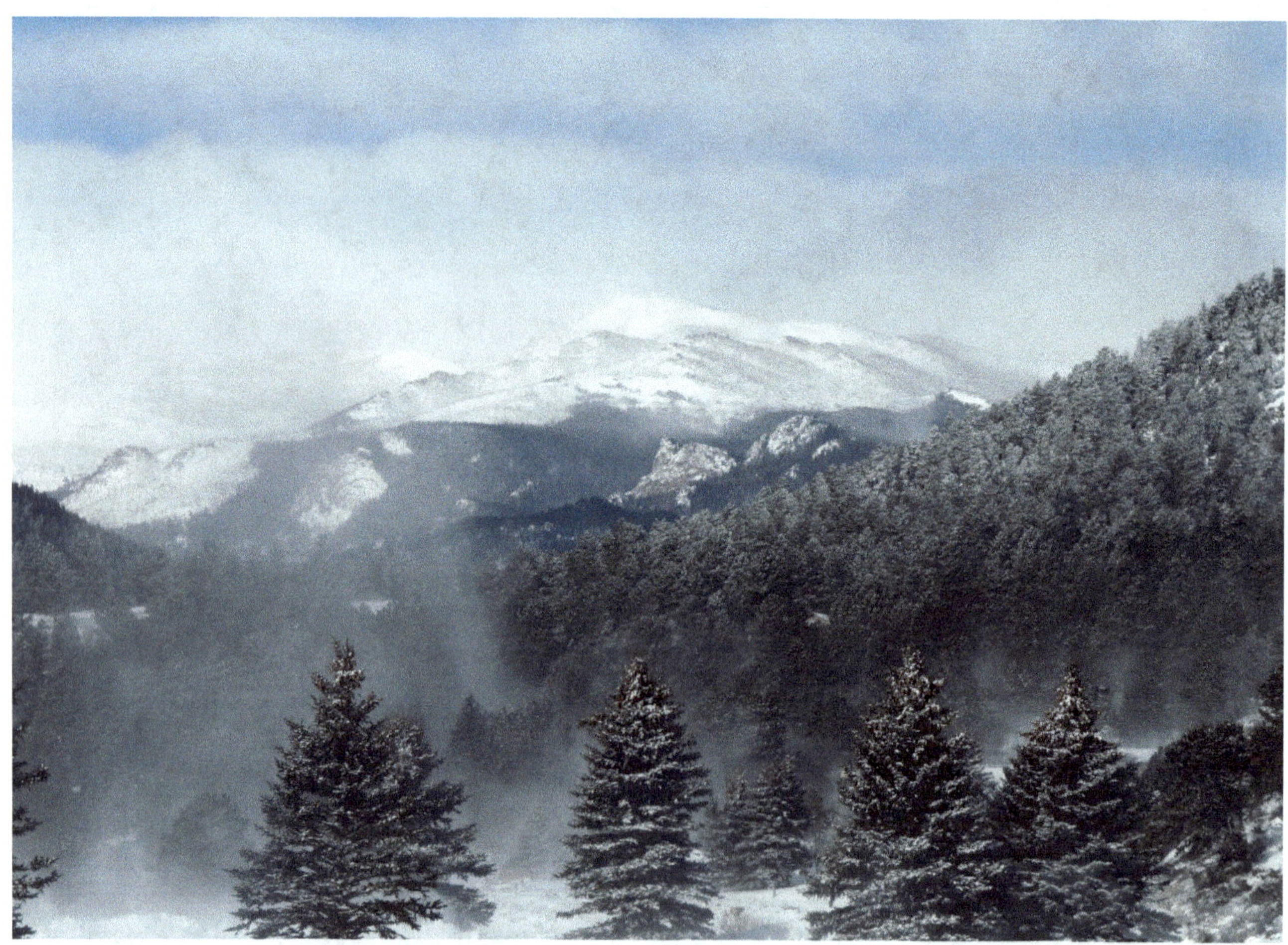

The Chicago Lakes Trail on the backside of Echo Lake became my favorite destination for snowshoeing and photography. As I mentioned, Highway 103 is maintained in the winter and parking at Echo Lake is never a problem. The trails in the area are generally safe and there is almost always someone hiking nearby in case of an emergency. In addition, there is beautiful mountain scenery to be photographed from both the Idaho Springs and Evergreen approaches to the mountain. I never fail to bring the camera along on one of these treks, the winter landscape in those mountains is just too fantastic to leave behind without taking a piece of it home! Each visit brings new wonders, whether it's the blazing blue Colorado sky against bright white snow, blowing snow, or the dark clouds of an approaching winter storm.

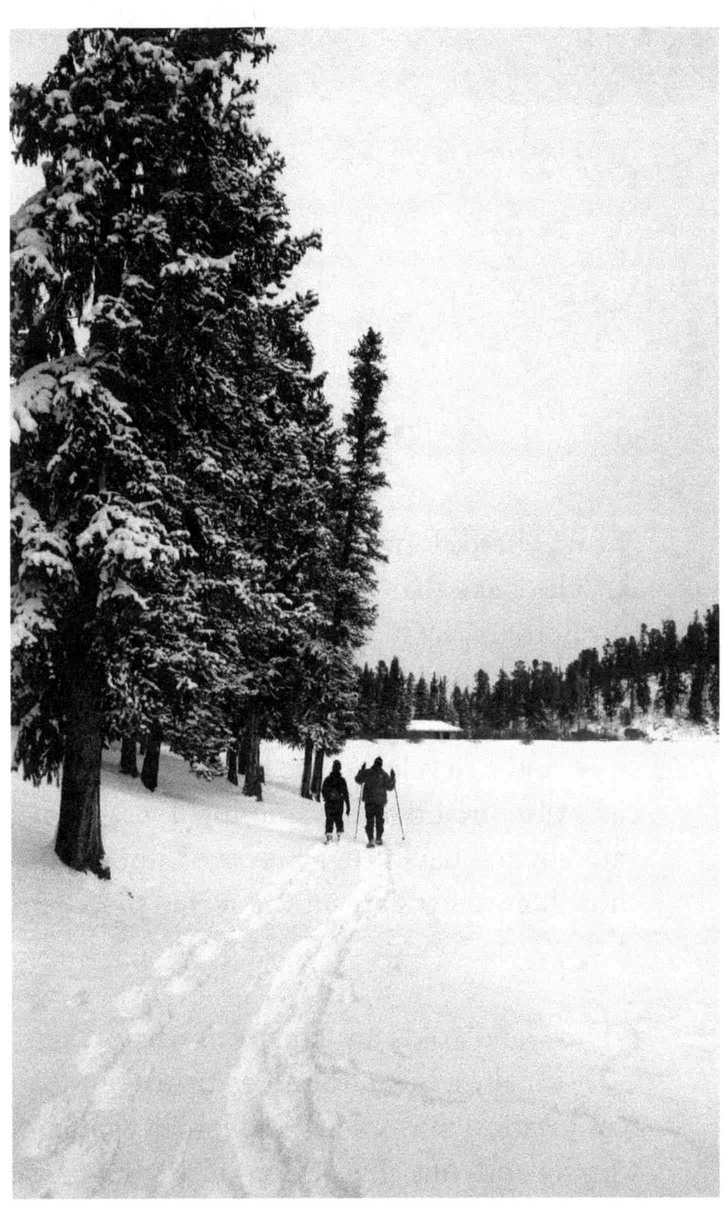

A quick trip around the lake is good way for beginners to get started with alpine snowshoeing or cross country skiing. The trails are usually snow packed along the icy shores and it's impossible to get disoriented and lost with the lake in constant view.

Slightly more difficult trails can be found on the west side of the lake where it's possible to put in additional mileage and gain experience in deeper snow. As you can see in the picture to the left, ski poles are helpful with pushing forward and maintaining balance in deep snow. Poles can also be used to search out buried trails ahead to prevent falling off the packed path and into deep snow. A winter hiker can expend a lot of energy fighting out of chest deep snow to get back onto the packed trail.

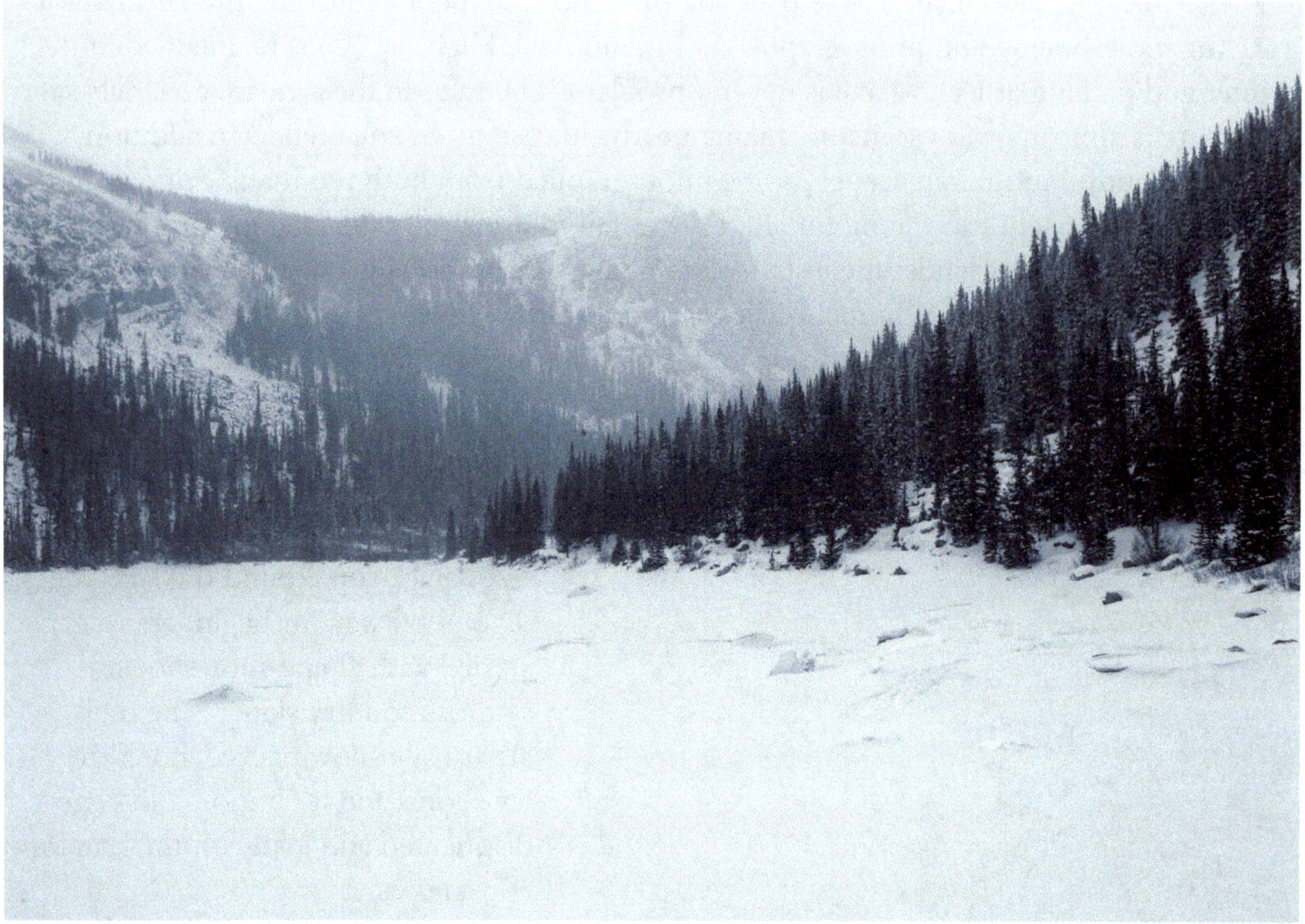

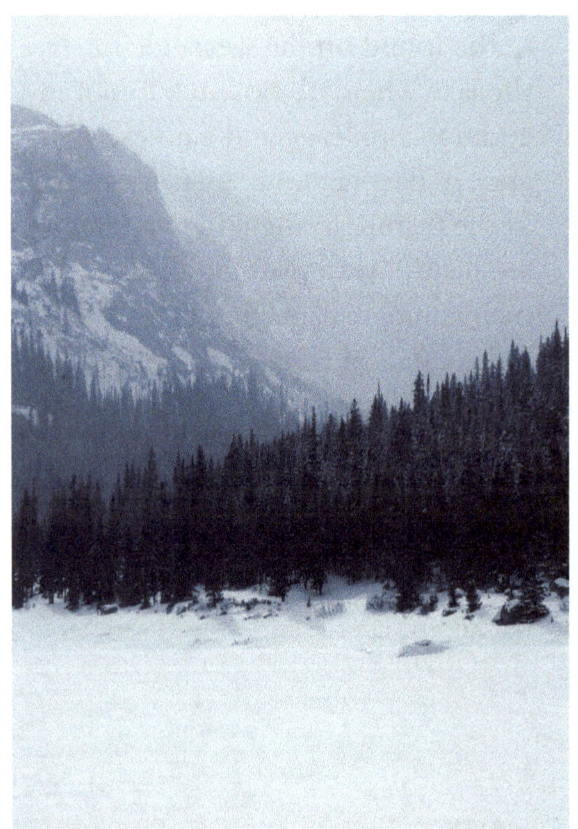

It was here along the shores of beautiful Echo Lake that I fell in love with minimalist photography in the snow and clouds of the Rocky Mountain winter. One cold morning I looked up as I trudged through the snow and marveled at the beauty of rugged cliffs obscured by snow and fog. I was captivated by the harsh ruggedness of unbroken snow before me and snow covered pine trees in the background.

Snow and cold can transform what is normally a bustling and colorful summer location into a stark and lonely winter wonderland, one that feels as if are the first person to ever witness it.

Stunning scenes can be captured even on perfectly clear mountain mornings as powerful winds howl over 14,000 foot summits, creating blizzard conditions in the powder covering beautiful pine trees below the tree line. I never tire of photographing the beauty of blowing snow against stunning blue skies only witnessed at extreme elevation. A sturdy tripod may be required to overcome camera shake in extreme winds such as these. Winter gales can become so powerful that holding a camera still is nearly impossible. Once while hiking up Mount Evans Road the wind was blowing with such power that I could barely keep my eyes open long enough to frame a composition. While trying to shoot the range north of the mountain my eyes were freezing shut faster than I could I could capture the scene. Fortunately I had a tripod along and was able to keep the camera steady by sitting on the ground and using only the thick upper segment of the legs to create a low center of gravity for maximum steadiness.

The images from that day remain among my all time favorites, so the extra effort was well worth the trouble. The lesson to be learned is that the Rocky Mountain winter can create extraordinary situations requiring extraordinary measures!

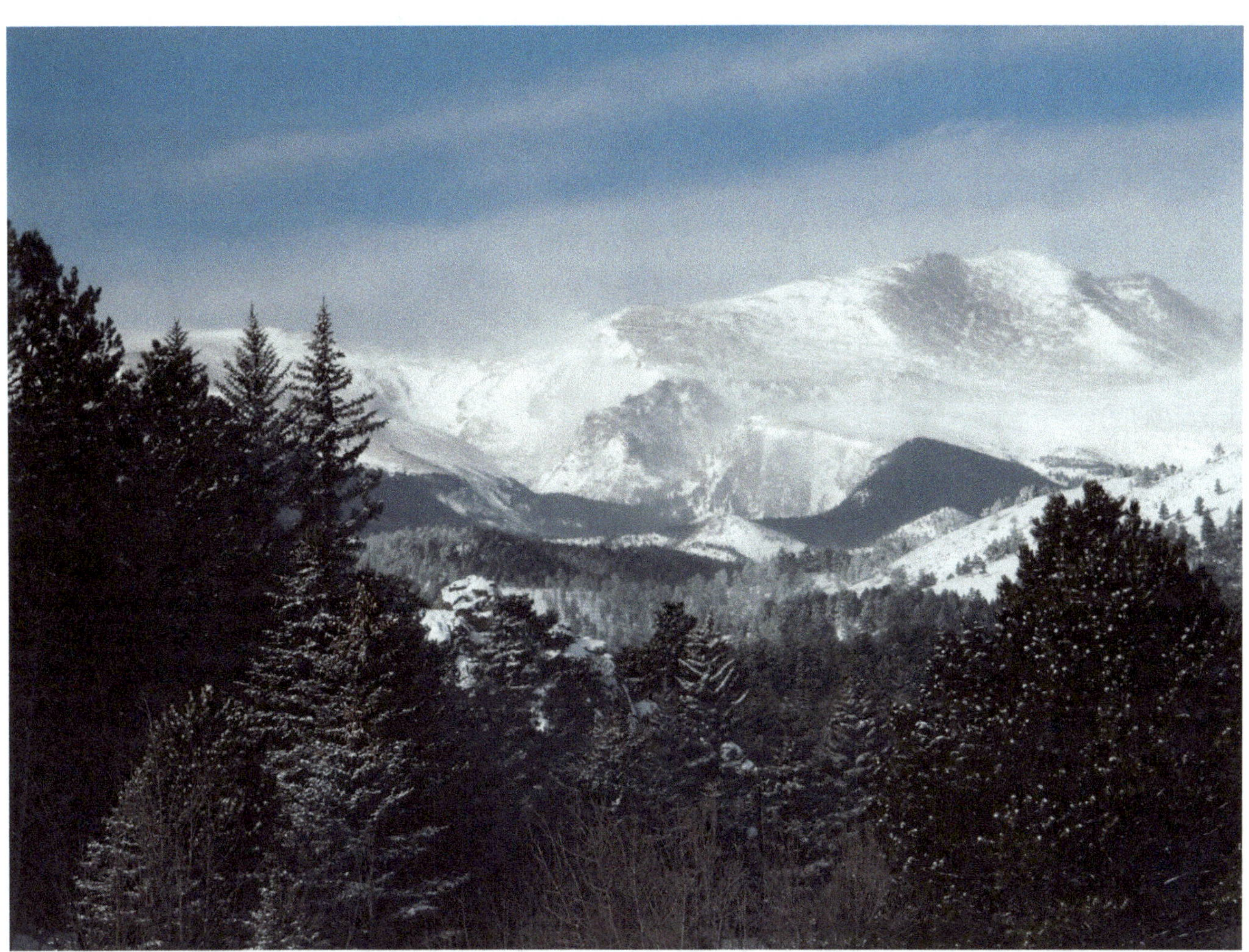

The Chicago Lakes Trail is an 11.3 mile out and back route with 3,330 feet of elevation gain if you complete the entire course. It took me a few attempts to actually find the trailhead because I was looking in the wrong place, but the mistakes were worth the effort to learn the lay of the land around Echo Lake. Many online trail resources now available to hikers would have come in handy then, even a good map and compass would have saved me a lot of frustration! These days I prefer Alltrails.com with it's detailed terrain maps, trail descriptions and wealth of pictures. I have also enjoyed countless hours of compiling my list of completed trails while searching for future prospects. If you can load the maps of your hike onto your phone before losing signal in the mountains, it's possible to use the GPS feature to track progress along the route.

To reach the trailhead just make your way around the south side of the lake and venture back into the trees on the west side. The trail follows the deep gulch through which Chicago Creek flows, so if you just stay near the top of the ridge behind the lake you will eventually cross the trail. There is also a nice sign marking the trailhead, and if there hasn't been a big snow in the previous few days there will also likely be a trail of snowshoe and micro spike tracks guiding the way. The trail eventually descends down into the valley with a series of steep switch backs leading down to Chicago Creek where the trail continues past Idaho Springs Reservoir and onward to Lower and Upper Chicago Lakes. If that isn't enough physical exertion for one day, it's possible to continue all the way to Summit Lake!

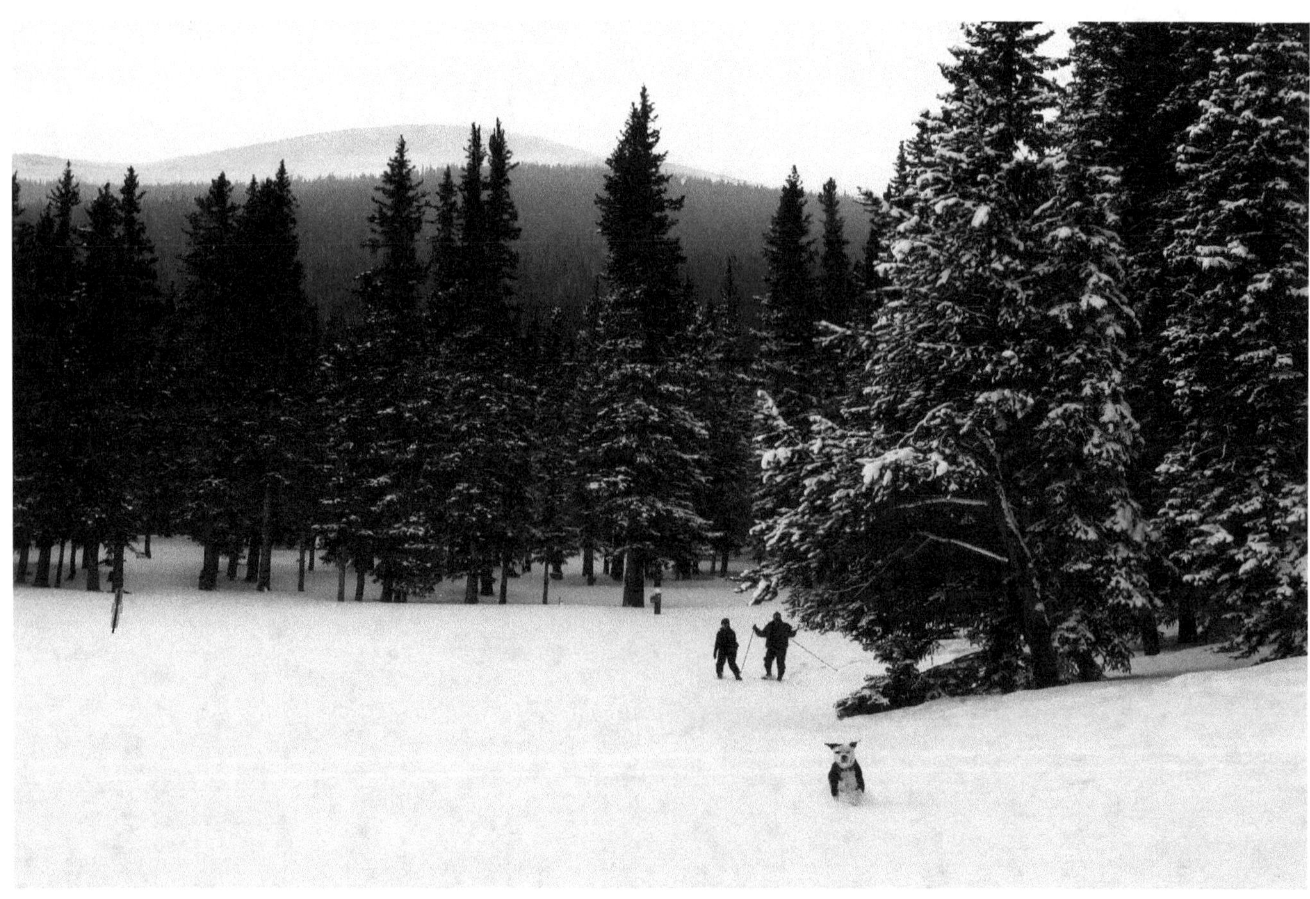

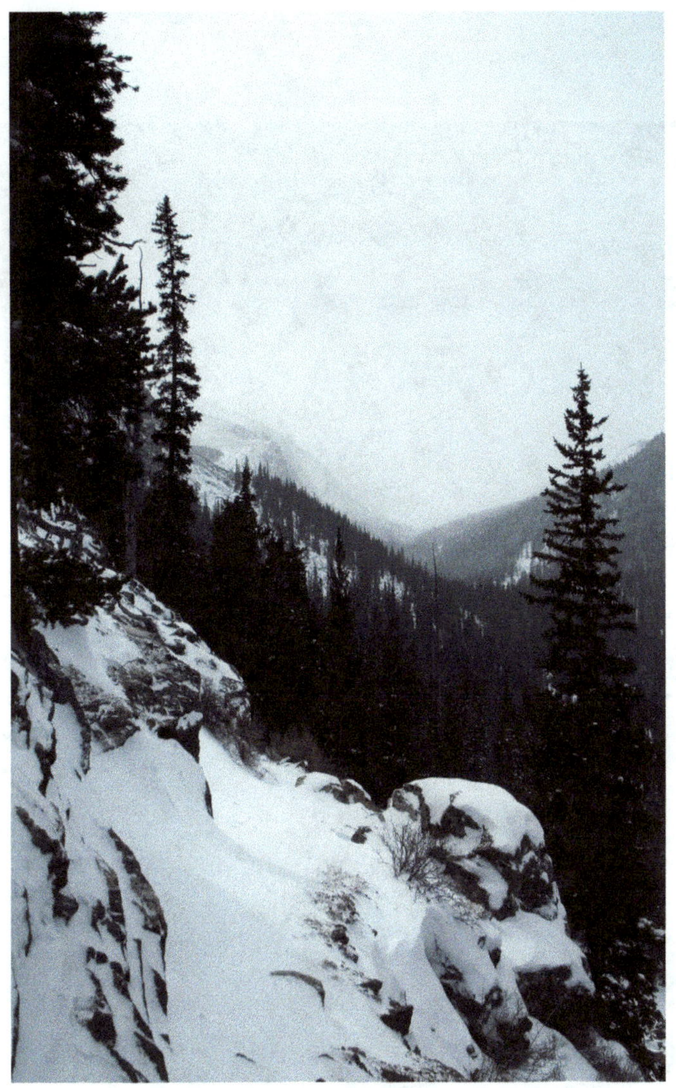

It was along this trail that I learned the hard lesson of choosing the right snowshoes for the task. I normally prefer my racing snow shoes for their light weight and excellent mobility, and those were what I was wearing on a day when heavy snow was forecast to arrive in the afternoon. The trip out to the lakes was great fun as I hustled down the switchbacks and along the creek to the lakes.

Snow began to fall about the time I was ready for the return trip but I wasn't worried, I was dressed for the occasion including a full Gor-Tex suit. It wasn't until I began climbing the switchbacks on the trail back up the ridge that I discovered cause for concern. As you can tell from the picture (left), heavy wet snow had turned a nice flat trail into a treacherous angled and slippery slope.

My racing snowshoes were designed for running on a packed trail, with only a single front claw for traction. The front claw provided insufficient stability on the sloped snow and with each step I ran the risk of slipping off the trail and tumbling down the steep mountainside with nothing to stop a long slide into the deep valley below. Fortunately I had my ski poles with me so before taking each step I would stab a pole into the snow ahead of me all the way to the rocks where I was confident of a stable anchor for my foot. One step at a time I safely made my way at least a quarter of a mile over the deep drifts before the trail once again turned upward onto better footing.

Since then I have invested in a more appropriate back country shoe, a pair of MSR Evo Ascent shoes with substantial front claws plus side rails to prevent slipping sideways or backwards down steep embankments. This model sports a snowboard style binding that is simple, easy to use and doesn't get all jammed up with ice. They are constructed with a heavy durable plastic decking that never wears out, unlike the soft vinyl material commonly used in other familiar brands and models.

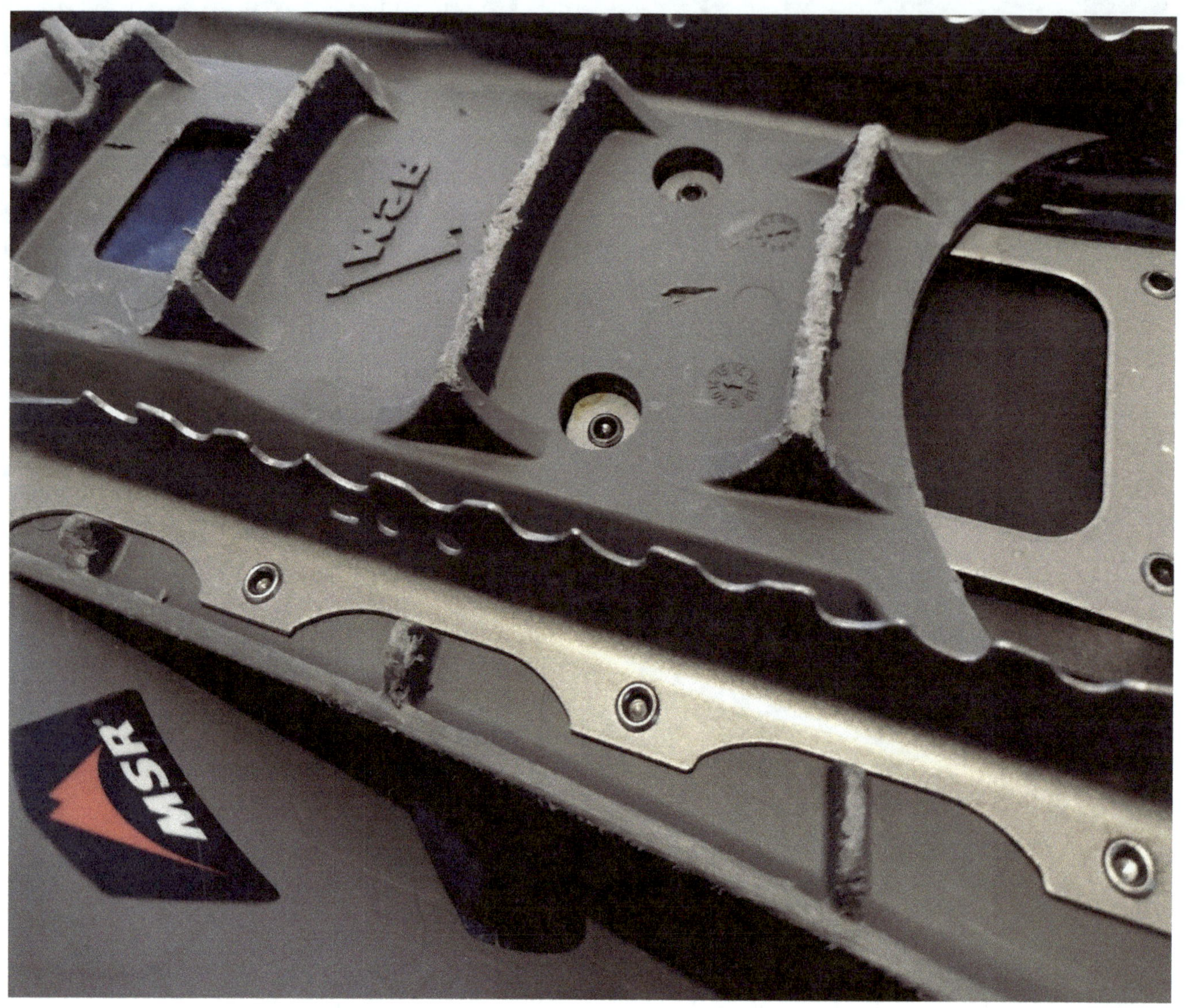

I can personally attest to the durability of this design, I've been wearing them for over a decade in all kinds of snow, including thin snow with rocks underneath. One time I even backed over them with my truck in the parking lot after carelessly forgetting to put them away and I'm happy to say they are none worse for the wear!

An apparently unremarkable reservoir on the barren plains just east of Denver is host to one of winter's most extraordinary events. **Barr Lake State Park** plays host to the annual bald eagle migration as dozens of the great raptors roost in tall cottonwoods surrounding the reservoir. Hundreds of Canada geese also call these icy waters home for the winter and each day they rise en masse in a great cloud as they depart in search of food in the surrounding fields. Wildlife photographers will also delight in a surprising variety of birds and mammals that occupy the high plains of Colorado in wintertime. The eagle migration can be expected between the months of November and March while these images were captured in February.

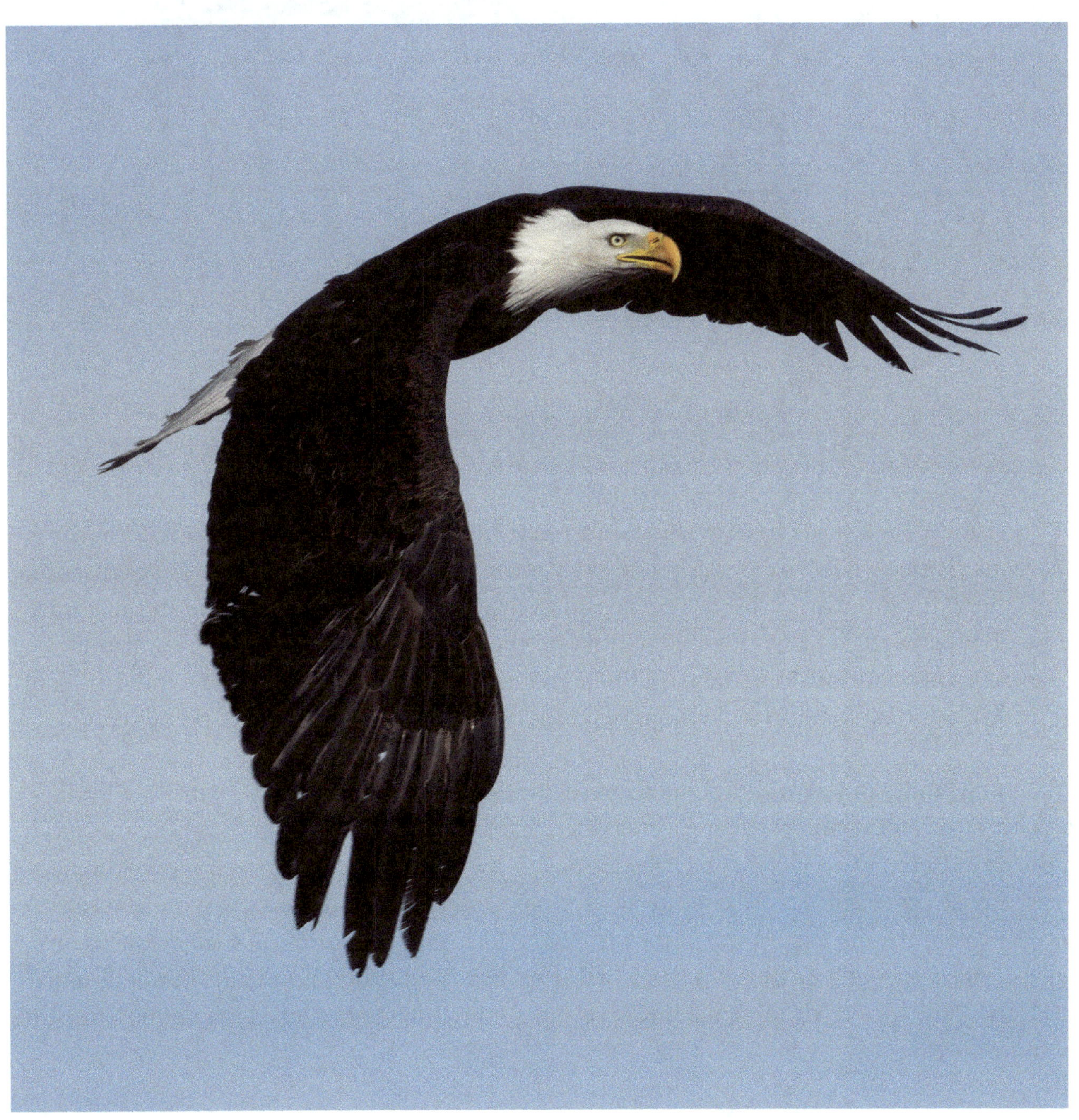

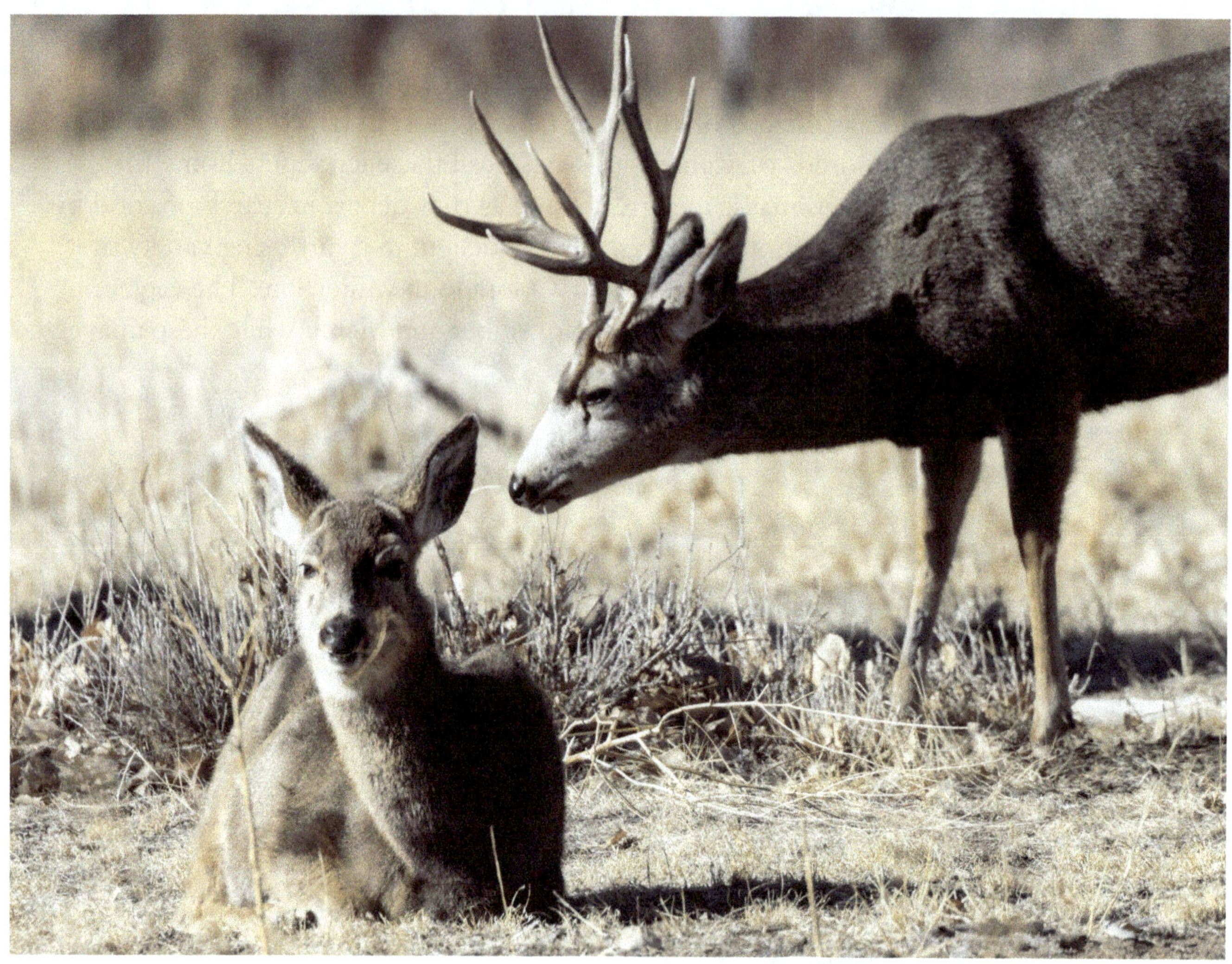

To visit the park take Highway 76 east just beyond the E-470 interchange and look for signs. Turn east on 152nd Street and then south on Picadilly Road to the park entrance. Once the state park day use fee has been paid at the kiosk, take the short drive to the nature center. Unfortunately it isn't possible to drive all the way around the reservoir, so plan to make your visit on foot along the paved bike trail surrounding the lake. Several miles of trail are available for exploration so I recommend touring on a mountain bike if possible.

A couple miles in you will find the main eagle viewing station, a lovely boardwalk leading onto the lake to the viewing gazebo where eagles can be seen along the shoreline and in the trees to the west. Unless an eagle decides to fly directly over the gazebo it will be necessary to use powerful glass to capture any meaningful images, but the view with beautiful Longs Peak in the distance is worth the visit even if close up captures of eagles don't materialize. Eagles roosting or flying in front of Longs Peak and other mountains in the distance make for some nice environmental images even if you don't have a lens long enough to bring them in close.

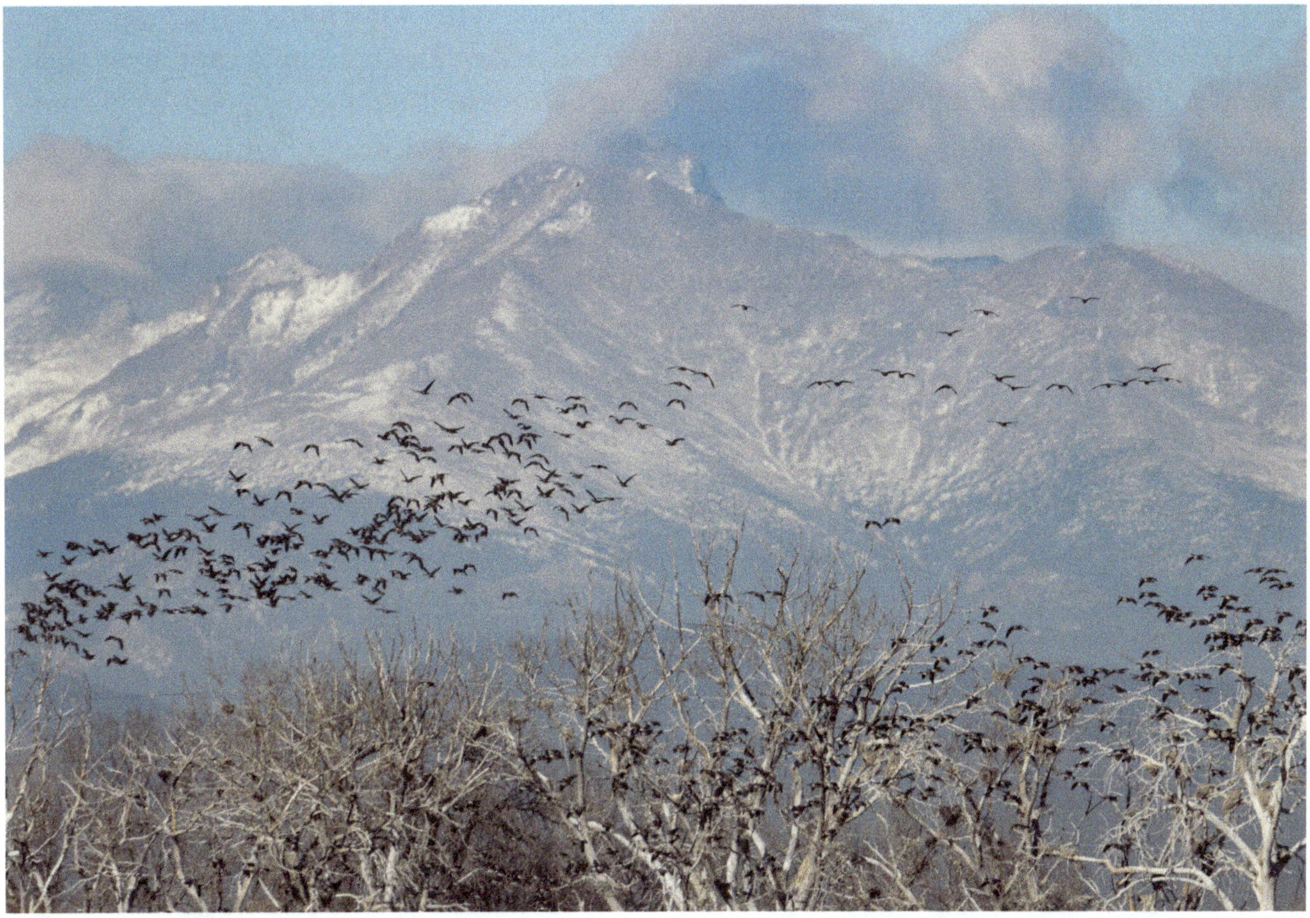

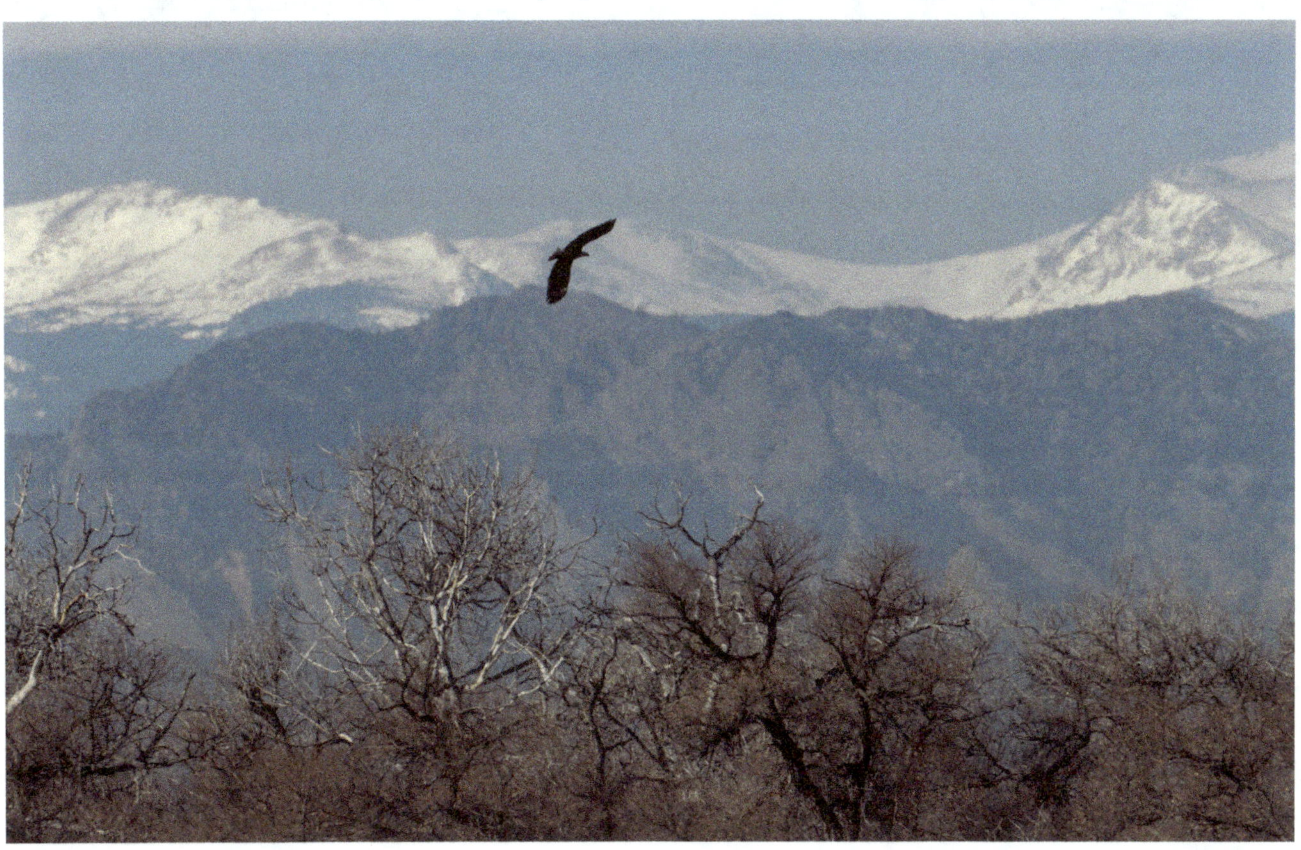

Naturally the bald eagles are the big draw for the park in the winter, but a mass ascension of hundreds or even thousands of Canada geese makes for an exciting capture as well! As you are watching and photographing bald eagles be sure to listen for the geese to become agitated right before their ascent. Excitement builds as they get closer to flight, giving photographers time to set up for the event. For this image I chose a fairly large center zone of focus, giving the camera plenty of subject material to lock onto. Firing several bursts at a fast frame rate assures several good captures of the entire event. Filling the camera buffer up in the first couple of seconds could result in missing the maximum spread of the flock as they ascend in a massive wave of wings and feathers, so shorter bursts give the camera time to catch up throughout the event.

An attractive backdrop for the image is also important, so as the event draws near it might be a good idea to move around to avoid unsightly objects and buildings in the background. If the camera in use doesn't have the most reliable auto focus, this would also be a good time to switch to manual and get focused on a point in the middle of the action. In the case of the image below, the birds on the shoreline are a good plane of focus. Choose a fast shutter speed for birds in flight, in this case a 1250th of a second worked well while allowing a very usable ISO value of 500 for low noise captures.

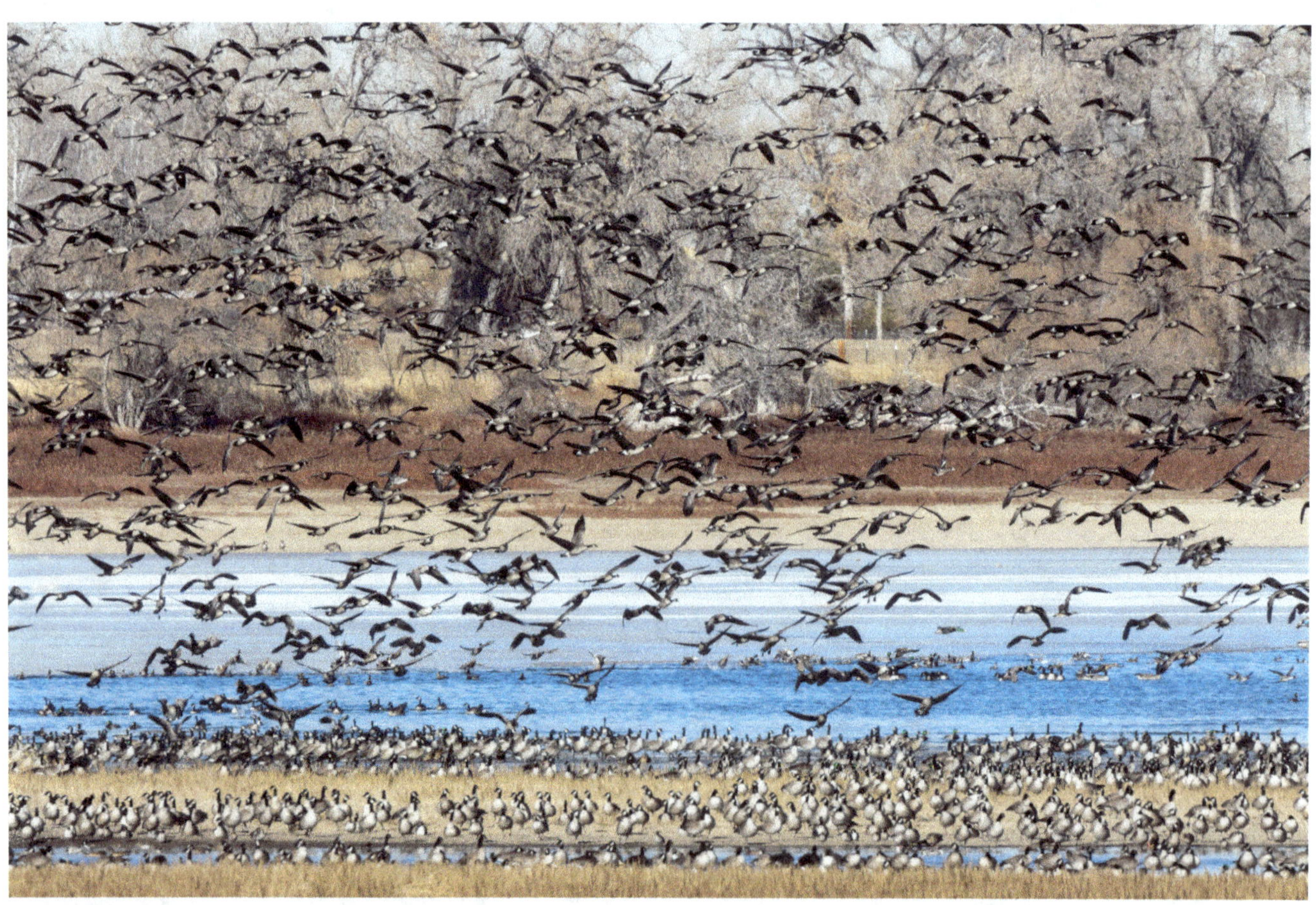

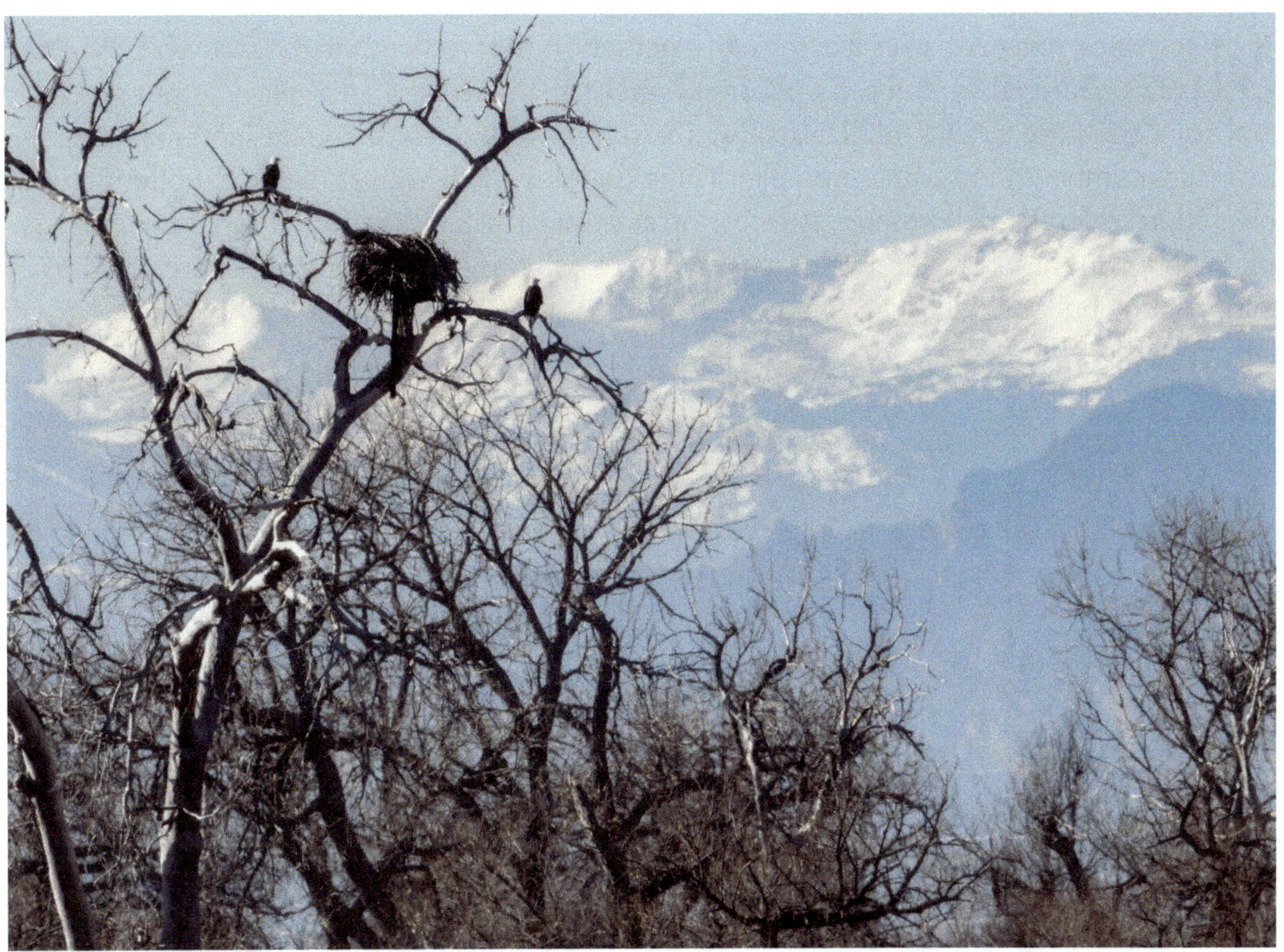

The viewing gazebo is nice, but much more dramatic captures can be acquired by moving closer to the action on the west end of the reservoir. This is where a mountain bike can come in handy, otherwise it is going to be a long walk back to the nature center on the hard paved path. The lake is host to at least one permanent nesting pair of bald eagles who raise a new eaglet or two each season. Unfortunately the above nest was tragically blown down in a windstorm but with the assistance of park staff the pair has since built a new nest and has resumed breeding.

A good tripod is invaluable when trying to capture sharp captures of such distant birds. When they are standing still on branches a tripod allows for a slower shutter speed, facilitating a lower ISO value. The above shot was taken at an 800th of a second at f/8, resulting in an ISO value of 320 and a very clear and noise free image.

As winter wears on, the pair returns to the nest where they concentrate on repairing and reinforcing their home for the annual breeding season. In another month or so from the time of this image, eggs will appear and one of the pair will be at the nest at all times until the eaglets can defend themselves against any possible threat.

Mature and juvenile eagles like to soar together on the west end of the reservoir. Picnic tables scattered around the western terrain of the park are a great place to put down your pack and have a snack while watching the skies overhead for the great raptors at play. Exposure compensation comes into play as the eagles fly high against the bright blue sky and low with trees in the background. A factor of at least +1 will be needed to avoid underexposing the birds in the sky, while a value closer to zero will provide the right exposure when trees comprise the bulk of the background.

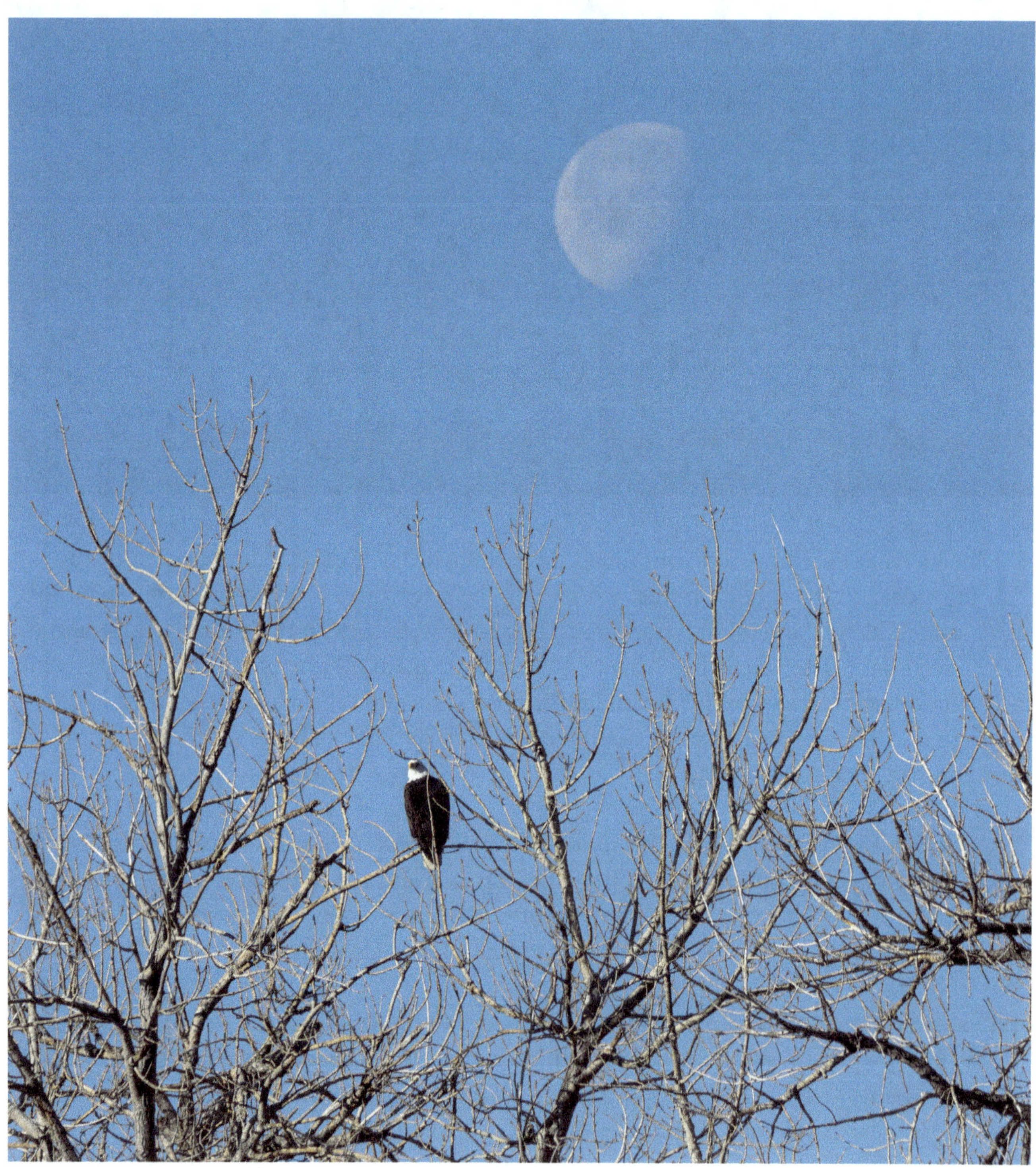

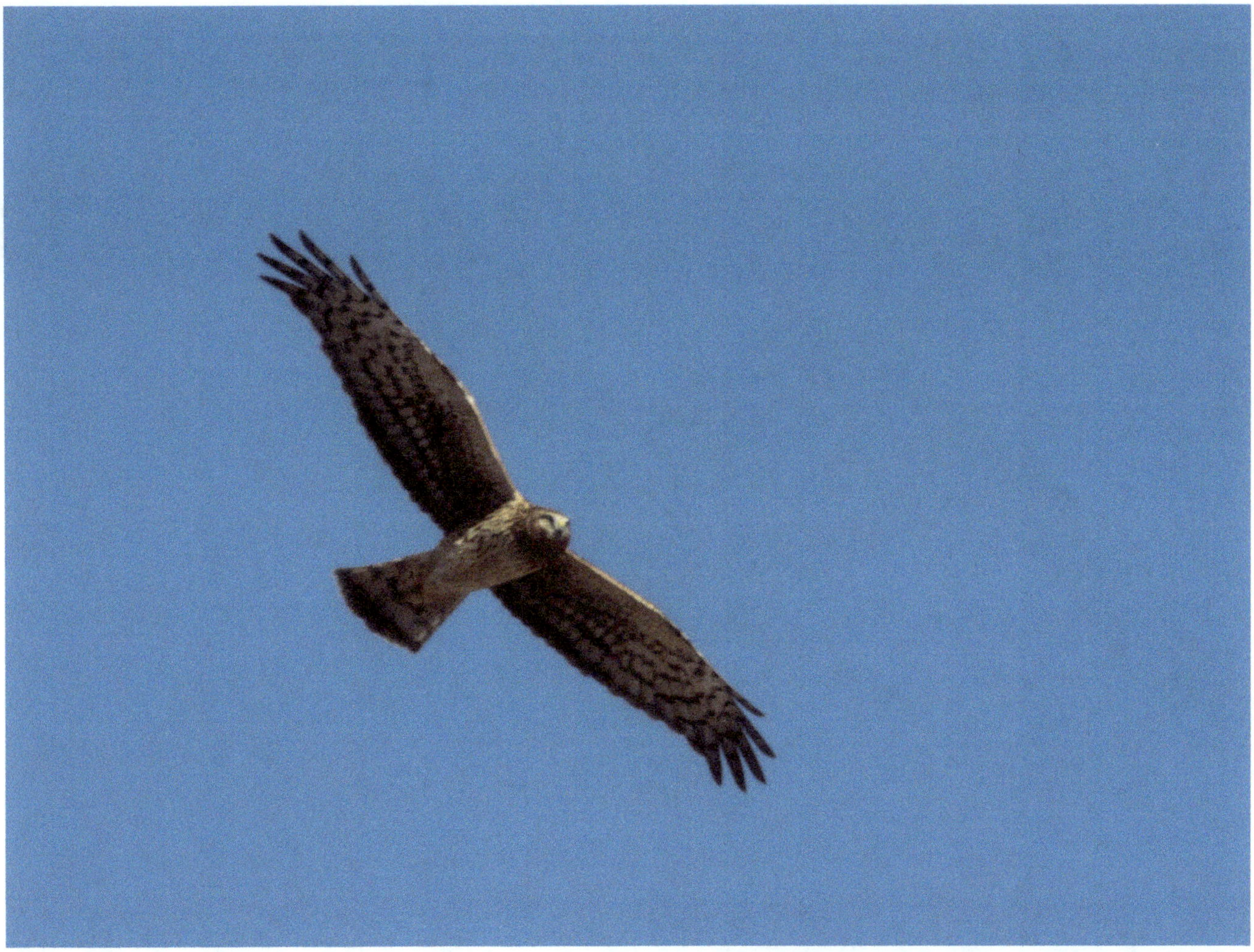

A healthy population of prairie dogs and other rodents on the west end of the lake attract a number of raptor species such as the beautiful northern harrier shown above, red-tailed hawks (next page), golden eagles and juvenile bald eagles. A 2000th of a second is a good choice for capturing these raptors in flight. They appear to be floating slowly in the sky but in reality they could be propelled by upper air currents at speeds approaching 100 mph. Make sure image stabilization is turned on in your lens or camera, it's difficult to avoid camera shake when tracking these speeding predators across the blazing blue Colorado sky. I enjoyed the challenge of trying to capture two subjects in a single frame.

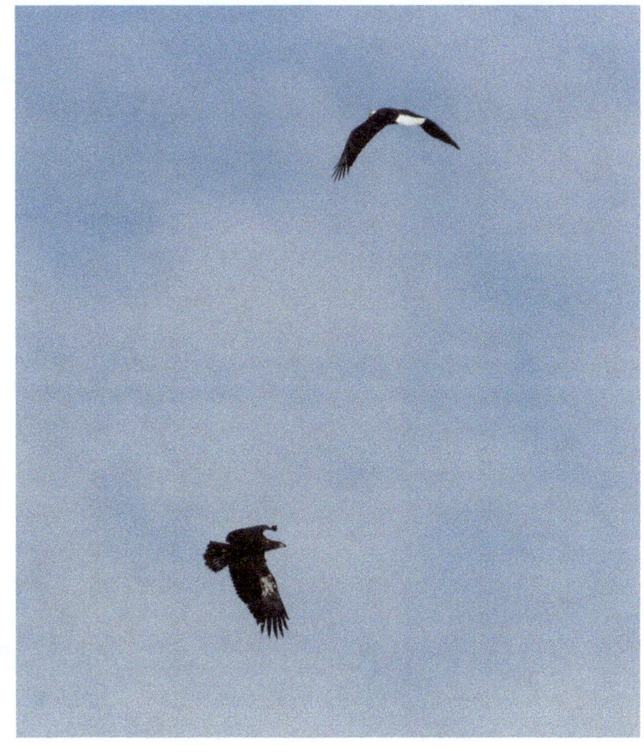

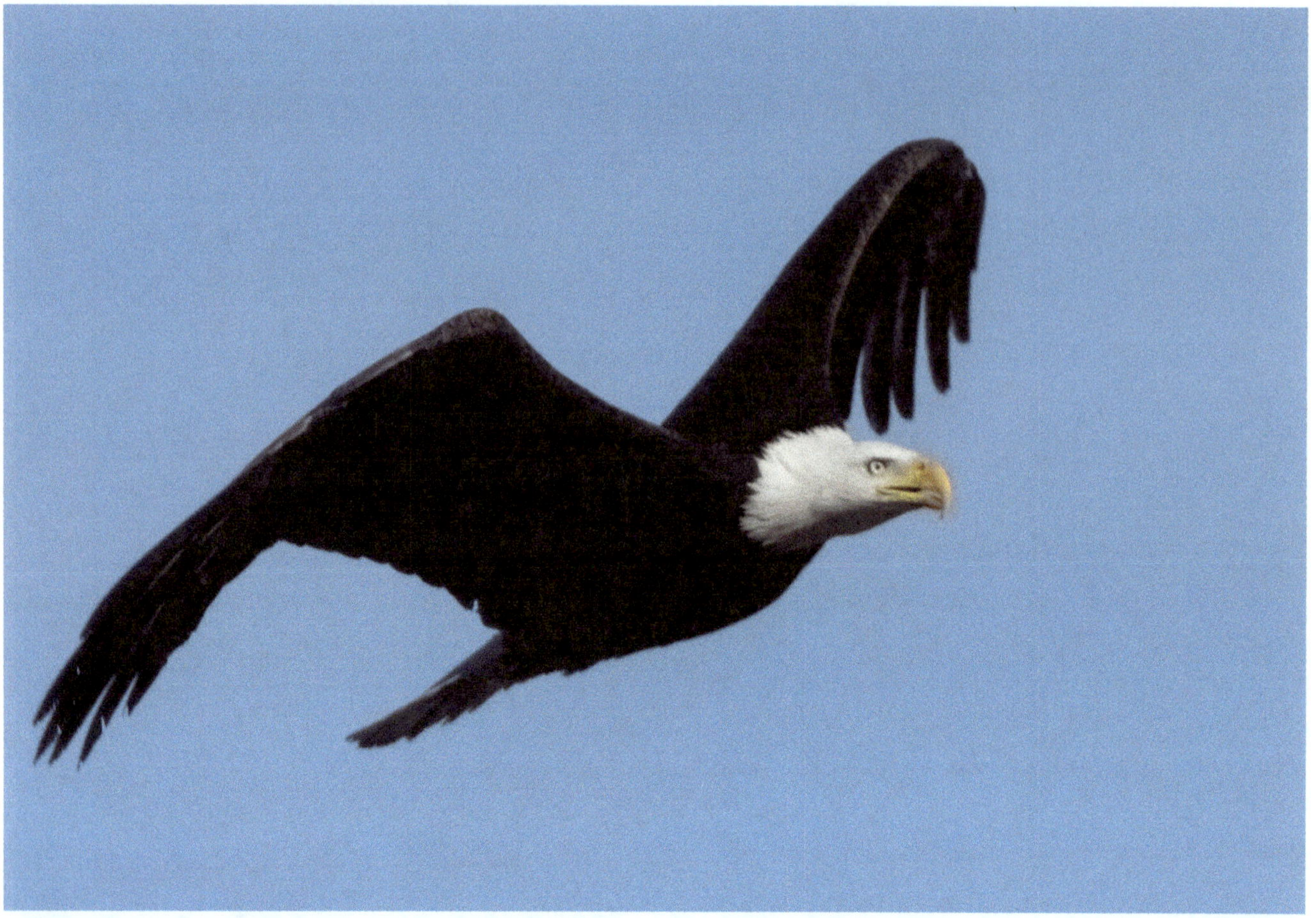

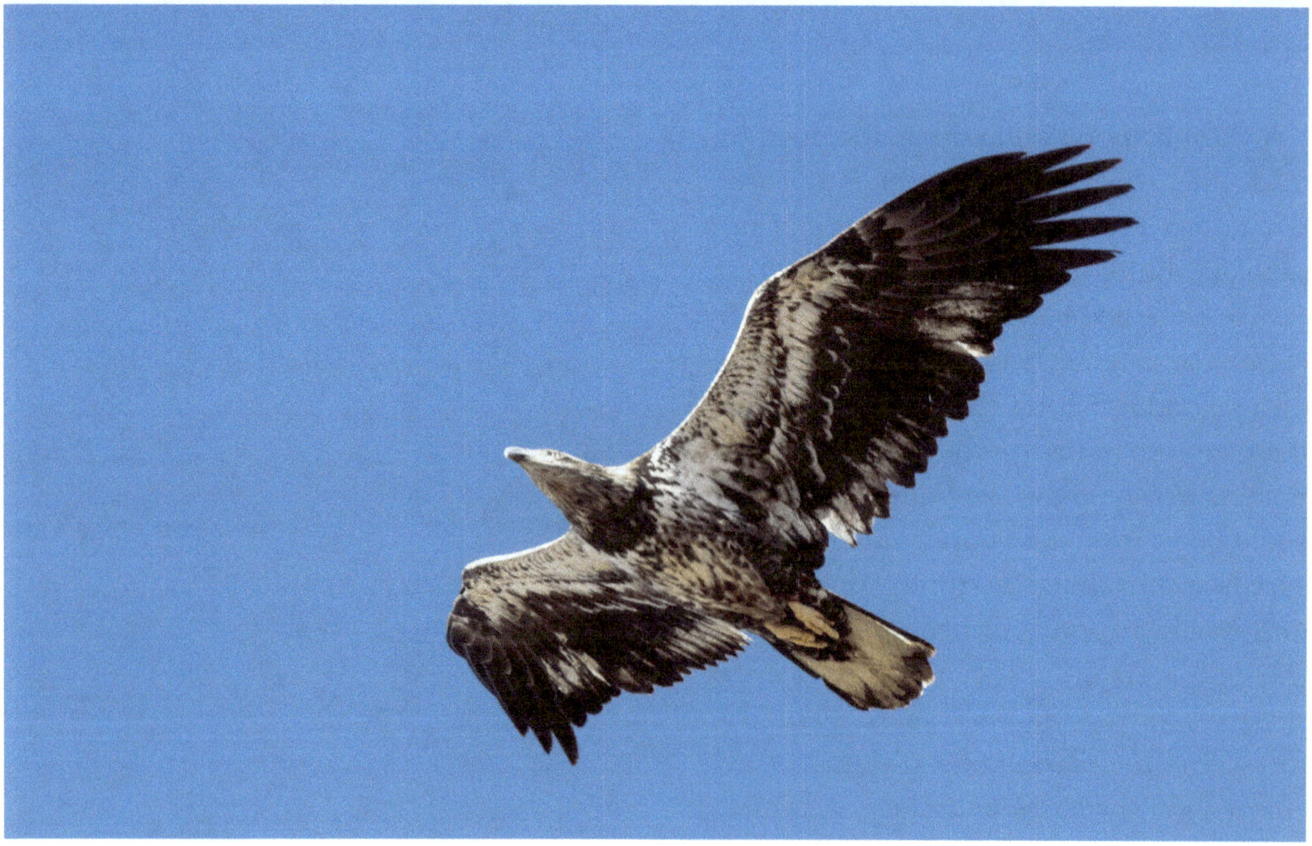

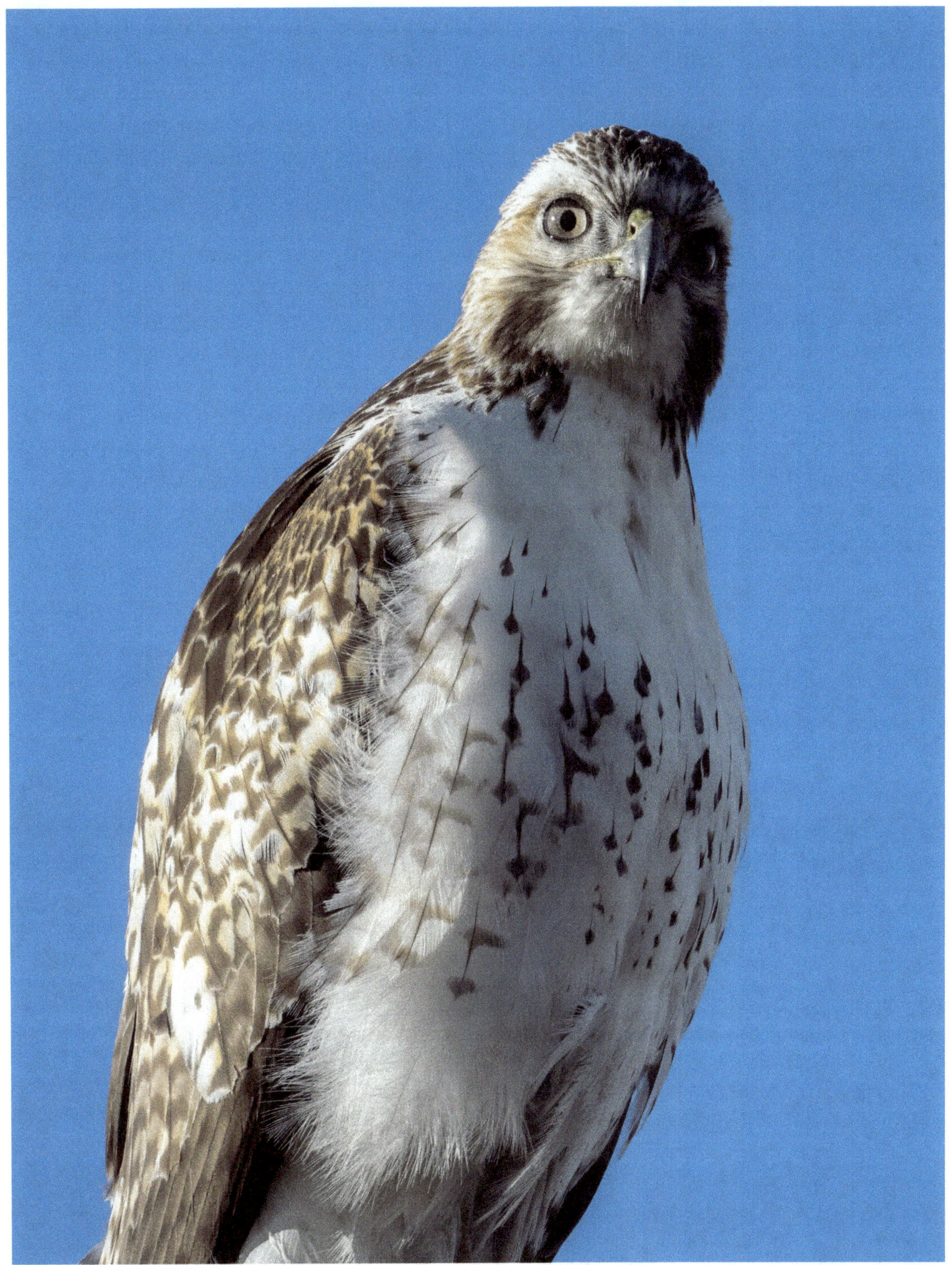

Winter conditions on the sunbaked spires of **Garden of the Gods Park** in Colorado Springs are a fleeting opportunity, but well worth the effort for diligent photographers. The beauty of sandstone rock formations with majestic Pikes Peak in the background in this free park is unparalleled. Although it frequently snows on the foothills of 14,115 foot Pikes Peak, winter conditions don't last long in the garden once the bright Colorado sun beams down on the snow.

The best approach to capturing winter conditions in the park is to watch the weather for a forecast of nighttime snow and arrive at first light long before the sun has the power to begin melting the new mantle of white. Often the snow is already gone by 10:00 in the morning, so photographers should have a plan to quickly identify which rock formations to shoot and from what vantage points. Great panoramic vistas are visible from the sign at the entrance on 30th street, the patio of the visitor center and the overlook on Mesa Road above the visitor center. Beautiful Pikes Peak stands watch over the Garden in all of these locations and is even more stunning than usual in snow capped winter glory. Snow also turns the normally dark pine forest at the base of the mountain into a magical picturesque winter wonderland.

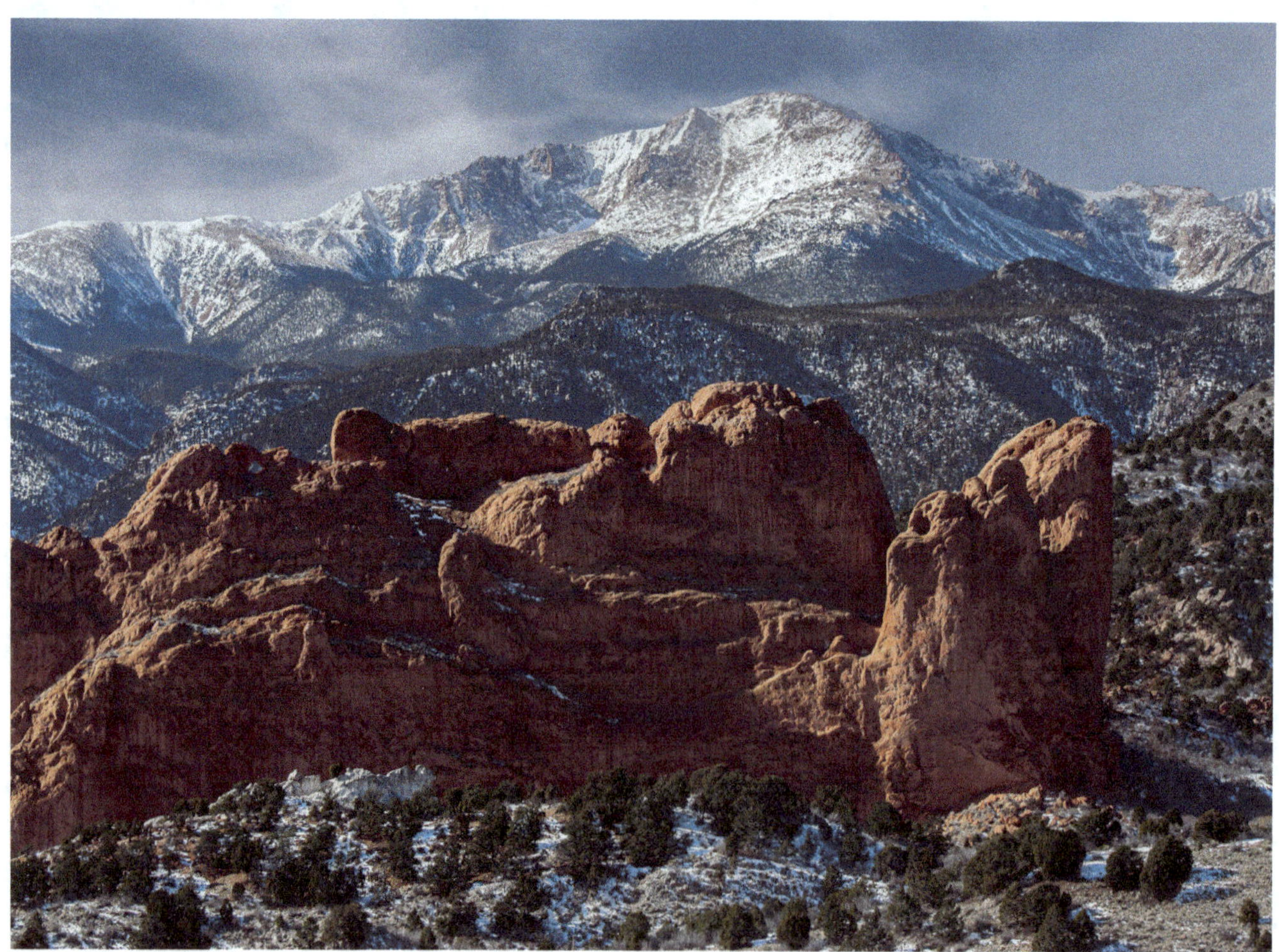

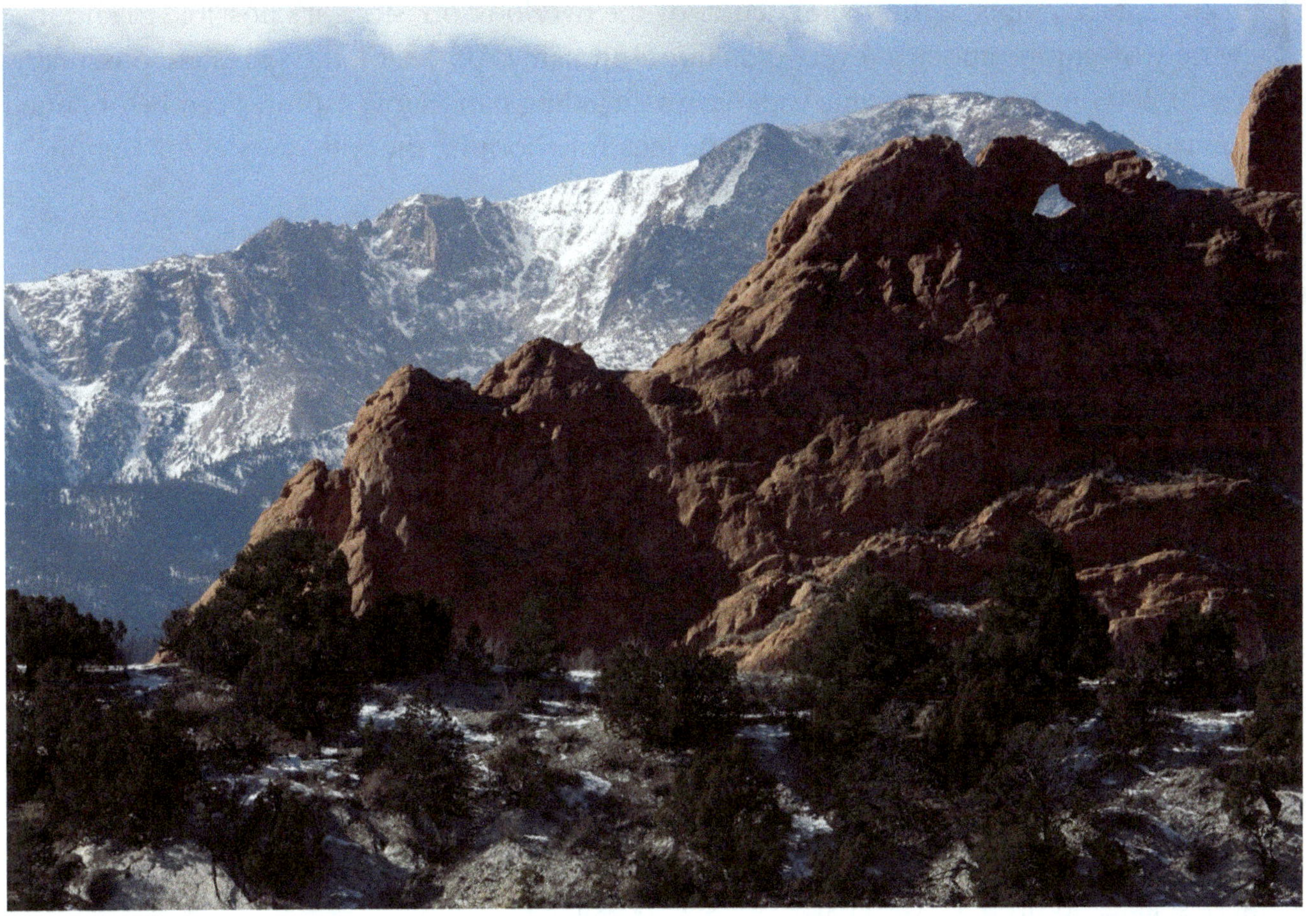

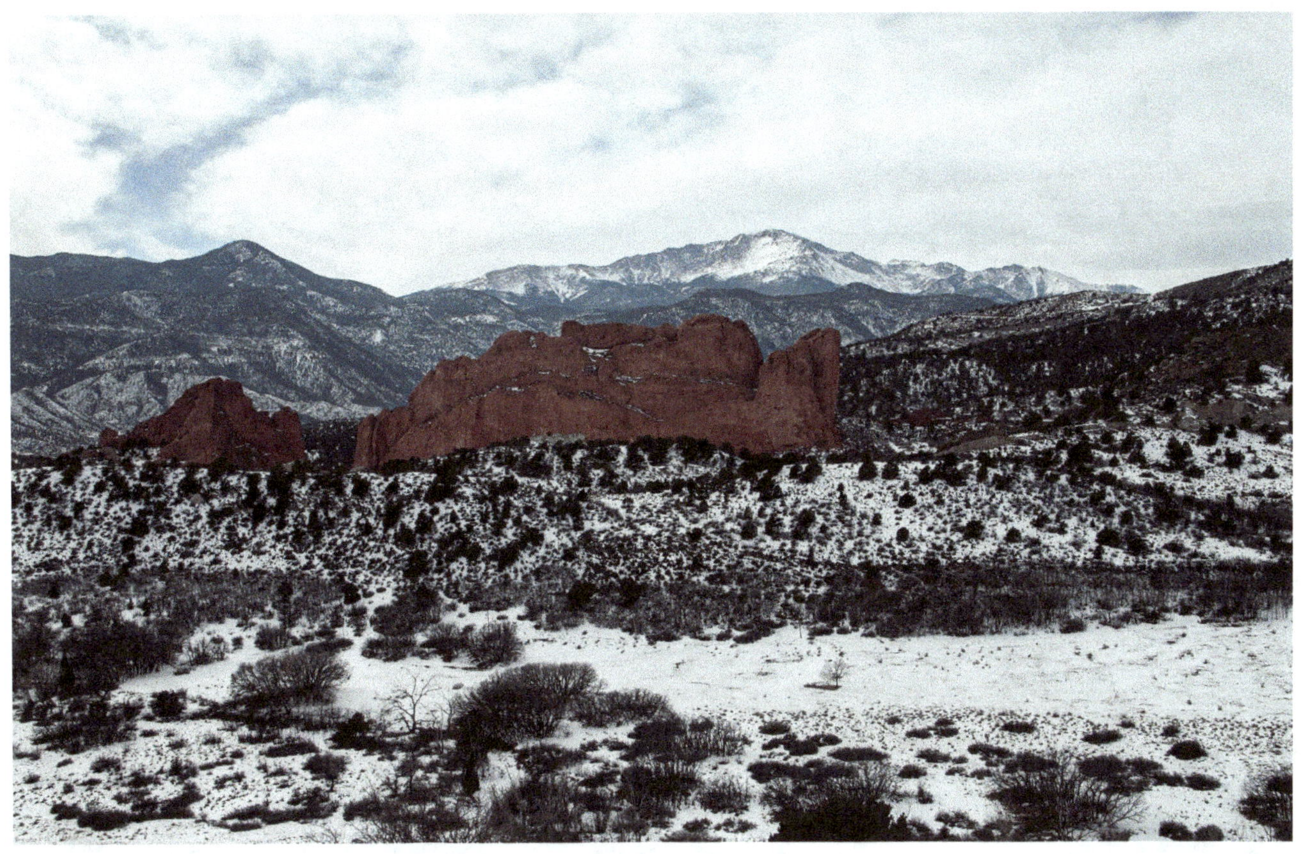

From vantage points at the visitor center or the overlook on Mesa, it's possible to shoot a variety of compositions in every direction. Intimate captures of the spires are possible with a 70-200mm zoom lens while wide views including panoramic captures can be obtained with a wide prime or zoom lens. My favorite lens for shooting the wide view is my Canon 24-105 F4L.

Shooting wide will make the peak in the background appear small while a longer focal length will bring it in close, displaying it much more prominently in the image. Clear blue sky mornings are nice but I like to have a bit of cloud cover to add drama to the scene. The lowest ISO value possible for the lighting conditions will yield the highest quality image and a smaller aperture such as f/8 will make nearby rock formations sharp while clearly rendering detail on the distant peak.

Camera shake might become an issue when using longer focal lengths if your chosen ISO value results in a slow shutter speed. The old rule of picking a shutter speed based on 1/focal length doesn't really apply these days with new high megapixel cameras. High pixel density sensors are very susceptible to recording the slightest camera movement even with stability options turned on, and I find 1/(3 * focal length) to be a better starting point. For the sharpest images I recommend shooting in live view or electronic shutter mode using a tripod with stabilization turned off. The two second timer or a cable release will also limit camera shake and produce the sharpest image possible.

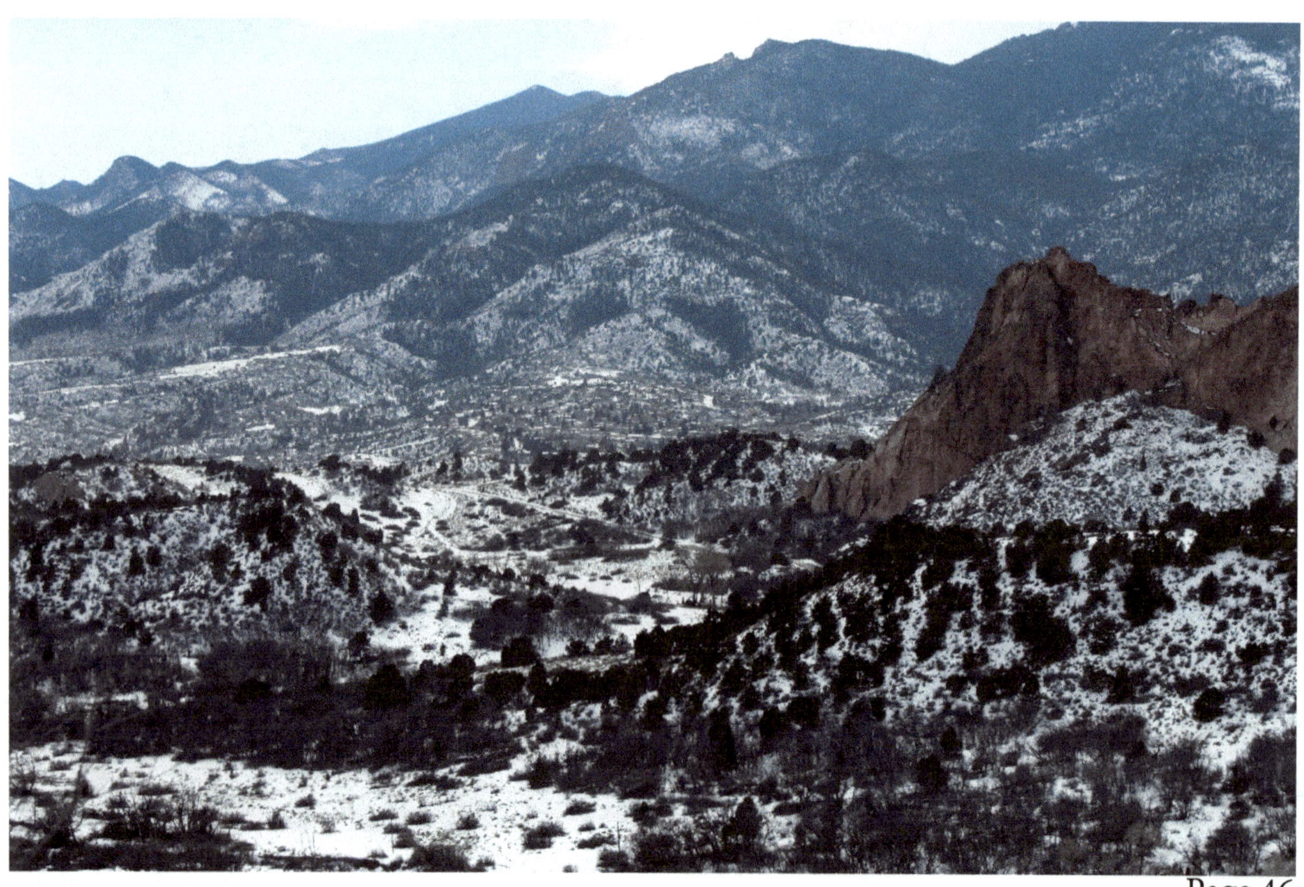

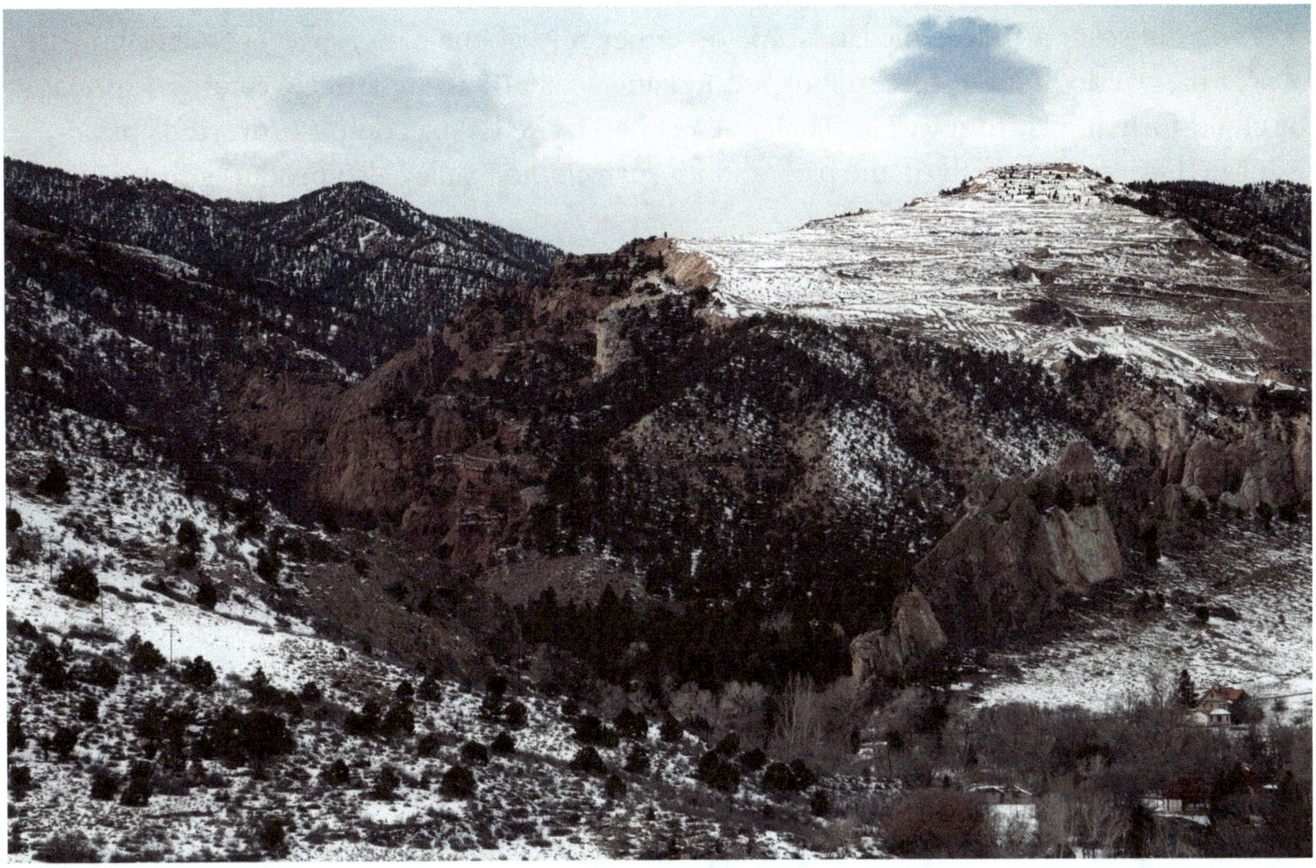

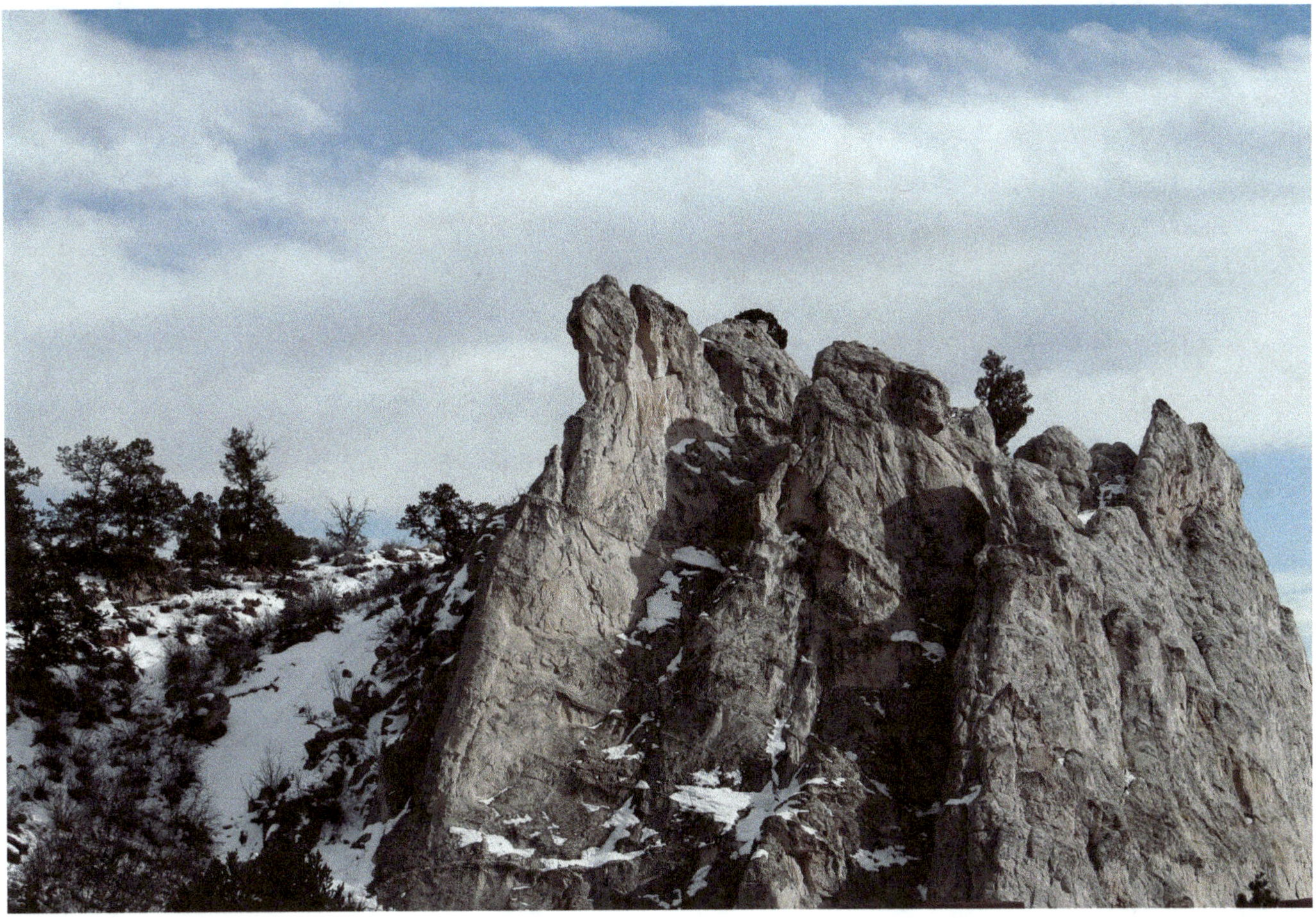

Beautiful scenery graces the landscape on either side of the park as well, so while you are at the overlook make sure to look around and see if there are attractive compositions or cloud formations from various angles. The Glen Eyrie Castle complex (previous page) is located just to the north of the park and it's surrounding valley also produces some nice compositions in the right light.

If you are lucky enough to still have snow after thoroughly working the overlooks, there are many views of individual formations from the road and hiking trails in the park. Keep an eye on the light and shadows and get into position to use the best angles to create the most interesting compositions. Wide angle lenses are the best choice for captures of nearby spires, but it's still a good idea to change the perspective using various focal lengths. I don't usually bother to carry a tripod on my treks around the park, aperture priority with f/8 and ISO 200 or so is going to result in a fast enough shutter speed in the brighter light of mid morning to avoid camera shake.

A short climb up to the Siamese Twins can produce some nice compositions, including the one below with snowy Pikes Peak in view between the towering formations.

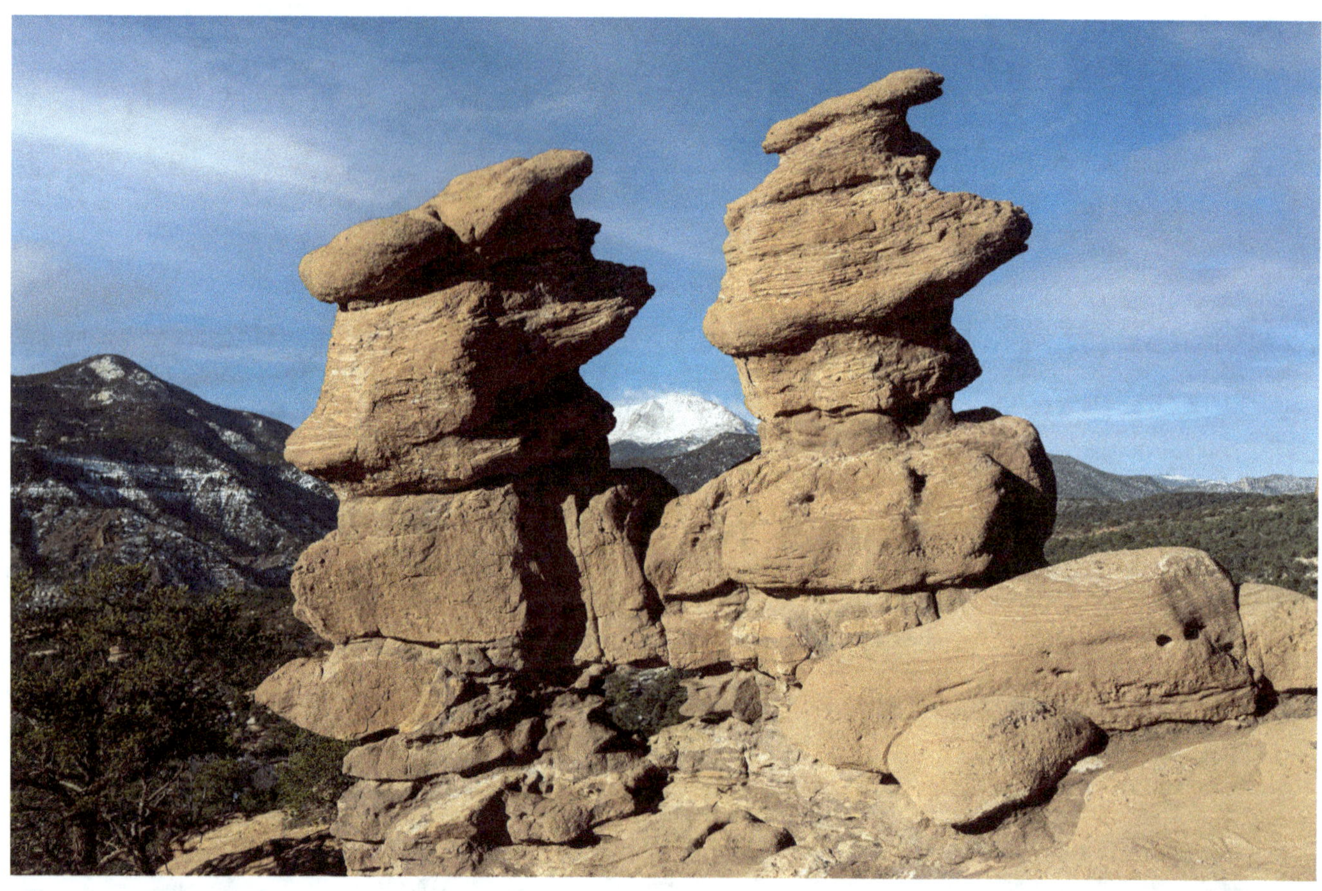

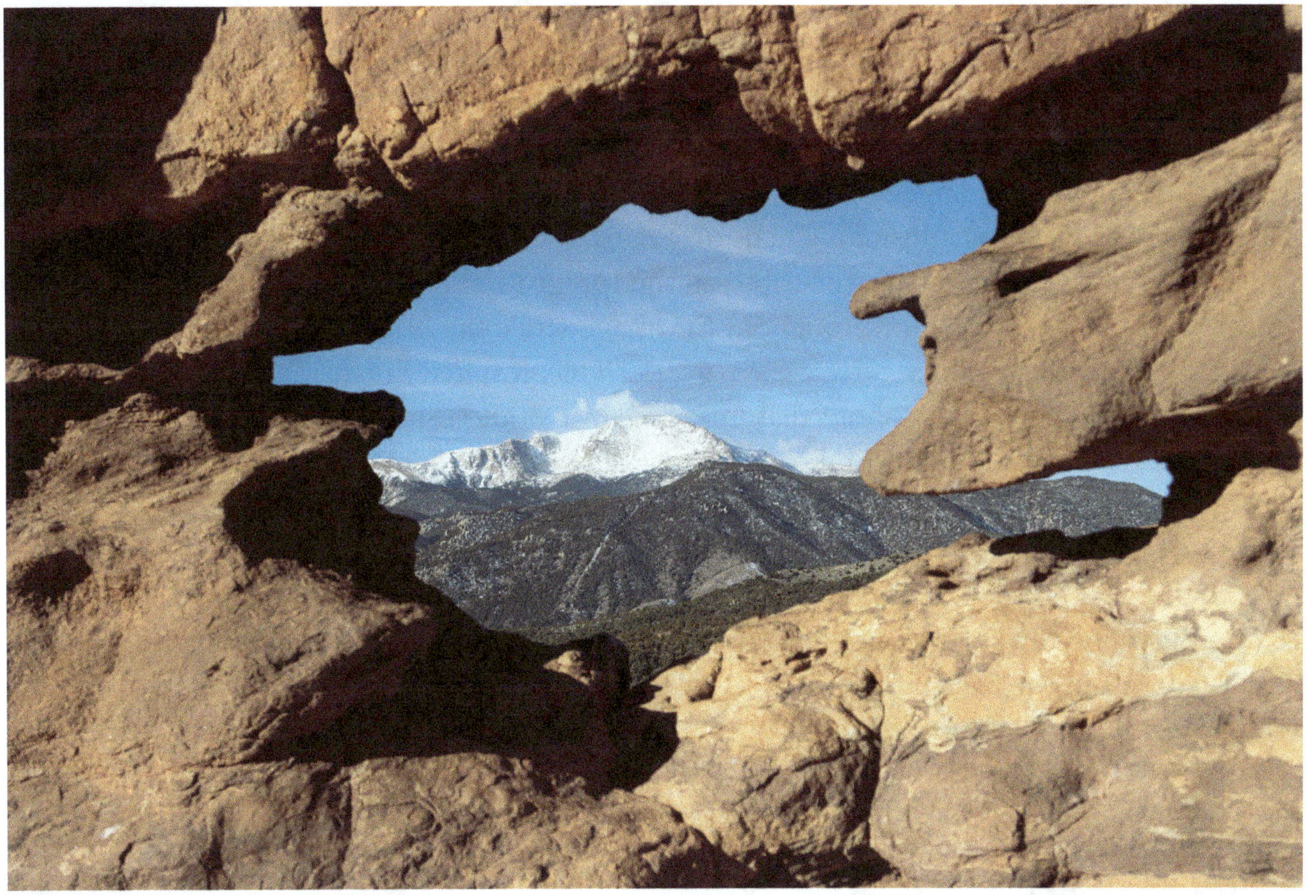

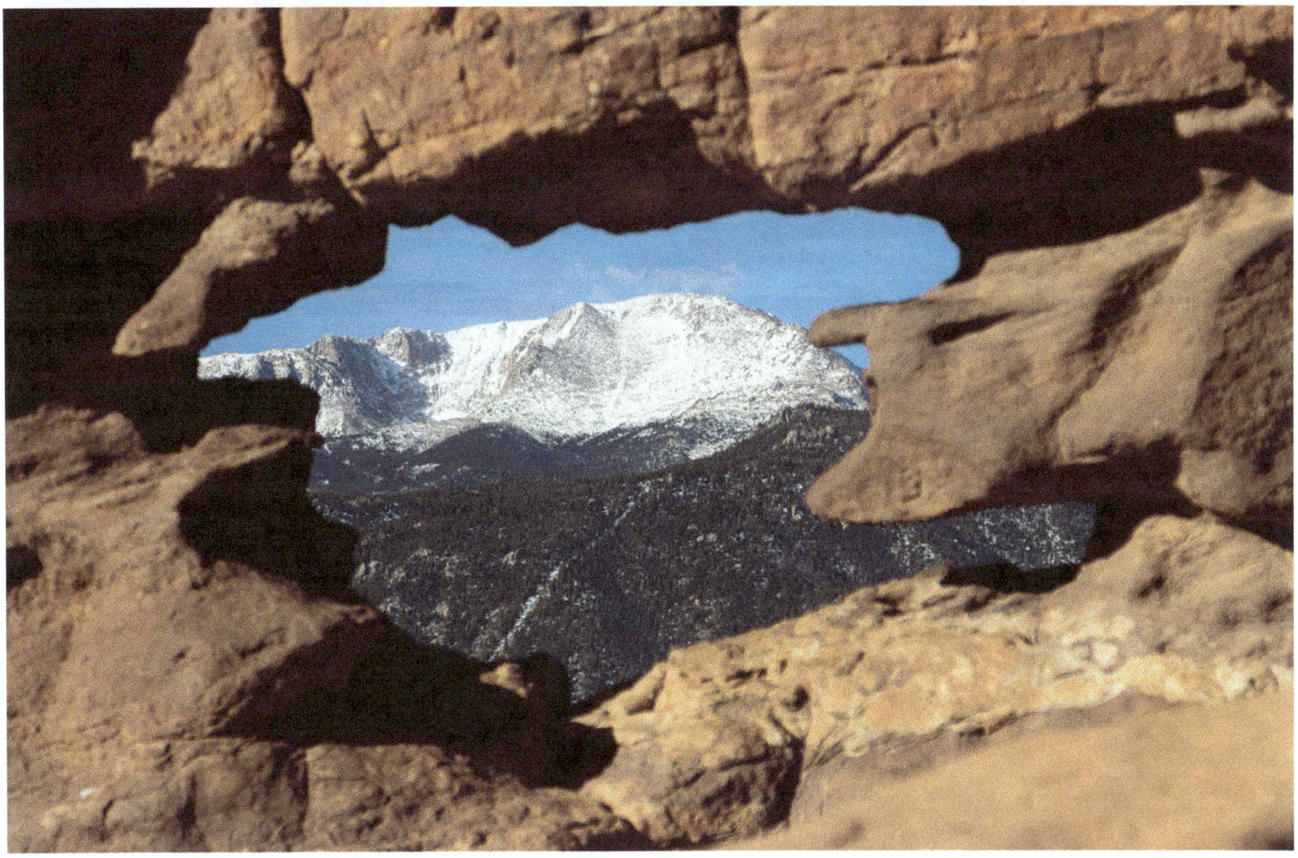

Winter is also the best time to shoot Pikes Peak through the keyhole between the sisters (previous page). It is of course possible in the summer, but the peak buried under heavy snow is much more attractive and dramatic. The keyhole is best photographed early in the morning when orange sandstone rocks and the peak in the distance are bathed in the golden light of morning sunshine. Focus on the peak in the background while using a wide aperture to get as much detail as possible on the foreground rocks. Notice the top image (previous page) is fairly sharp throughout the image while the bottom composition using a longer focal length to increase the size of the peak has resulted in blurring of the sandstone in the foreground. Were I to shoot that image again I would use a tripod and shoot two exposures, one for the mountain and another focused on the sandstone. The two images could then be focus stacked in post to produce a sharp foreground and background.

A bright blue sky provides wonderful contrast for both the white mountain in the background and the amazing colored rocks in the foreground, while a few wispy clouds add a bit of drama in the background.

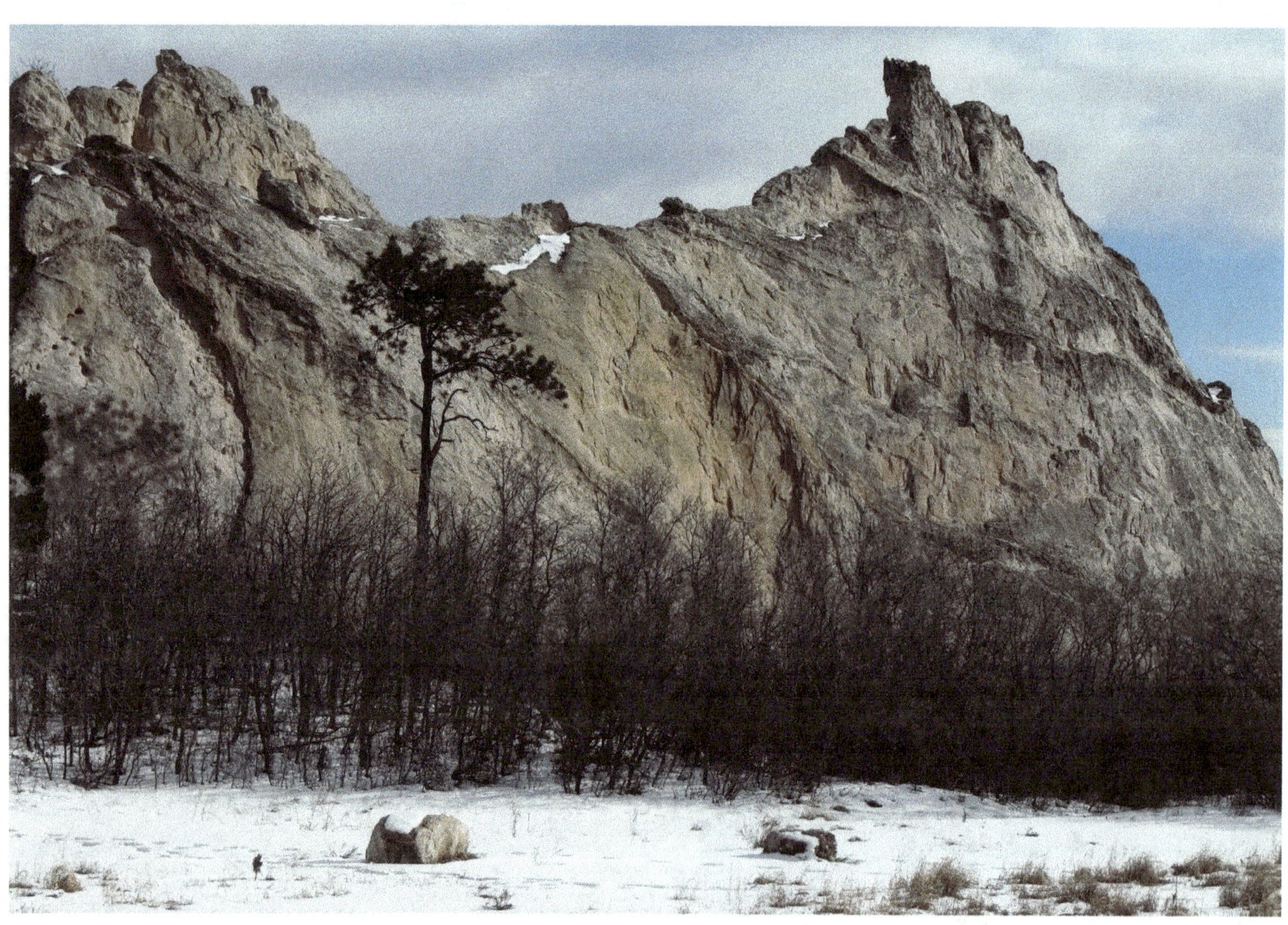

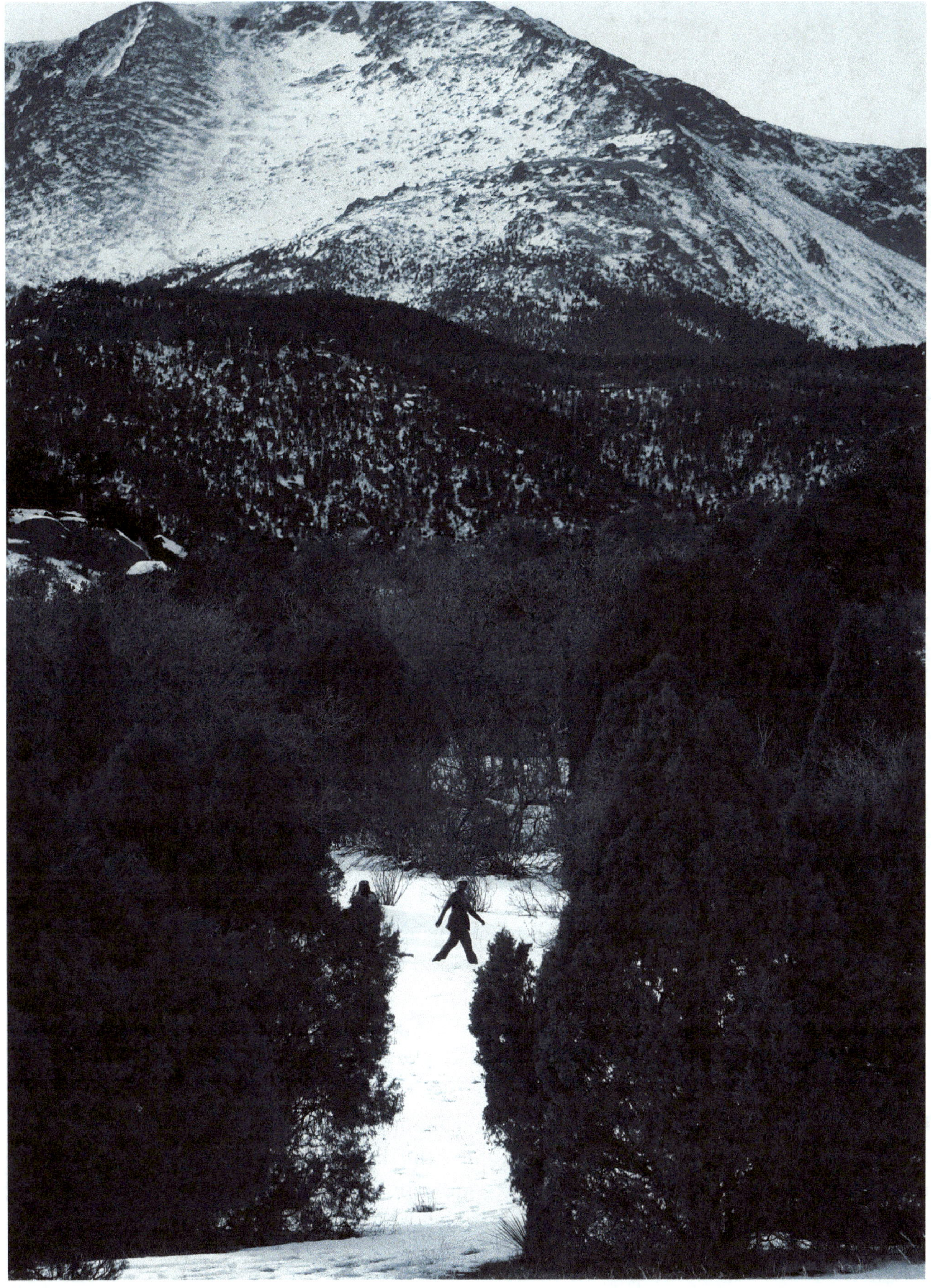

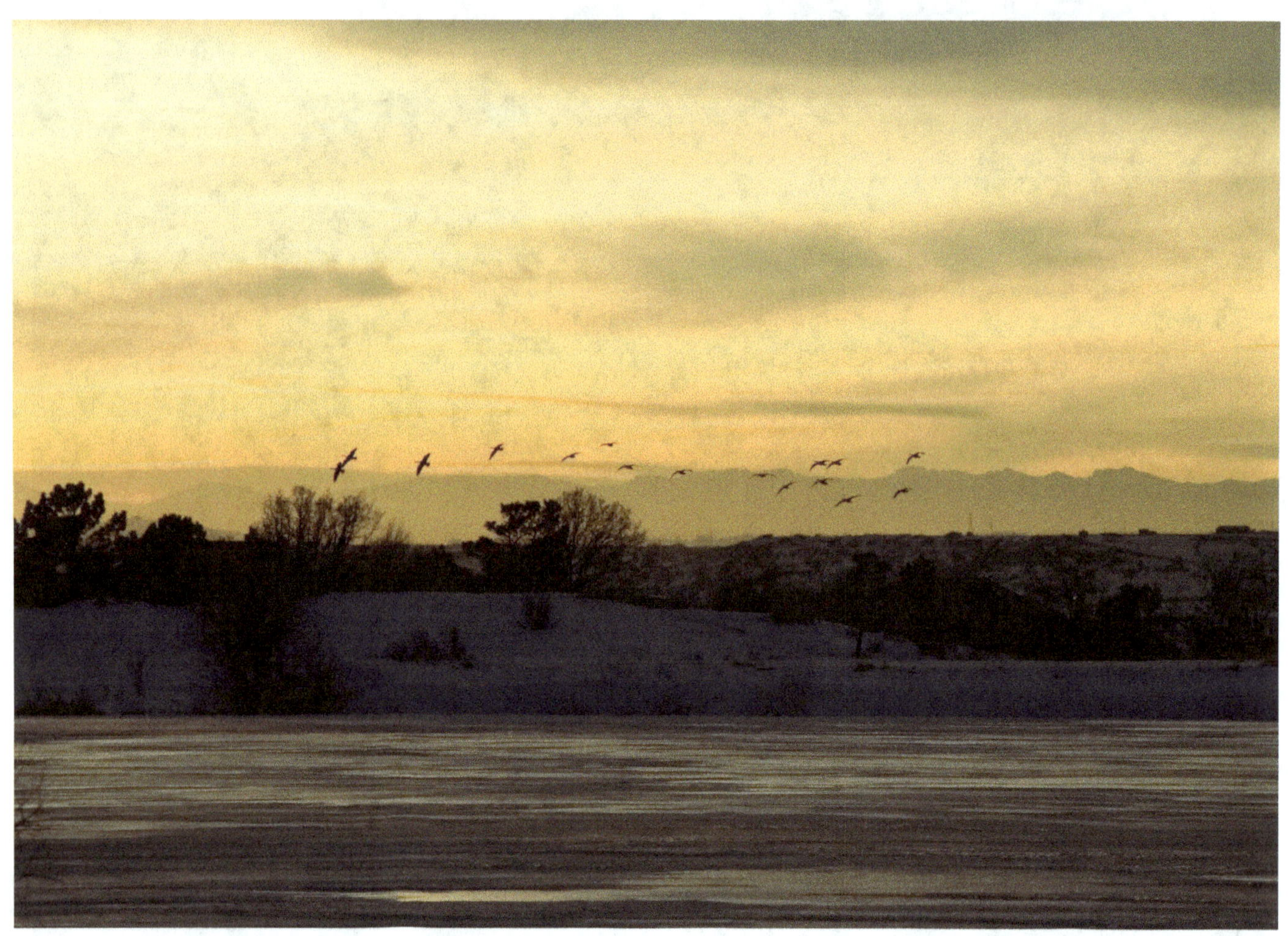

Icy sunsets on Front Range lakes are another worthy subject if you don't mind standing in the cold for a few minutes waiting for the show to develop! The beauty and solitude of the setting sun shimmering on frozen lakes with no one else around is simply exquisite. Canada geese flying in for the night against the golden sky and mountains to the west make for such a beautiful tranquil setting that it can't help but shine through in the images.

The most important part of sunset photography in the winter is to dress warm. The temperature drops like a rock as the sun dips behind the mountains and that's when the show is just beginning! I like to put the camera on manual exposure mode with an ISO value of no more than 400 and aperture set to f/8. Then I adjust the shutter speed and check the histogram often to assure that my exposures remain correct even though the light is rapidly fading.

Expose for the sky and don't worry too much about detail on the hills. Sometimes the mountains will be silhouetted and other times the distant haze will become illuminated from the reflection of light in the sky. Foreground exposure and detail can be adjusted in post using image editing software.

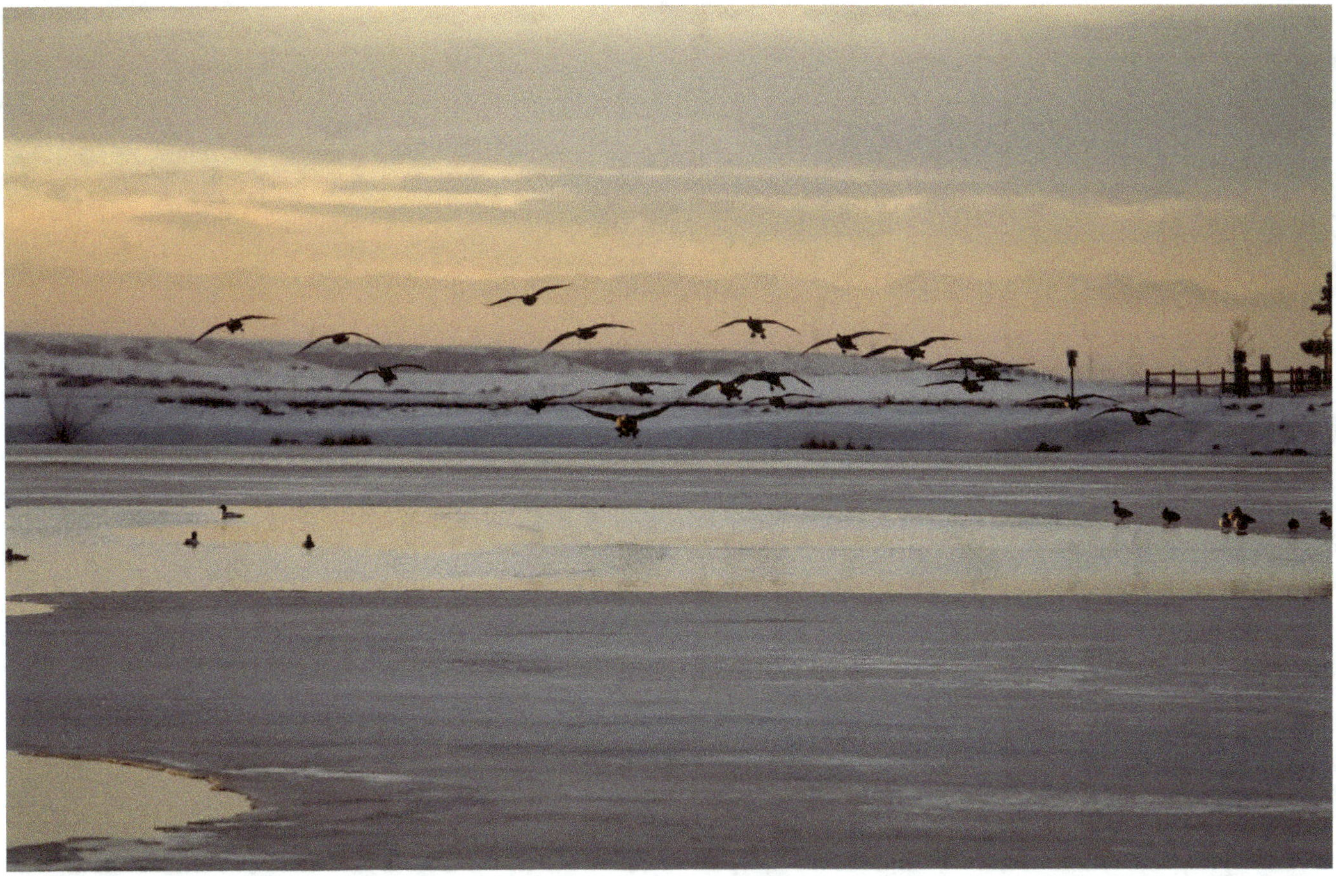

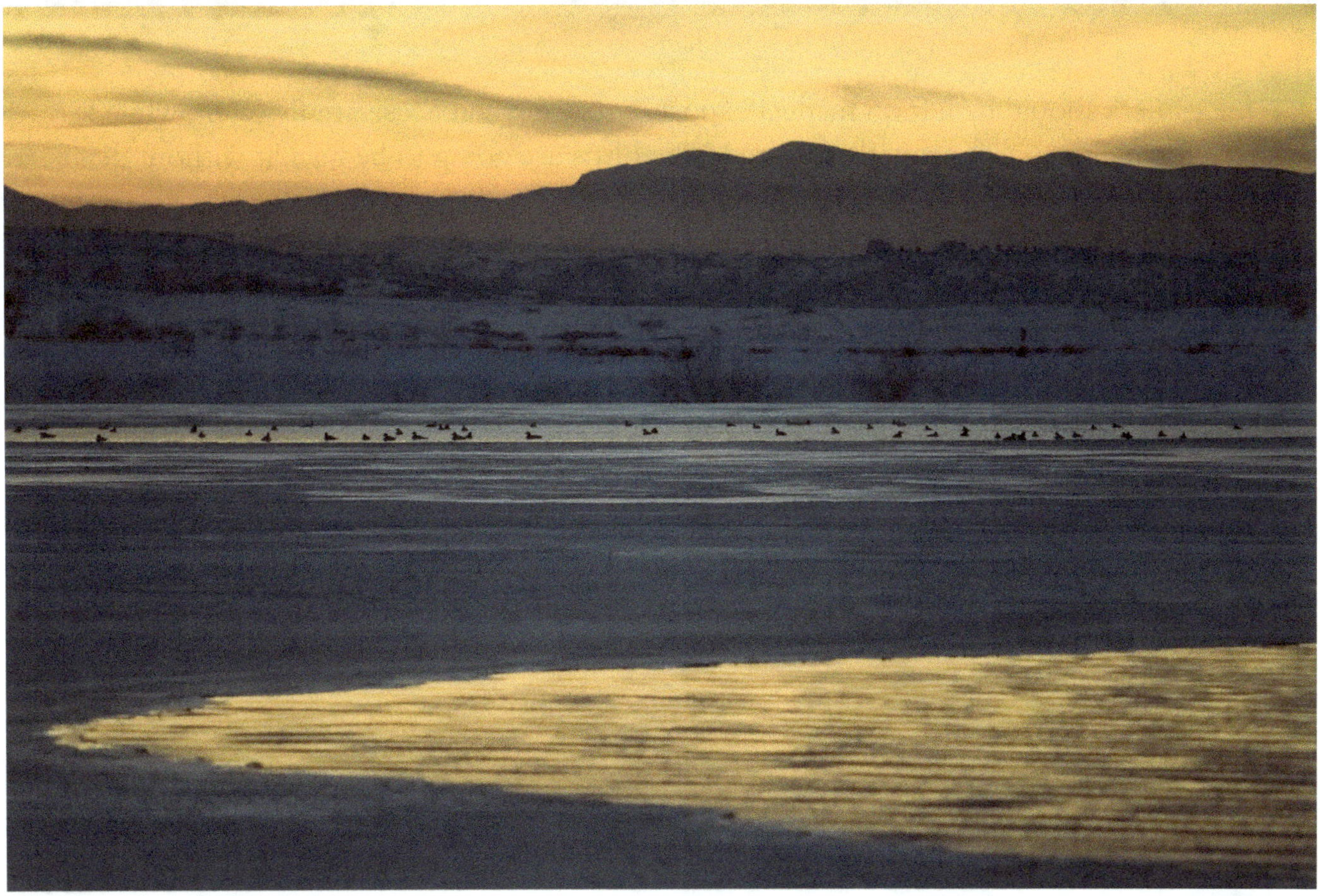

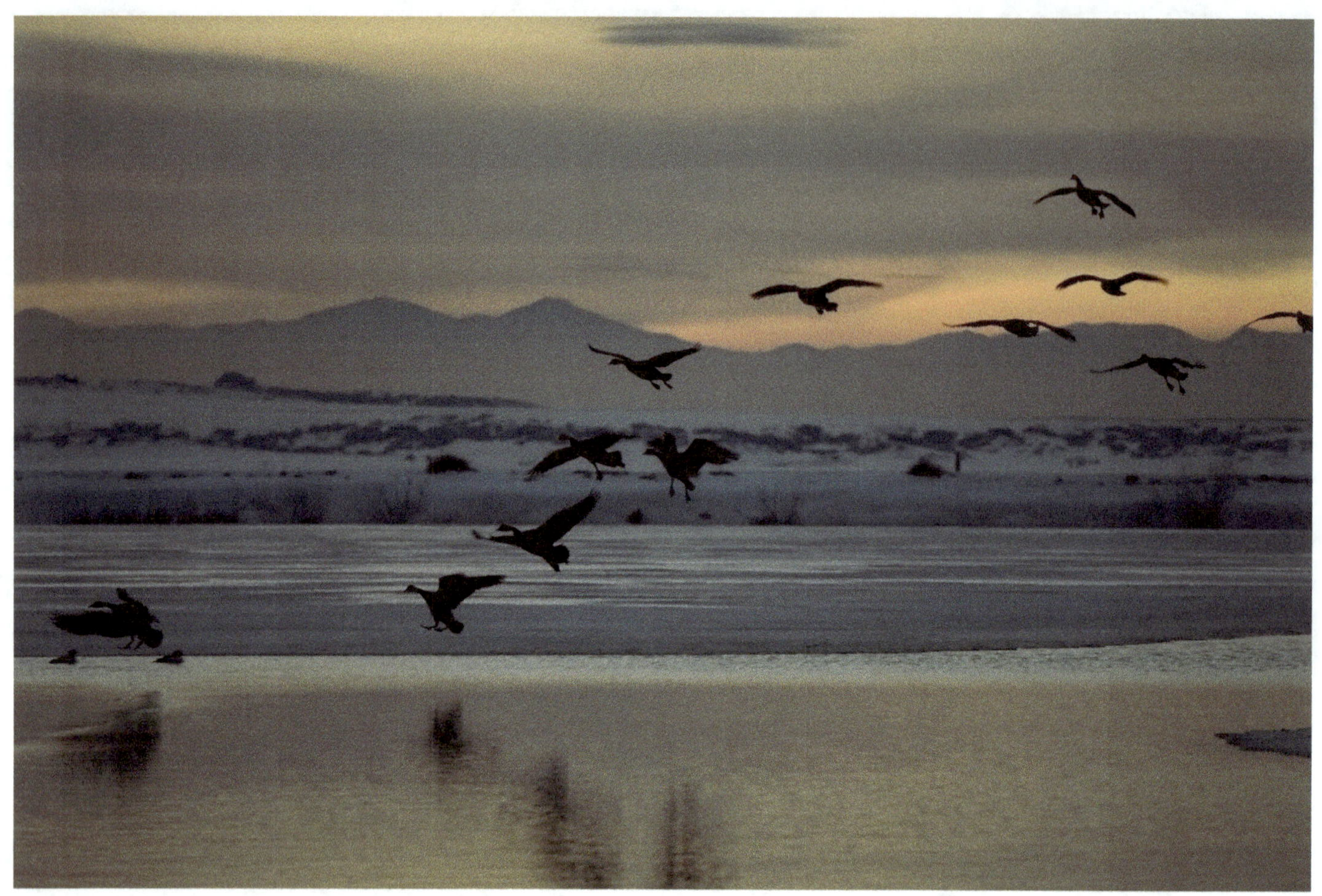

The camera should be left on manual exposure mode when geese are flying in, while leaving the overall scene properly exposed. The birds are going to be backlit without detail anyway so it's fine to expose them as silhouettes. But if you know your image is going to show them in flight it's a good idea to use a higher shutter speed to keep them from blurring, such as these images using 160th of a second at f/4 and ISO 200.

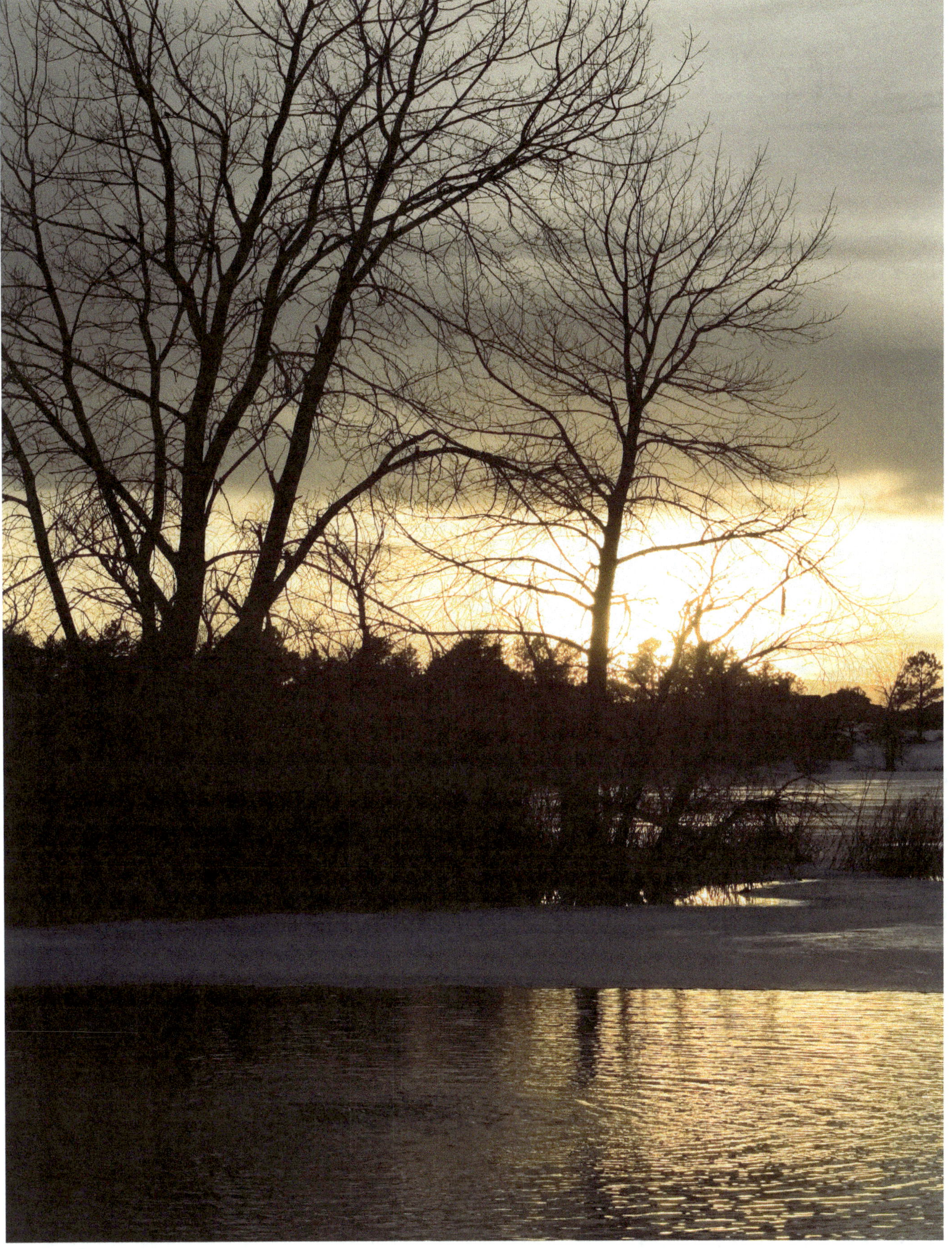

The Boulder Ranger District

Not everyone thinks of the **Boulder Ranger District and Arapaho & Roosevelt National Forests** as a place to visit in winter, but snowshoe and cross country ski trails, rugged mountains, front range railways and amazing scenery can make for a veritable winter wonderland in the coldest part of the winter. The Flatirons are stunning in fresh snow and trains making their way west to the Continental Divide are one of my favorite winter photography subjects. Boulder County with it's vast grasslands and livestock at the base of beautiful mountain backdrops is spectacular in winter and well worth a photo adventure!

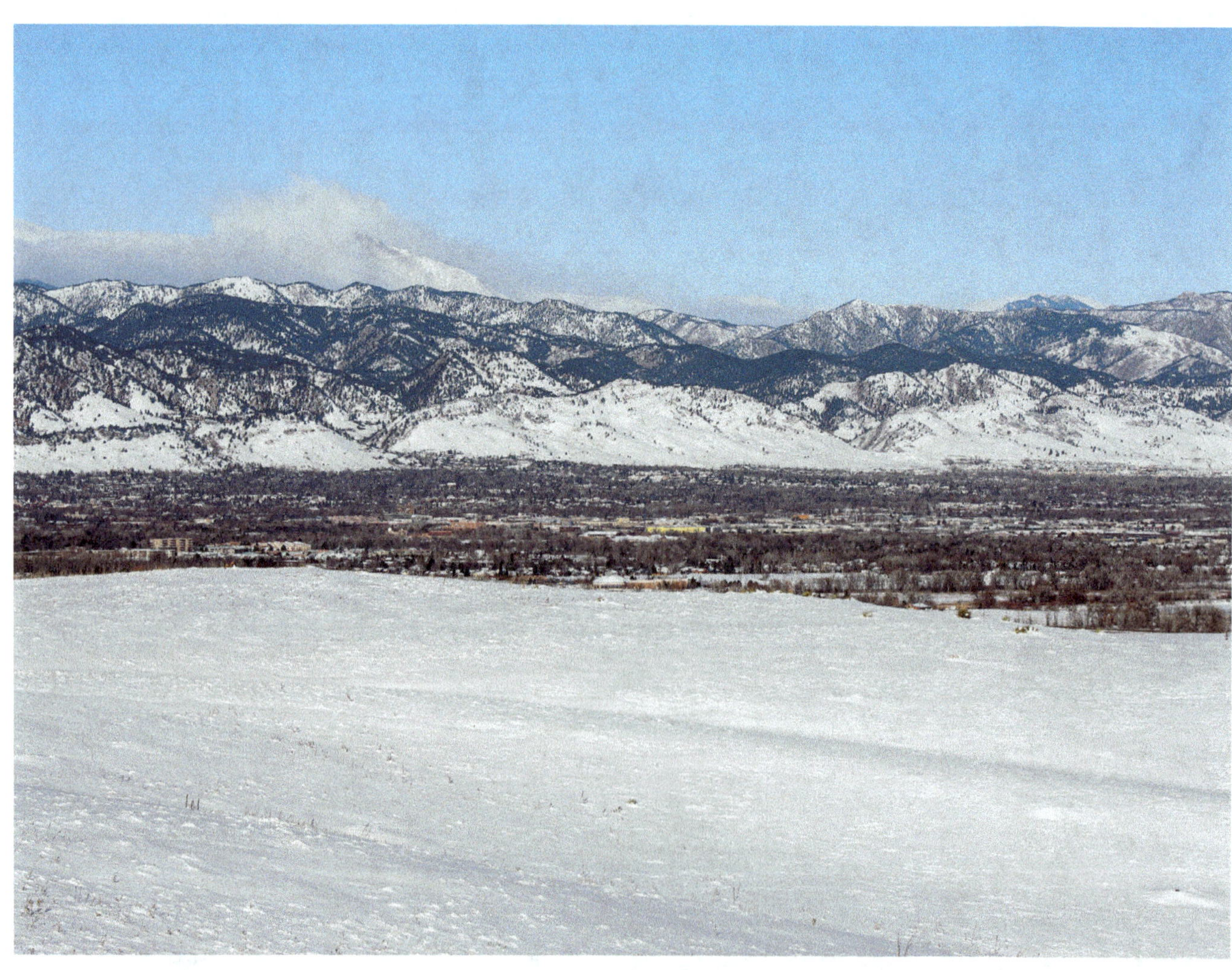

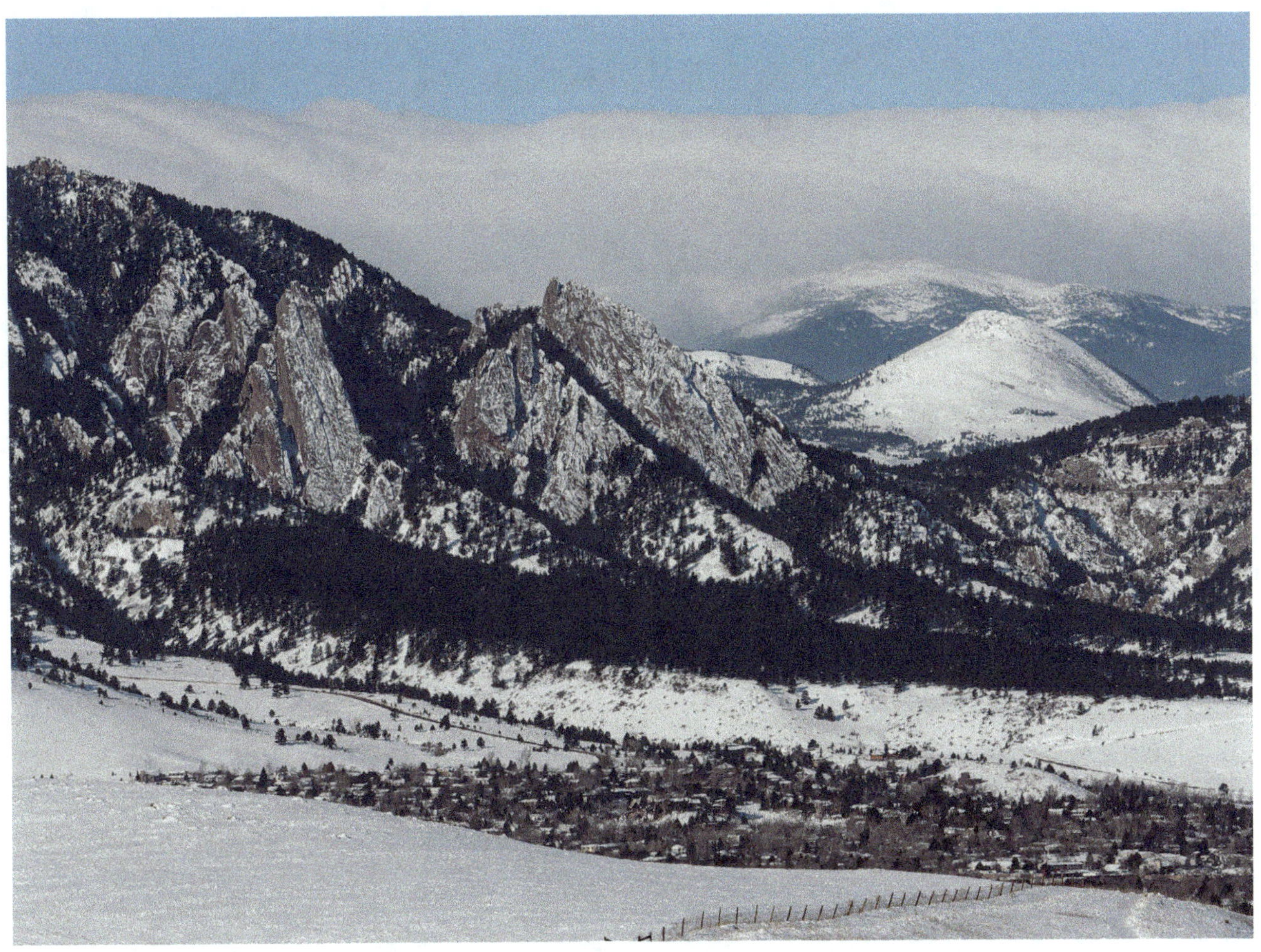

Be sure to take in fabulous views of Boulder and the Flatirons from Highway 36 and also from Highway 93 between Golden and Boulder. The summit of 14,259 foot Longs Peak (left) would be visible in the picture above if it weren't for the heavy cap cloud that has descended upon the Front Range mountains. Be sure to bring both a wide angle and a long lens to work the scene. Tremendous winds along the Highway 93 corridor may make it too difficult at times to hand hold a camera so be sure to bring a heavy tripod that won't blow over.

With such beautiful foreground and background scenery, it may be necessary to shoot two or more images of the same scene to focus on the foreground, details in the middle and the majestic Front Range mountains in the background. Once you are confident the scene is adequately captured, use the focus stacking capabilities of your image editing software to stitch together a stunning image sharp throughout the entire focal range.

I especially enjoy days right after a heavy snow when the tall pines are still laden with fresh snow. The bright Colorado sun won't tolerate the snow long, so be sure to get out early when the air is still cold and the shadows long.

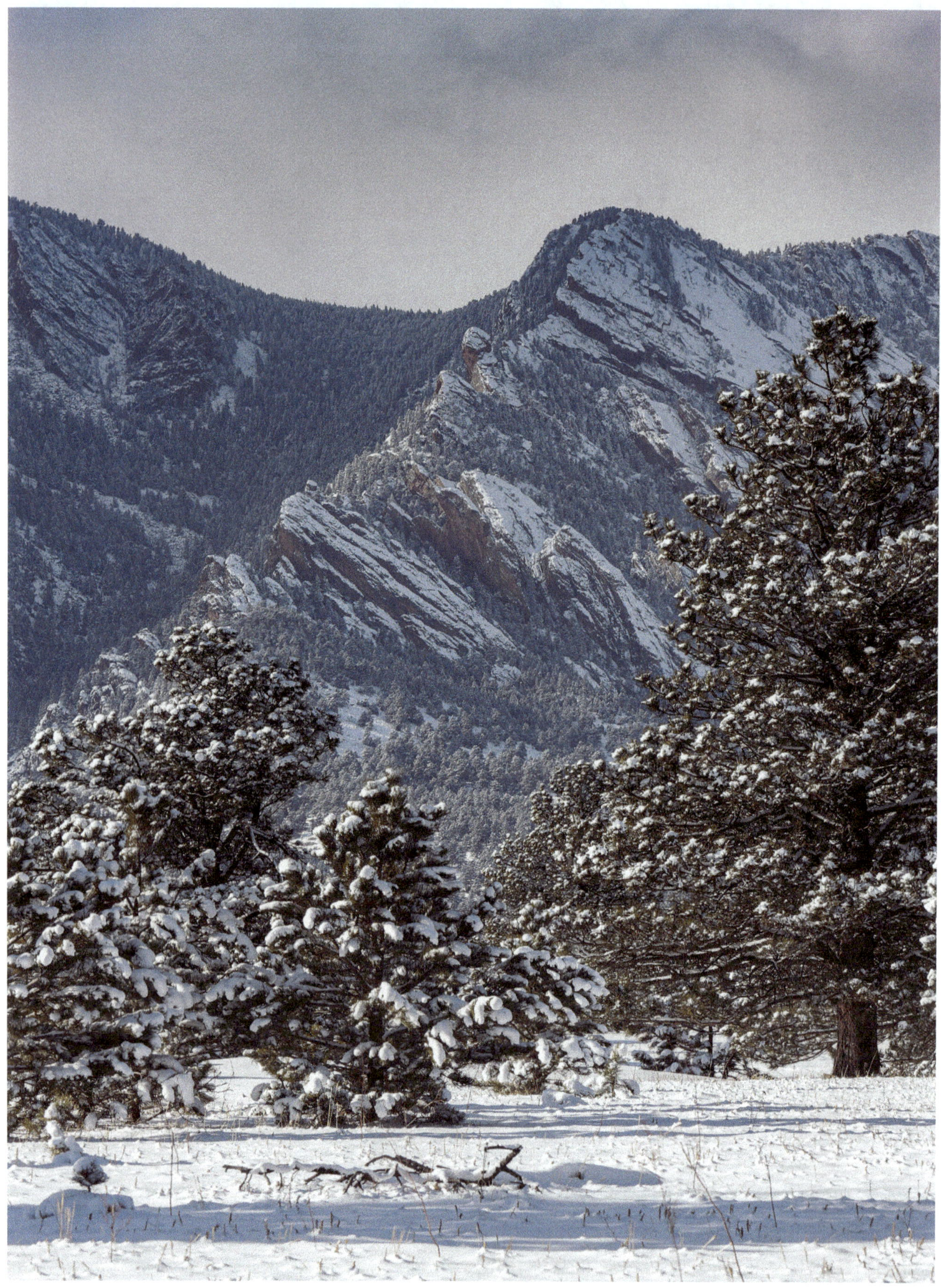

Warm clear days are nice if comfort is what you desire, but there is nothing like storm clouds and fog to add drama to a scene which is why I like to pick the stormiest days for my winter images. When the foreground is dark and the sky bright, a variable neutral density (ND) filter can come in handy as well. In the image (below), the clouds would have been nearly invisible without the use of the ND to darken the upper half of the image. I was fortunate to get this image, as you can see the snow is already starting to melt off the trees where the sun is shining directly upon them. A few more minutes and the pines would just be dark featureless figures in the foreground.

The barren expanse of eastern Boulder County with it's livestock and picturesque trees is great for the kind of stark minimalist imagery I like to capture. Animals in the foreground (next page) provoke emotion and provide scale at the base of the tall mountains of the Colorado Front Range. A polarizing filter can help moderate highlights in the snow on the mountains and retain detail in the clouds overhead.

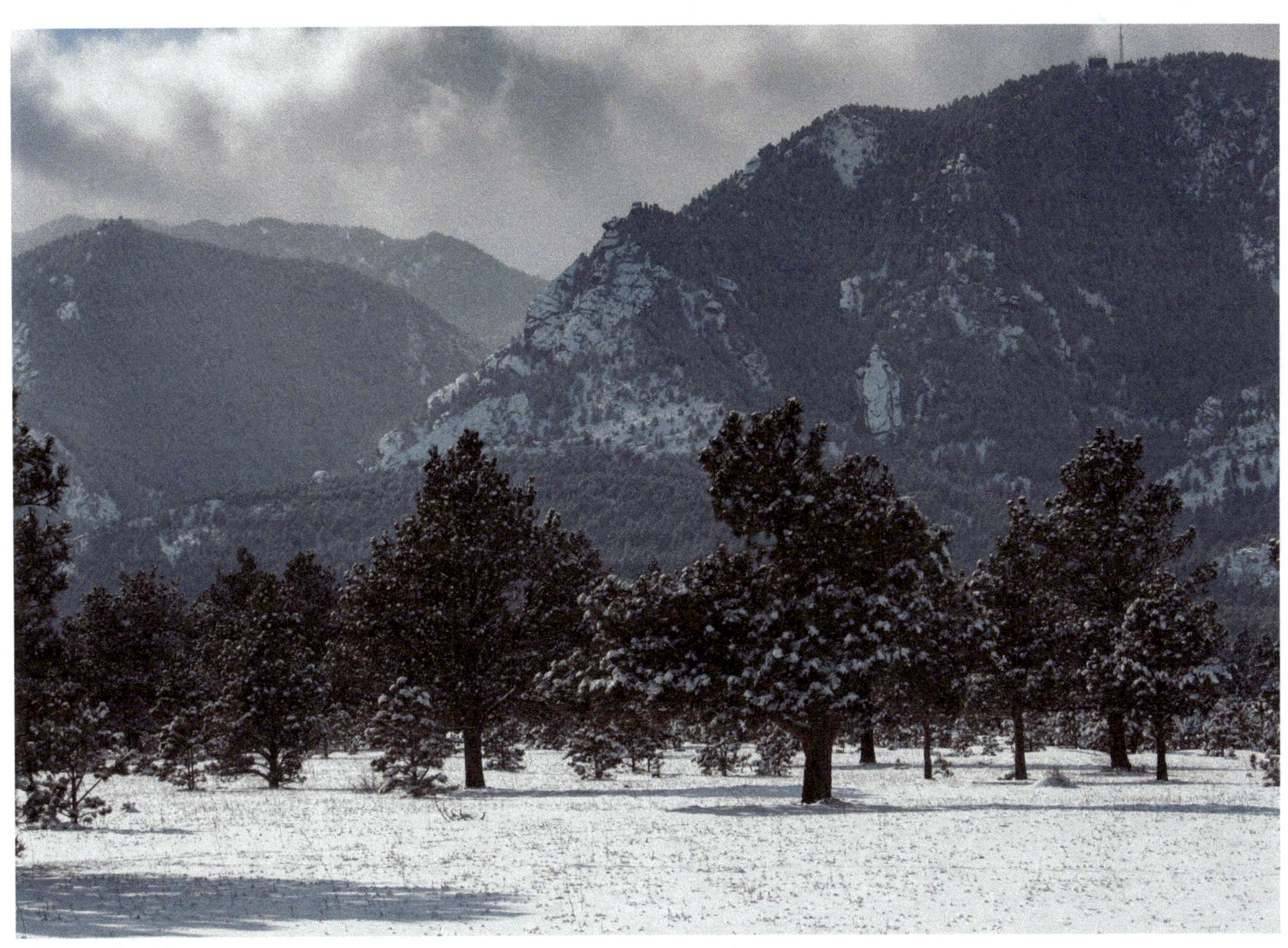

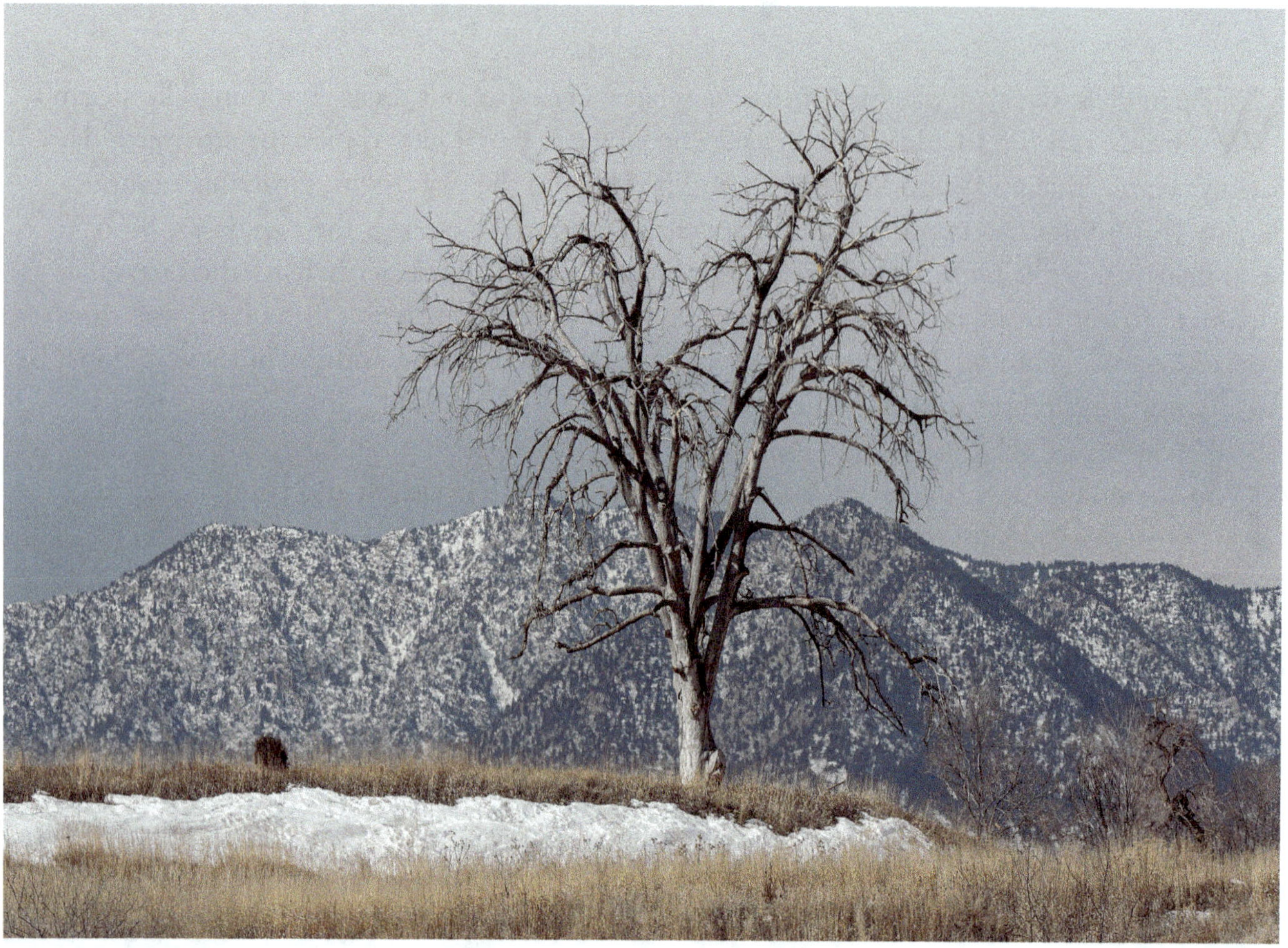

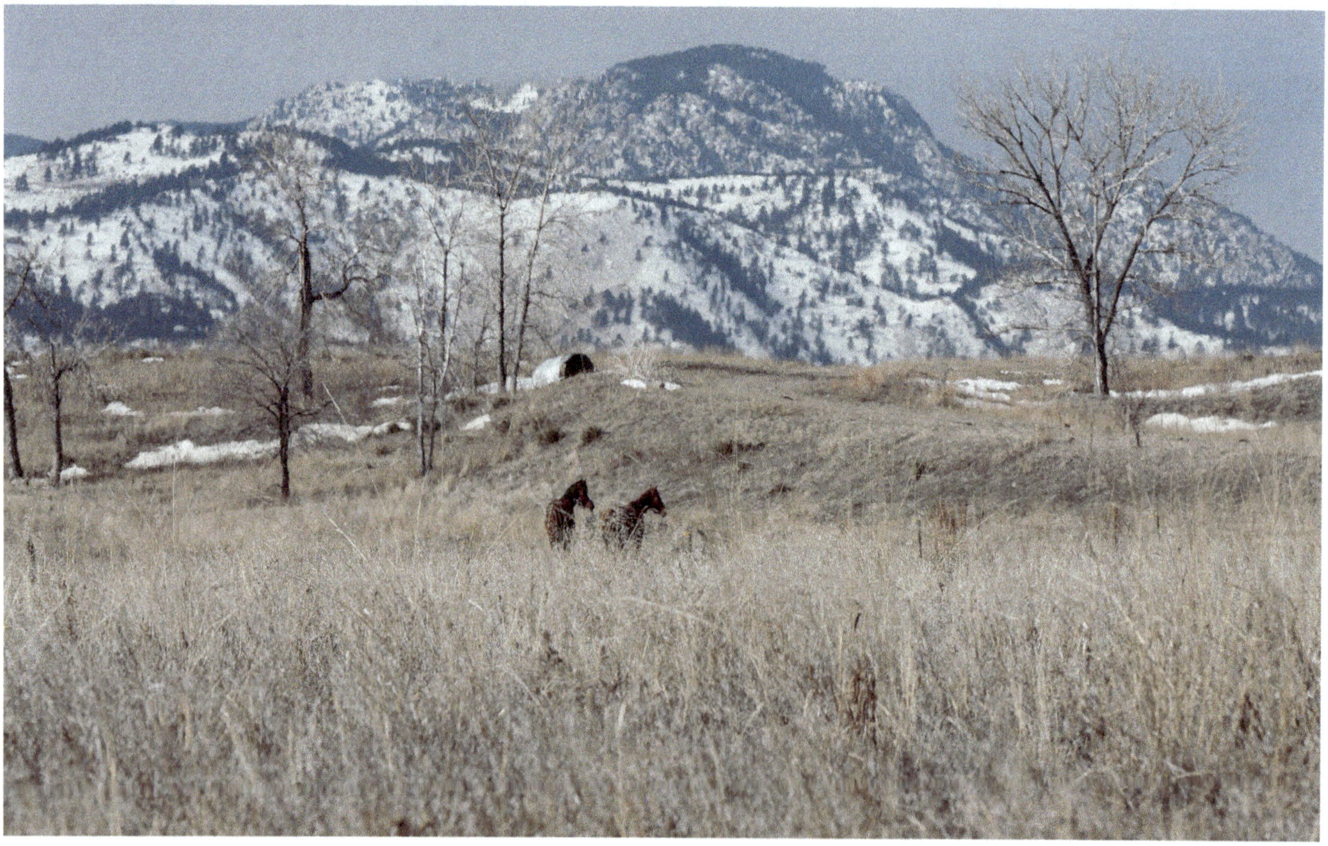

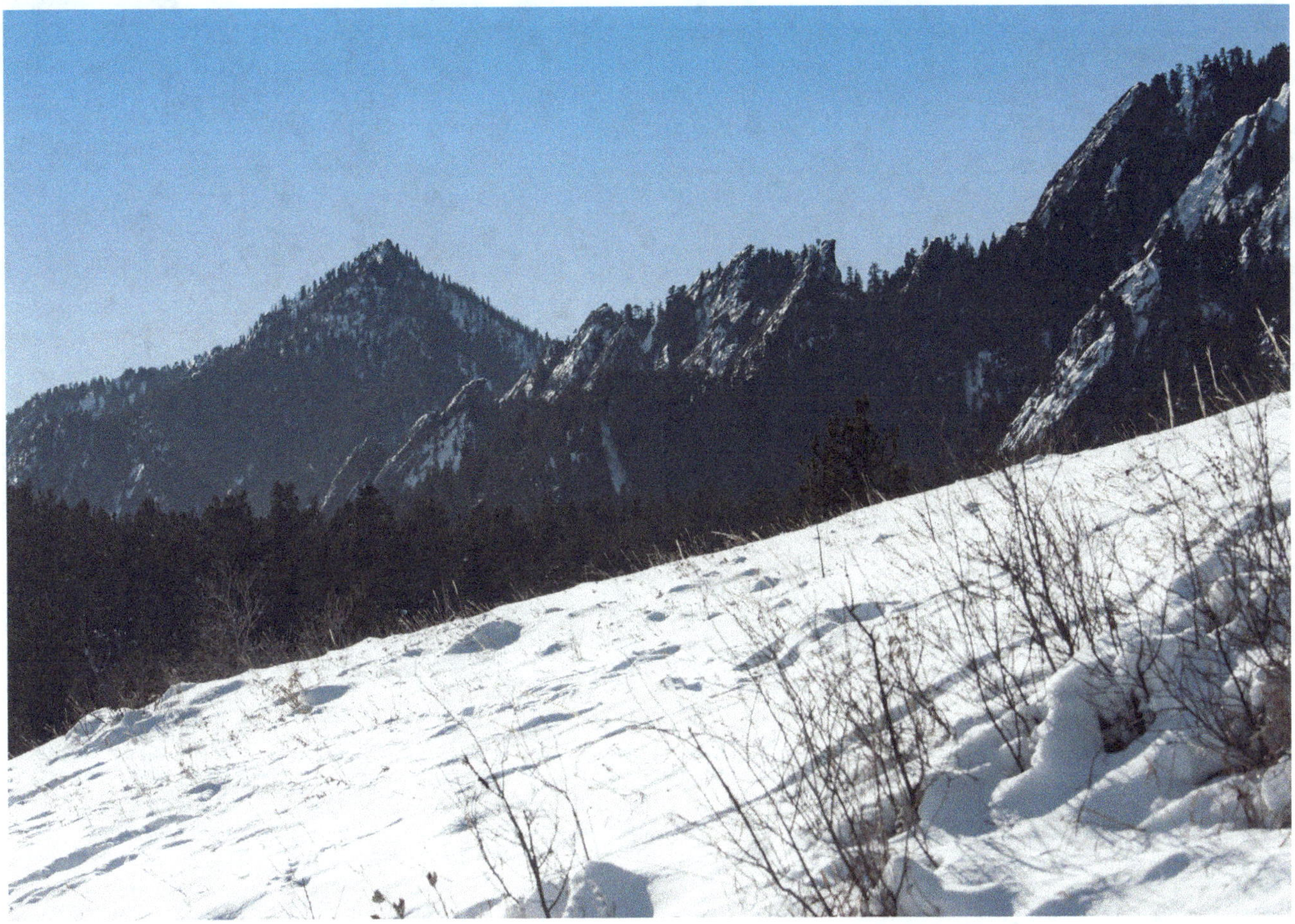

The Flatirons and Bear Peak are magnificent in snow, and once again a graduated ND filter could come in handy to tone down the white snow in the foreground while retaining detail in the mountains.

The Flatirons are a popular destination for thousands of university students and outdoor enthusiasts and soon pristine snow (above) will be marred by footprints criss crossed with snowshoe and cross country ski tracks, ruining the appearance of solitude in the scene. As always, the early bird gets the worm!

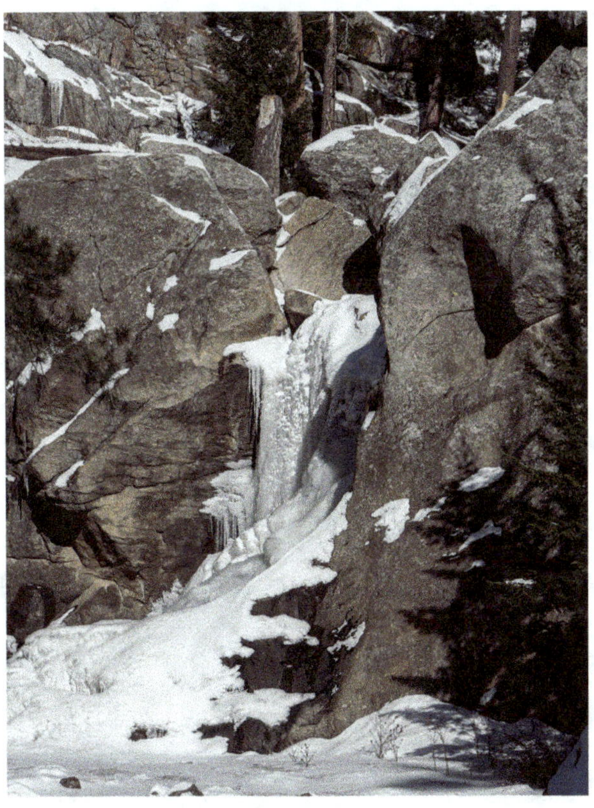

The roaring water of Boulder Falls is silenced in winter, replaced with a quiet frozen monument to it's summer power.

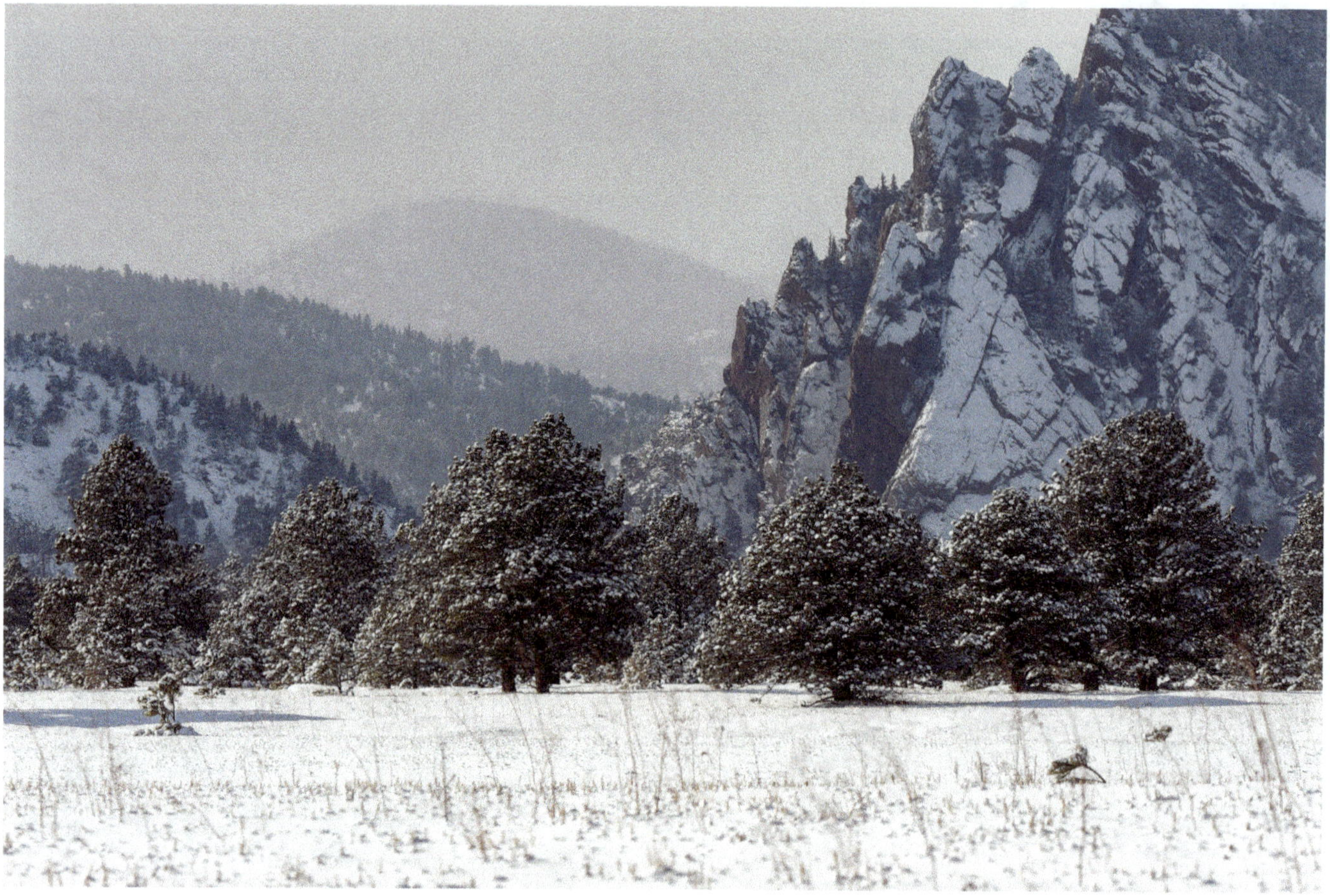

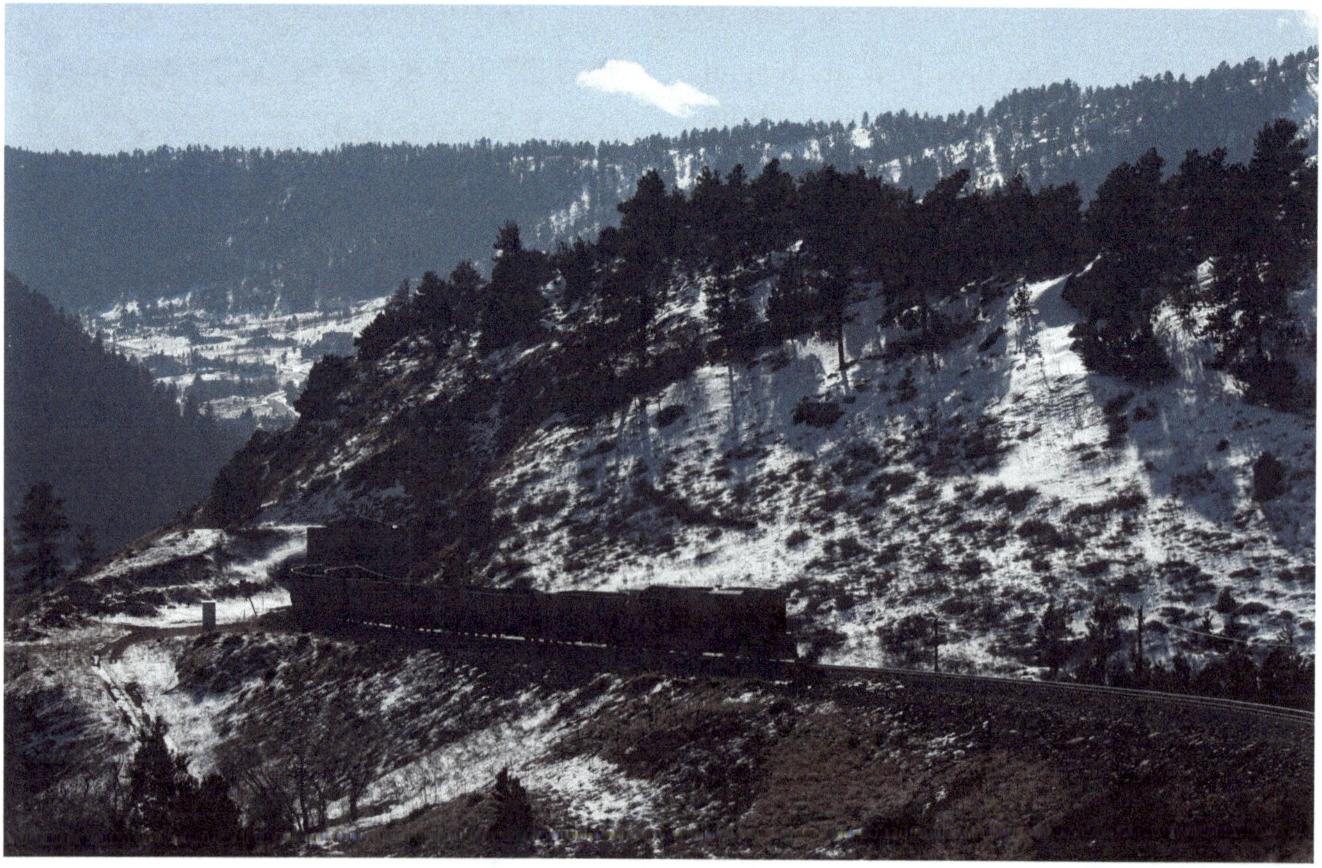

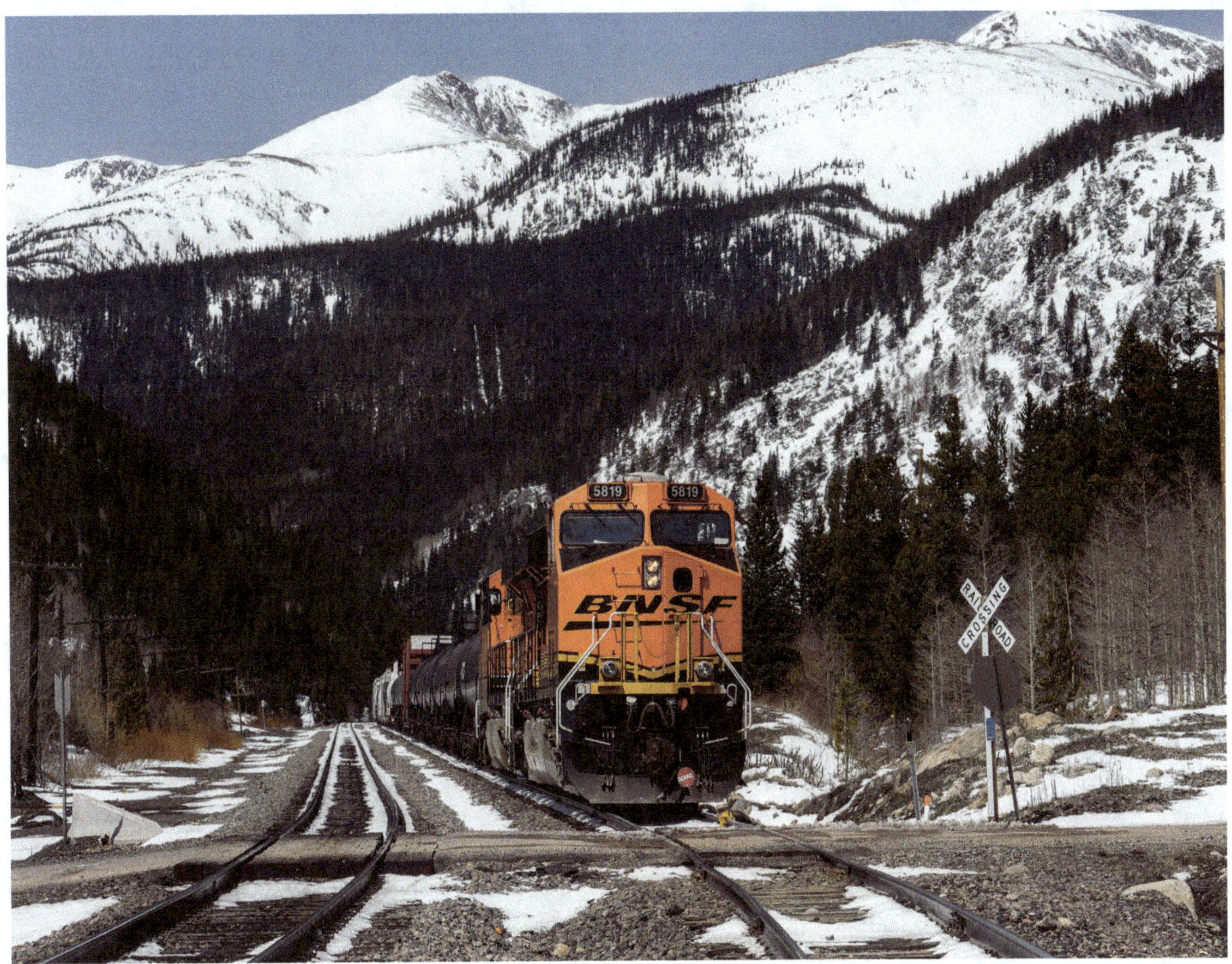

To me there is no more compelling subject than the nations railways, and deep snow only adds to the mystique of living history snaking it's way through the towering peaks of the **Indian Peaks Wilderness**. Rollins Pass just west of Rollinsville in the western part of the district is one of the most beautiful places on the planet, and my favorite location for train photography. A BNSF coal train steams through the Indian Peaks Wilderness on it's way down from the Moffat Tunnel as blowing snow fills in and highlights crevices around the tracks.

A fast shutter speed is required to freeze a train's motion and I like to take care not to blow out the bright headlights. Be sure to use manual mode and a static ISO value or the camera meter will see the glowing headlamp and underexpose the image. The trick is to meter the scene ahead of time using a low ISO number and a fast shutter speed. The train powering through the dark storm (next page) was exposed with an 8000th of a second at f/4 and ISO 400. The brightness of the headlamp accentuates the darkness of the stormy scene while snowflakes are frozen in time. Using a slow a shutter speed would have streaked the snowflakes, creating more of a foggy appearance than a snowstorm.

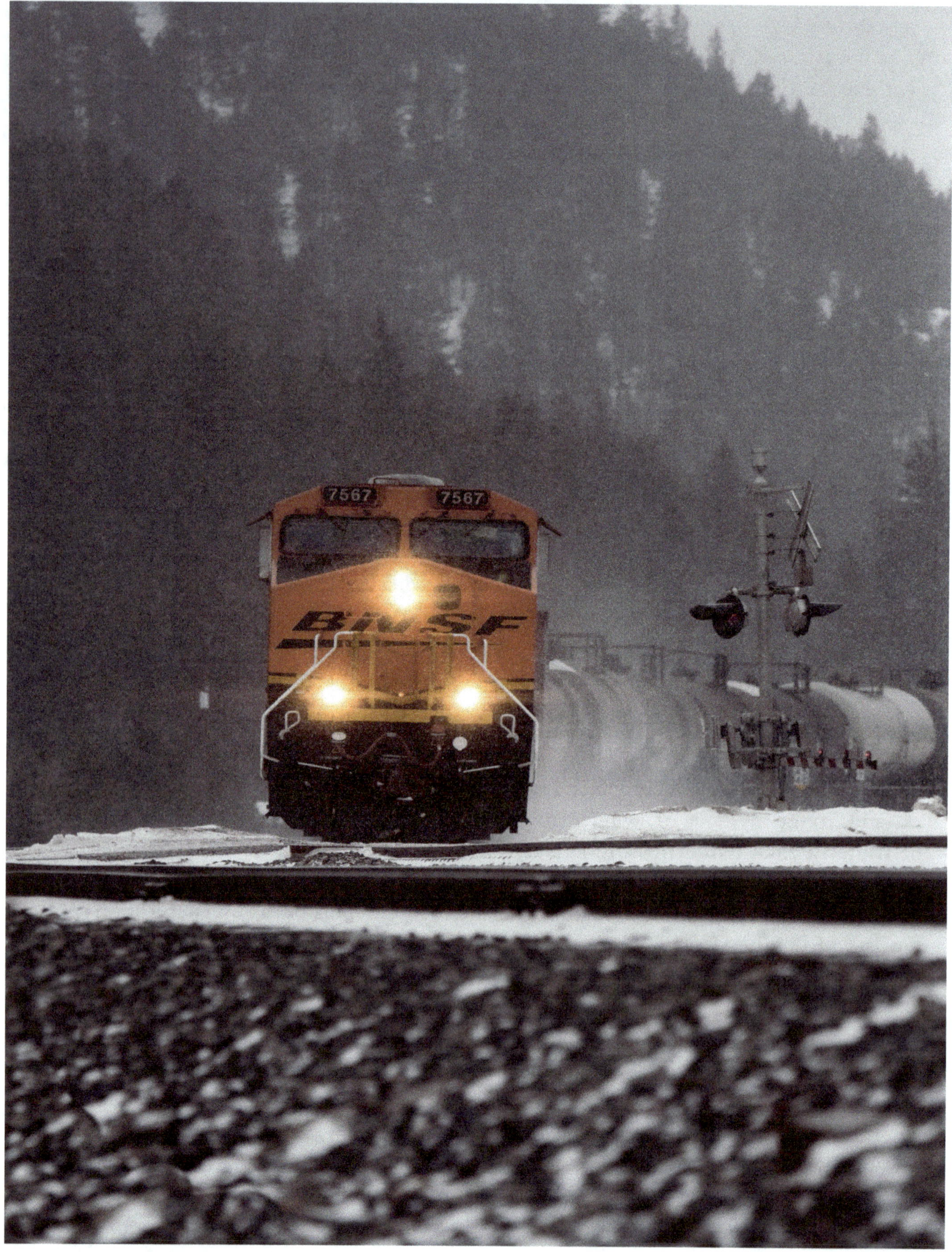
7567
7567
BNSF

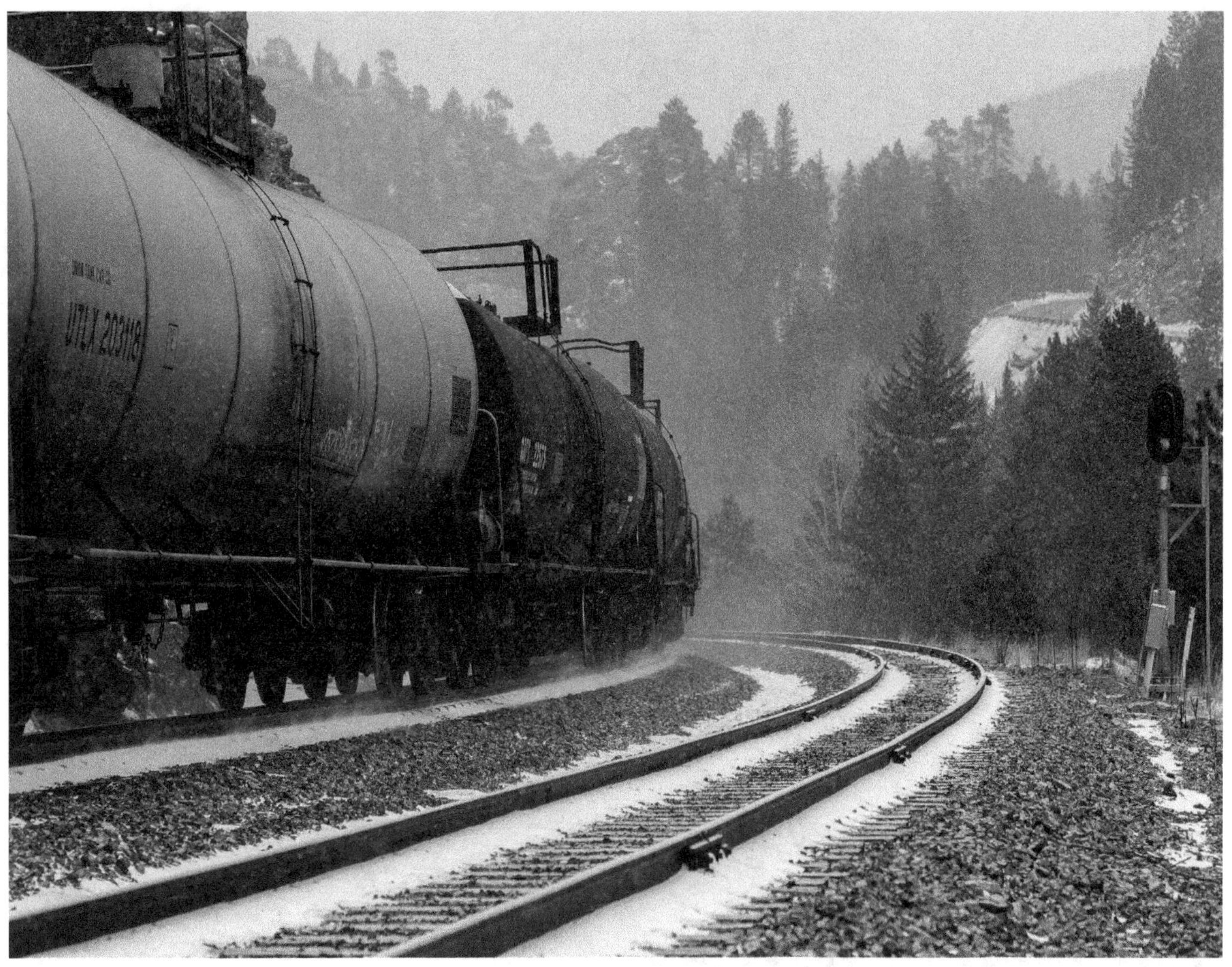

Don't be afraid to get out and shoot in bad weather, just make sure you and your gear are protected from the elements. Heavy snow on this day necessitated the use of a Gor-Tex suit for myself and my heaviest rain cover for the camera and lens. I knew I would be out in the snow all day so affixing my Aquatech rain cover and weather sealed eye piece was an acceptable burden.

There is a decision to make when shooting images like this one. Do you use the tripod and shoot for motion blur on the train or do you freeze motion with a fast shutter speed. On this particular image I wanted to make sure the falling snow didn't render as streaks so I chose a 1000th of a second at the widest aperture on the 70-200 F4L which is of course f/4.

The Moffat Tunnel is the crown jewel of train tunnels in Colorado. A rough drive to the very end of Rollin's Pass is well worth the effort to get a chance to capture a train passing through this amazing feat of engineering (next page).

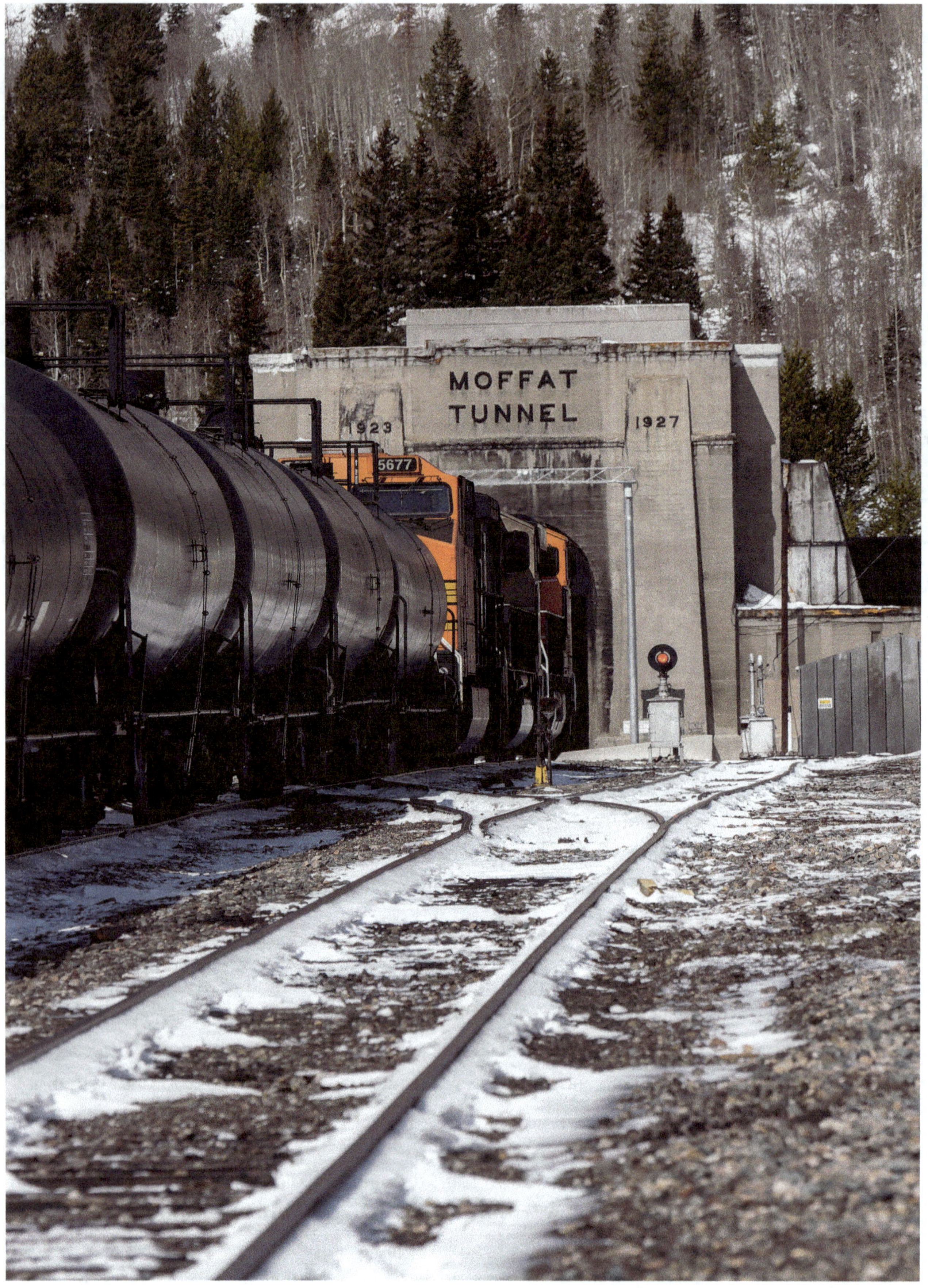
MOFFAT
TUNNEL
1923
1927
5677

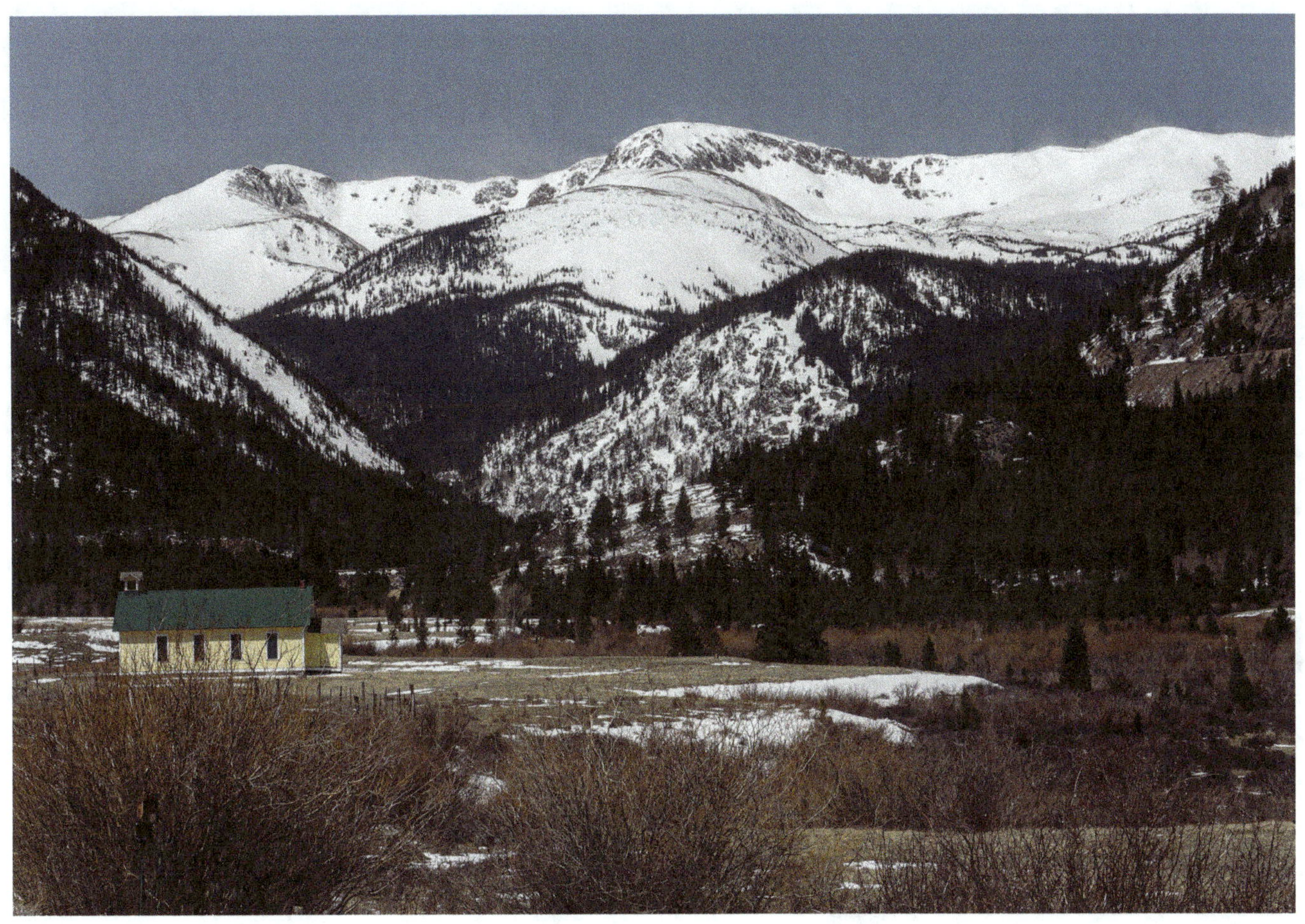

As I made my way toward the destination at the tunnel I couldn't resist stopping to photograph this old church seen along Rollins Pass Road. On this tremendously windy morning, snow powered by hurricane force wind shear can be seen blowing over the peaks. The sunny foreground belies the severe conditions often encountered at high elevation.

There are many beautiful images waiting to be captured right from the road on this drive, including several railroad crossings where patient photographers can wait for a train to round out a beautiful mountain landscape image. There are also many wilderness trails in the area for the more adventurous, those willing to brave the cold and strap on a pair of snowshoes or cross country skis. The famed Crater Lakes lie in the high peaks off to the north for those with the skills to negotiate rugged snow covered terrain. I've seen the lakes in summer but wasn't quite prepared for such a difficult undertaking on this winter day!

Rocky Mountain National Park

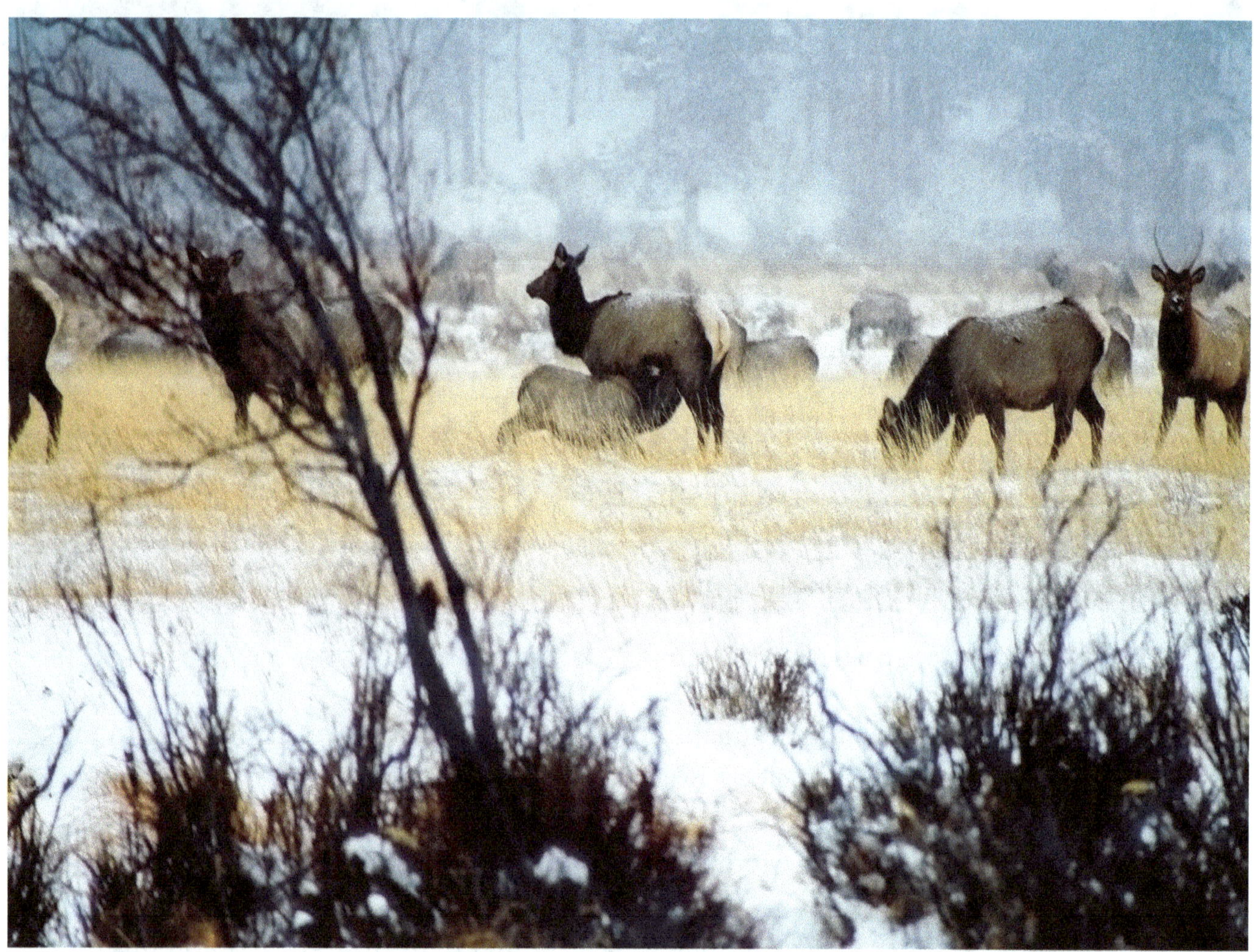

Rocky Mountain National Park is a wonderful place to visit in the winter, as long as you aren't planning on driving over landmark Trail Ridge Road which is closed from the first big snows of the season until spring. However the east side of the park remains a popular destination for winter sports including cross country skiing and snowshoeing. The best part of a winter visit is the absence of huge crowds and timed entry permits. Bear Lake Road is maintained all winter and many of the popular summer trails are groomed for winter sports when the deep snow arrives. Popular trails along Bear Creek Road include Bierstadt, Sprague and Bear Lakes. Unlike the congested summer months, there are no parking issues or shuttle buses to negotiate in the winter.

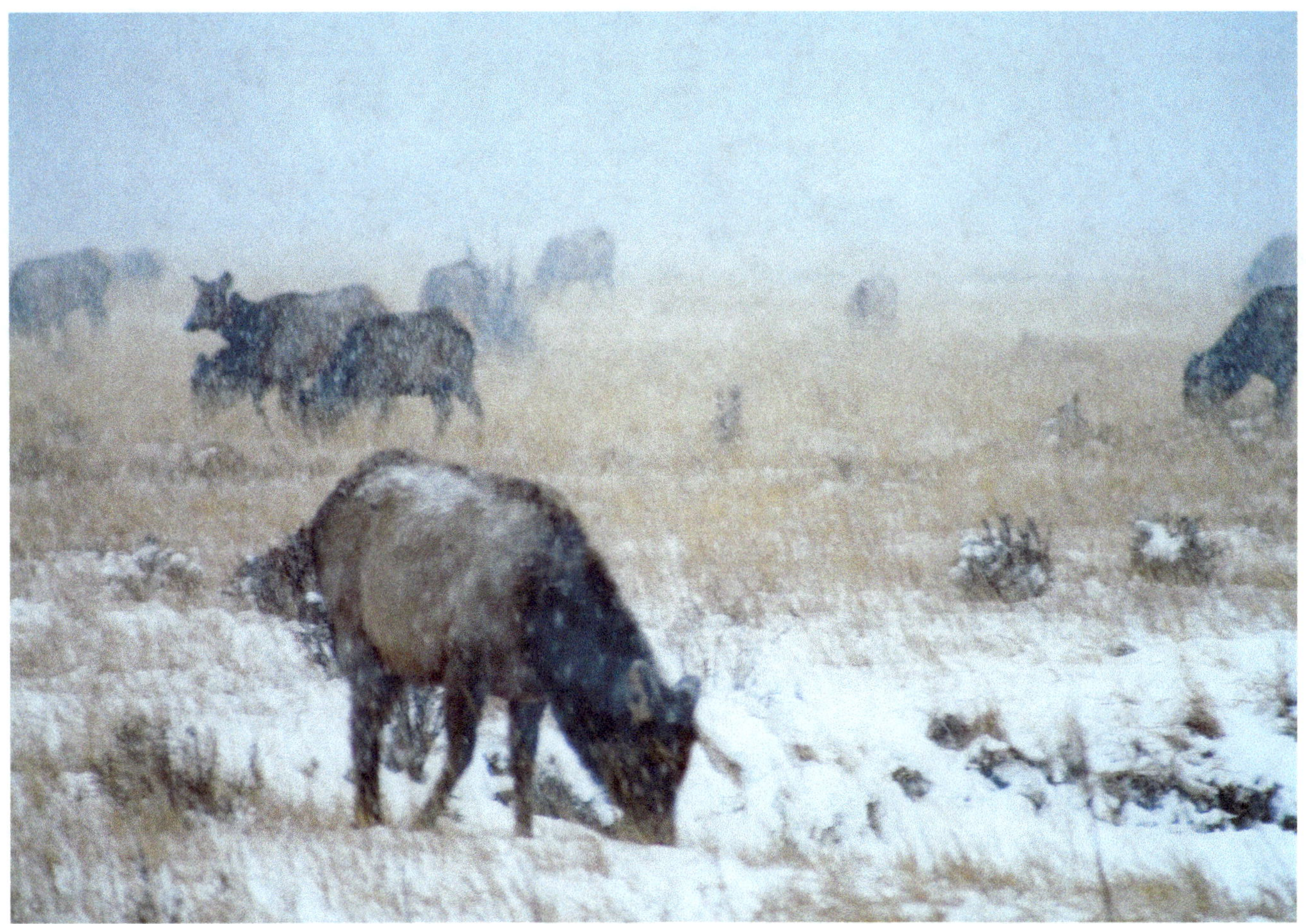

Winter is an awesome season for wildlife photographers in the park. The elk herd is forced out of the high country, gathering en masse in Moraine Park where there is safety in numbers and access to a food source. Snow was falling hard on this stormy morning and the elk paid absolutely no attention to me as I worked my way around capturing all the images I could have ever desired. Pictures of elk in autumn are nice with colorful leaves in the background and the rut in full swing, but I don't enjoy competing for the best locations with dozens of other photographers trying to do exactly the same thing at exactly the same time. In the winter it is likely you will have the park to yourself, especially during inclement weather. I was thrilled to make my way around on snowshoe with only the falling of snow and an occasional grunt from the animals to break the silence.

Coyote and fox are also out roaming around during daylight hours, fighting for their own survival. They too are so intent upon overcoming the harsh winter that little attention is paid to a lone photographer. Short seconds granted to you for pictures in the summer can turn into long minutes when the weather is cold and crowds are sparse. I just love those days when the shooshing of my snowshoes is my only company, save for the animals that accept me without notice as part of their herd.

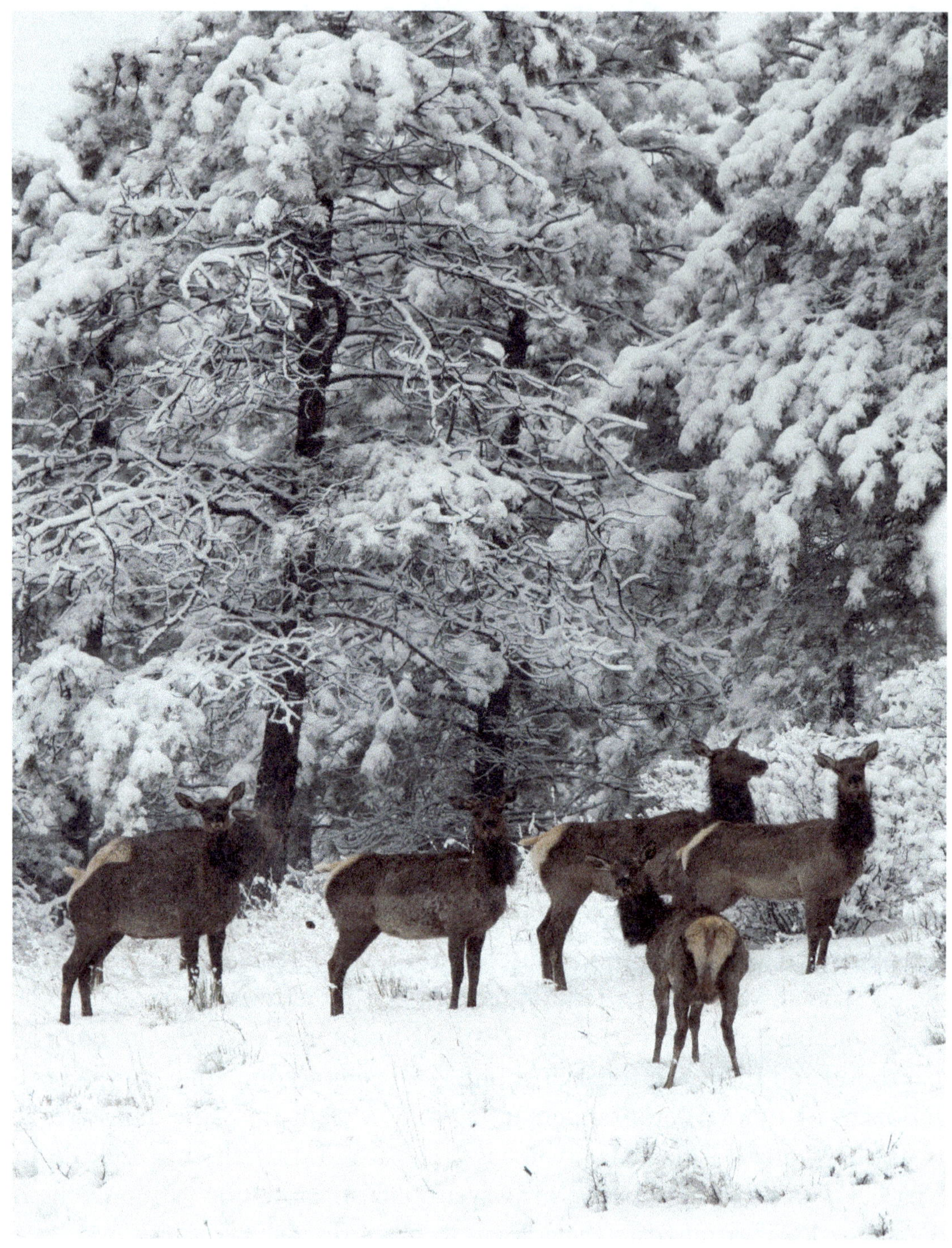

This was one of my very first winter weather digital photo shoots (previous page) and I wasn't quite sure how to capture the falling snow. A relatively slow shutter speed rendered the wind driven snow as streaks, which in a way captures the essence of the severity of the storm that day. On a less wind swept day a faster shutter speed will produce a more magical snow globe effect. That's completely an artistic decision that each photographer will need to make based on conditions and the desired result.

It was on a snowshoe hike to Bierstadt Lake that I witnessed one of the most stunning natural phenomenon I have ever seen in my entire life. It was a cold cloudy morning in the park and snowflakes had already begun to fall by the time I was ready to start my snowshoe trek. Snow was falling steadily at Bierstadt Lake but my son and I decided to extend the trek and push on to Bear Lake anyway. Eventually the trail cleared the ridge and a massive white bowl opened before us with the lake at the bottom.

As we stood still taking in the beauty I could hear a powerful wind gust in the trees approaching from the north. As the gust passed over and blasted into the giant bowl, a huge wall of snow swooped into the valley before being whipped thousands of feet into the sky by the fierce gale. Twenty years later I remember it like it was yesterday. As I stood watching in awe at the spectacle the only word I could think to utter was simply, "Wow!". It was as if the breath of God Himself had filled the valley with unparalleled grandeur for that moment in time. Fortunately I had my camera at the ready and was able to capture of few images of the amazing scene (below).

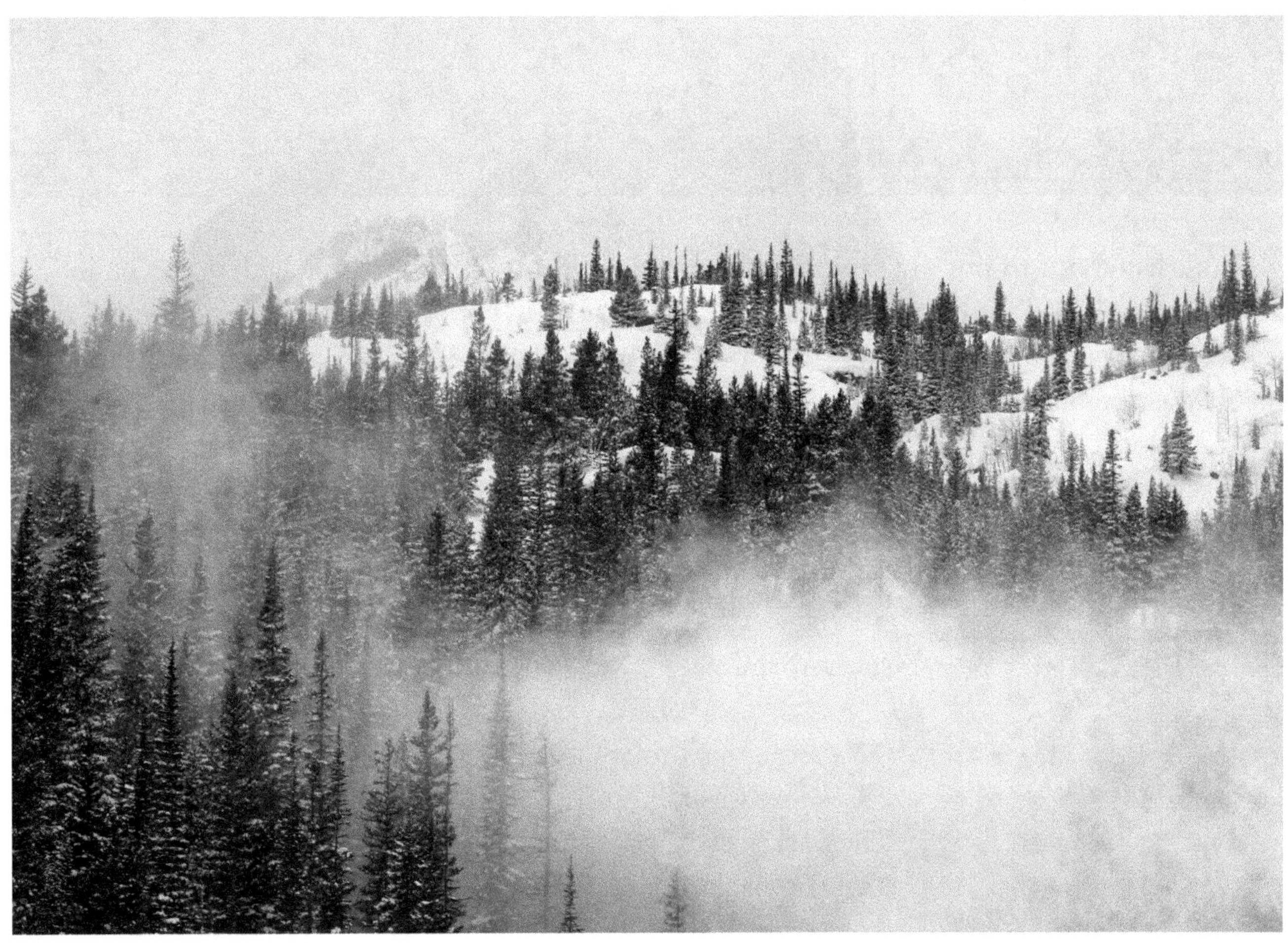

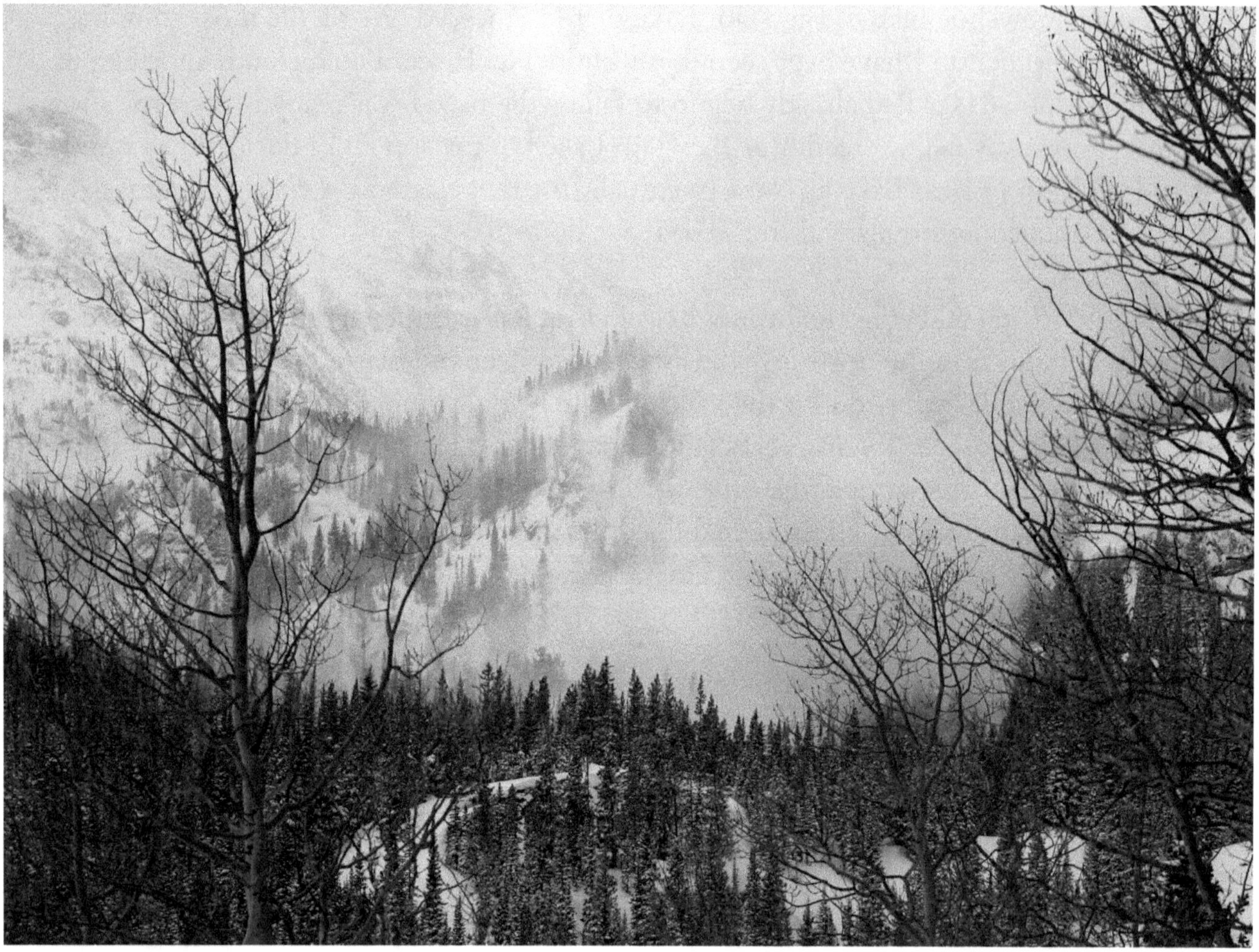

I also learned not to put my camera in the pack with the lens hood attached, not even in the reverse position. Plastic and glass become brittle in extreme cold, and torquing of the front element in the pack by the lens hood cost me a $100 B&W sky filter that day. I'm just glad it was the filter that cracked and not the lens! Having learned from that mistake, I leave the hood loose over the lens whenever I put the camera in the pack, even in warm weather!

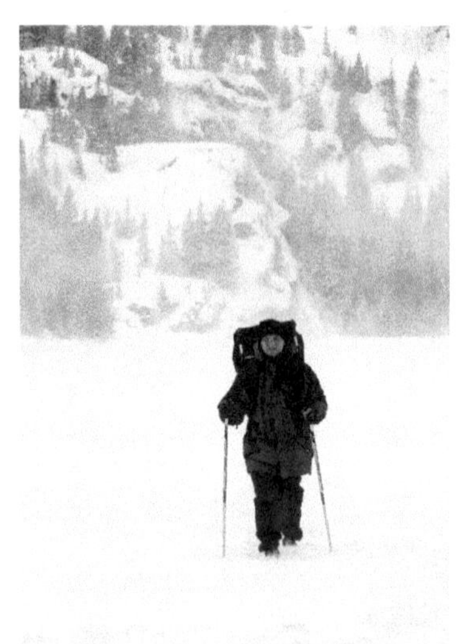

Eventually we made our way down to the lake and of course had to take advantage of a photo op on the lake in the snowstorm!

There wasn't much at all to see on the return trip, by then snow was falling so hard it was almost a total whiteout. The park service continued to clear the road though, so the return trip back to Estes Park wasn't an issue once we were back to the vehicle.

The west side of the park is open in the winter as well, at least to the **Kawuneeche Visitor Center**. Many trails between Grand Lake and the visitor center are accessible in winter, but a call to the park service or use of a good trails application like All Trails would be a prudent idea before taking a long drive only to discover the road is closed due to weather.

The west side of the park is teeming with wildlife though, and a road trip from Grand Lake to the visitor center always offers the possibility of a profitable photo trip with beautiful winter scenery and a variety of birds and animals along the way.

In fact the entire road trip to the west side of the park is a scenic winter adventure! The route from the city up I70 to Highway 40 over Berthoud Pass through Winter Park and then on to Grand Lake via Highway 34 takes you through some of the most scenic terrain in Colorado.

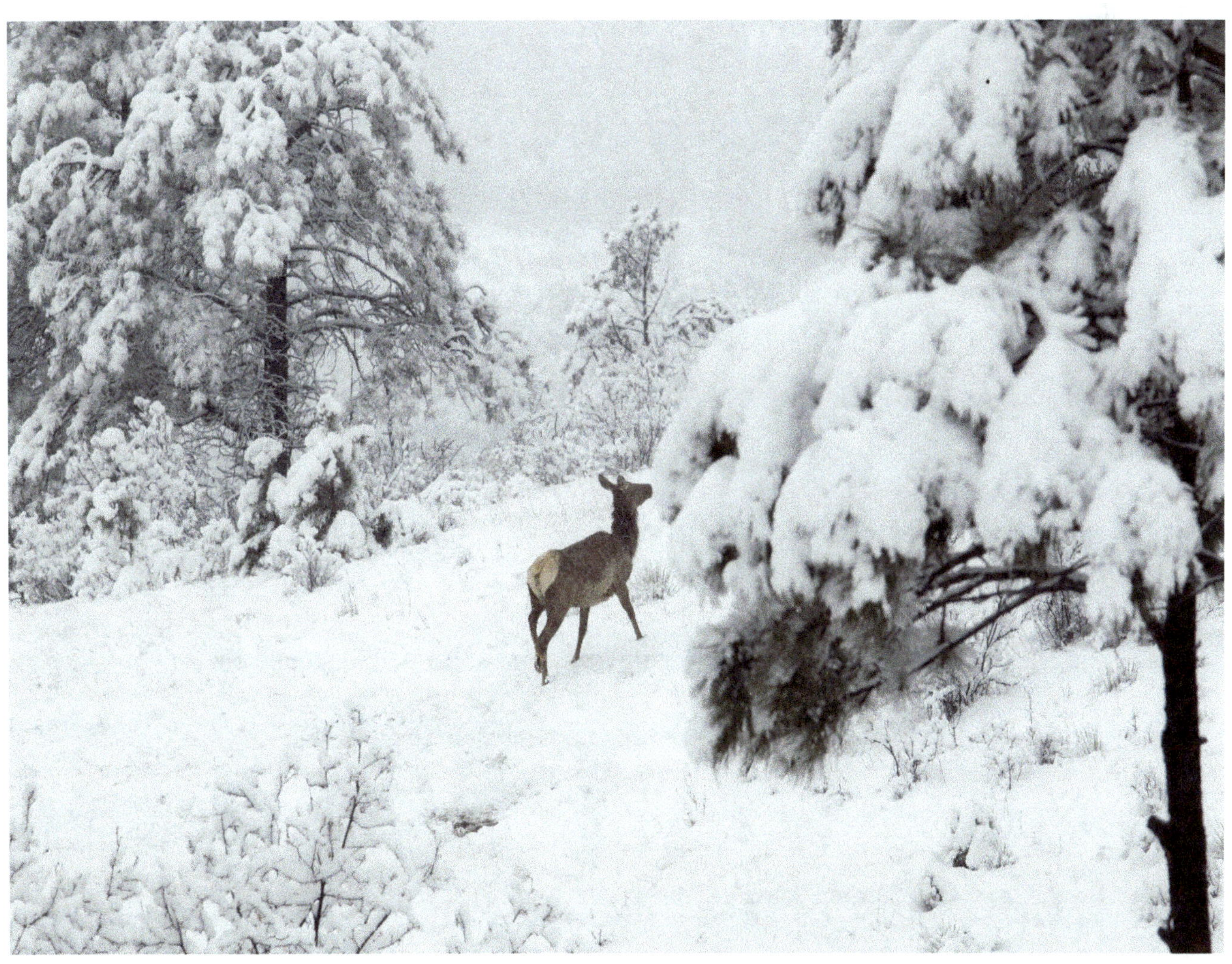

Trail opportunities are almost limitless in the **Berthoud Pass** and **Winter Park** vicinities including the Winter Park Nordic Center, and a quick check of your favorite trail guide on the internet is the best way to plan a back country snowshoe or cross country ski trek. I need to stress here the importance of extra safety precautions in the cold months. If you make a mistake in the summer and take the wrong trail there's the chance that you might have to spend a night in the mountains. If you make that mistake in the winter, an uncomfortable overnight stay can suddenly become a life threatening fight for life.

I recommend old school fire starting materials such as a flint and steel and a magnetic compass as staples in a winter pack. Matches can get wet and butane lighters can run out of fuel but a Firebiner or flint and steel are easy to pack and they never fail. Detailed waterproof topographical maps of your intended area can also be obtained from a high end mountaineering store such as REI, and these maps combined with an inexpensive magnetic compass can save your life when the batteries on your high tech GPS device or phone become weak from the extreme cold.

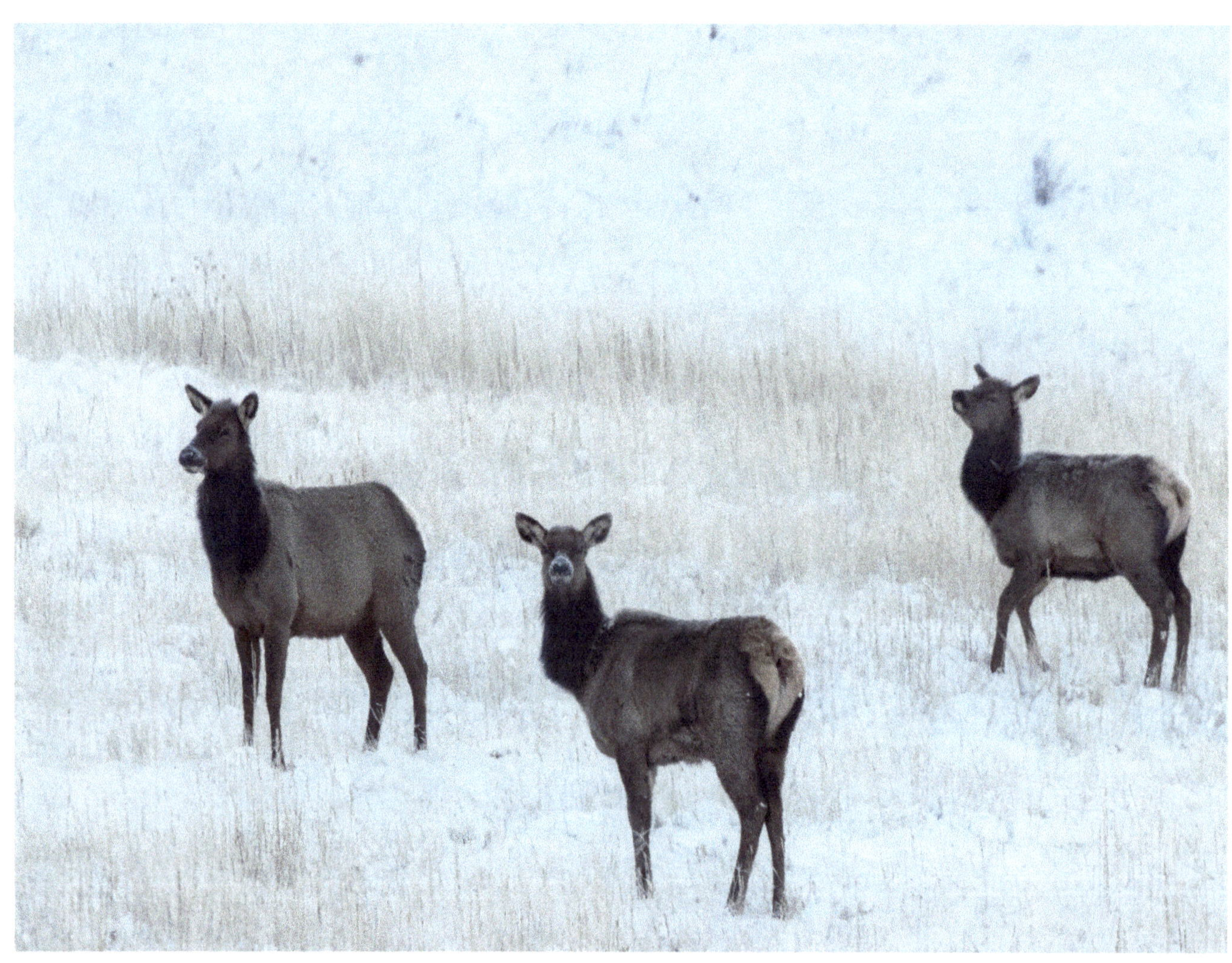

The Pikes Peak Region

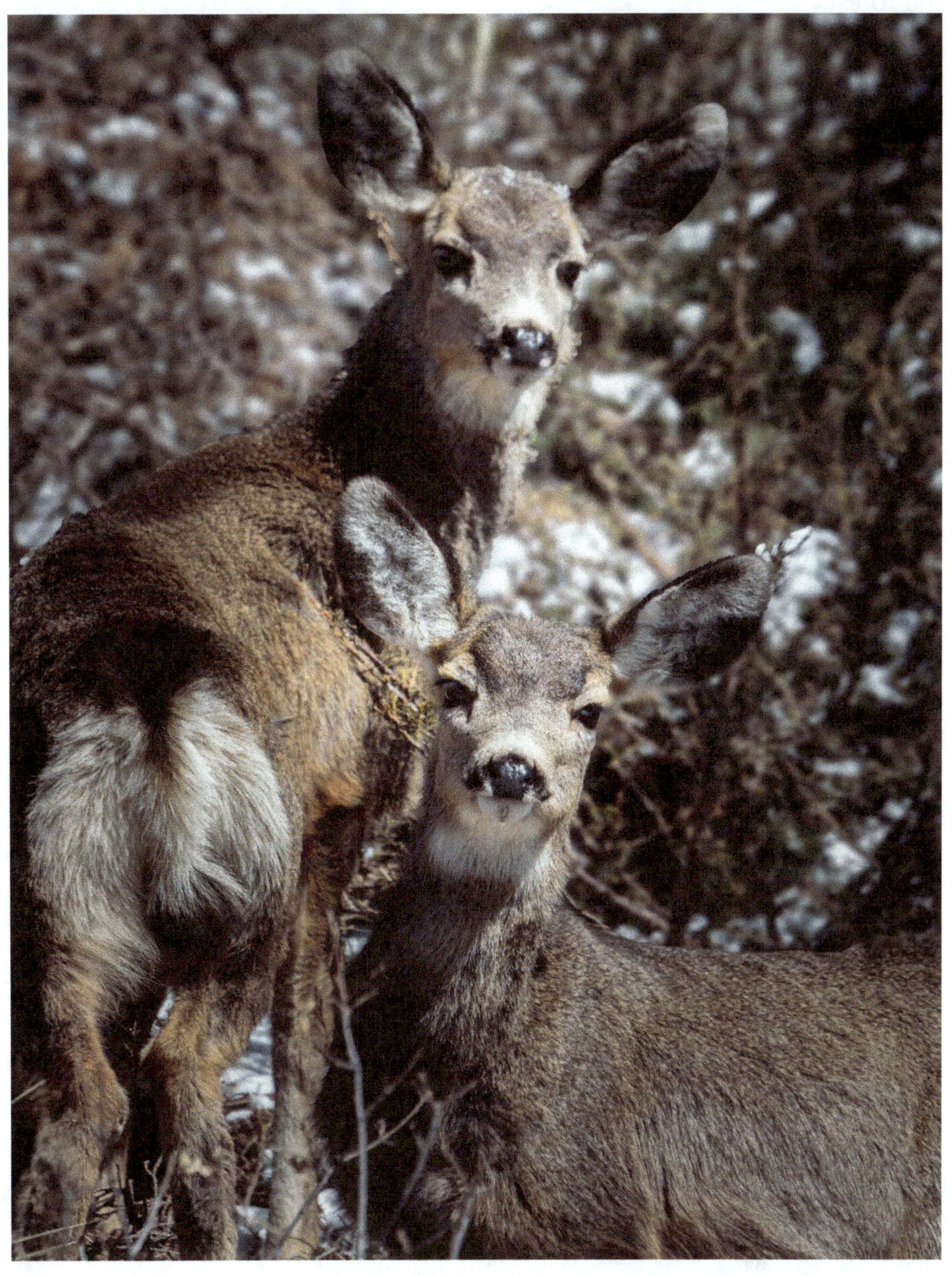

Easy access to mountains and trails in the Woodland Park and Cripple Creek area after relocating there has been a real boon to my wildlife and mountain landscape photography portfolio. Deer, elk and many species of raptors and various little birds call this area home and of course winter is my favorite season for capturing images of the rugged peaks, rivers and forest.

Garden of the Gods Park and Red Rock Canyon Open Space at the base of Pikes Peak were among the first attractions to capture my interest in this location and I made the best of easy access to those places. Pikes Peak stands tall over Woodland Park and it seems the great mountain is always putting on a spectacular show, providing photographers with an almost limitless opportunity for stunning winter imagery.

The great mountain often produces it's own weather, other times it's towering elevation splits weather systems moving through the area from the west. Clouds drifting past the north face of the peak and mist filling the valley from weather systems below provide something interesting to shoot almost every day. Beautiful sunsets grace the towering cliffs on the north face and make for beautiful imagery on days when the weather systems fail to develop.

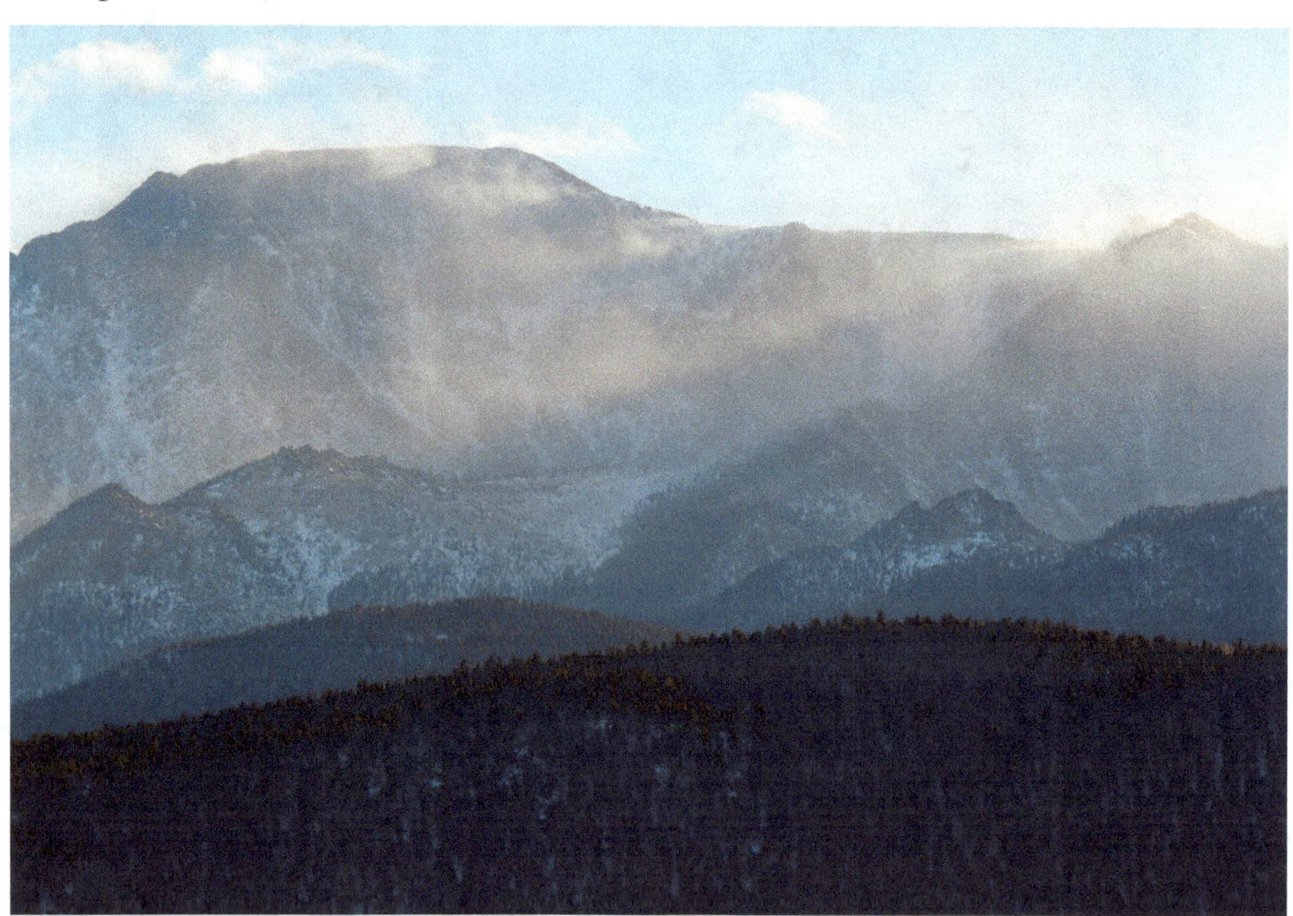

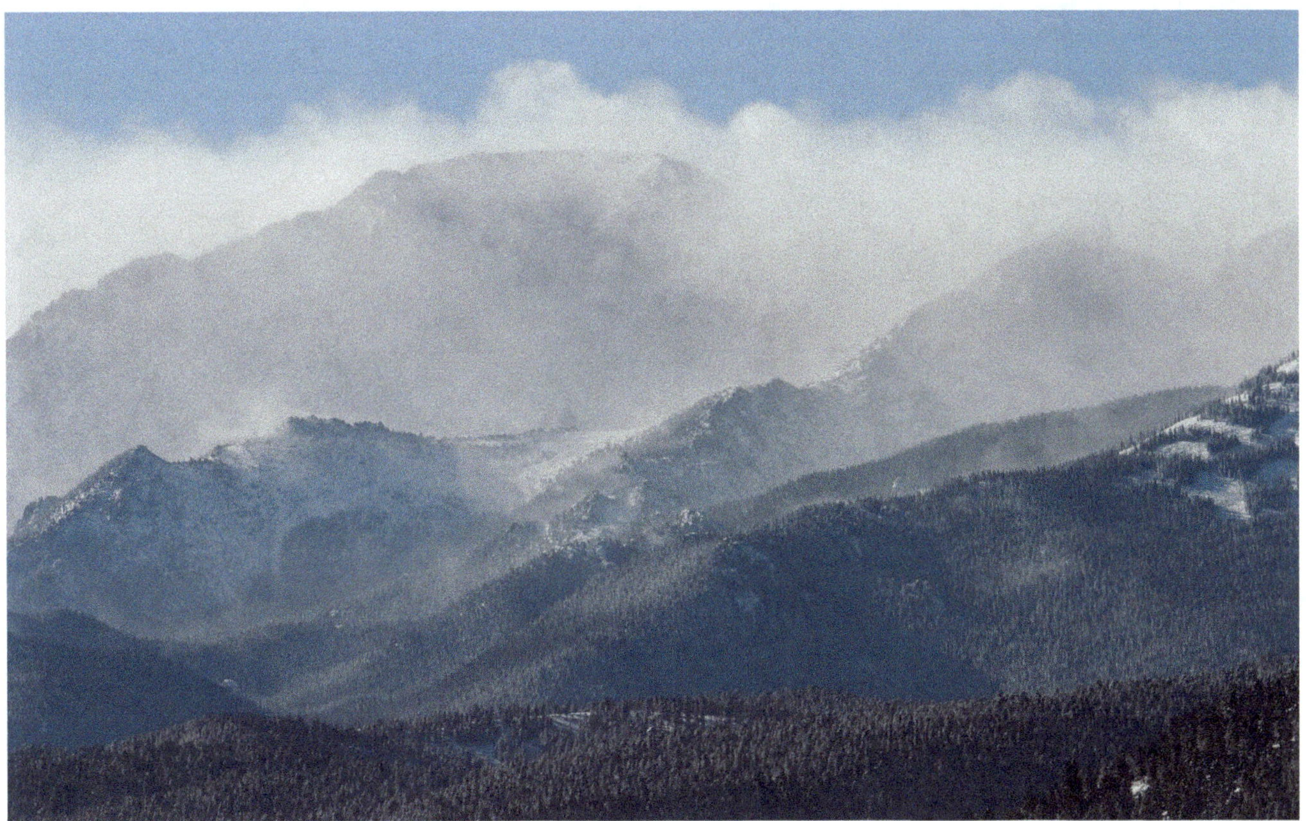

A nice network of trails on the northern slopes of Ute Pass provide a wonderful venue for photographing deer and elk and every possible view of the north face of the peak. Each day seems to present some new phenomenon begging to be photographed. I found it best to have my camera at the ready at all times, weather on the mountain is very unpredictable and fantastic images can appear at a moment's notice. One problem with the Ute Pass Valley though is that the mountain is so high that the peak is in the dark from solstice to solstice. Some neighborhoods on the south side of the valley see no sunlight at all throughout the day. Trails on that side of the valley are inaccessible without professional ice climbing gear.

One of my favorite trails leads from just north of Crystola to the summit of Bald Mountain. The trail can be accessed from the top of 3rd Street on the north side of Highway 24 and also from Kings Canyon Road at Paradise Open Space Park as well as another lesser known trailhead at the southernmost end of Kings Canyon. Photographers wanting to take in the spectacular views of the peak without a long hike can visit with a drive up Rampart Range Road which leads right to the summit.

The trails on the north side of the pass are exposed to the winter sun on it's southern travels, so snowshoeing and cross country skiing often give way to regular hiking with occasional use of microspikes in the shady valleys. However the north facing slopes of the pass and the peak with it's foothills are almost always covered in snow for beautiful winter landscape photography.

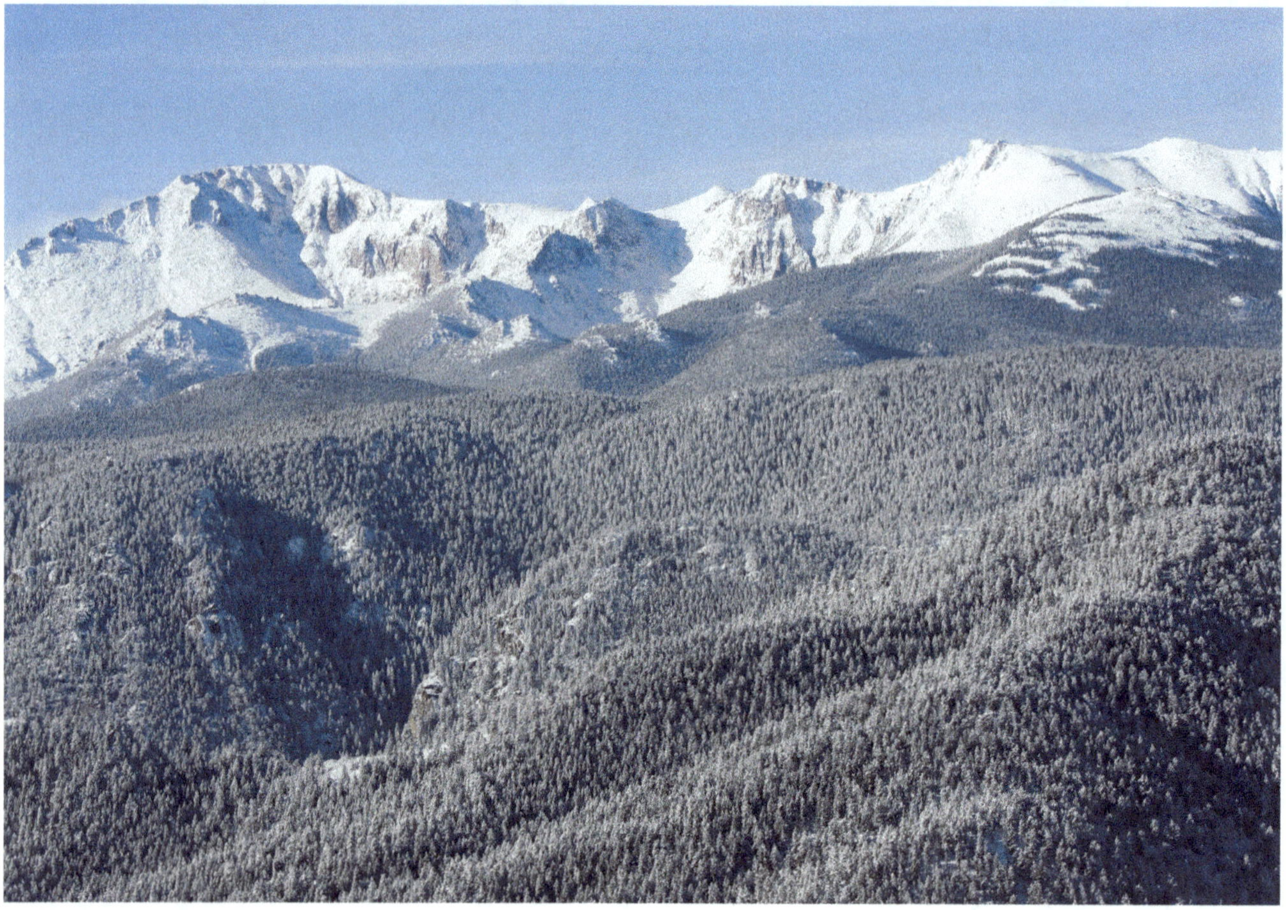

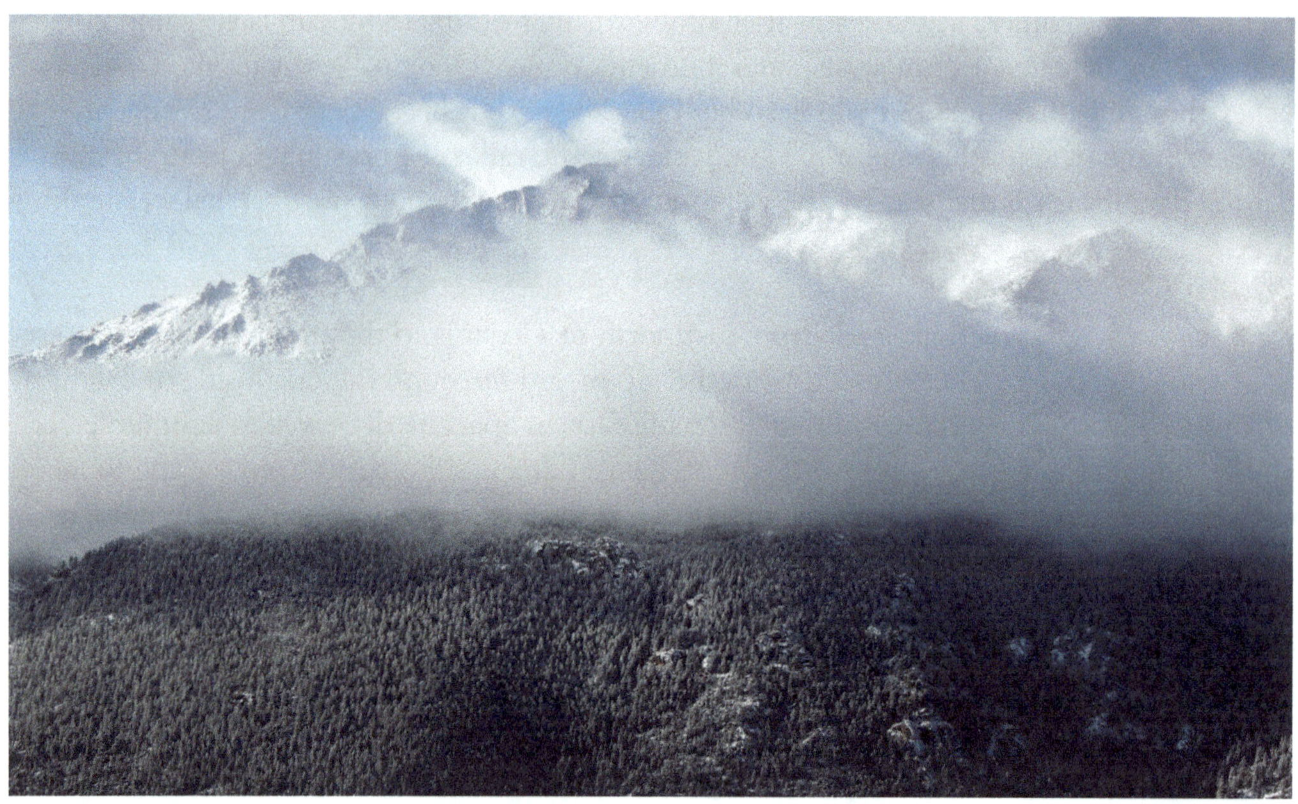

Mule deer along the trails are somewhat accustomed to people and will often stop and stare when they see a hiker approaching. There are many beautiful bucks inhabiting the area and I was able to obtain many of my best deer images while enjoying these beautiful trails. Elk however are elusive beasts, and even though I see sign of them everywhere I find it very difficult to actually photograph them. When deer get spooked they run a short distance and then stop for a look back to see if anything is actually chasing them. Knowing this helps one to prepare for the moment when the perfect capture becomes available. If you do manage to spot an elk in the Pike National Forest it's best to quickly capture whatever you can before they flee. Once elk begin running they don't look back and they don't stop until there are miles between themselves and any perceived threat.

One memorable day though my luck with the elk changed. I was snowshoeing in a heavy snowstorm fully clothed in a Gor-Tex suit, with my camera and 200mm lens protected by the Aquatech rain guard when I came across a sizable herd. The massive beasts seemed to understand that they had the advantage in deep snow and posed for a few captures before meandering slowly up the steep mountainside.

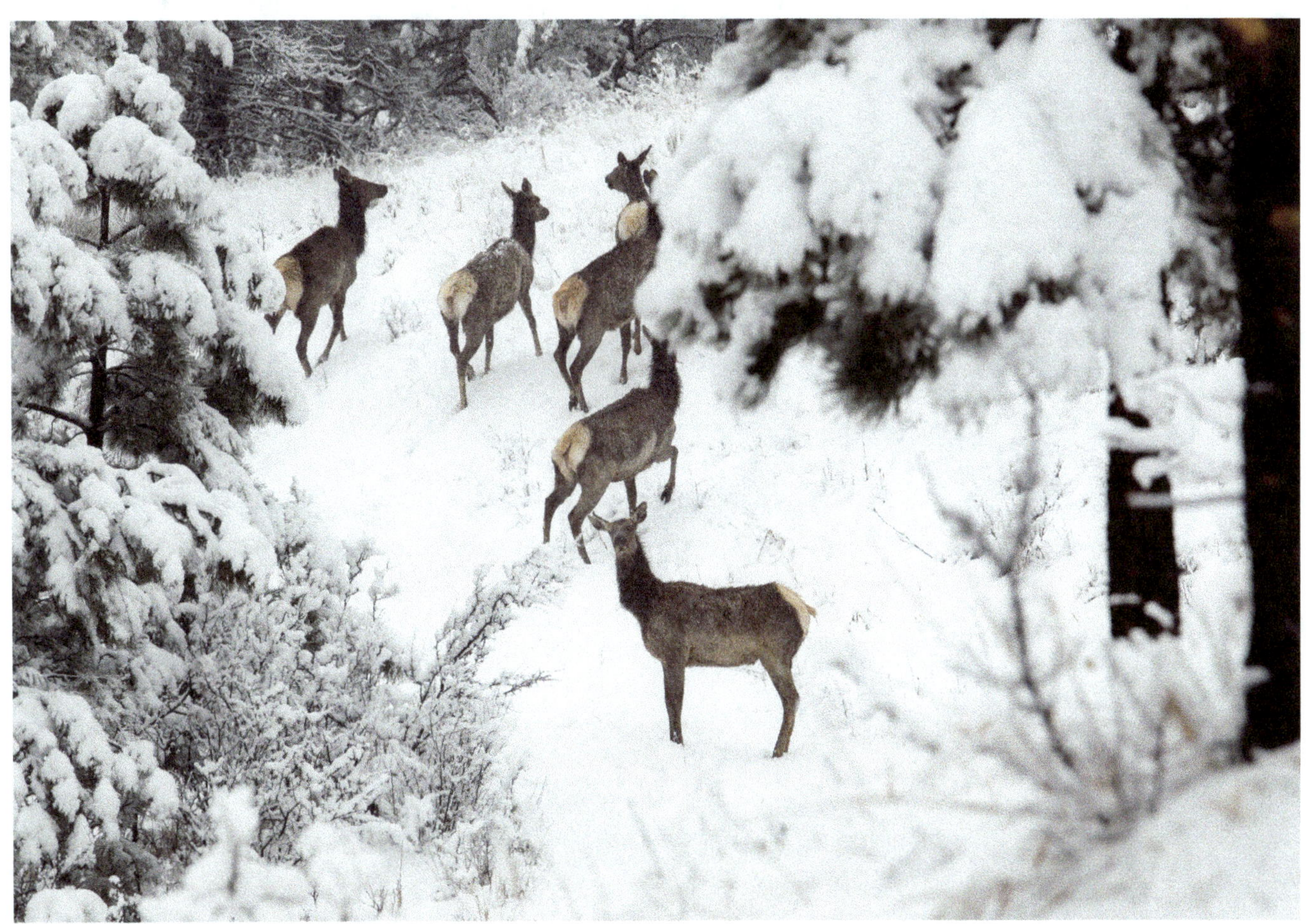

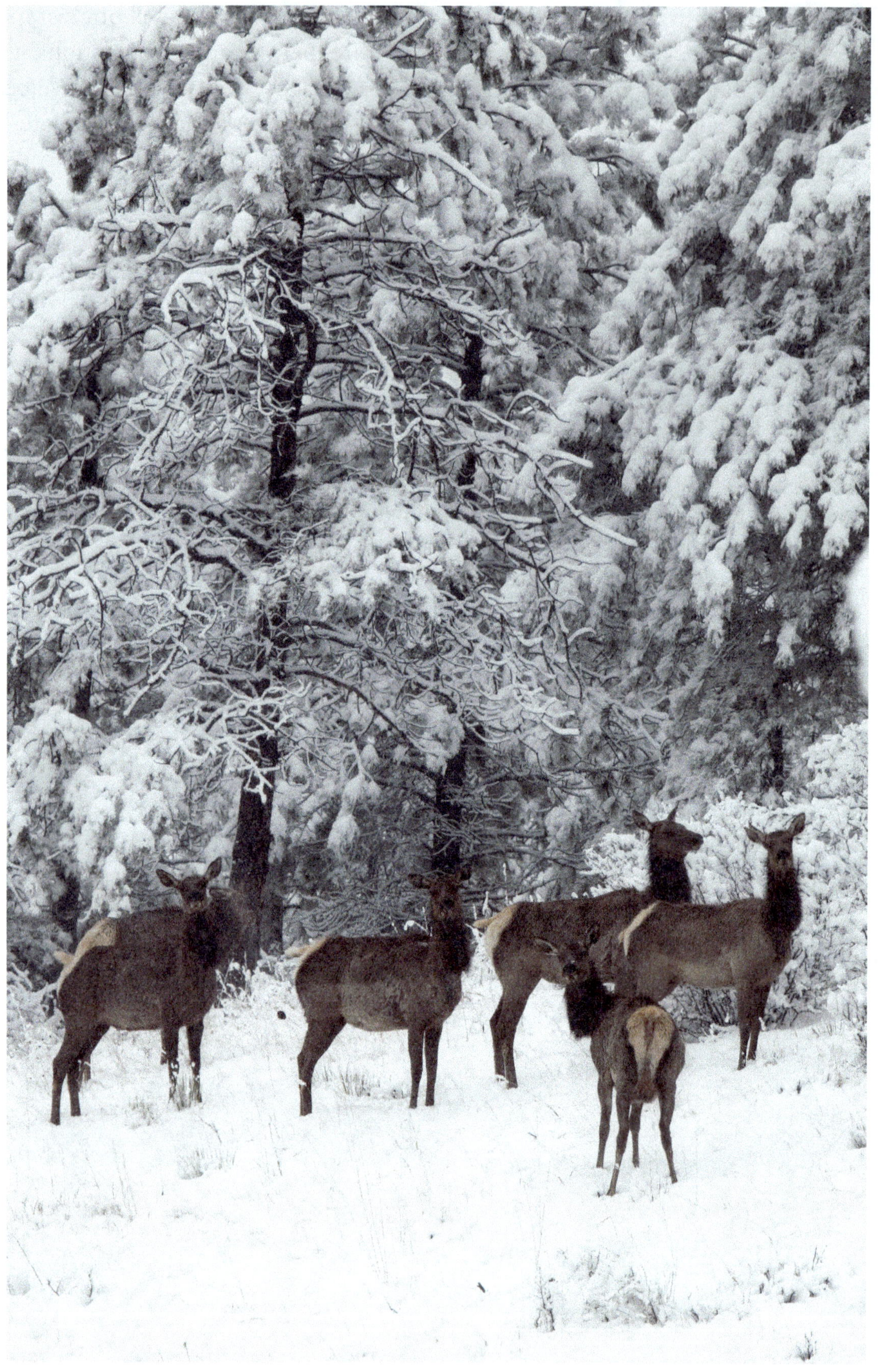

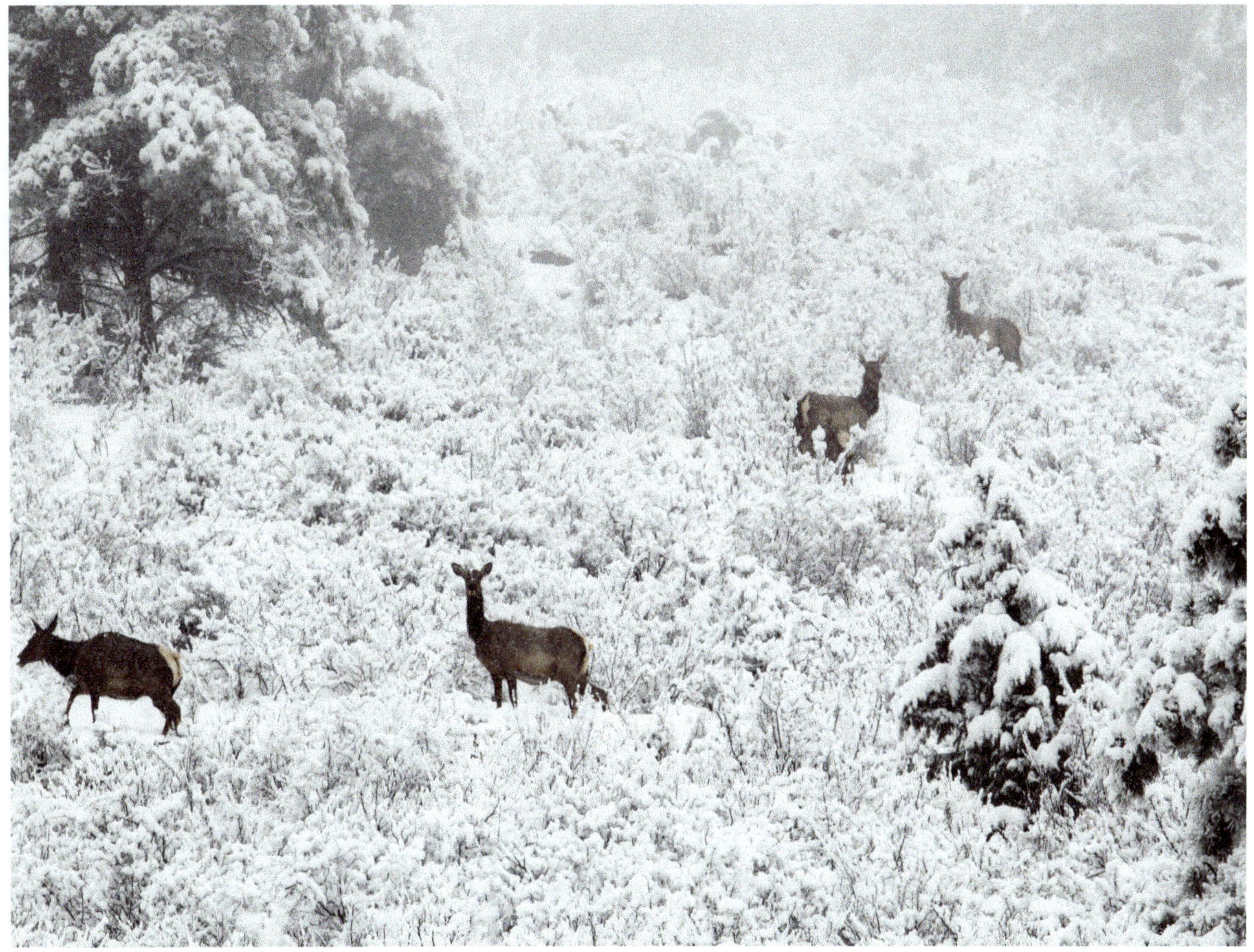

During my years of hiking these trails I found my Canon 70-200 F4L IS lens to be the most useful, along with the essential Aquatech rain guard. A longer lens was not often necessary in the close quarters between the highway and the steep mountainside and the 200mm focal length also seemed to be the perfect amount of magnification to best capture Pikes Peak and it's foothills across the valley only a few miles to the south.

In the above image the fairly wide F4 aperture allowed a capture at ISO 400 with a shutter speed fast enough to freeze the motion of the snow. Unfortunately the snow was coming down so hard that I wasn't able to capture detail in the animal's eyes. In fact for most of the animals, it appeared they were deliberately keeping their eyes closed for protection against the driving snow. However, for this session the snow allowed me to get shots of animals that would have normally fled at the first sight of me. At times the snow was too heavy to even see the animals but patience was rewarded by breaks in the wind blown snow long enough for some memorable images.

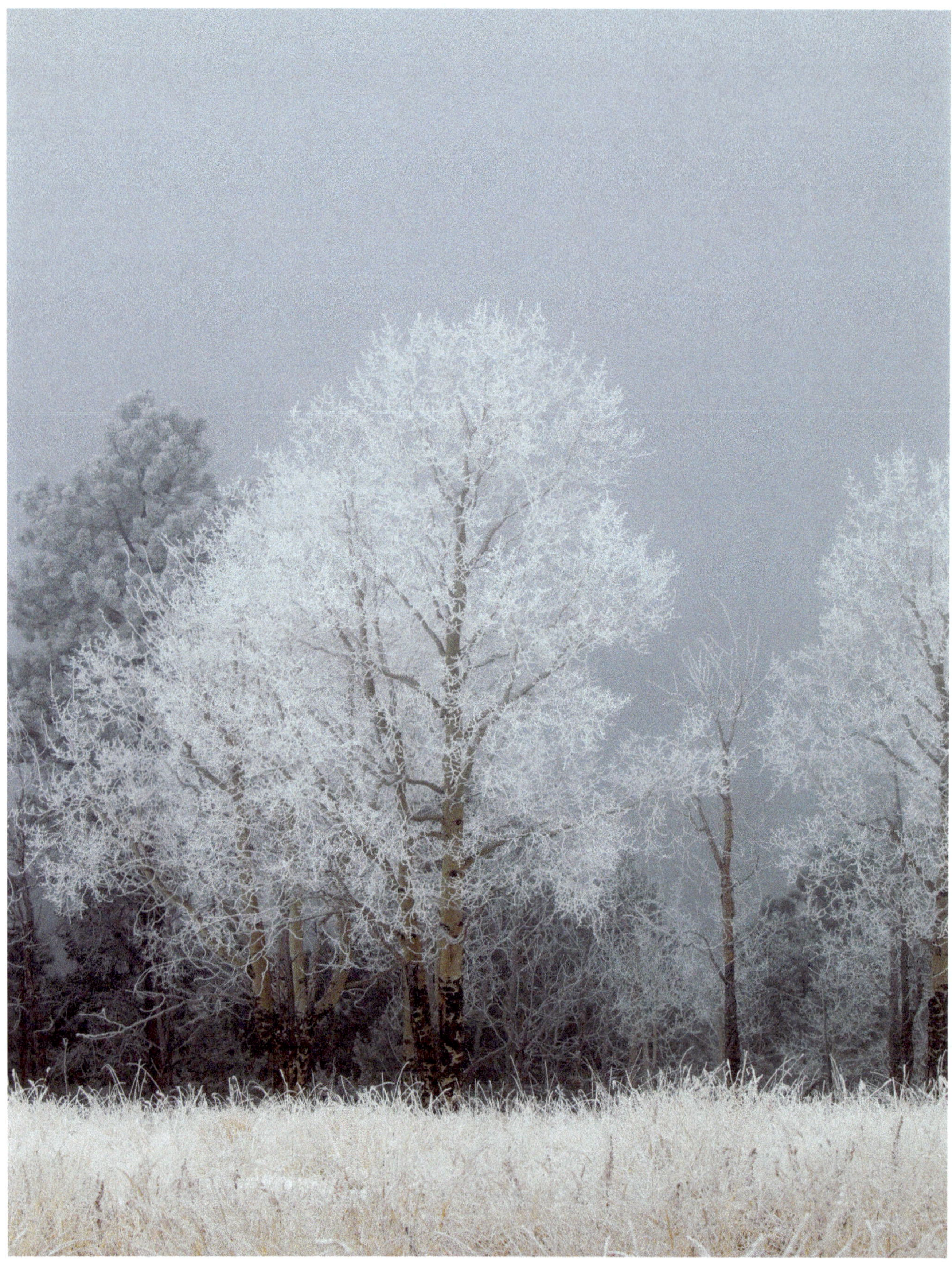

A beautiful little aspen stand at the top of Ute Pass often provided me with subject matter for minimalist imagery, not so much in the summer but certainly in the fall and winter seasons. Autumn of course with it's magnificent colors makes a beautiful foreground for captures of distant Pikes Peak, but as always winter is my favorite time of year to photograph aspen trees. In these images, ghostly frozen branches stand guard over the hidden depths of wilderness within.

I awoke to a misty Thanksgiving morning one year, the type of morning when dense fog might embolden the deer and elk to resist fleeing while enshrouding the woods in a soft blanket of white mystery. I set out early to assure that I would capture a few images before the morning sun had a chance to burn away the mist, but nothing would prepare me for the beauty I would encounter near the top of the ridge. The fog began to clear as I climbed the last few yards out of the pine trees and onto the summit of the mountain, and it was there that I viewed the exquisite artwork that the weather phenomenon had left behind. Overnight the freezing fog had covered the branches of the aspen grove in a stunning white garment of ice and snow that I could scarcely believe with my own eyes.

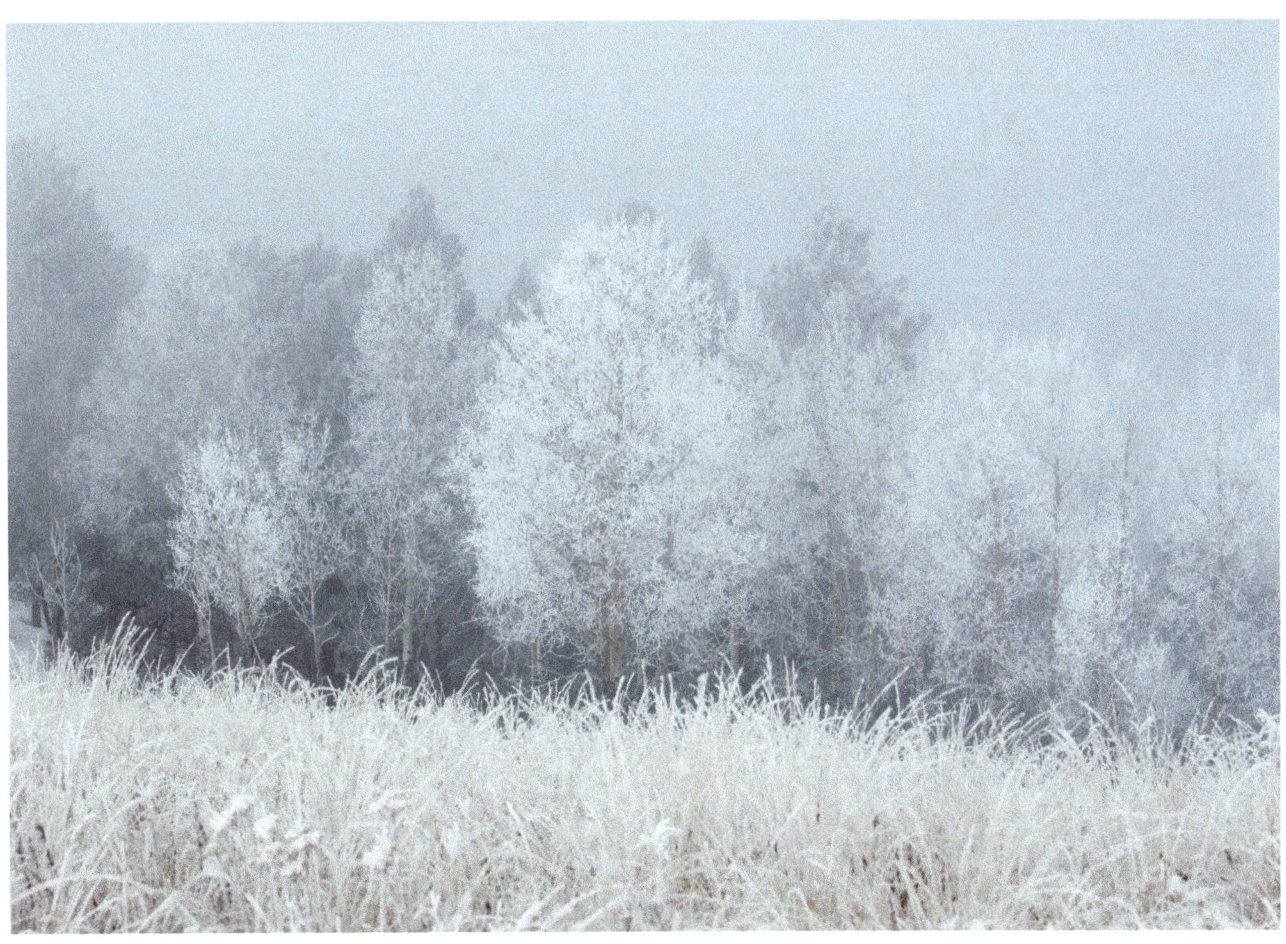

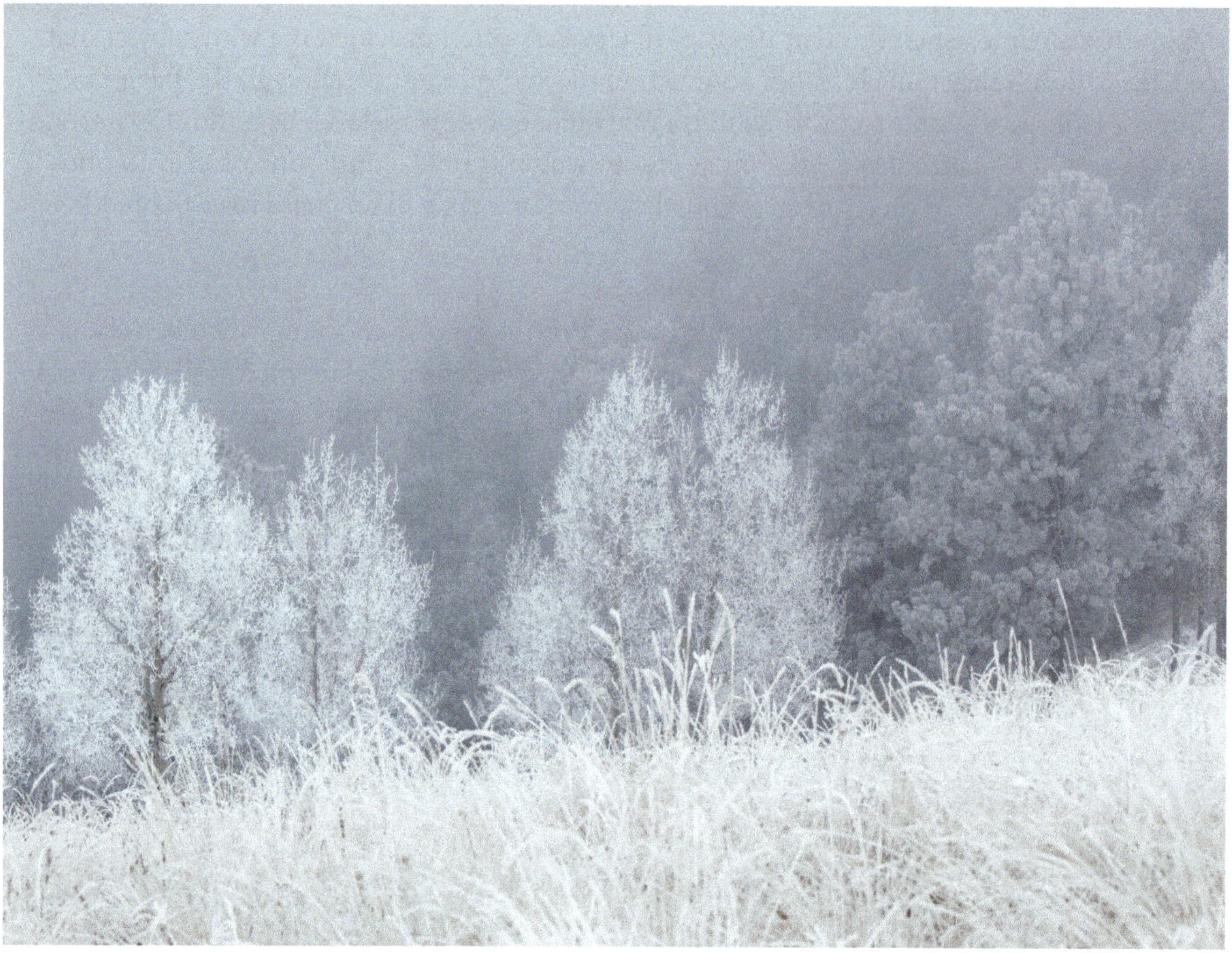

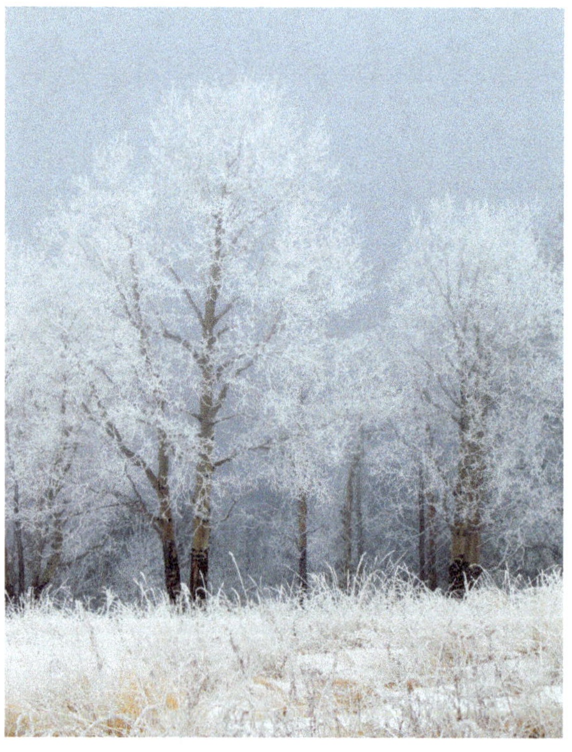

The mountain grass in the foreground was also cloaked in ice while the trees and mountains in the background were hidden in the ethereal beauty of mountain mist.

At a time like this a photographer should leave nothing to chance. After shooting a few images with customary settings to assure a capture, put the camera in full manual exposure mode and carefully choose an aperture that will render the closest trees sharp while allowing a dreamy bokeh effect in the background. Check the histogram after a couple of captures and adjust the shutter speed and ISO as desired while leaving the aperture in it's sweet spot for sharp focus.

The best views of the north face of Pikes Peak await just ahead as the trail steepens and trees become sparse near the summit of the grassy mountaintop. It is here that the snow is deepest and the reward the greatest. As you climb above the trees an unobstructed view of what seems like half the state opens in a splendid panorama including the foothills of the valley to the south and east, Pikes Peak itself and even the mountains of the Continental Divide to the west.

My 70-200mm zoom lens proved to be the perfect tool for this scene, able to capture the foothills at the wide end as well as intimate views of the fierce weather conditions pummeling the summit at 11,000 feet and above when fully zoomed to 200mm. With four stops of image stabilization and a maximum aperture of f/4, most captures are possible hand held even during the darkest of winter storms. The most amazing aspect of the peak and this view is that there is a new show to experience every day, it seems the Cantankerous Old Lady has a different look every time you look at her! The peak (below) is just a ghost seen through a low level snowstorm invading the Ute Pass Valley.

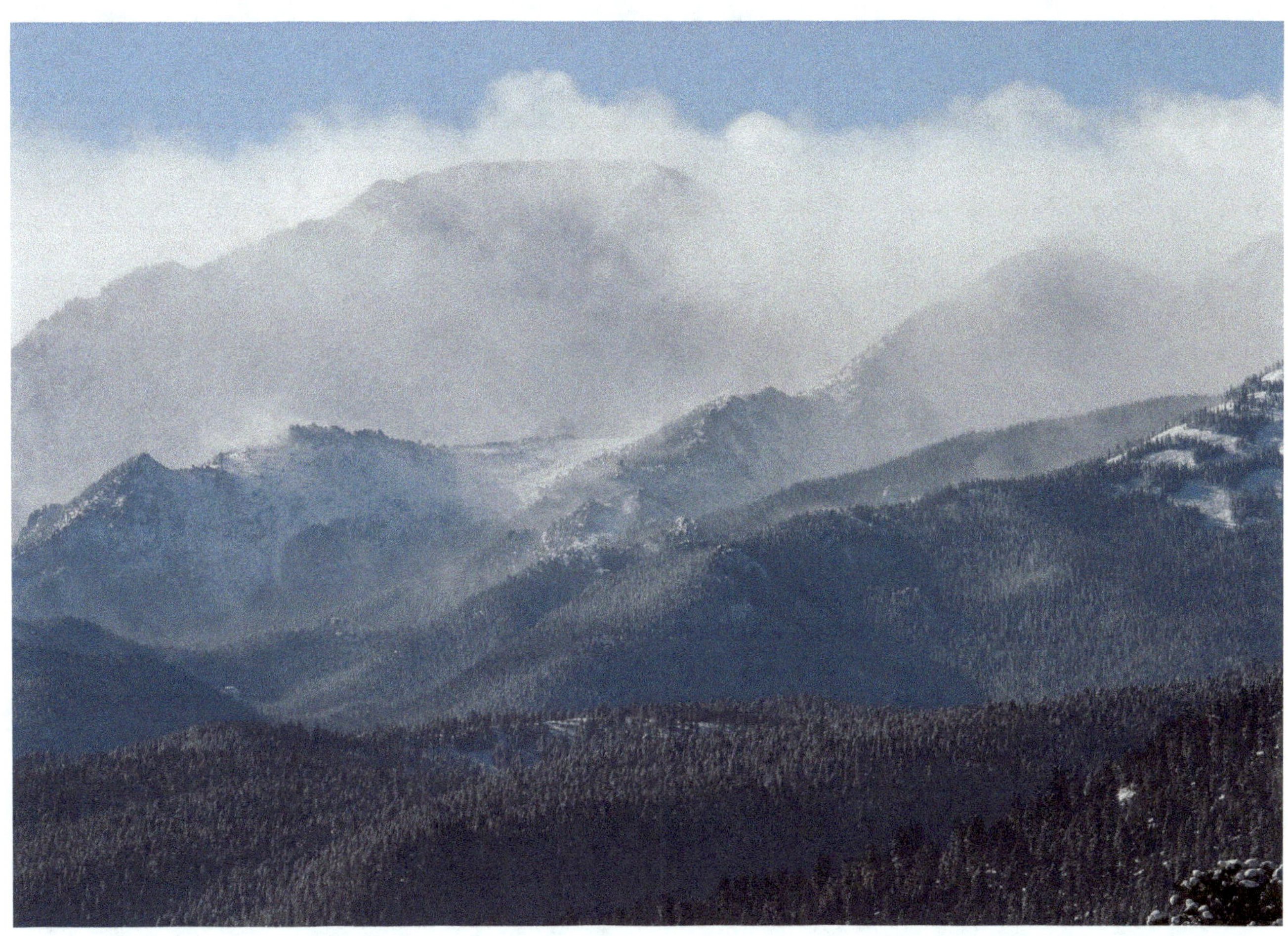

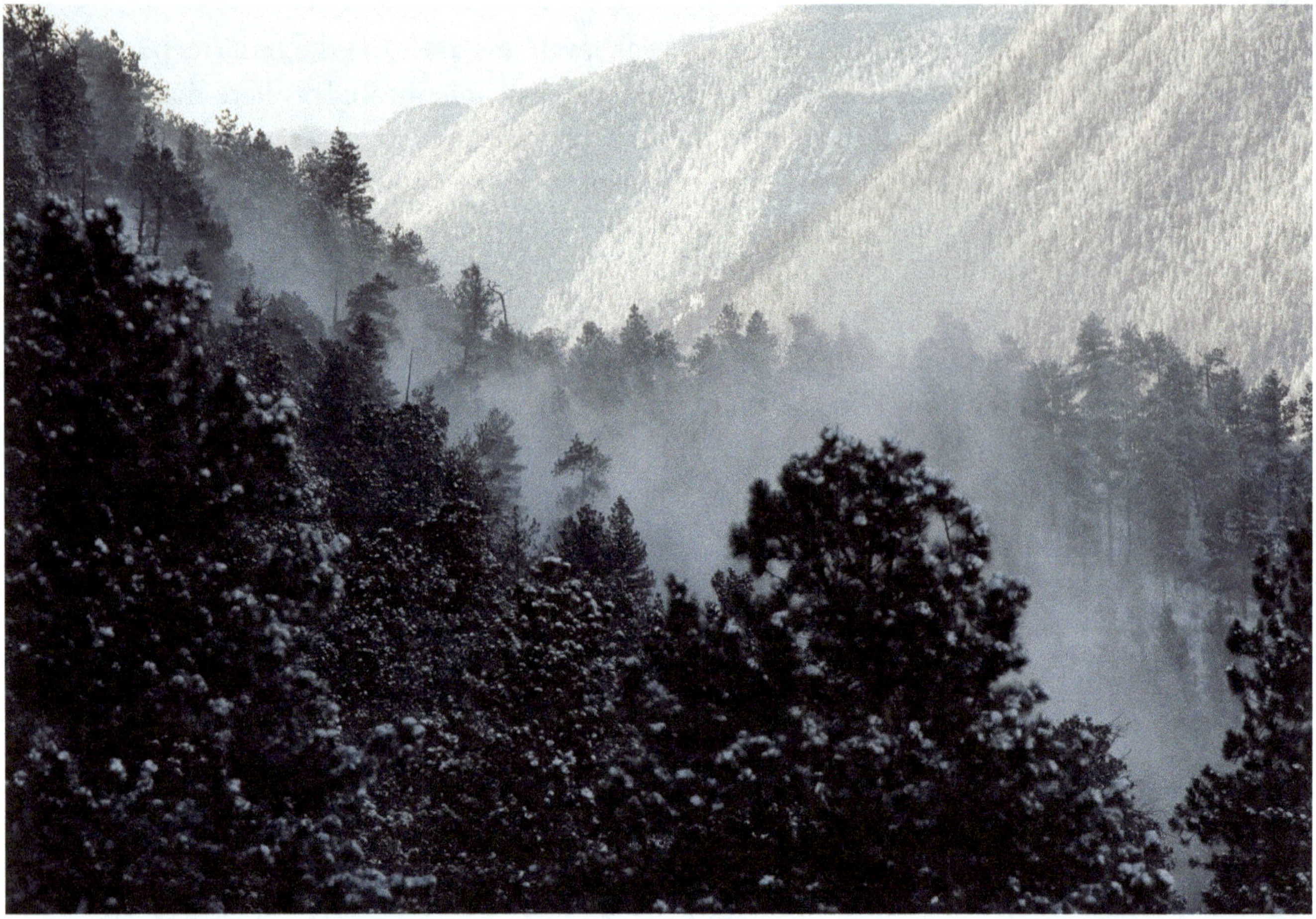

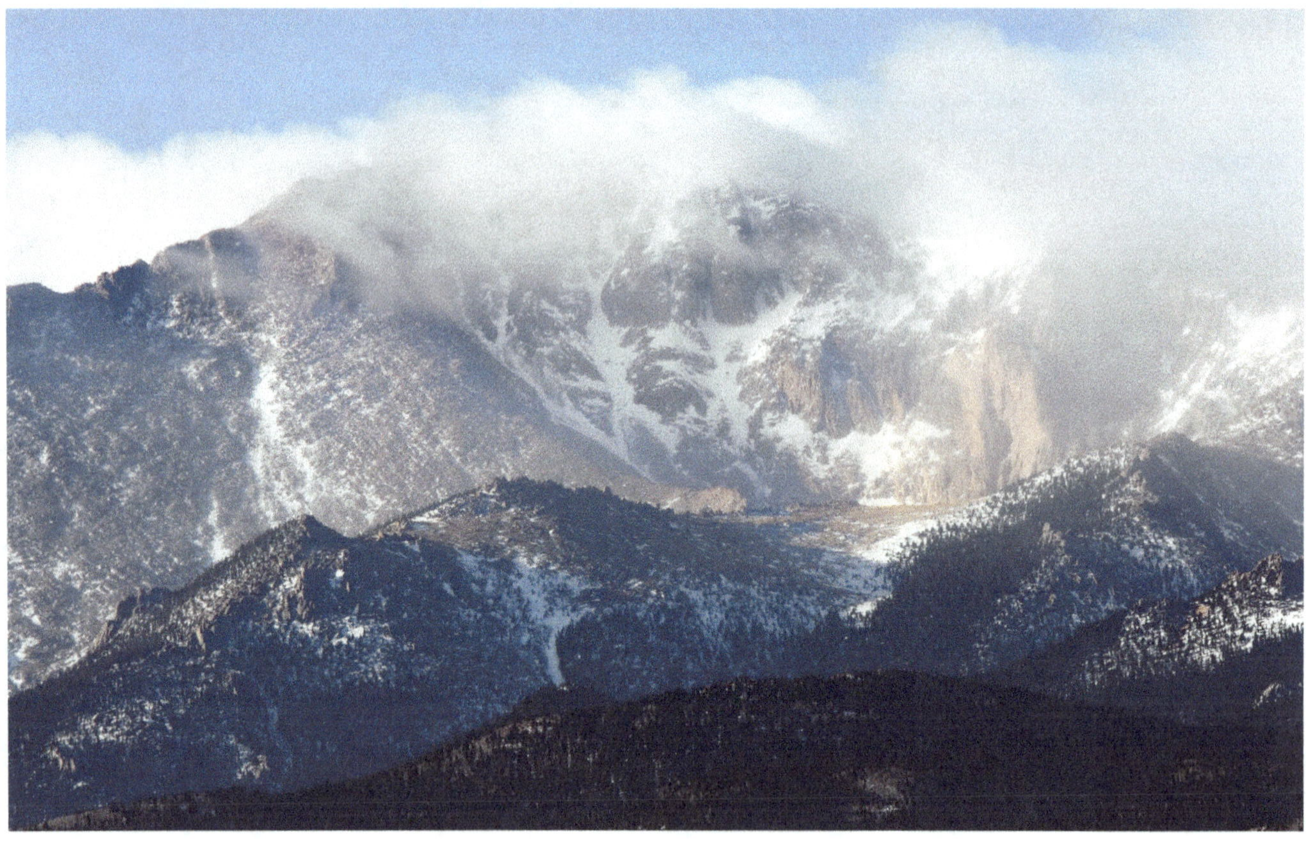

The **Manitou Incline** in Manitou Springs is a great winter sports and photography destination. Climbing the incline should be high on any outdoorman's list of things to accomplish and it was prominent in mine as well. For years I pondered the steep slash on the side of the mountain and vowed someday to tackle it myself.

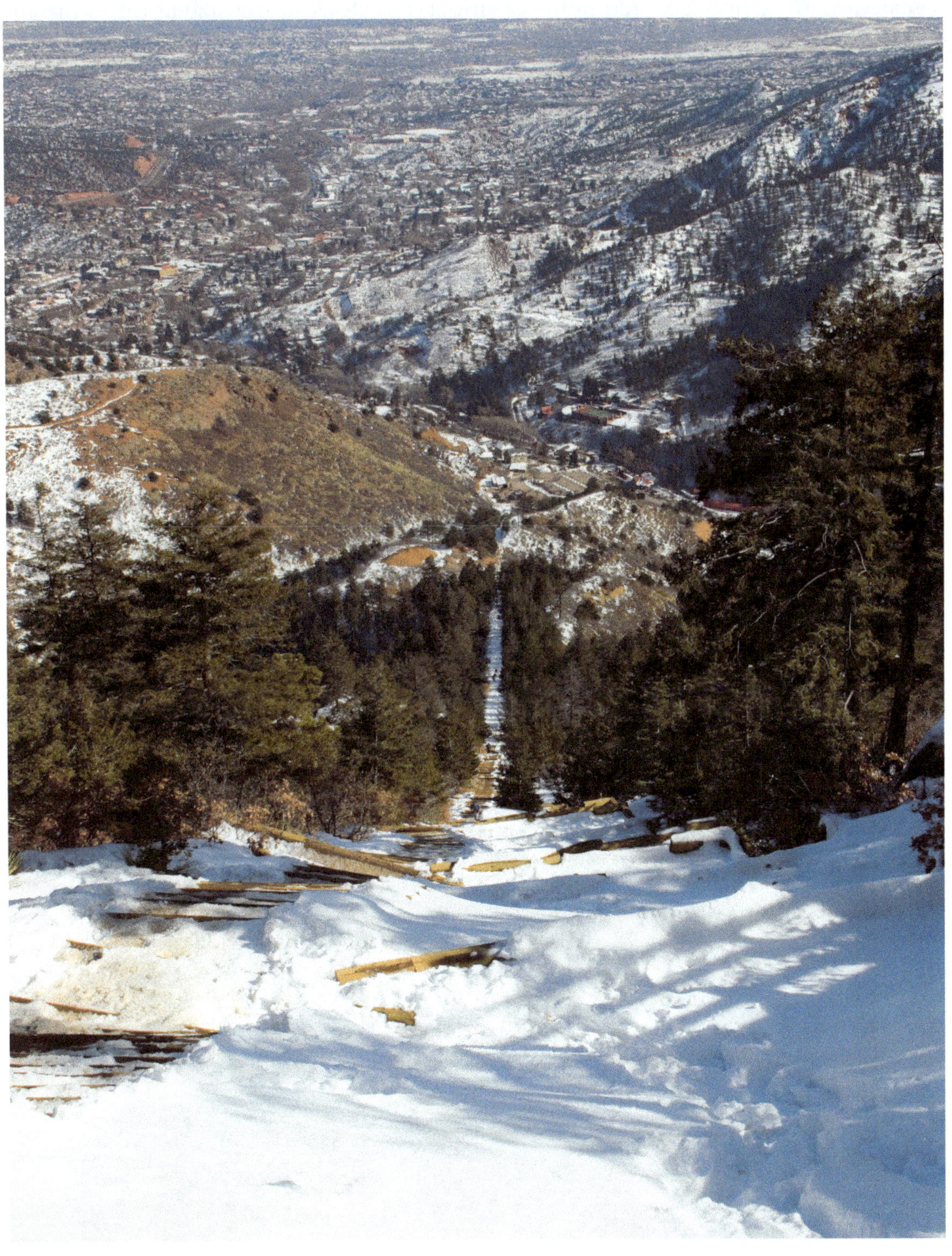

However stories of crowds and parking problems had always caused me to shy away from the experience, until of course I discovered microspikes. One day while perusing winter gear reviews I came across an article about microspikes, a simple winter traction device set in rubber that can be pulled over any pair of hiking boots to provide extra safety on icy trails. The model reviewed by the article was the Ice Trekker brand diamond spike model, which just so happened to be in stock at my local REI store. A quick call to the sales staff revealed that the now coveted item was indeed in stock in my size at our store in Colorado Springs, and I was soon on my way down to snag a pair of my own!

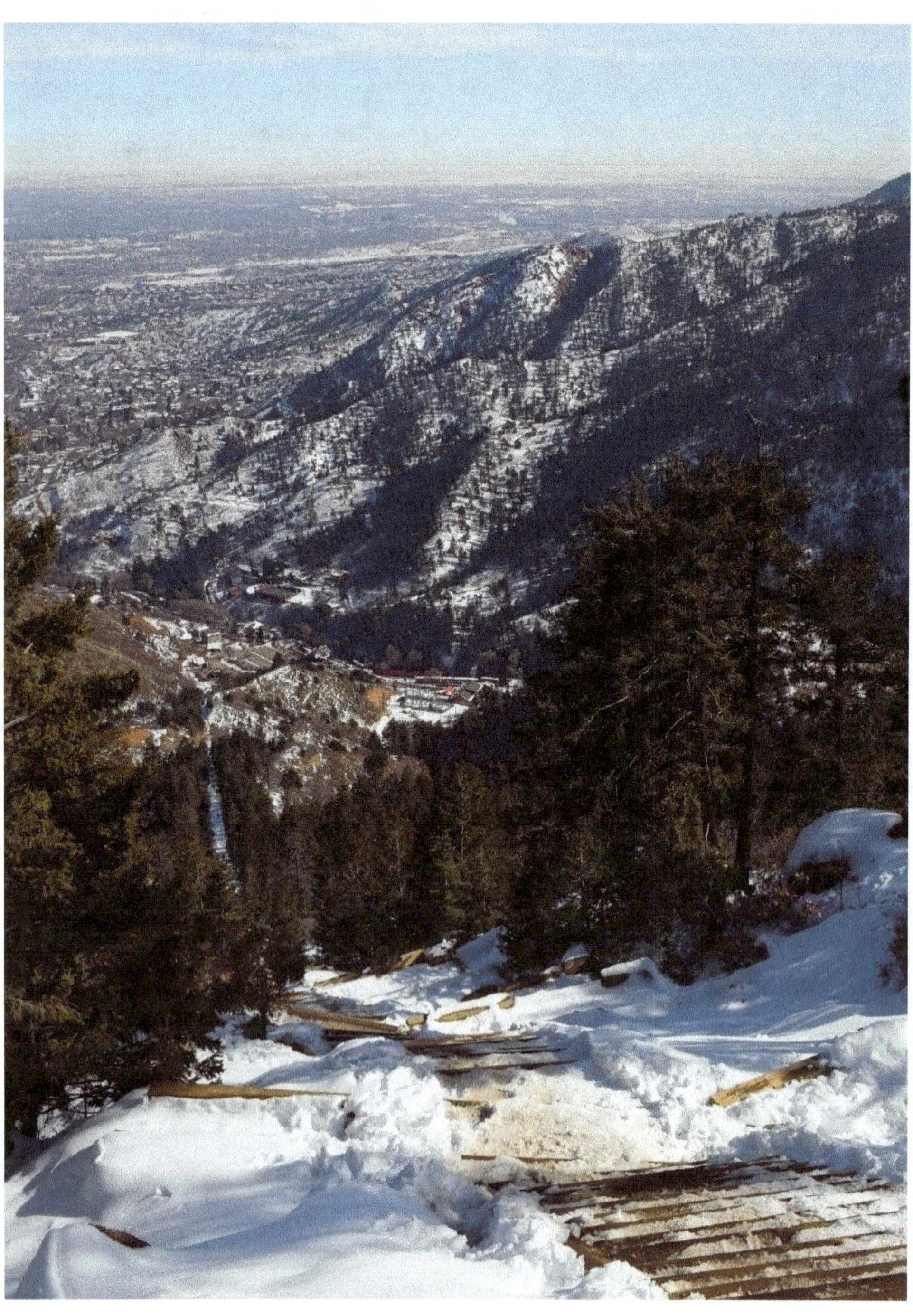

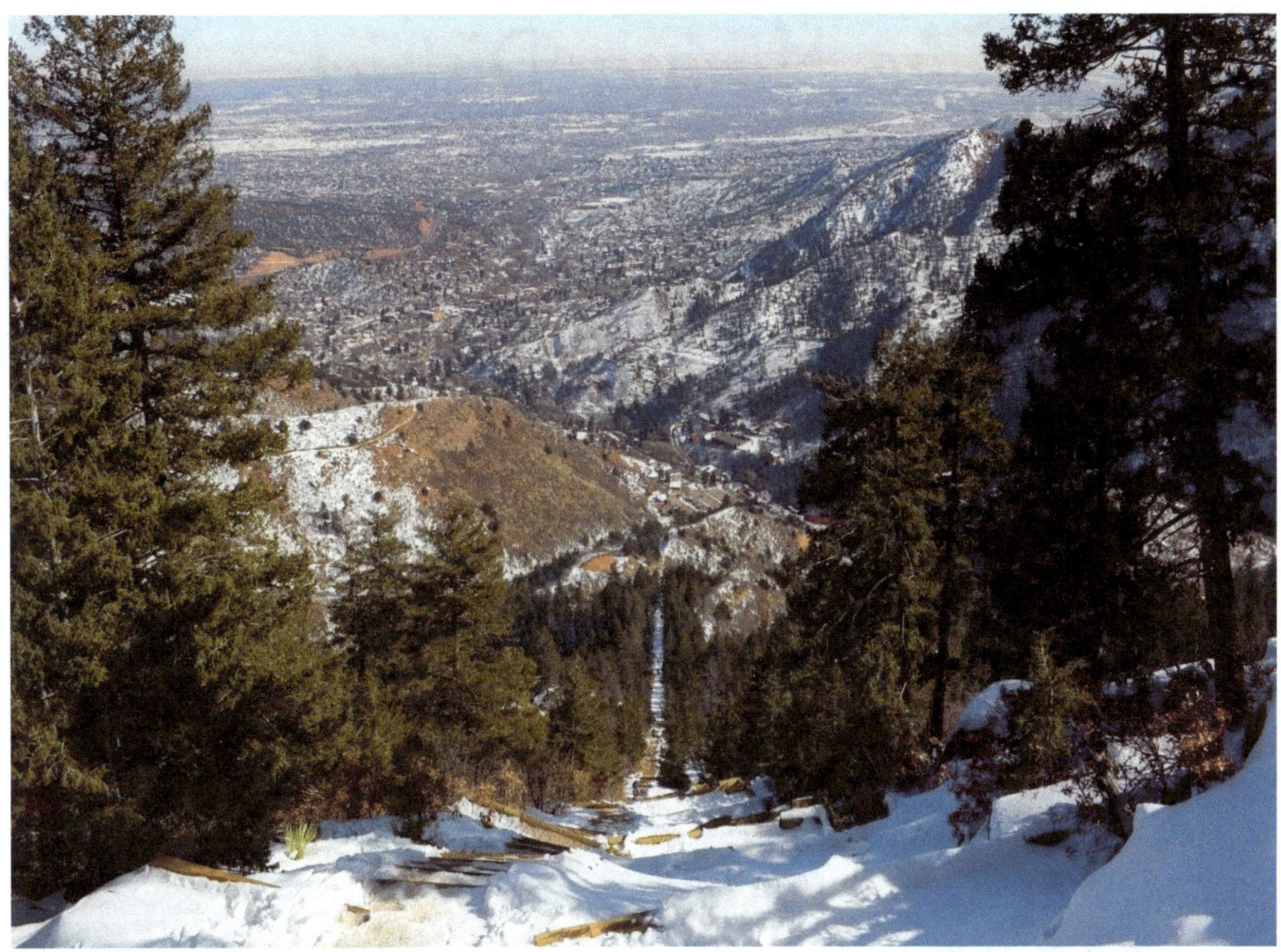

It would be impossible to climb the rugged stairs in snowshoes so I had never considered a winter climb of the famous landmark, but with microspikes a winter ascent is very possible. In winter there are no crowds and parking isn't an issue. I knew the climb would be a tough one and weight on the steep stair steps would be an issue so for my inaugural trek. I chose to leave my long lens home, packing only my light plastic 18-55mm kit lens. Even though the stairs are narrow, the view from upon the mountain is huge. I wanted my images to take in details on the snow covered stairs in the foreground all the way to Manitou Springs below, plus the red spires of Garden of the Gods and beyond to the expanse of the city on the plains all the way to the horizon.

One other item I felt might be worth the extra weight to pack was my trusty monopod / trekking pole. When you are gasping for air the monopod helps to steady the camera for epic shots of the great adventure, and it is also a good tool to assist with balance as climbers claw their way up and down the slippery slope. I recommend hiking the alternate route on the Barr Trail back to Manitou Springs. Signs at the top of the stairs indicate the route to the trail, a much safer choice for the descent. Trekking poles and microspikes will be invaluable as one navigates snow and icy patches along the way down the steep trail back to the parking lot.

The Mining District

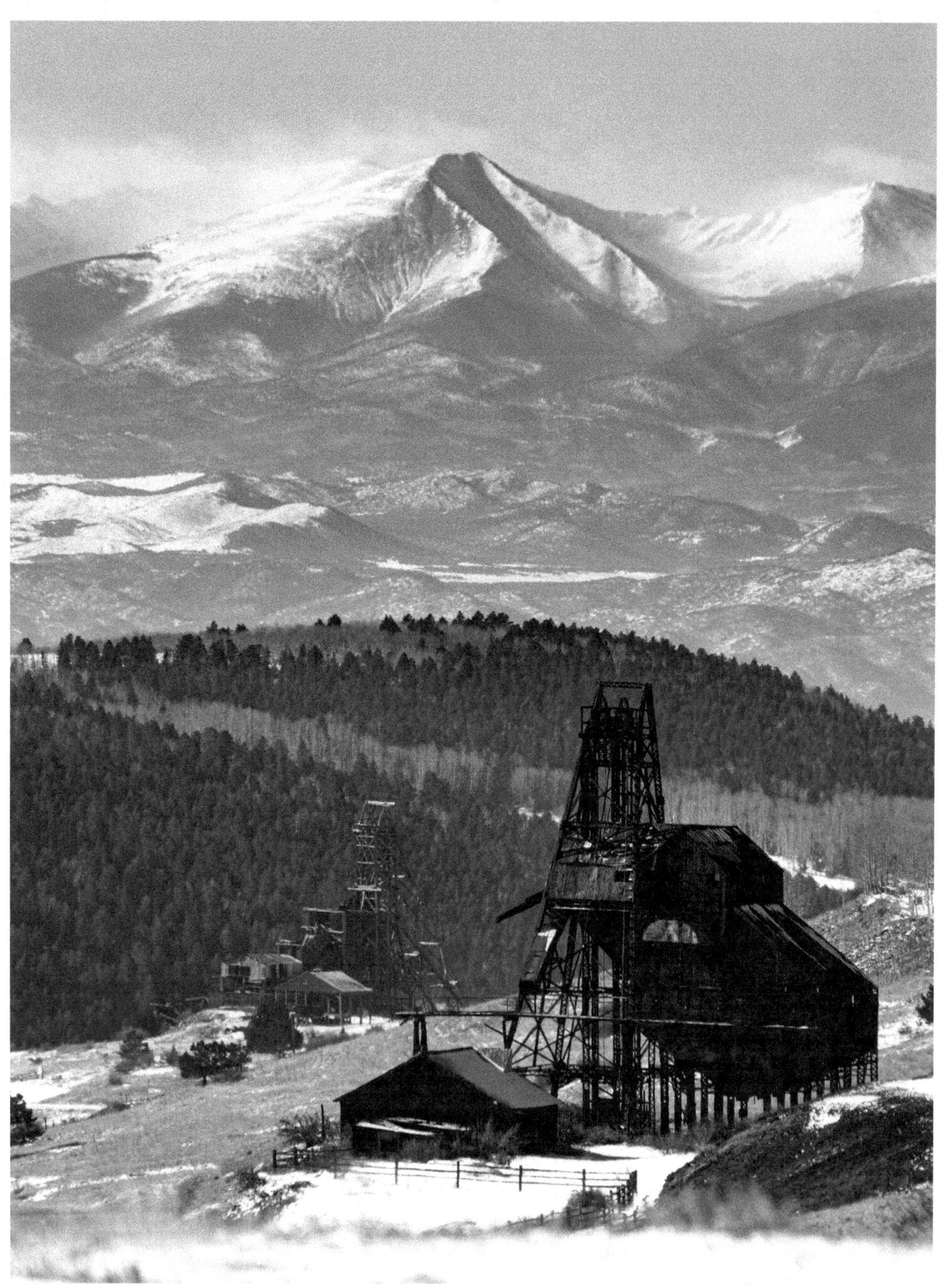

My travels throughout Colorado would eventually take me beyond the north side of Pikes Peak to mine country on the south side, the **Cripple Creek / Victor** and Goldfield historic gold mining district. The district is a beautiful combination of sparse population, great beauty and unlimited winter adventure. Nestled between the Sangre de Cristo Range to the South and Tenderfoot Pass and Pikes Peak to the north, the tiny mountain town of Cripple Creek seemed like the perfect place to settle in for a while. I fell in love with this place the first time I descended from Tenderfoot Pass, and the Backbone of the Nation came into view. The rugged Sangre de Cristo Block Fault Range juts out of the Arkansas River Valley to the south as the Collegiate and Mosquito Range peaks stand tall in the west.

The high peaks are always magnificent but are especially stunning when covered with snow and storm clouds in the winter. This beautiful winter wonderland would take time to explore and to discover all the best roads, trails and views, and I wasted no time getting to know my new surroundings.

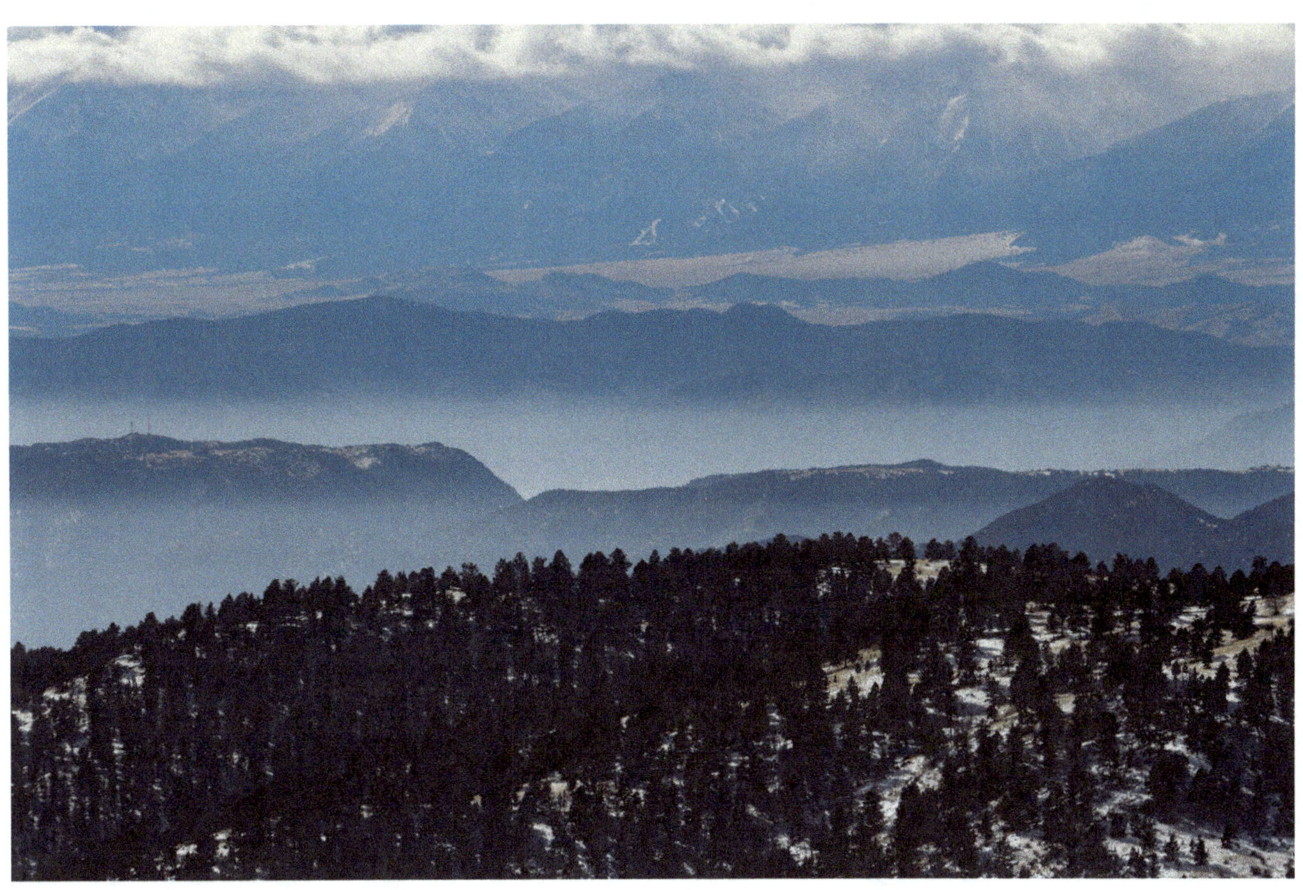

At first I was most enthralled with finding all the best views of the stunningly beautiful Sangre de Cristo Mountains. Magnificent panoramas are visible from a number of locations along highway 67 between Tenderfoot and Victor Passes, as well as more remote views from little known hiking trails dispersed throughout the area. The first and most obvious opportunity is of course the Cripple Creek overlook on the drive from the north on Highway 67 to the descent into the gambling town of Cripple Creek. From here the entire town of Cripple Creek is visible including the original old buildings, most of which have now been converted to casinos. To the southwest, the Sangre de Cristo Range is visible and to the west the Collegiate Peaks can be seen in the distance.

There are a number of ways to capture the tall peaks of the great divide in a compelling image, including both wide and tight views. Use a wide angle lens to include the town and foothills while a longer lens will accentuate the rugged mountains. A good 70-200mm lens will provide sufficient detail in the mountains, while a 400mm lens or longer will yield intimate details of the distant ranges.

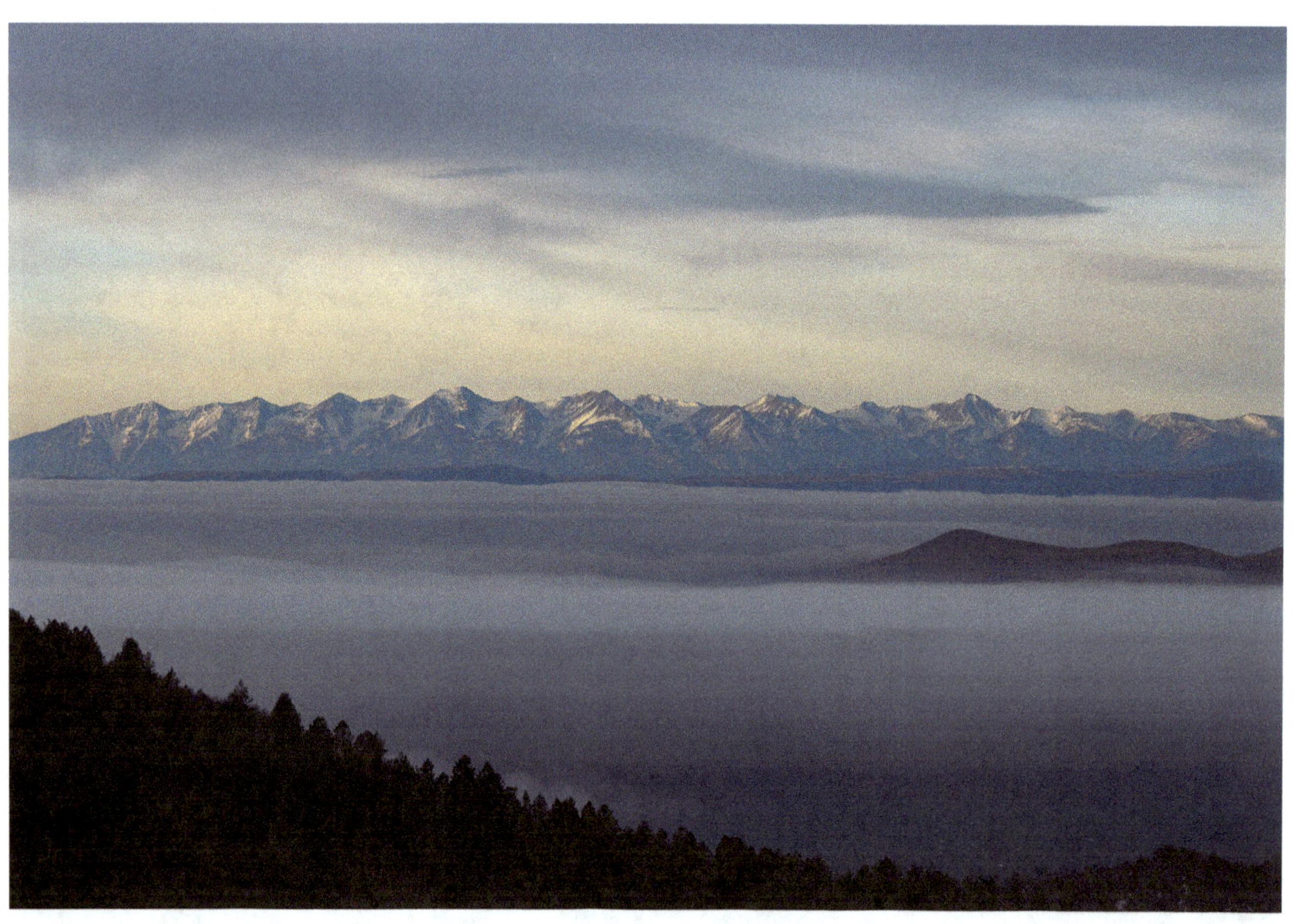

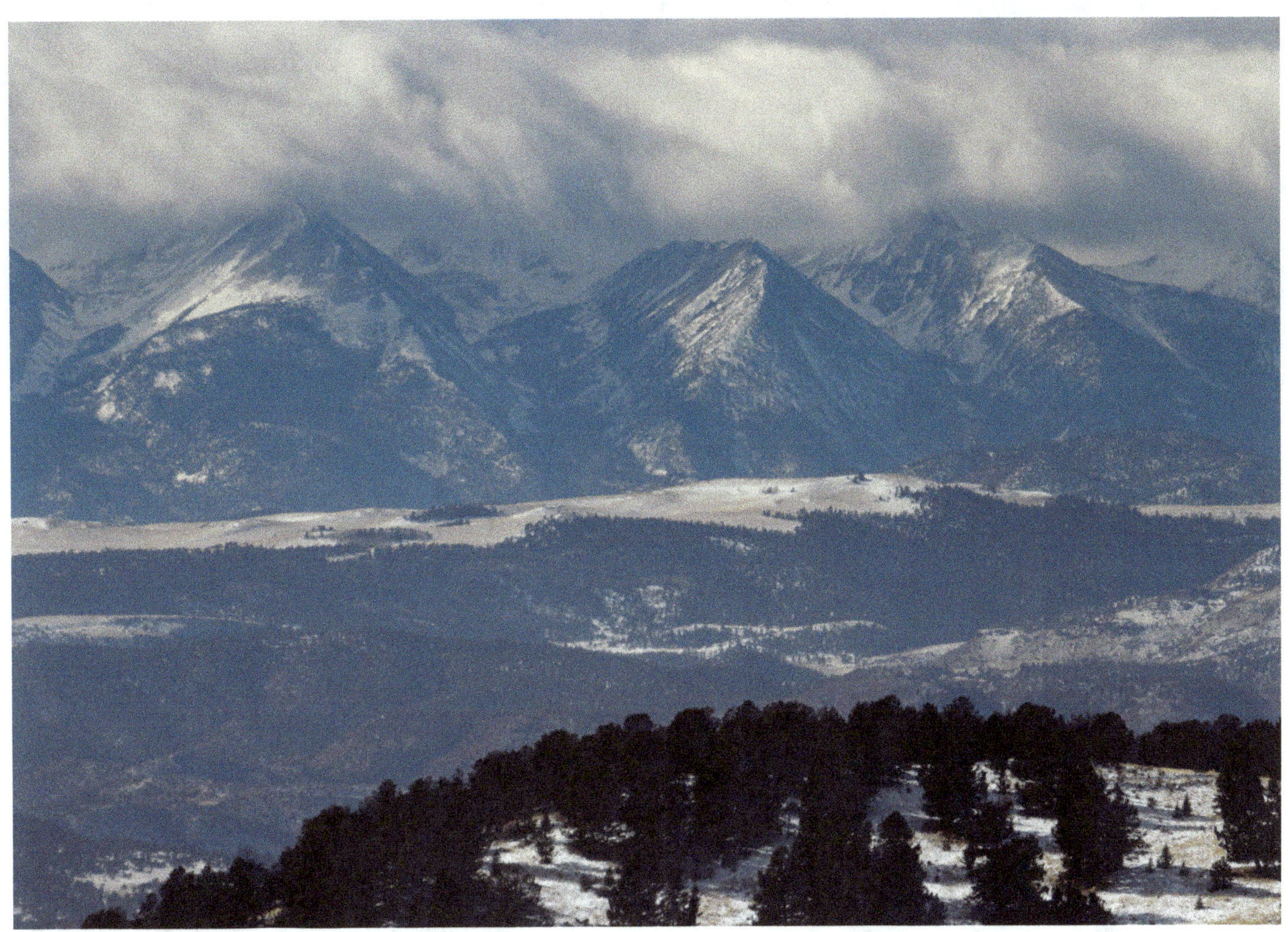

I like to use a heavy tripod to photograph distant scenes like the one above. From Cripple Creek these mountains are many miles away and the slightest camera movement at that range will cause significant motion blur. Most features in an image like this are going to be at the infinity limit on any lens so there is no need to use an extreme aperture like f/22 to get a sharp image. I find it better to use the sweet spot for best results with the lens I'm using. For example, my Canon 70-200 F4L seems to be the sharpest at around f/6.3, while my 400 F4-5.6 works well at f/8 or 9. A high quality polarizer will bring out details in the clouds, cut through haze and limit glare from the bright snow.

Another thing to consider with distant or tiny subjects is mirror slap. For photographers still using SLR cameras whether digital or film, the camera must move the mirror out of the path to the film or sensor before exposing the image. This violent movement can cause significant camera shake even with a steady tripod. Fortunately these cameras often come with a setting for raising the mirror separately from actuating the shutter which is good practice. With digital cameras the easiest solution is to switch to "live view" mode which brings up the mirror and displays the image on the rear LCD. Film camera users aren't as lucky, once the mirror is raised the photographer is shooting blind. Modern mirrorless cameras can simply be switched to electronic shutter mode, completely circumventing any mechanical camera shake issues.

The drive from Cripple Creek south to the gold rush era town of Victor is filled with awesome views of mines and distant mountain ranges. There is one main overlook with a parking lot about halfway to Victor but a watchful eye can spot a number of great spots to pull over and shoot.

Changing temperatures and a calm morning breeze often contribute to wonderful misty foggy conditions in the Arkansas Valley below, and on the rugged mountain range in the distance. At times a blanket of white will cover the valley below while other times the clouds will invade the mountains in a beautiful swirling mass of moisture.

Earlier in the day the valley (below) was completely obscured in fog, but eventually the fog drifted lower into the valleys, leaving behind a frozen scene worthy of an oil painting.

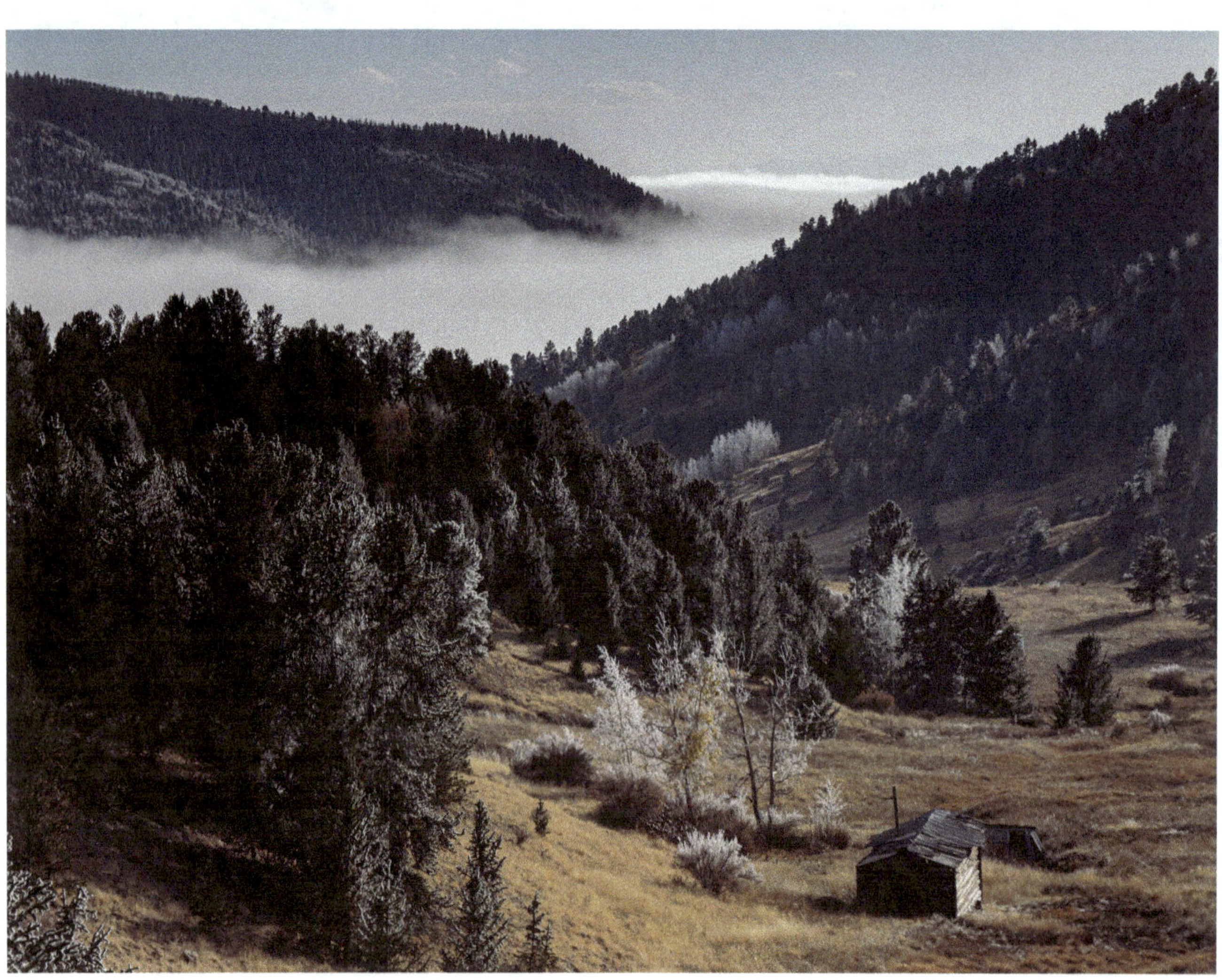

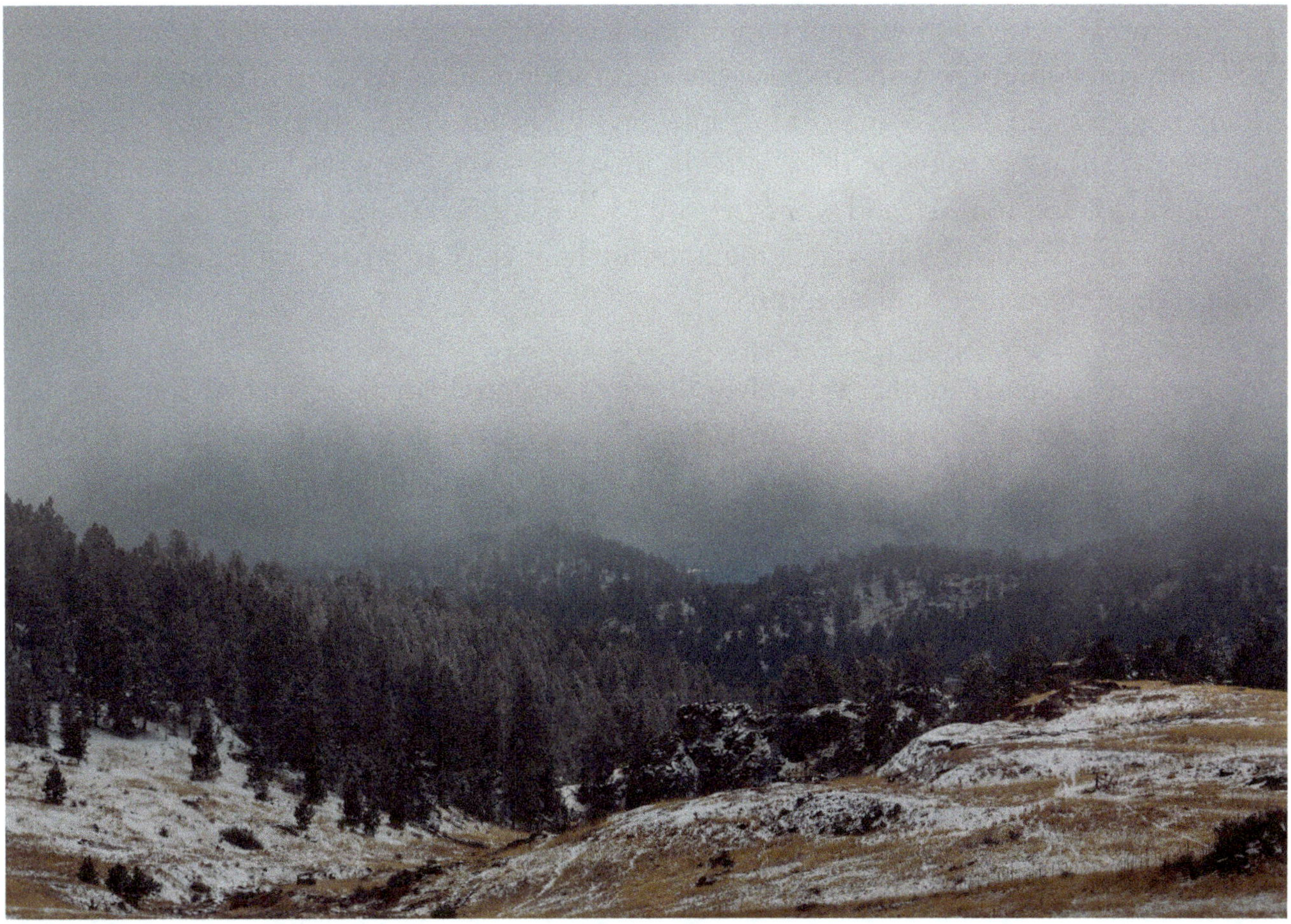

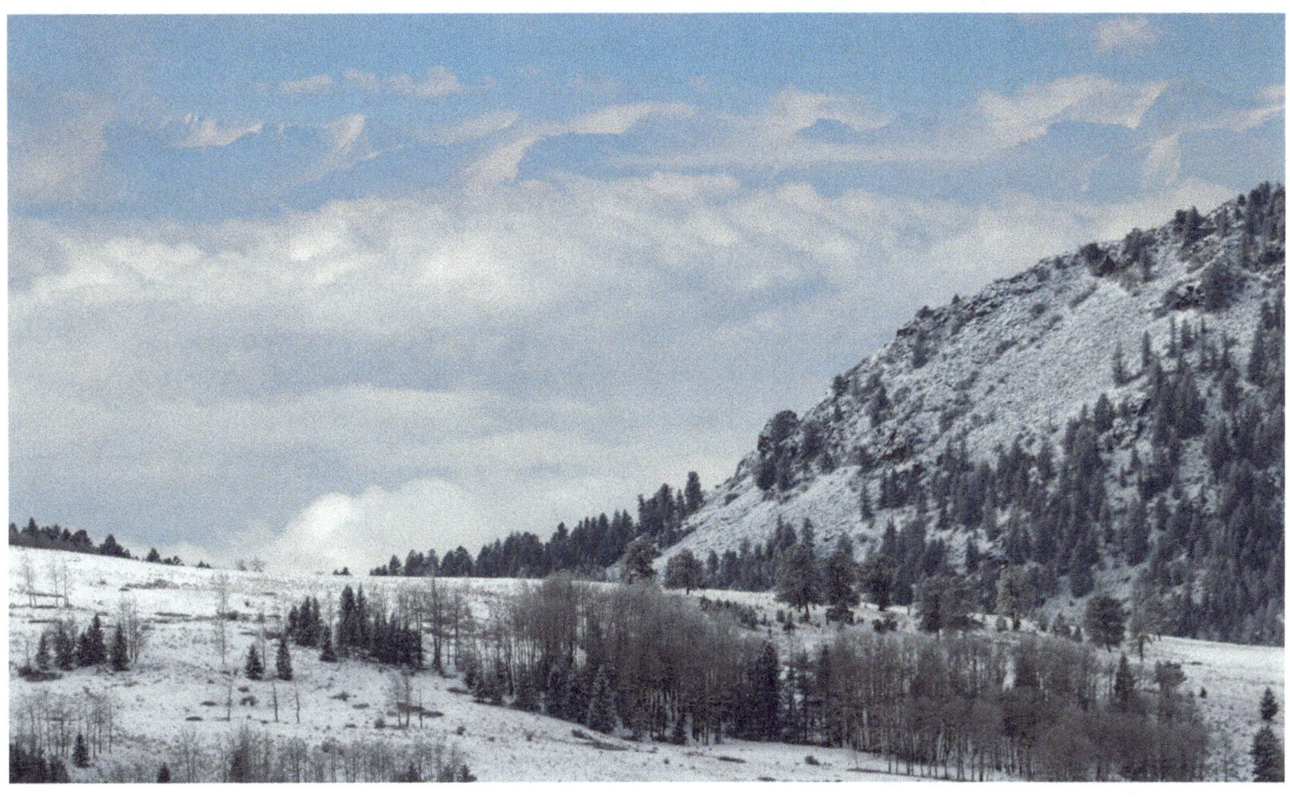

Unfortunately frequent weather conditions developing between the valley and the mountains often interfere with image clarity and contrast. Some correction is possible by adding contrast and de-haze in post but sometimes it just isn't possible to capture sufficient contrast or attractive colors in the winter. In these cases it might be helpful to shoot monochrome or convert to black and white in post. Monochrome images are a lot more amenable to severe contrast corrections, and sometimes the faint color in a hazy winter scene actually detracts from the power of the capture.

A graduated filter is another valuable tool for capturing dramatic images of the Sangre de Cristo landscape, bringing bright skies and snow on the mountains into balance with the dark pine forest in the foreground. But unlike the polarizer, a graduated filter can easily be recreated in post with an image editor so it may not be necessary to part with the funds for an expensive glass filter. I myself prefer the linear filter in Adobe Camera Raw which can be applied to any portion of the image necessary, and can also be angled to accurately fill only the brightest area of an image that can most benefit from the effect.

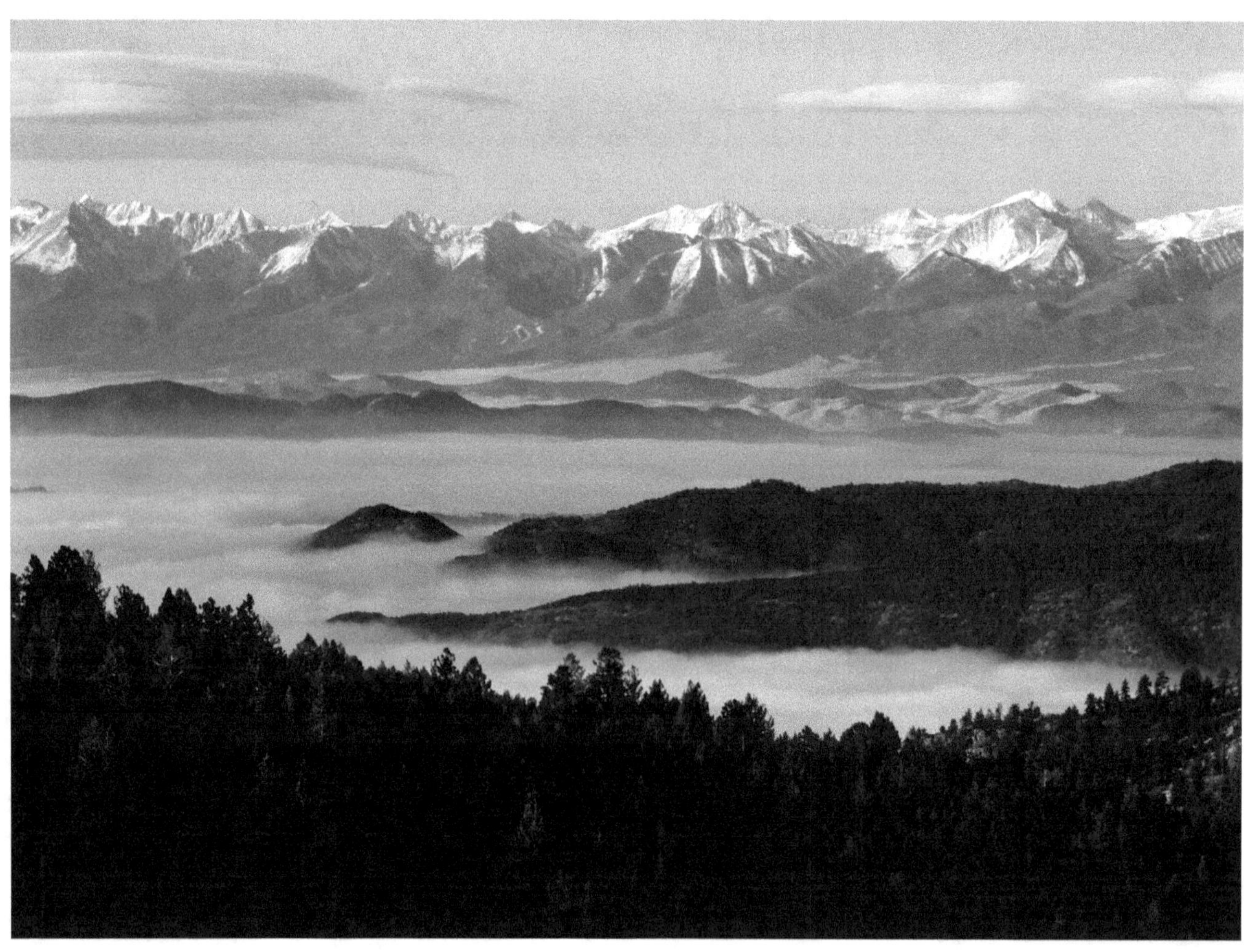

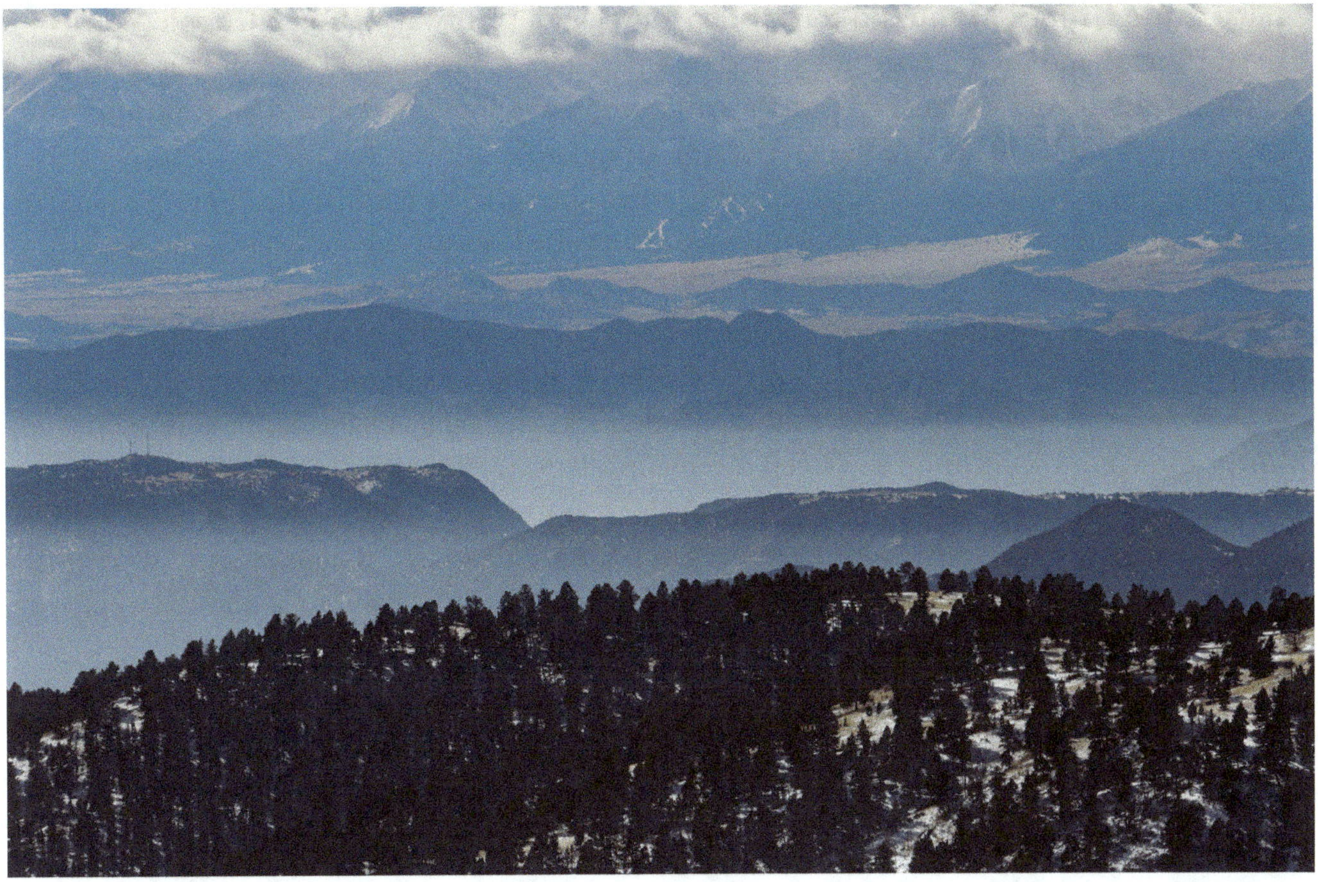

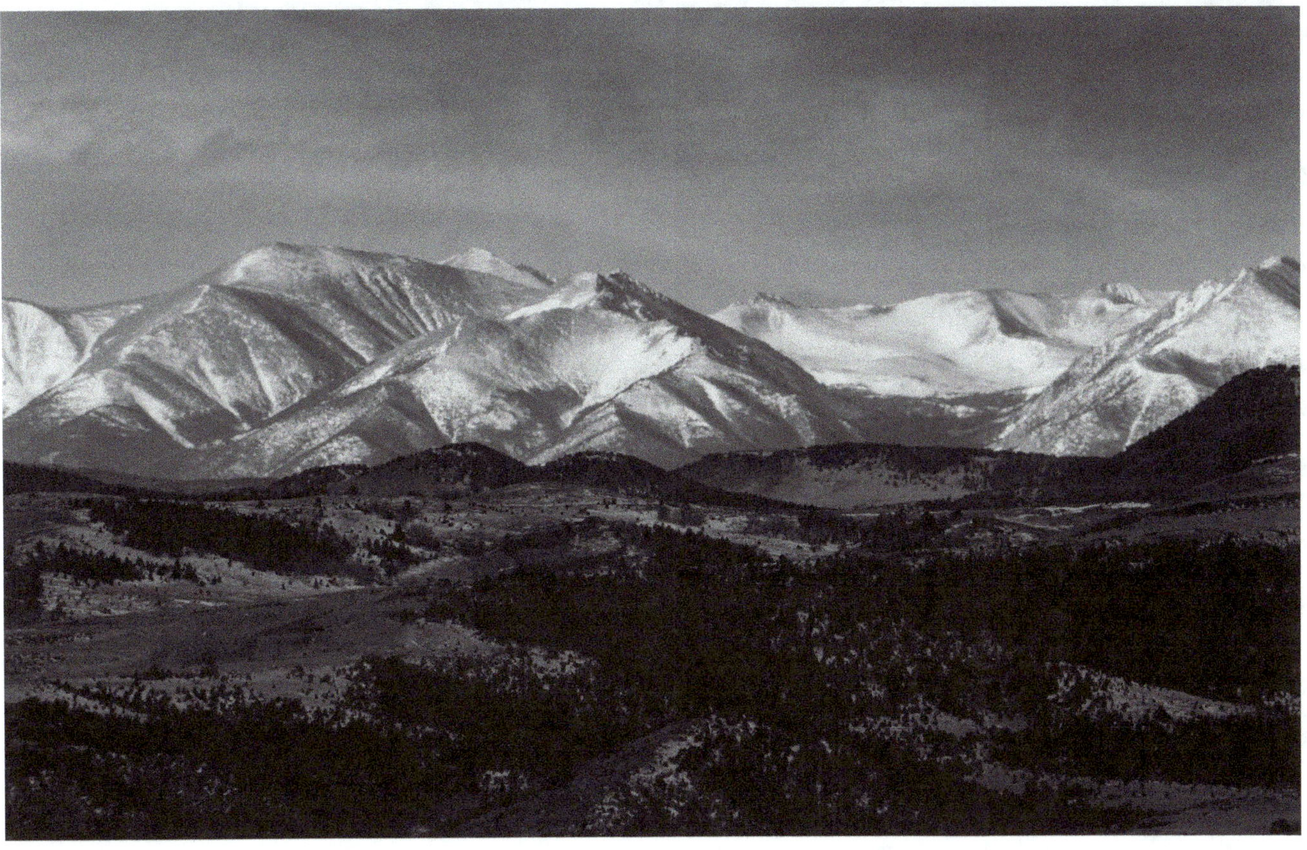

The **Little Grouse Mountain** trailhead is found about halfway between Cripple Creek and Victor and can be easily identified by a parking lot surrounded by split rail fencing and the display of old mining equipment with interpretive signage. A dirt road winds up from the lower parking lot to an elaborate replica of an old gold mine complete with another parking lot and more interpretive signage. Keep in mind though, the road to the upper parking lot is steep and often unmaintained so getting there by vehicle in the winter isn't guaranteed.

Hiking trails begin from both parking lots and vary in difficulty. The easy trail departs from the lower parking lot toward the southeast along a jeep road over rolling hills and ends near the Victor Cemetery. Another trail tracks the valley to the south and the most difficult route goes straight up the steep mountainside to the mine replica. The most scenic trail begins at the upper parking lot and proceeds west to a beautiful overlook where there is an unobstructed view of the Collegiate Peaks and Sangre de Cristo Range. Be sure to visit the metal peak finder mechanism just below the mine where a needle can be positioned to identify the names of distant mountain peaks and landmarks!

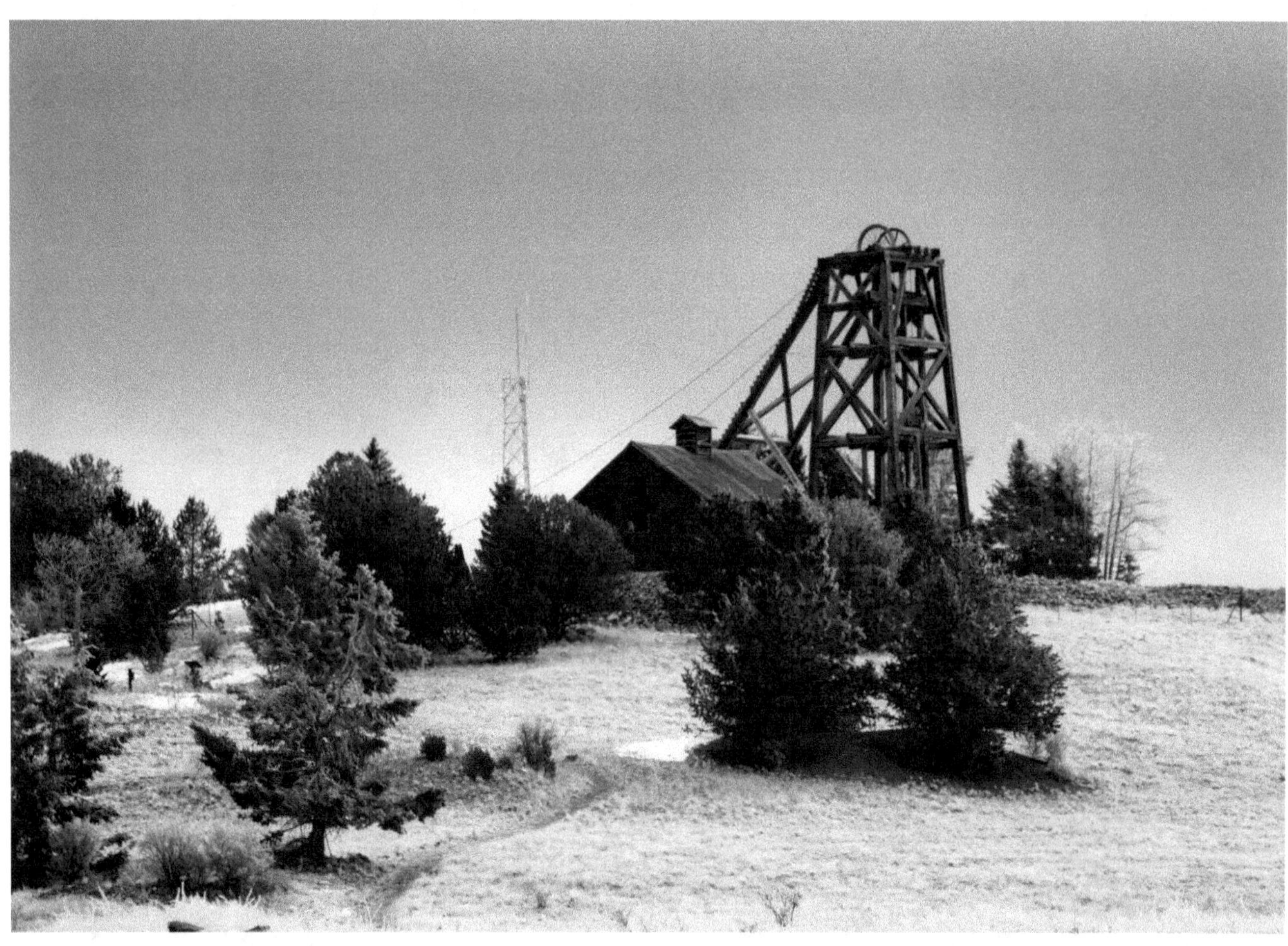

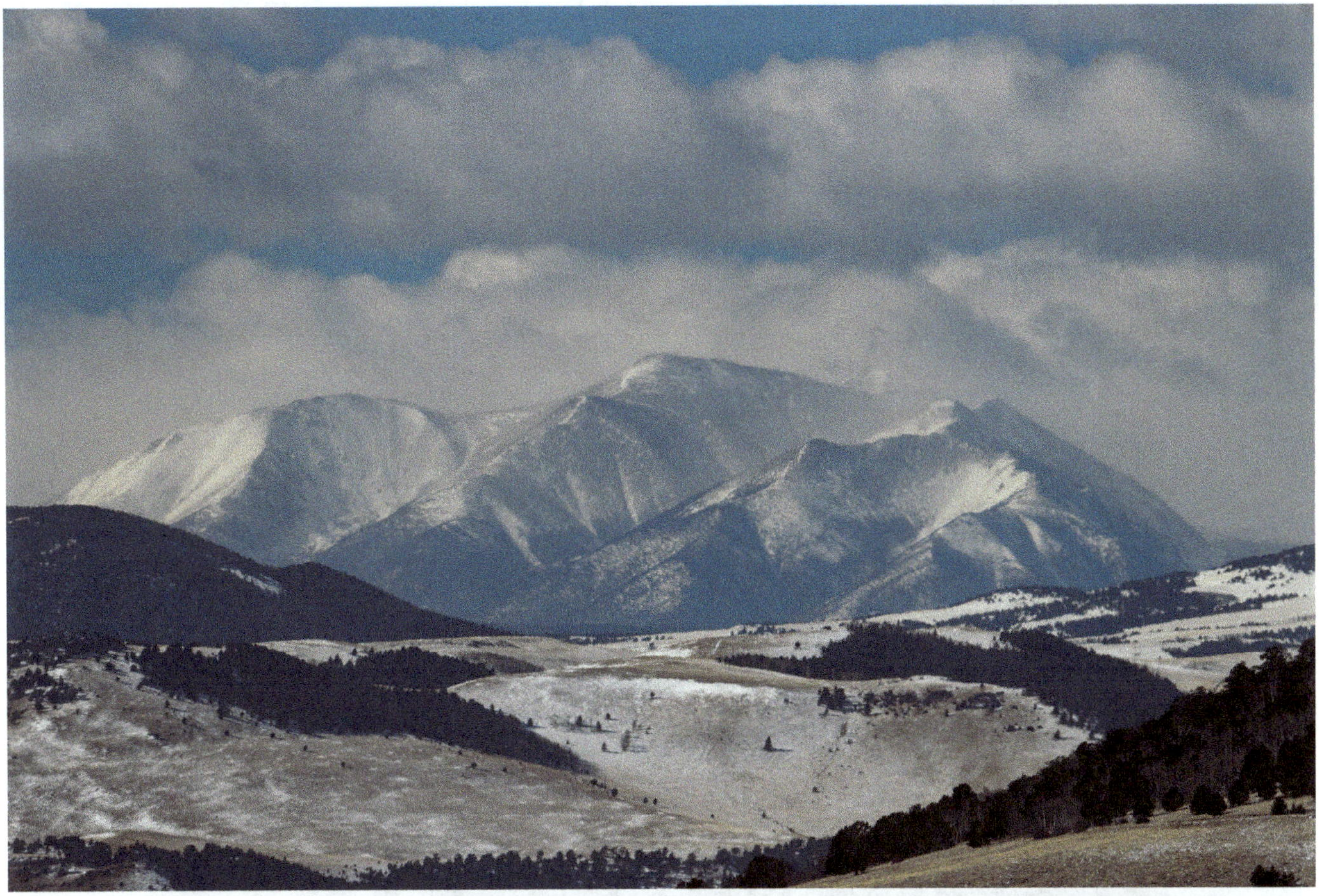

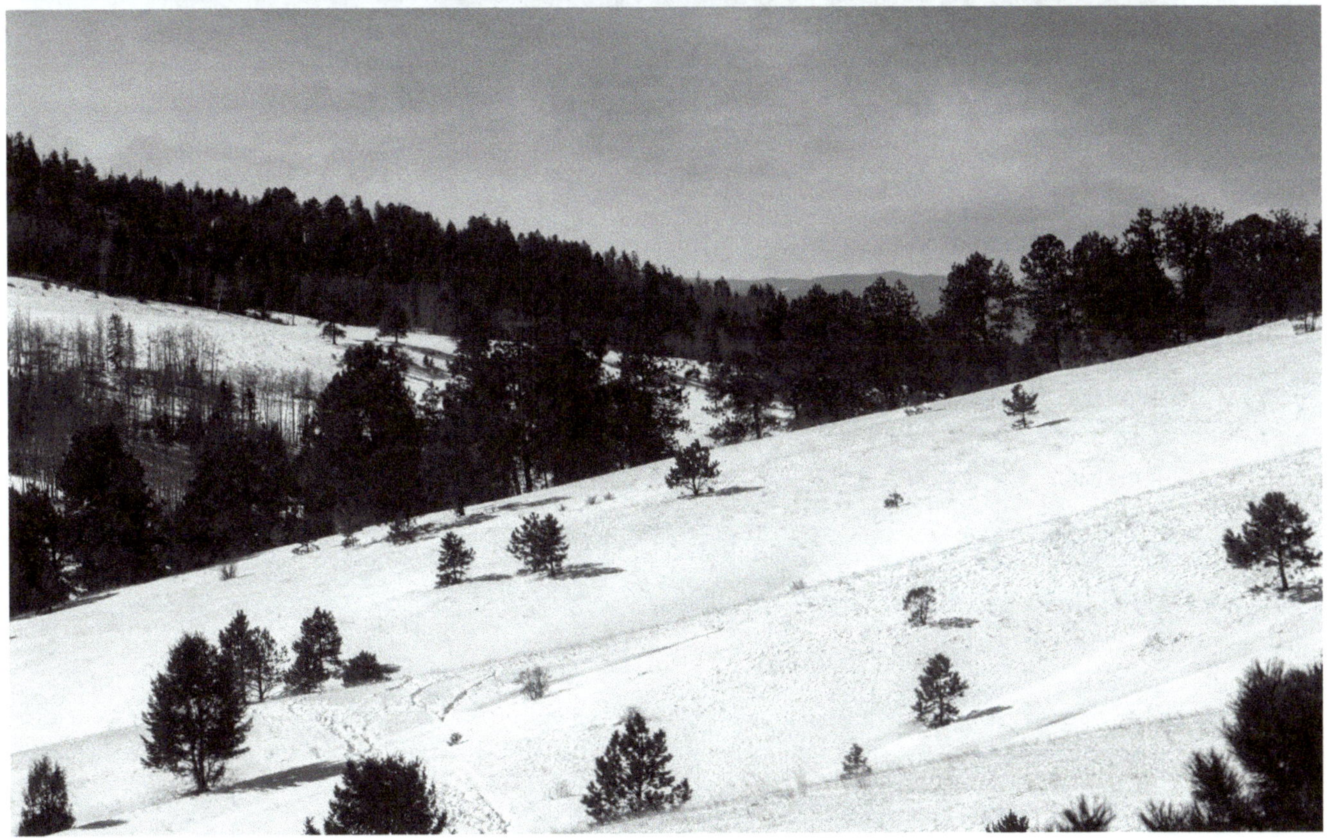

The trails are all within the easy to moderate skill level and any reasonably fit person should be able to negotiate them. However snow can get quite deep in the winter and snowshoes may be required. I prefer to start at the lower trail with my snowshoes and climb the steep trail to Little Grouse, pass by the mine and follow the trail back down the mountain on the other side to return on the lower trail through the valley. Being a fan of cold and snow, I also like to snowshoe the trail during snowstorms to capture interesting formations in the drifting snow. I am always careful to pack my Ruggard weather cover to protect my cameras and lenses in these conditions!

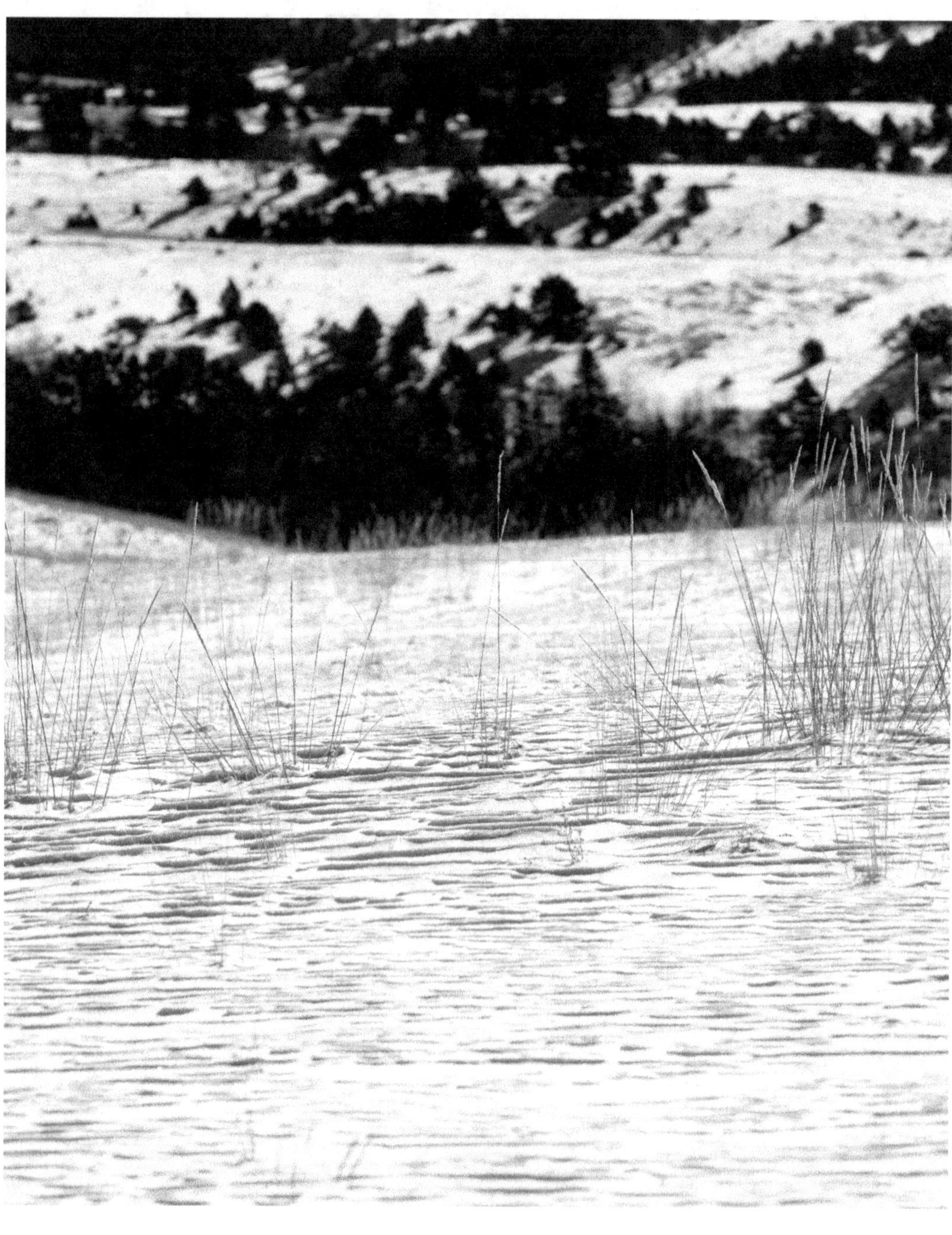

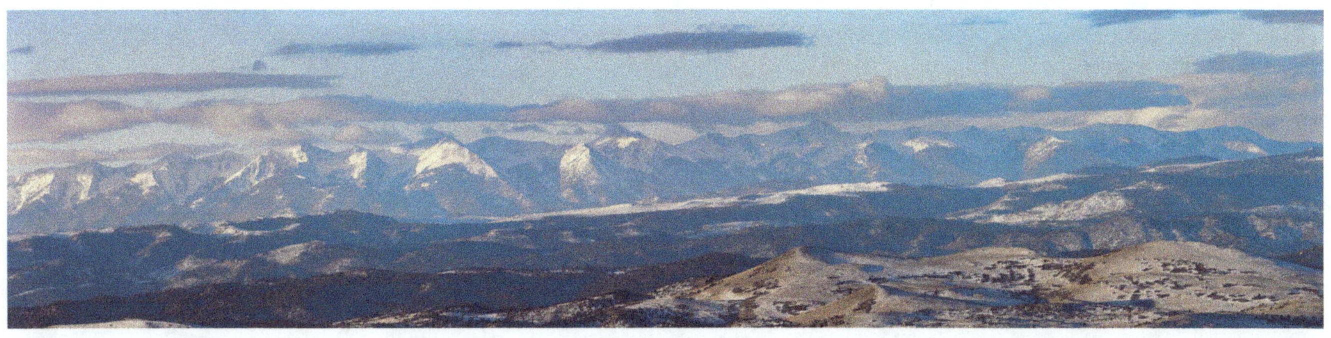

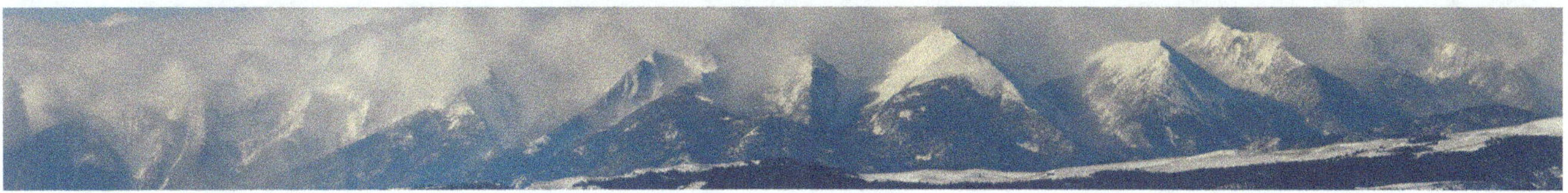

The sheer scale of vistas from this scenic stretch of countryside is perfect for panorama style images. Naturally it's best to use a tripod for such intricate work, but it's actually possible to shoot a series with a handheld camera that can later be stitched together in post. However a level tripod is the best tool to minimize inevitable cropping that will occur when mismatched images are stitched together.

To best capture images in a series for a panorama, be sure to accurately level the tripod using the spirit bubble. Set the camera to manual exposure and focus mode using a reasonable shutter speed like a 200th of a second, unless of course you are trying to depict cloud movement requiring a slow shutter speed such as a second or so to make that possible. An aperture in the f/8 range will be good for maximum sharpness along with a low ISO value such as 100 or 200. None of your exposure values should be left on auto or the exposures in the sequence might not match. Be sure to remove the polarizer if you are using a wide angle for the captures as the filter will cause aberrations in the color and luminosity in the sky. It's also a good idea to use the two second timer or a cable release to minimize camera shake from pushing the shutter button.

Once the camera and tripod are ready to go, just shoot an image and make a mental note of the boundaries for that frame to orient the next capture. Rotate the camera accordingly and repeat until the entire scene has been photographed. Positioning the camera vertically will render the largest area in the completed image. I shoot a blank frame before and after my series so I can easily identify the frames that were shot specifically for the panorama itself.

At the computer I perfect all the parameters in Adobe Camera Raw for the first image and then select the remaining captures for the series and use the "set to previous conversion" option to make sure all the images use the same values. Then just submit the images to the software to go to work stitching them all together! Consult the manual to see how to accomplish that with your particular software.

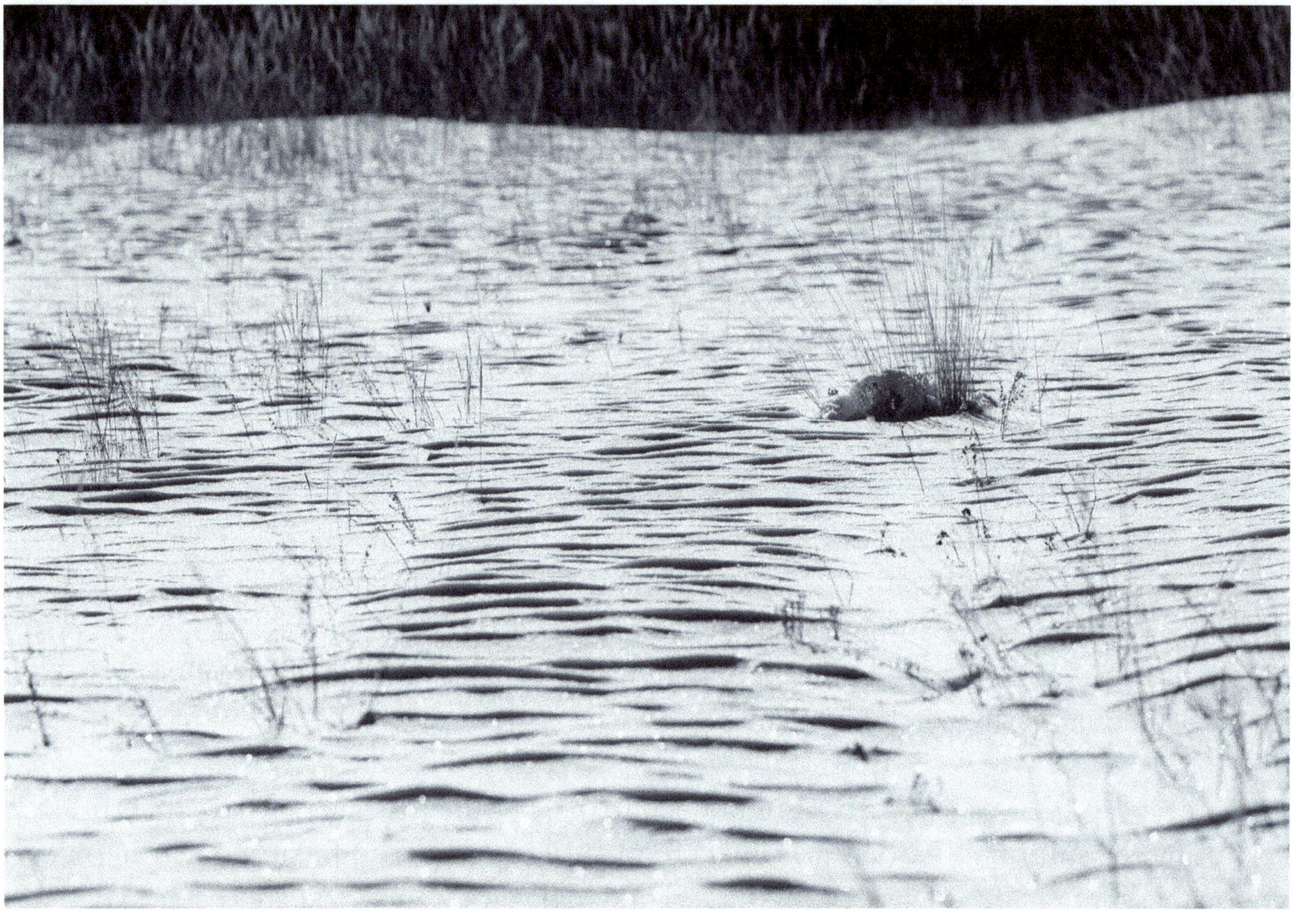

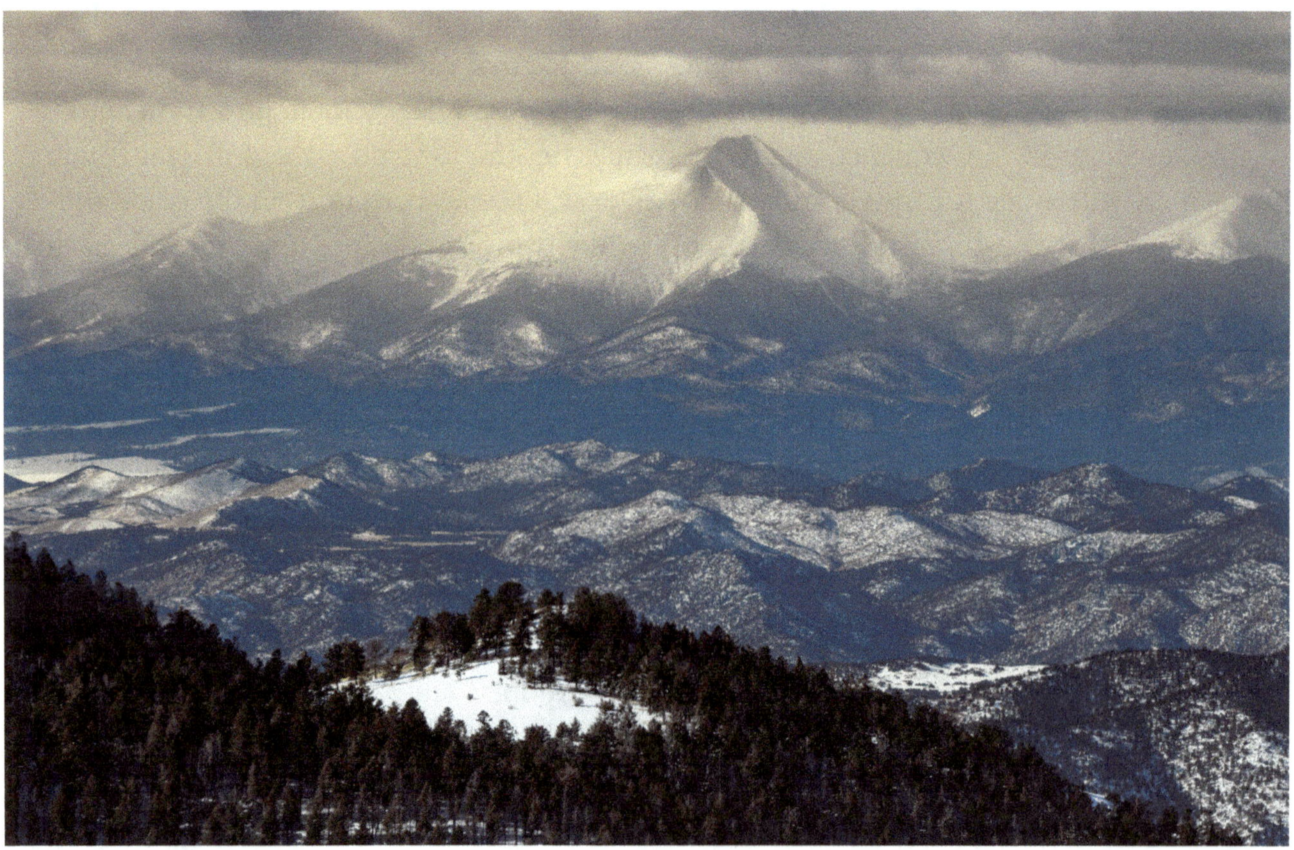

Mornings following snowstorms are a great time to visit the area as there are often dramatic clouds accompanying the fresh snow to add drama to the pictures. It's even better at sunrise when there is still some golden light spilling over the ridge to the east, adding color to the scene.

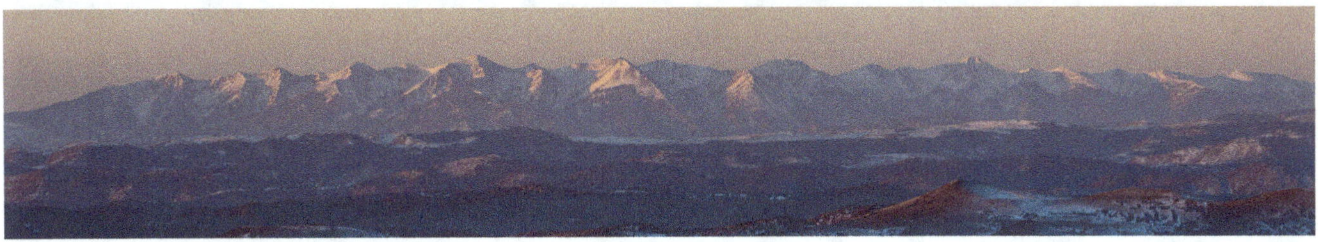

Dawn during the winter months is also the best time to capture the phenomenon called **alpenglow**, and interestingly the reason behind the name of this beautiful mountain range. According to the Encyclopedia Britannica website, "The mountains were named in 1719 by the Spanish explorer Antonio Valverde y Cosio, who, impressed at sunrise by the red-tinted, snowy peaks, supposedly uttered a fervent "Sangre de Cristo" ("Blood of Christ").".

As the sun rises in the east, ice particles in the western sky are illuminated and take on the distinctive red glow. If one can arrive on scene early enough, a red band will be visible in the sky, and as the sun rises the band of light descends. If you are ready with your camera it's possible to photograph the red glow as it eventually descends upon the mountain range turning it a beautiful red color, hence the name "Blood of Christ". In these images I was able to shoot an entire series for the panorama before the phenomenon was burned away by the full glare of the morning sun.

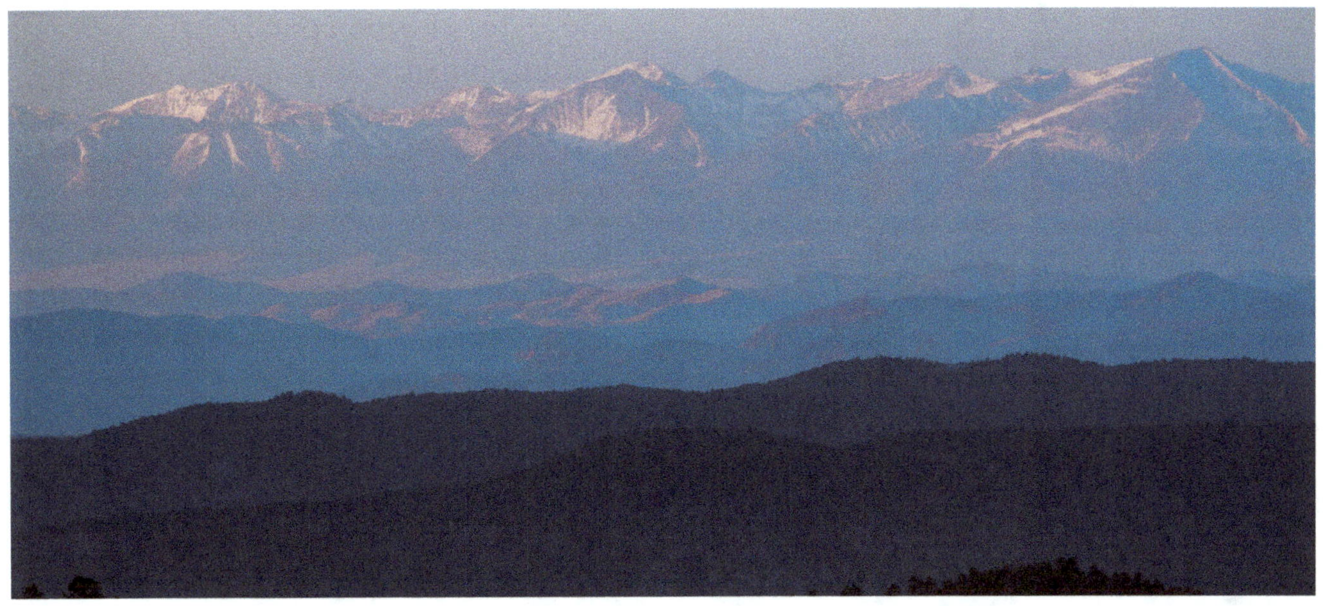

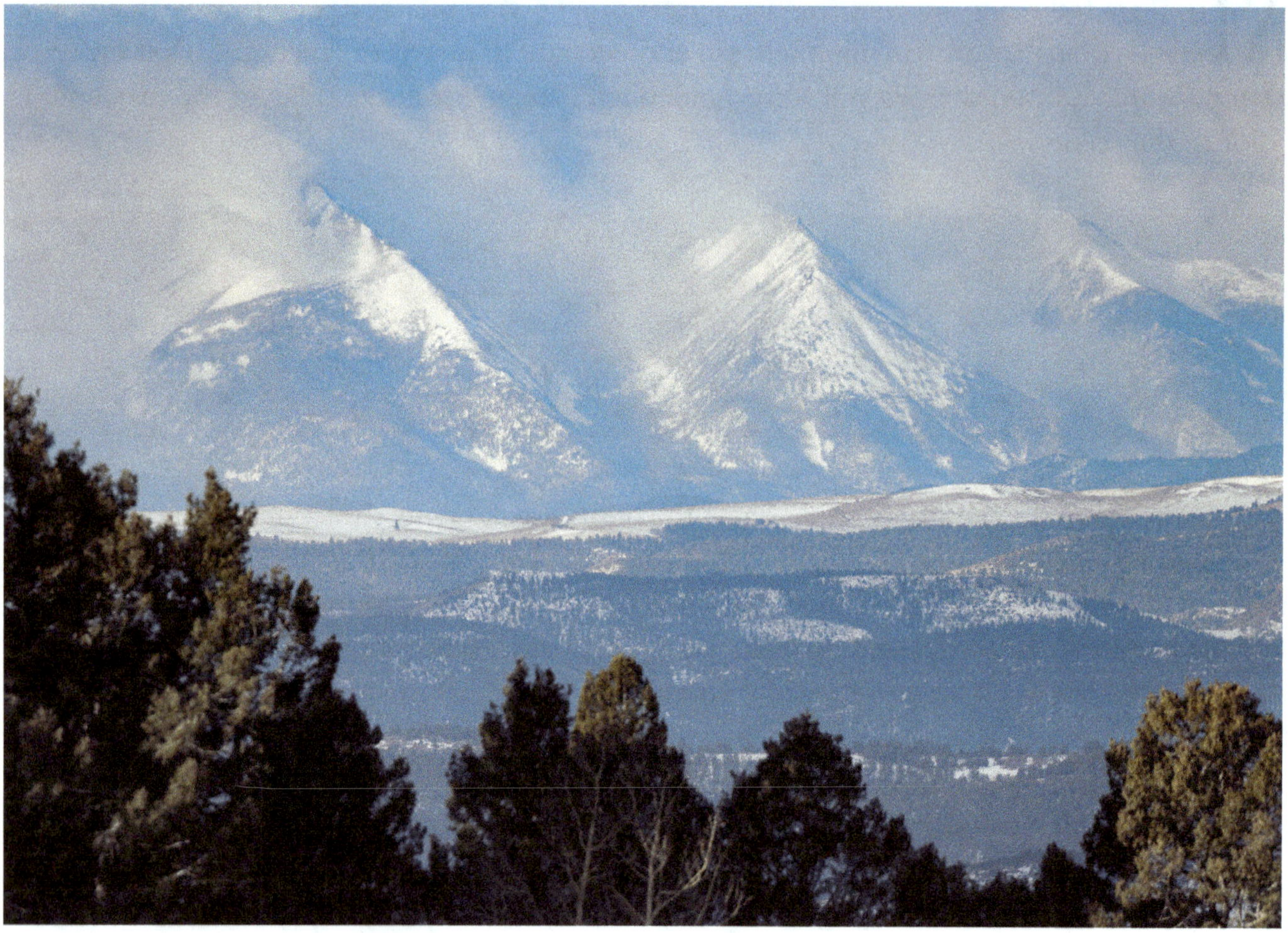

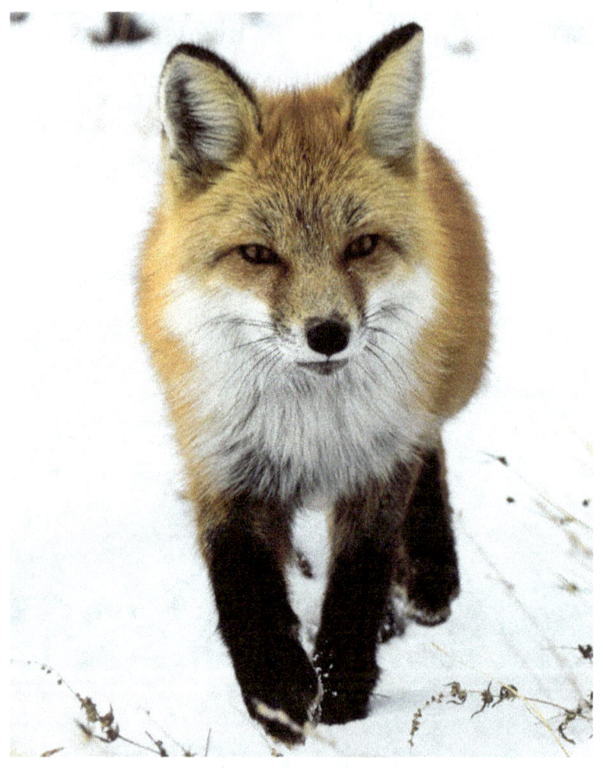

As one continues along the road toward Victor, the scenery seems to get even better! Just before the town there is a pullout for the Newmont mine that I like to frequent that provides a different angle and higher elevation on the scene with a different perspective of the Collegiate Peak range directly to the west.

For the early riser, a wide variety of wildlife can be seen doing their best to survive the winter snow. Elk, deer, coyote, fox, raptors and plenty of small hardy birds all call the mining district home.

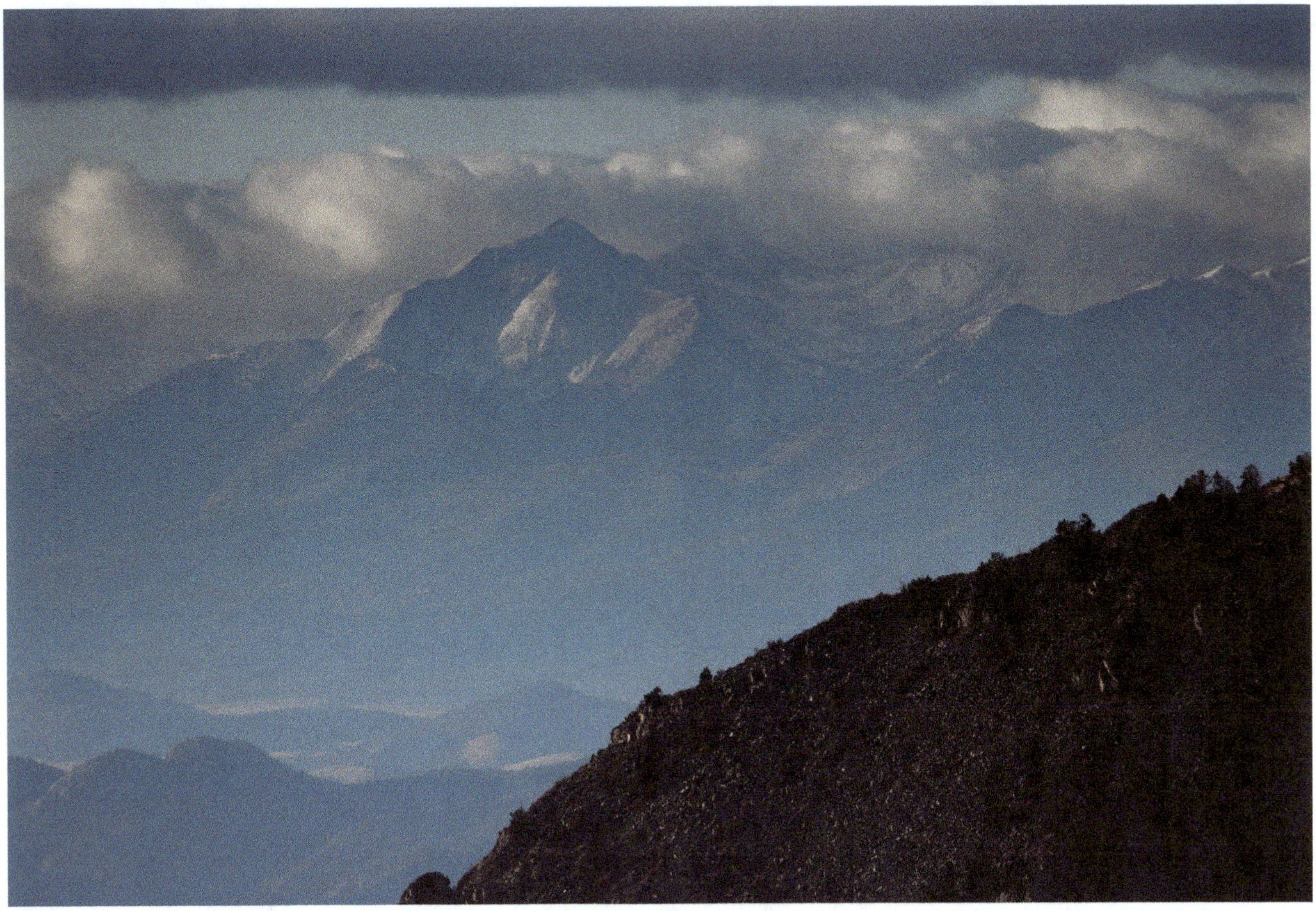

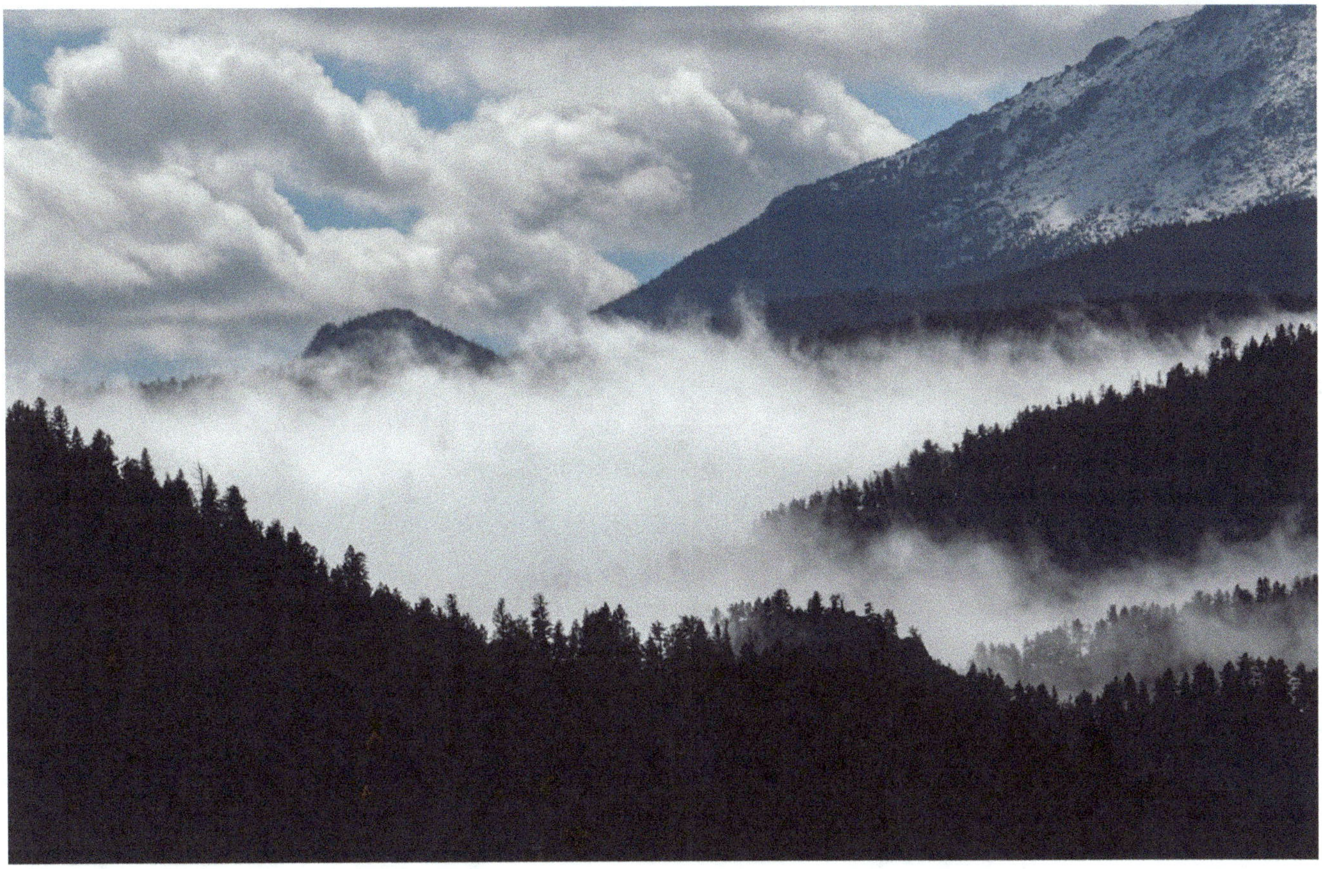

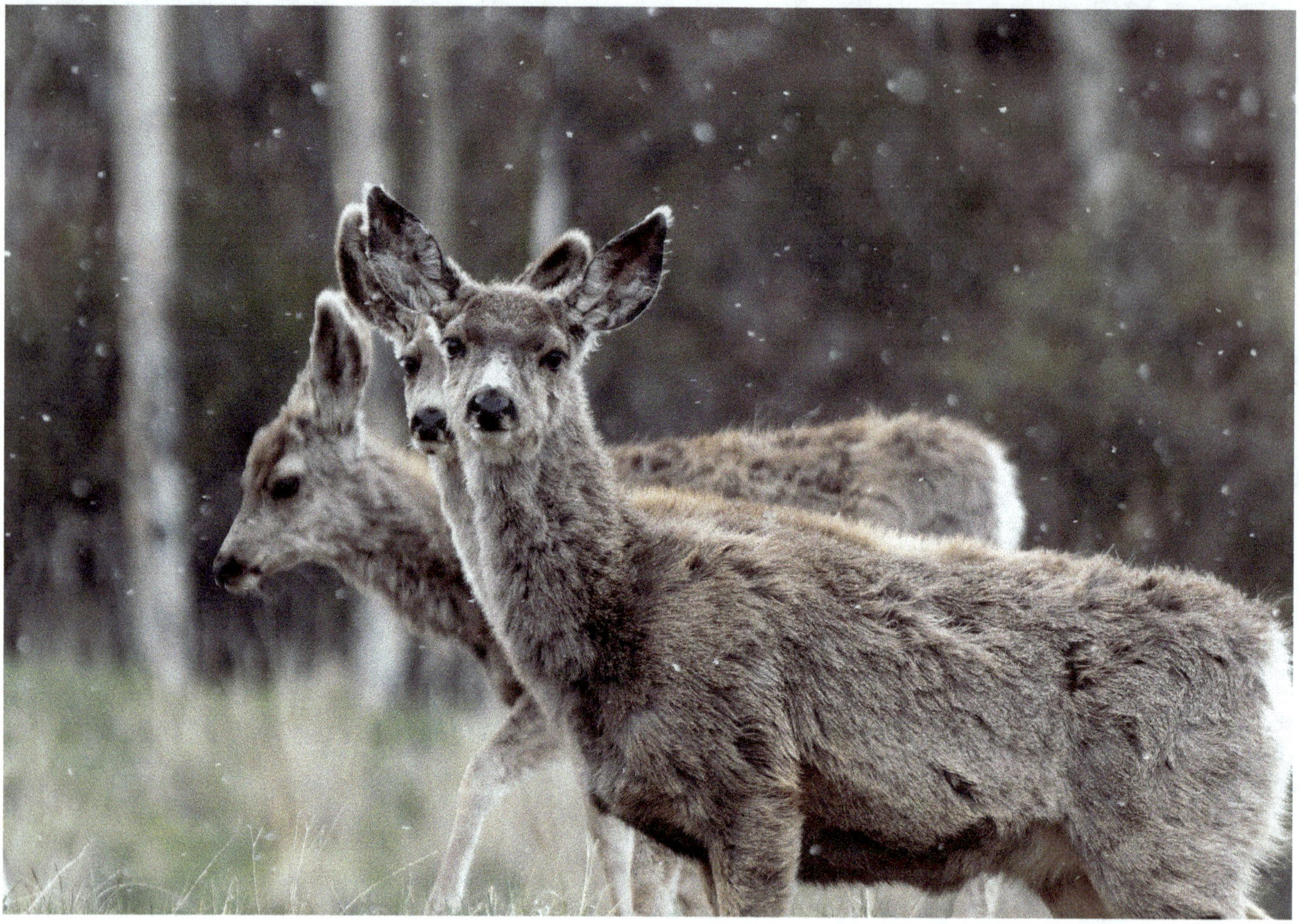

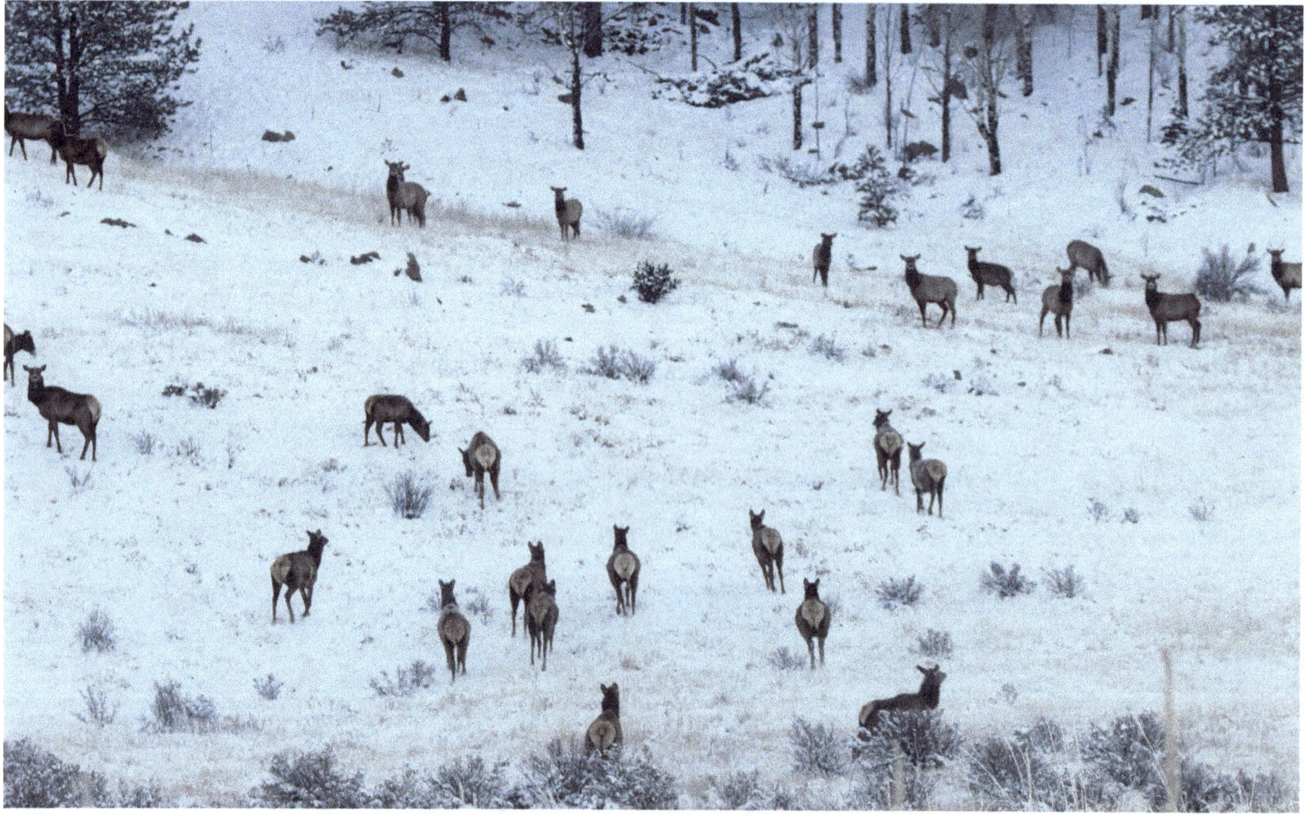

The journey continues through the old west mining town of Victor and on to the historic mines of **Goldfield**, Colorado where the major mines from the gold rush era have been preserved in an amazing park, complete with miles of trails and interpretive signage. I find foggy and snowy weather the best for photographing these ghostly figures and believe they often look the most dramatic in monochrome. Occasionally I'll even use the sepiatone filter in Adobe Photoshop to give the images that old west authenticity.

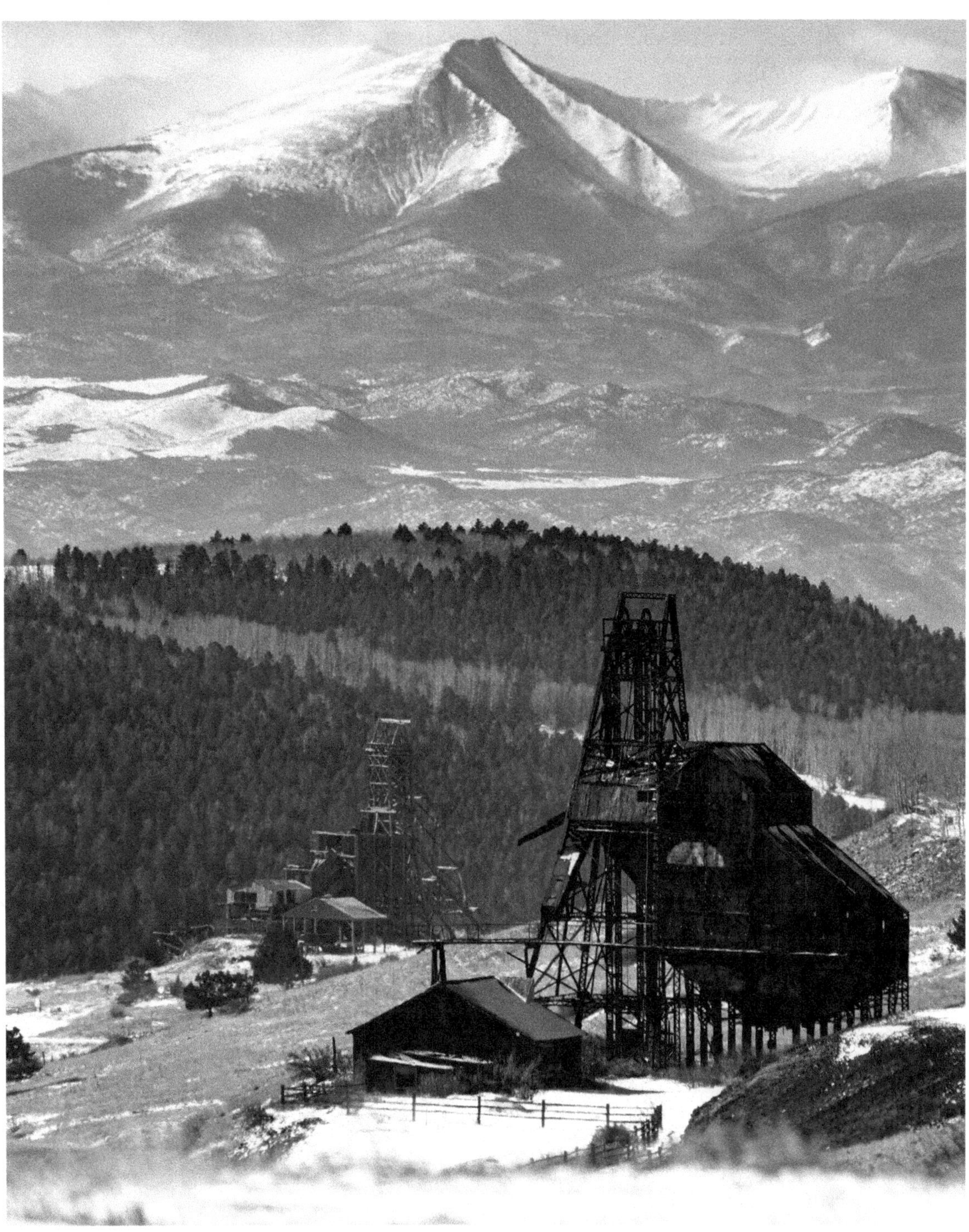

A wide angle lens works best when walking the trails which offer close up views of the head frames. The Canon 24-105 F4L is my lens of choice for the trails while a longer lens such as a 200 or 400 mm focal length might work best for more distant shots such as the one below. Longer lenses compress the scene and accentuate the rugged Sangre de Cristo Range in the background. Had a wide angle lens been used for this shot, the dramatic mountain scene would have appeared tiny and insignificant. Perspective makes all the difference when shooting these old head frames and each photographer will need to decide how he or she wants to depict the scene. Serious architecture photographers might want to consider using a tilt and shift lens for the close up images so as to avoid distortion inherent with photographing extreme angles.

Another advantage of shooting in heavy snow and fog is the ability to hide unsightly power poles and lines which are an inevitable obstacle when shooting a large area near towns such as with this place. For unavoidable obstructions that detract too much from the beauty of your images, I recommend using the "content aware fill" feature of Adobe Photoshop. The tool can be used to quickly and accurately eliminate unwanted objects like power lines.

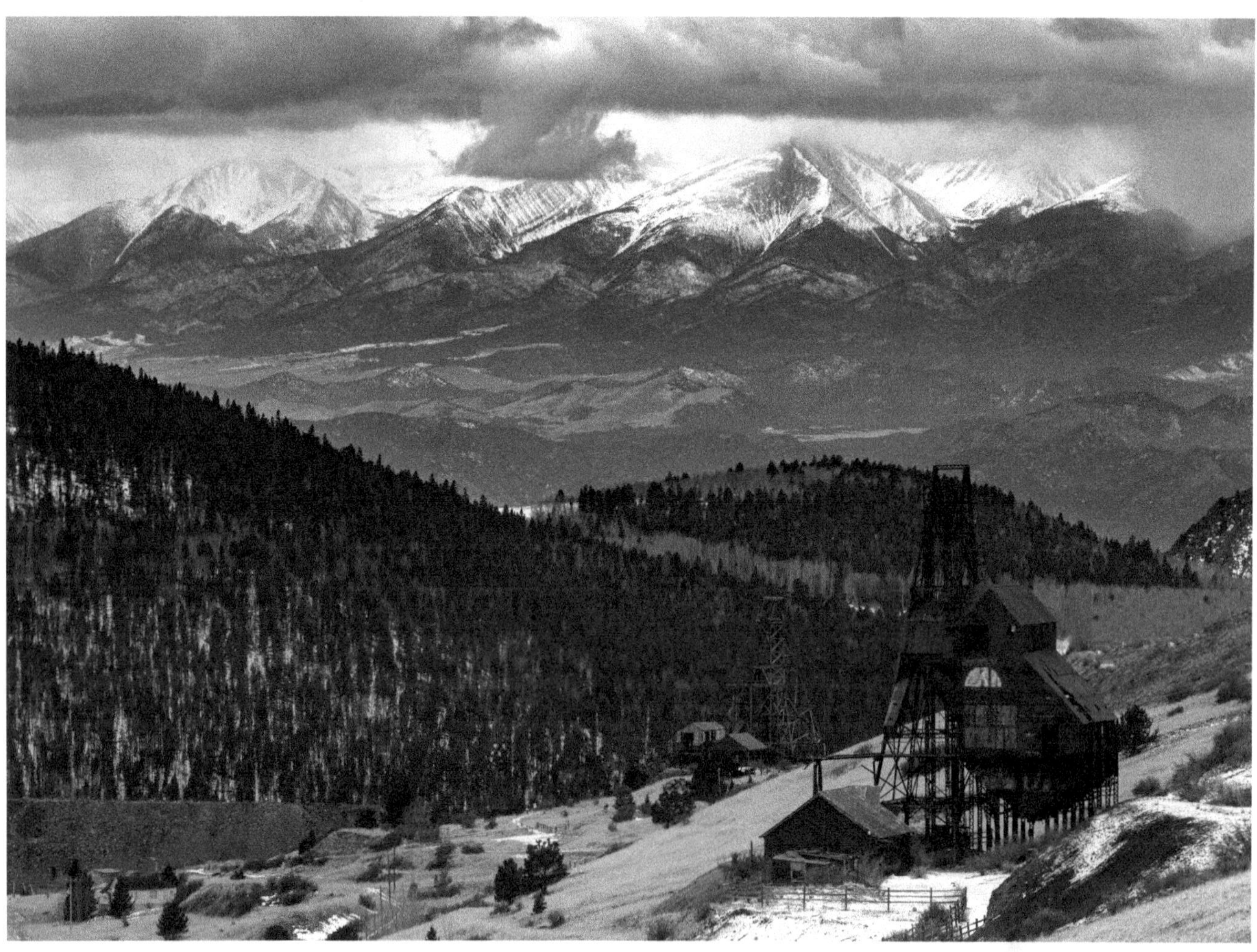

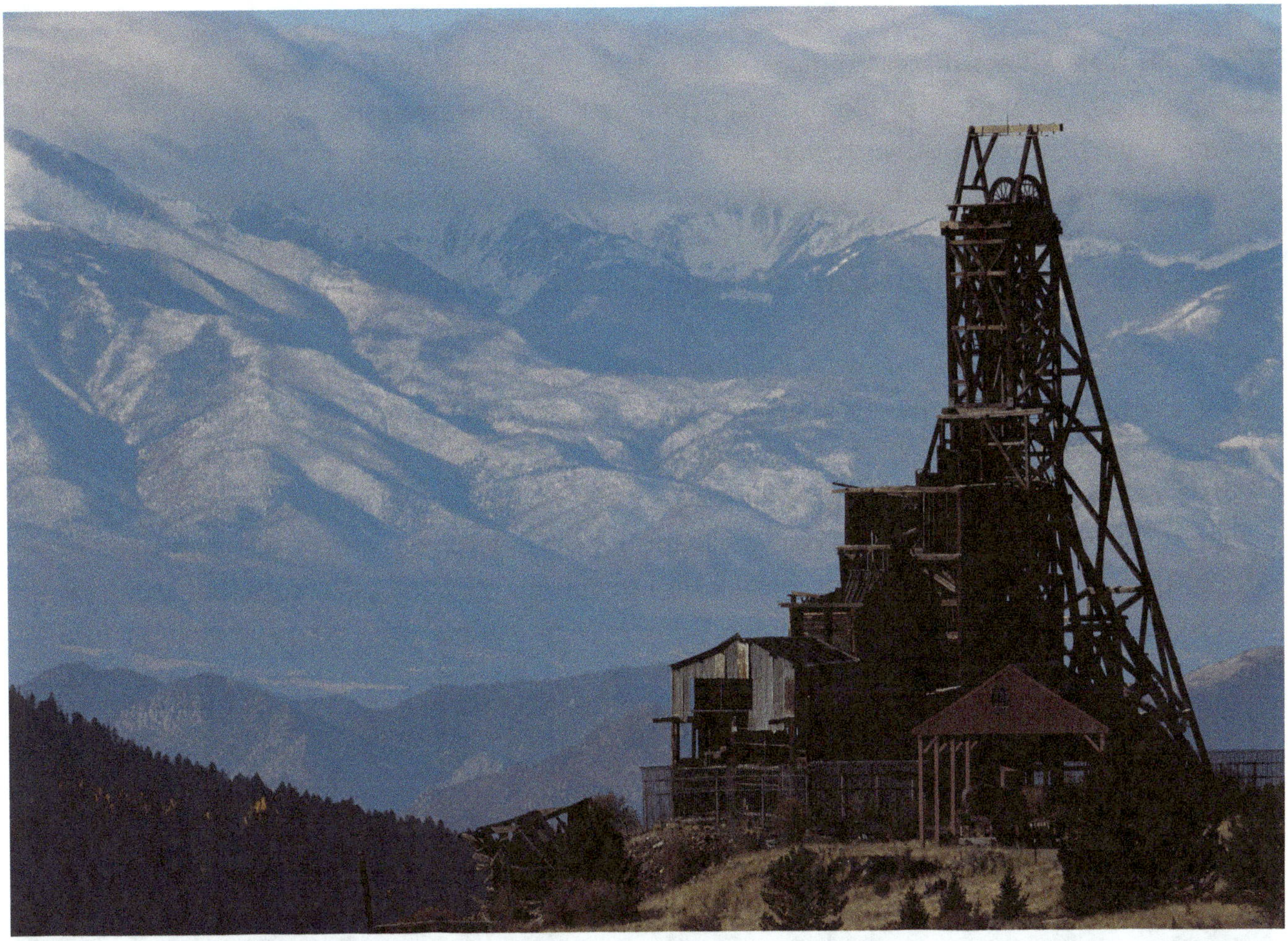

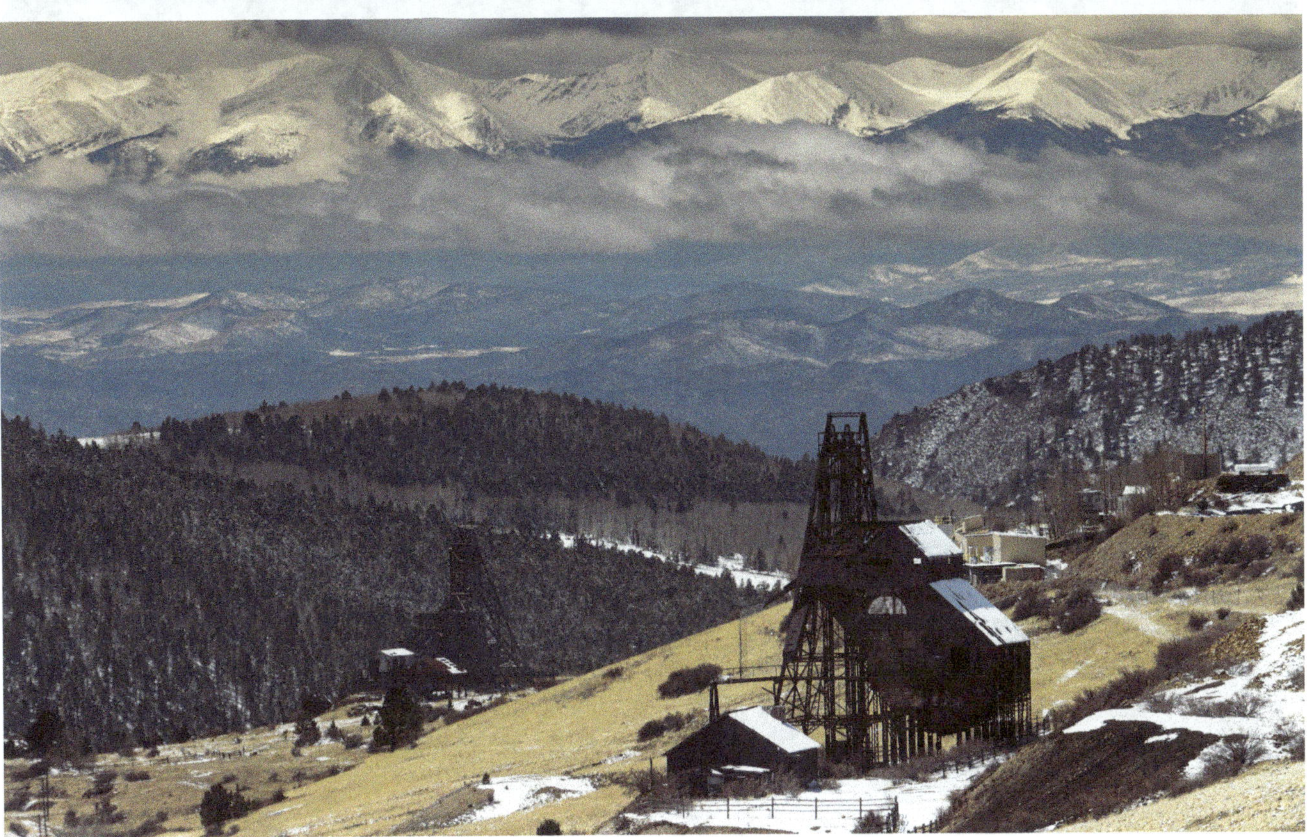

Eleven Mile Canyon located just south of Lake George is another Pikes Peak region favorite, although most would probably prefer to visit this beautiful canyon during warmer seasons! Cold air flowing down from Eleven Mile Reservoir can be brutal in the winter. One morning I encountered -27 degrees fahrenheit at the mouth of the canyon when it was well above zero in the rest of the Pikes Peak region! But the wealth of photographic opportunity available in this magnificent marvel of nature fades any discomfort into insignificance.

The access road to the canyon is about eight miles in length, and depending on the timing of a visit it could be anywhere from icy and snow packed to impassable. It's possible that there won't be many people back there, especially during inclement weather so it's imperative to be prepared for any kind of emergency. There is little cell phone access so it's possible if something goes wrong that you might have to hike out, and you won't want to be caught without the gear necessary to accomplish a hike in sub-zero weather. Visitors that aren't in the physical condition for a self rescue should bring enough supplies to survive in vehicle until help eventually arrives.

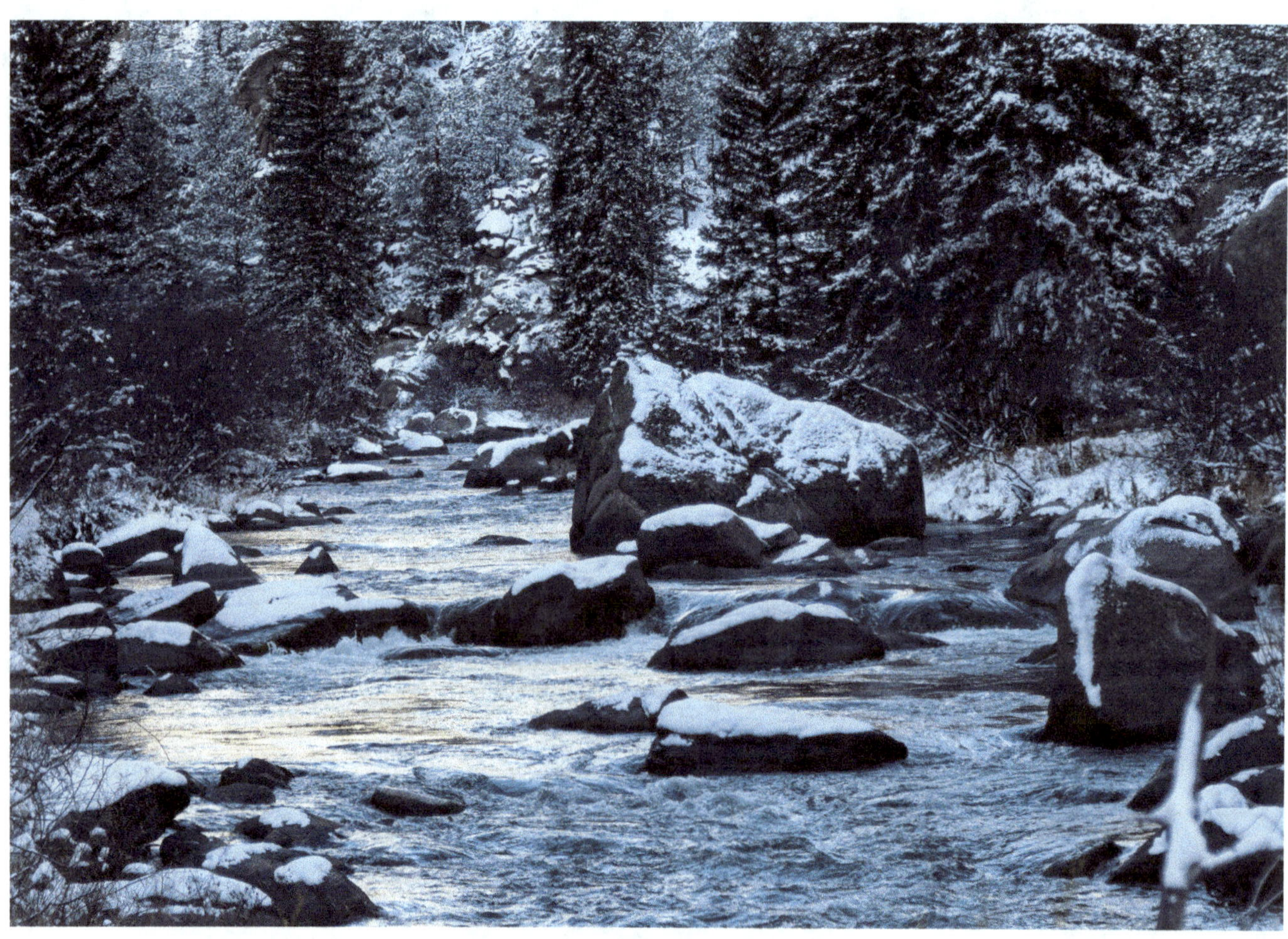

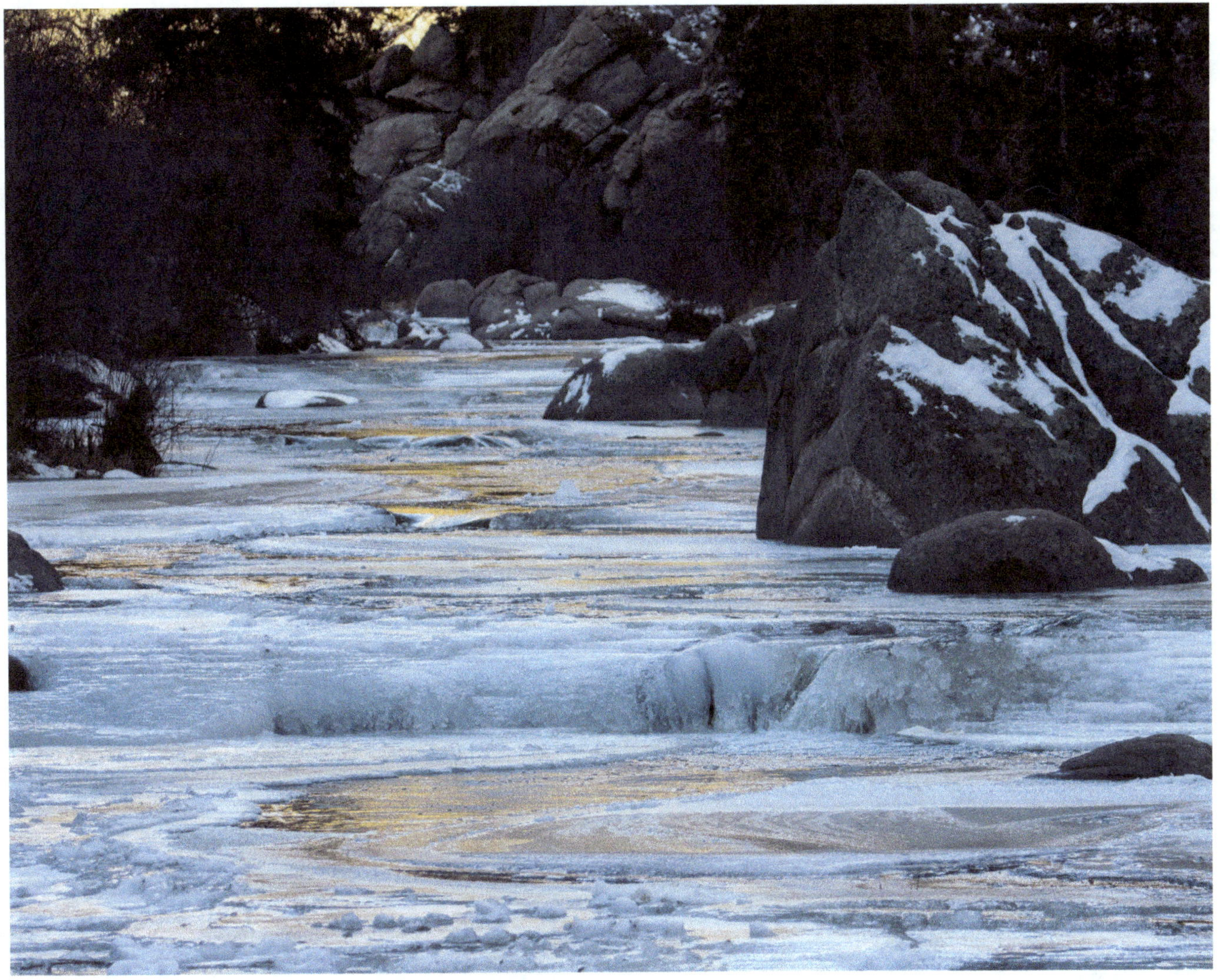

The blue hour, just before the sun clears the canyon wall to the east is the best time to capture the river itself. Once the bright sun begins reflecting off the snow on the mountainsides, white balance and contrast become problematic. It's best to capture the scene when the entire frame is filled with even white balance and contrast throughout. I was fortunate to capture the above image just as the morning sunshine began to fill the valley with faint golden light just starting to illuminate the pristine water. A few minutes later and the rocks at the top center of the frame would have been brightly lit, throwing the exposure out of balance and making a pleasing image impossible.

Winter conditions in the canyon are so harsh that most mammals avoid the river corridor, preferring the warmer forest land of the Florissant Fossil Beds to the east. However there is one hardy resident that thrives in this frigid stretch of river. The bald eagle is quite at home on the many barren branches lining the riverbed. The flowing water remains largely free of ice even in the coldest part of winter, making it possible for eagles to continue fishing year round.

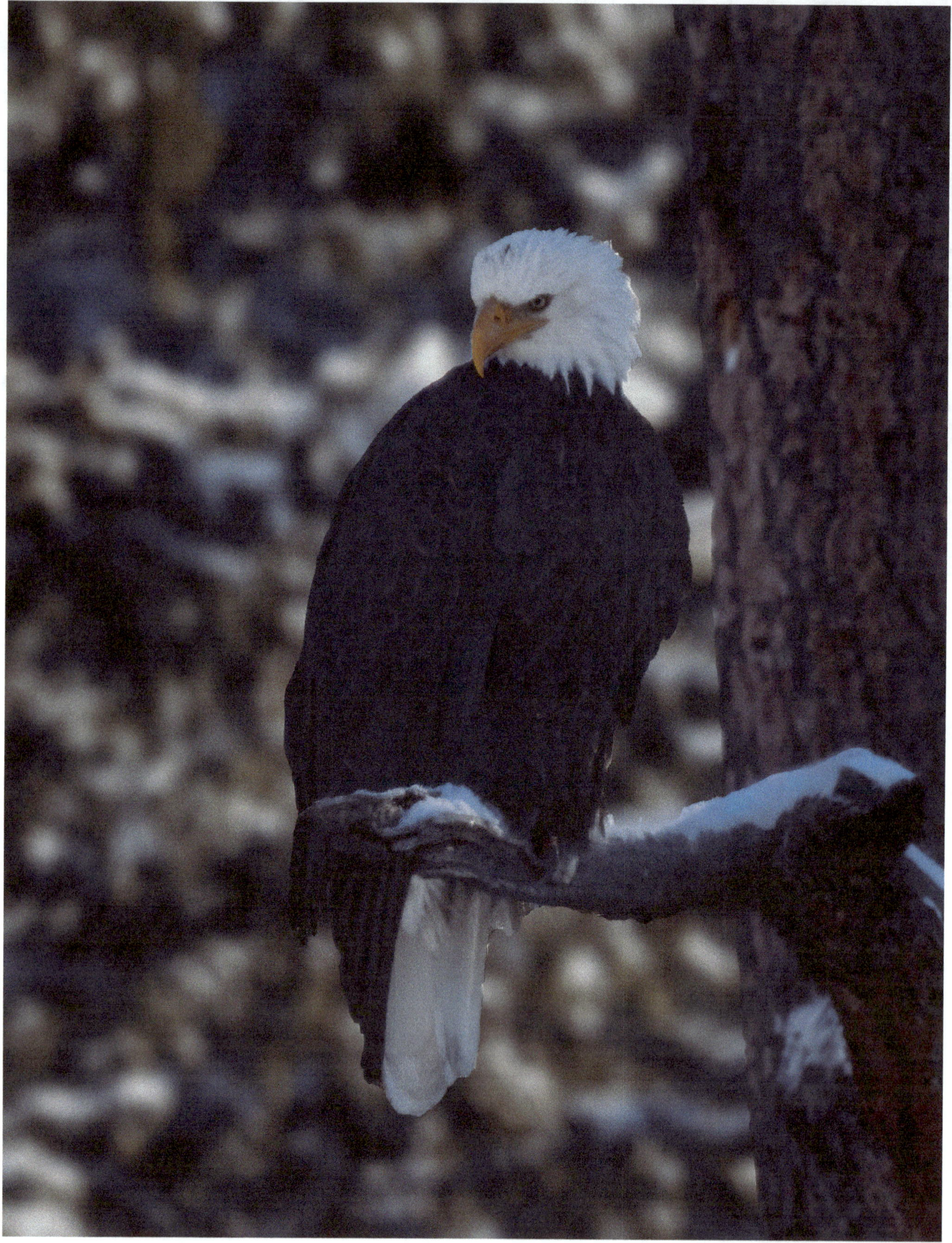

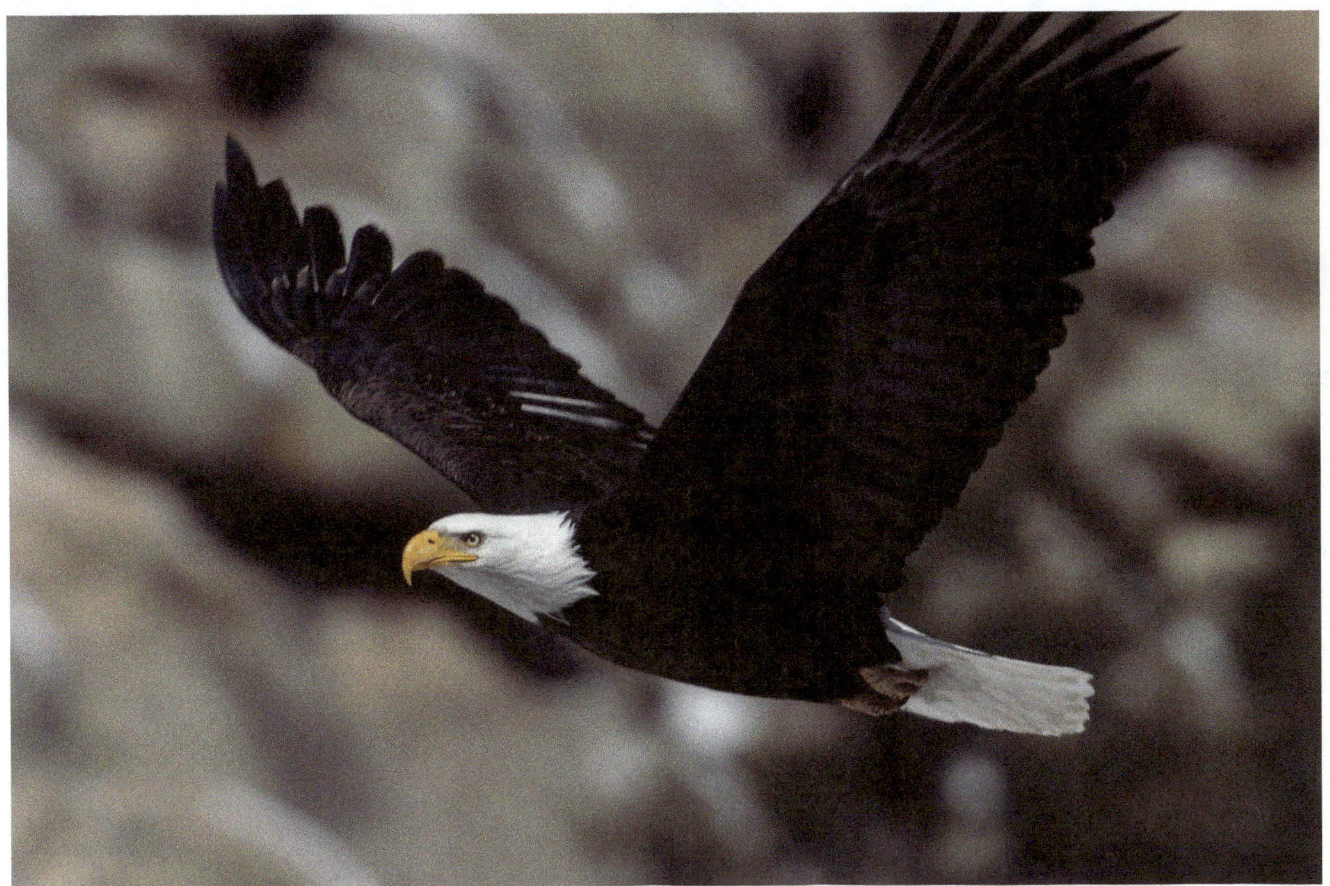

Eleven Mile Canyon is home to a healthy population of bald eagles, one of my favorite subjects to photograph. The narrow canyon limits distance to subject material, resulting in some of the most dramatic raptor pictures in the state. Capturing compelling images of these beautiful birds of prey requires a lot of patience, but the results can be quite rewarding for photographers willing to endure the cold.

Two permanent nesting pairs call the canyon home, one at each end of the river valley. There is a large nest at the entrance to the canyon and another one somewhere near the huge dam at the reservoir, and a rarely seen golden eagle lives near the middle of the park. The nest at the entrance can be spotted in a tall dead tree just west of the access road, and from March to early summer it is likely one of the pair will be there either sitting on eggs or babysitting young ones. In my years watching this pair I have seen anywhere from one to three eaglets mature to flight age. To my knowledge no one has ever seen the nest at the south end of the canyon, where the eagle known to locals as Speckles and his mate reside during breeding months.

Eagles take turns tending the nest while the other is free to hunt, fish and gather construction materials for the nest. Photographers can choose whether to watch the nest for compositions or to venture into the canyon to capture the action there.

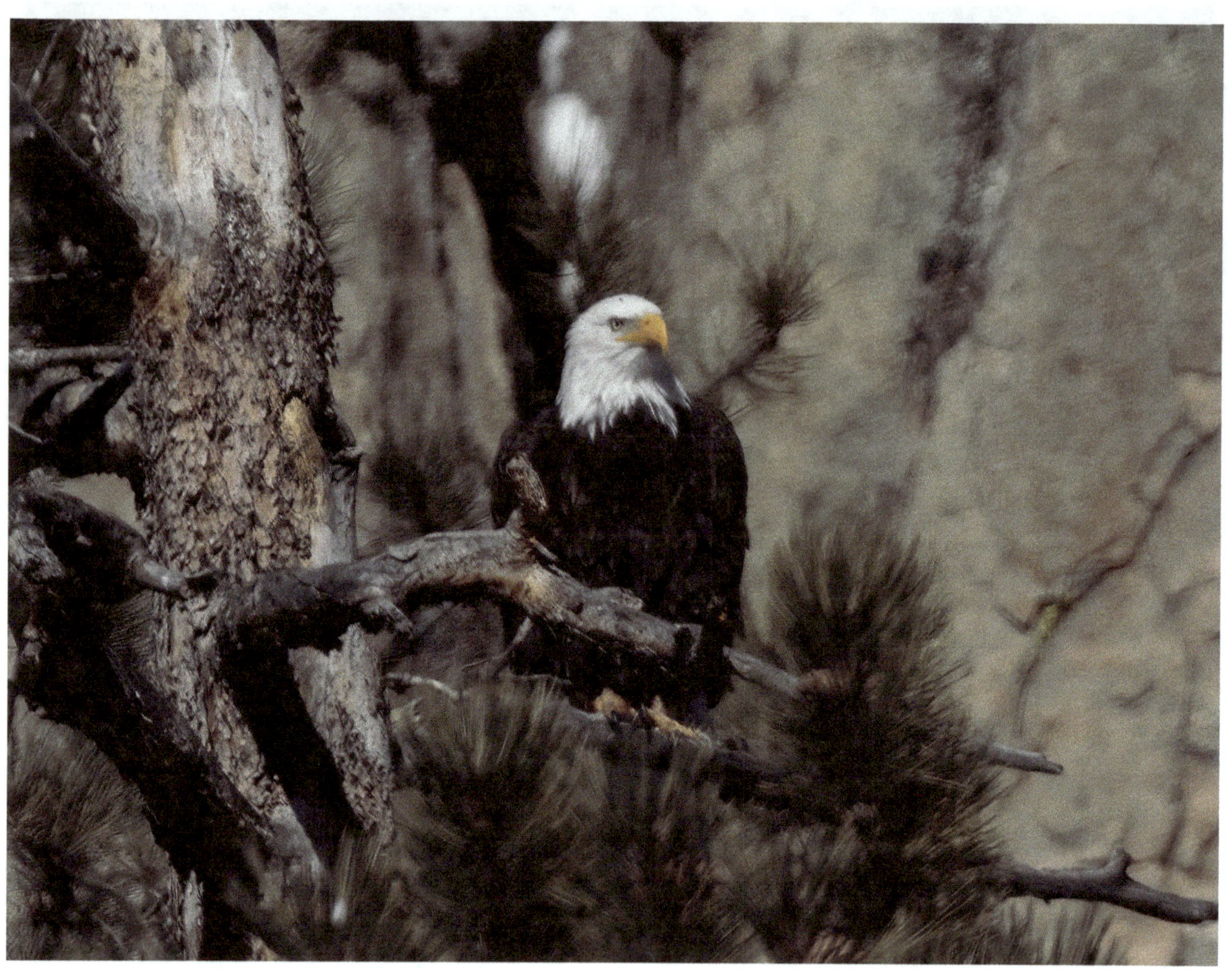

When an eagle is spotted, a photographer never knows whether the encounter will last just a few seconds or if the eagle will decide to remain perched for an hour or more. Given the brutal cold conditions normally present in winter, it's best to dress for a long wait in the cold. After a few minutes of standing still watching and photographing the great birds, ears, fingers and toes will begin to tingle and burn. The eagles will watch your antics with contempt, waiting for the perfect moment when you are distracted to take flight and ruin your chance for the coveted hero shot with those massive wings spread wide. The second you look away or try to warm your hands or get out a tripod, the highly intelligent bird will take the cue to fly away. Pray that your sighting is the rare one, when the eagle has been at that perch for a long time and is already preparing to take flight.

Occasionally eagles will alert you that they are ready to look for a new branch. Defecation is sometimes a sign that they are considering a take off while other times they will become restless and change positions on the branch. After watching them for an hour or more they will often suddenly turn around on the branch and fly in the opposite direction just to spite you.

But if you persevere, eventually the conditions will be just right and the giant raptor will fly right at you and you will capture the giant wingspread and fierce glare, and for a moment wonder if those sharp talons will soon be tearing at your own flesh.

No matter where you go to photograph eagles, serious equipment is necessary to get the most dramatic images. I recommend a focal length of at least 400mm, 600mm is even better and even 800mm is not too much. My main lens is a 100-400mm professional Canon zoom and I almost always have a 1.4x teleconverter attached. I also have a 2x converter available for the times when I need 800mm to bring in the subject to an acceptable size. The unfortunate side effect of teleconverters is one stop loss of light for the 1.4x and two full stops for the 2x, effectively turning my f/5.6 lens into an f/8 or f/11. High ISO values and digital noise are also the price paid in the early hours when eagles are most active and light is low. A fast prime lens like a 600mm f/4 would provide better results but fast lenses are expensive, often commanding prices in excess of $10,000. Each photographer will need to ascertain his or her own budgetary situation.

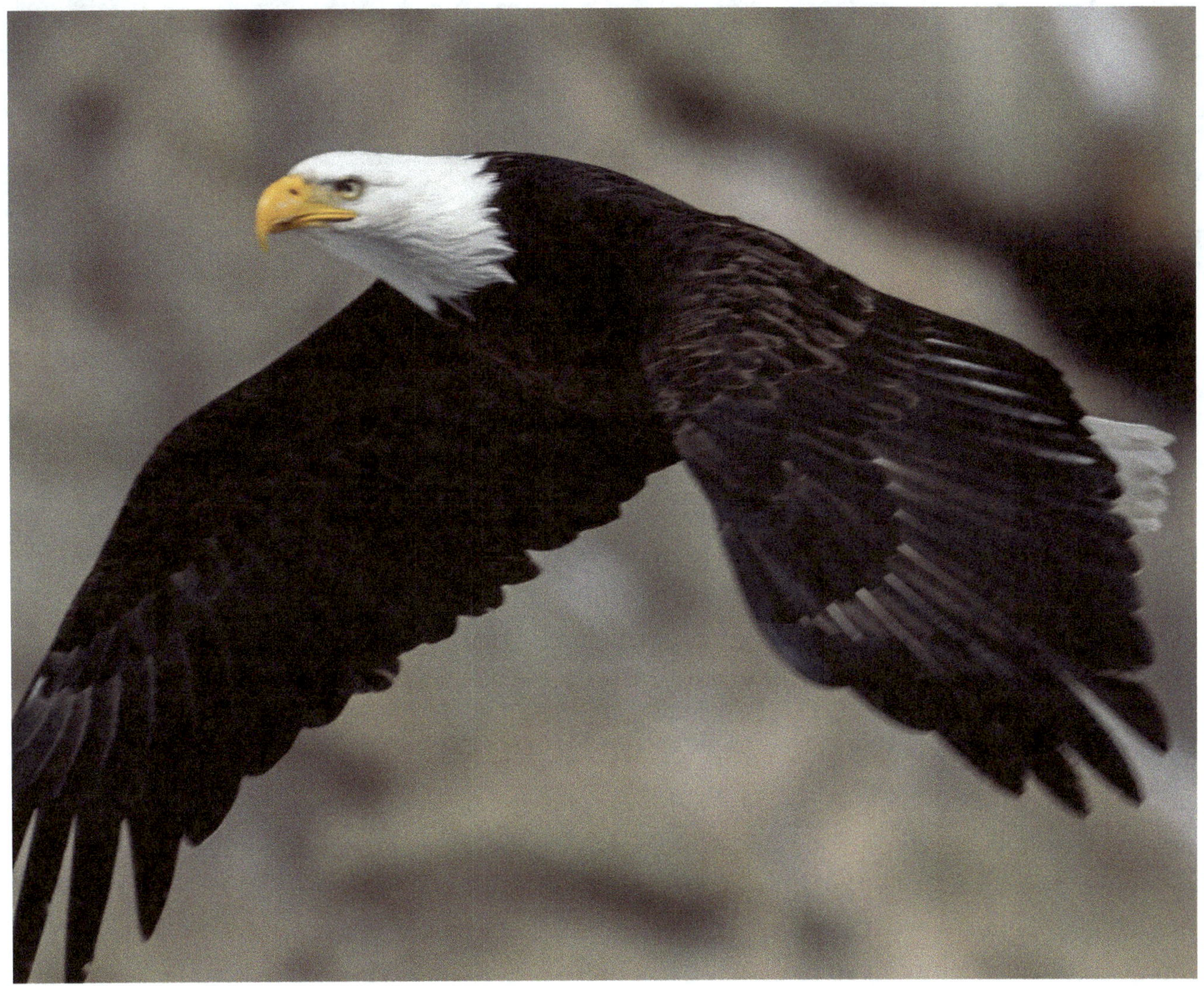

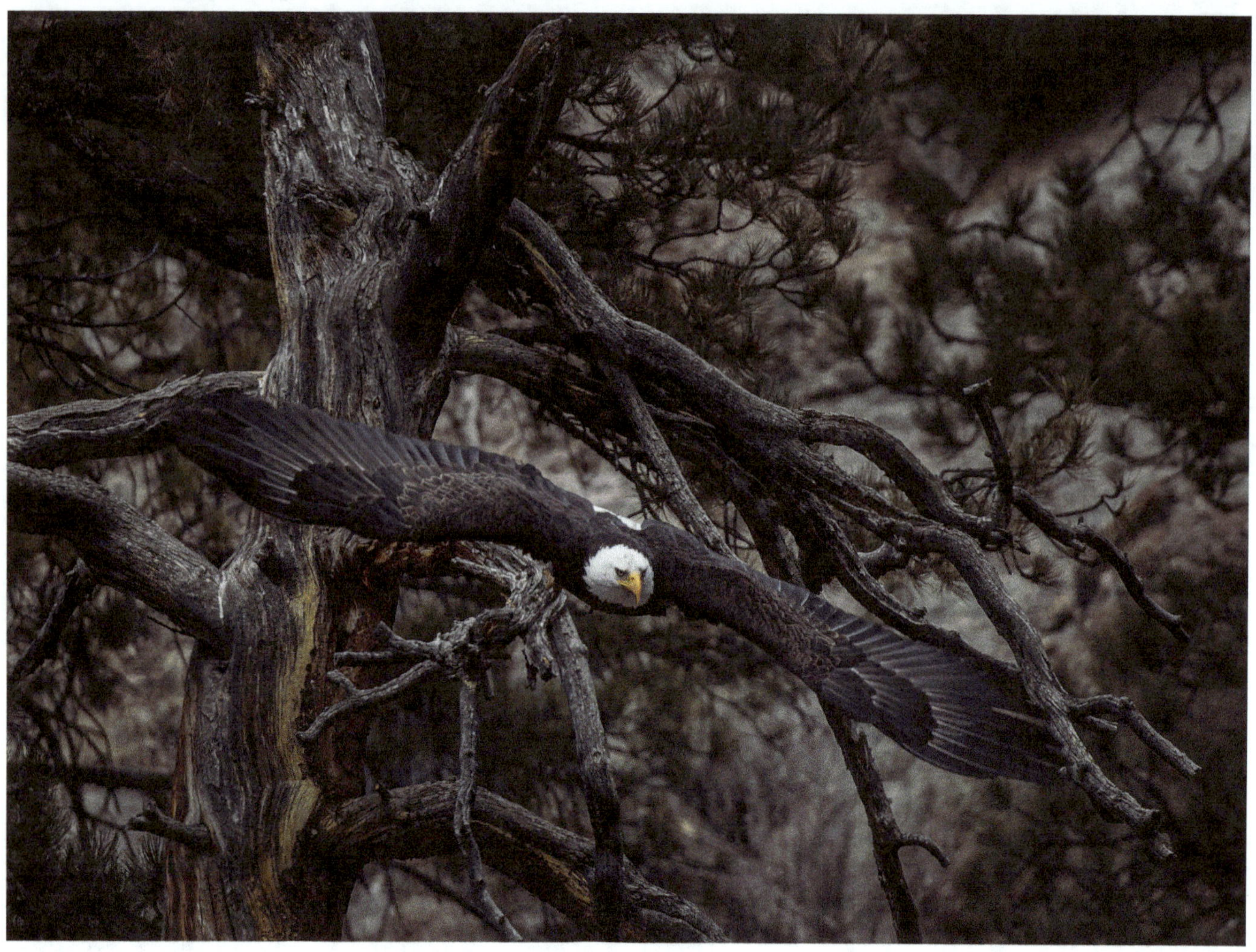

Maintaining focus on a bird flying directly toward the camera requires advance planning. The focus system will need to be set up for action prior to the session, there won't be time to fiddle with buttons once the show begins! I keep my Canon bodies set to back button focus in servo mode, which means as long as I have the button depressed the camera will continue to acquire focus. Focusing on wildlife has been made much easier by animal tracking and eye detection available in many of he newest mirrorless camera models. Many photographers now program the half press shutter button function to include eye detection along with metering. Each manufacturer has their own terminology and button layout so consult your manual to find the best settings for your camera make and model.

A fast shutter speed is required to freeze the motion of a bird in flight and I recommend at least a 1600th of a second, a 2000th might even be better. Aperture will depend upon available light, keeping in mind that every stop down may result in increasing noise in low light conditions. A fast lens wide open will yield clearer images while stopping down might avoid a blurry eye if the camera happens to focus on a wingtip instead of acquiring direct focus on the bird's eye.

Fast shutter speeds in low light result in high ISO values no matter how much light is available, but modern digital cameras have such awesome low light capacity I don't even worry about it anymore. I just set the ISO to auto and let it float to whatever the shutter speed and aperture require. Some photographers prefer to control both the shutter speed and aperture in manual mode while I prefer shutter priority (Tv mode). Manual mode will be the better choice if you have a really fast lens that you don't want sacrificing depth of field by opening up to it's widest openings of f/4 or f/2.8. Manually selecting f/5.6 or smaller will strike a compromise between depth of field and faster shutter speeds.

Digital noise is an inevitable result of low light shooting with high ISO values and if it becomes problematic in your images we are fortunate these days to have some really great tools for correcting that type of problem. I find I get the best raw images with DXO Pure Raw in combination with the AI tool set provided by Topaz Labs. Each photographer will have to determine the best software for his or her own needs. I find for my needs, Pure Raw is usually enough to provide a quality image in most lighting conditions.

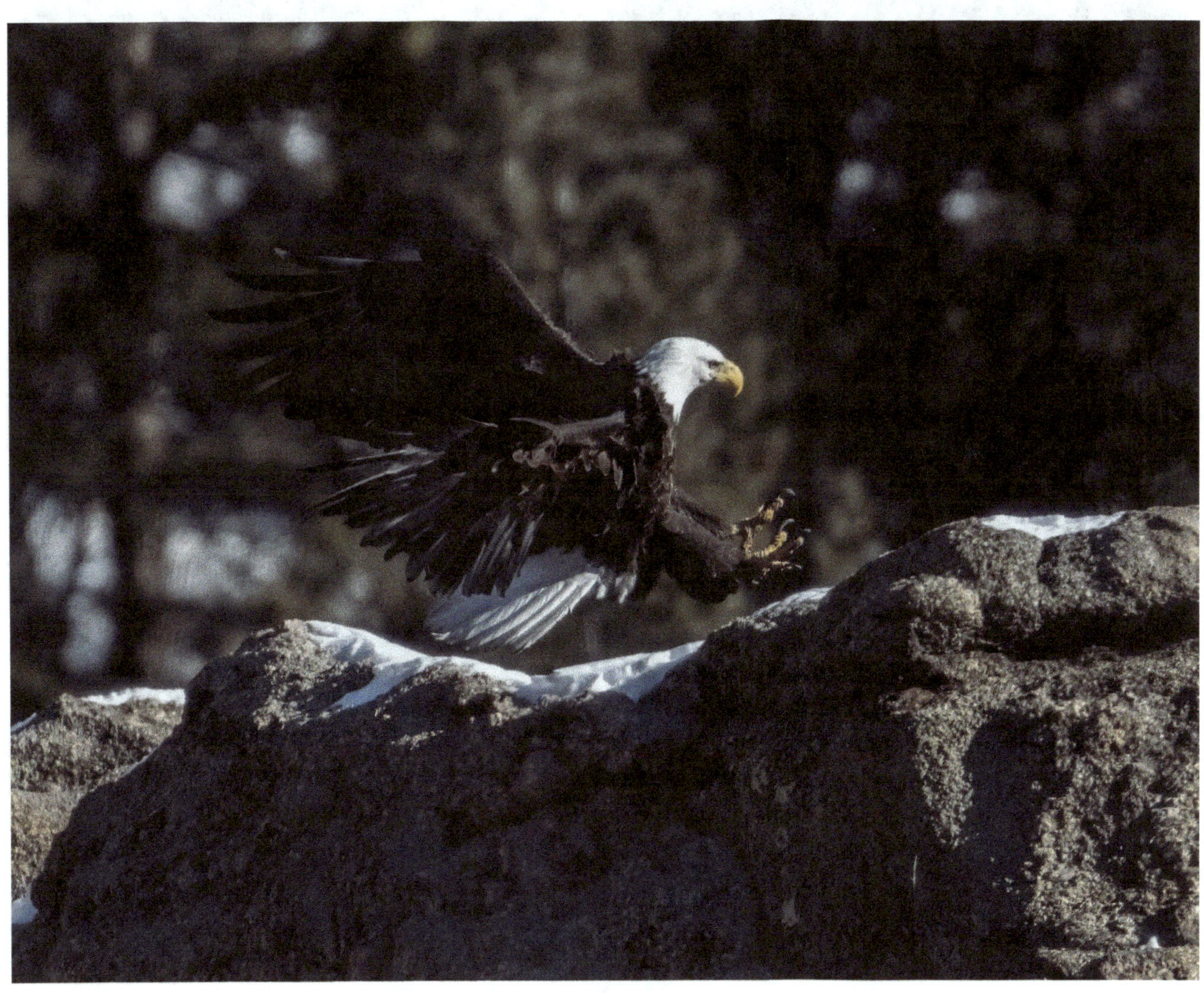

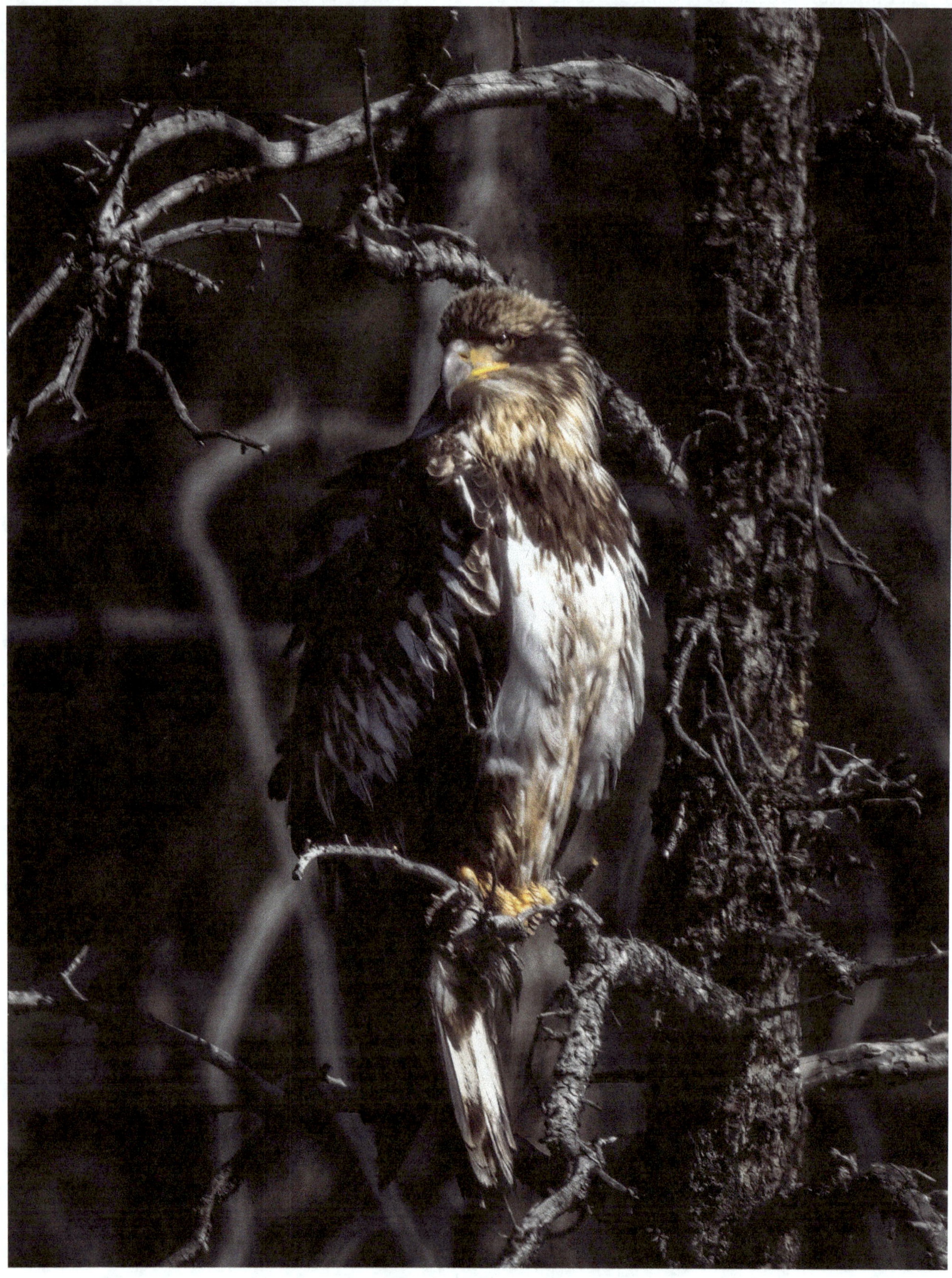

Eleven Mile State Park and Reservoir is the body of water that feeds the canyon and is also an interesting place to make a winter photo excursion. Unfortunately there isn't a direct route from the canyon to the state park so getting there requires passing through the town of Lake George on Highway 24 to the Highway 92 turnoff to the south. The road is approximately 10 miles of paved two lane leading all the way to the entrance of the state park where visitors can either use a season pass or pay the day fee of about $10, depending on the current rate. As you pass through the village there is also a left turn to the Coyote Ridge parking lot where there are a number of nice hiking trails of varying distance and difficulty. For climbing on the rocky trails I recommend the use of micro spikes for extra traction on the packed snow and icy sections of trail.

The reservoir is home to a number of animals species including coyote, fox, pronghorn antelope, raptors including eagles and red-tailed hawks, deer and of course all kinds of small animals and birds. This lone bison (below) actually lives on a ranch located on the west side of the park as you exit and head back toward Highway 24 on the west side of Wilkerson Pass. Occasionally pronghorn will be grazing within the boundaries of the park while other times it may be necessary to search northwest of the park or on the road over to Spinney Reservoir.

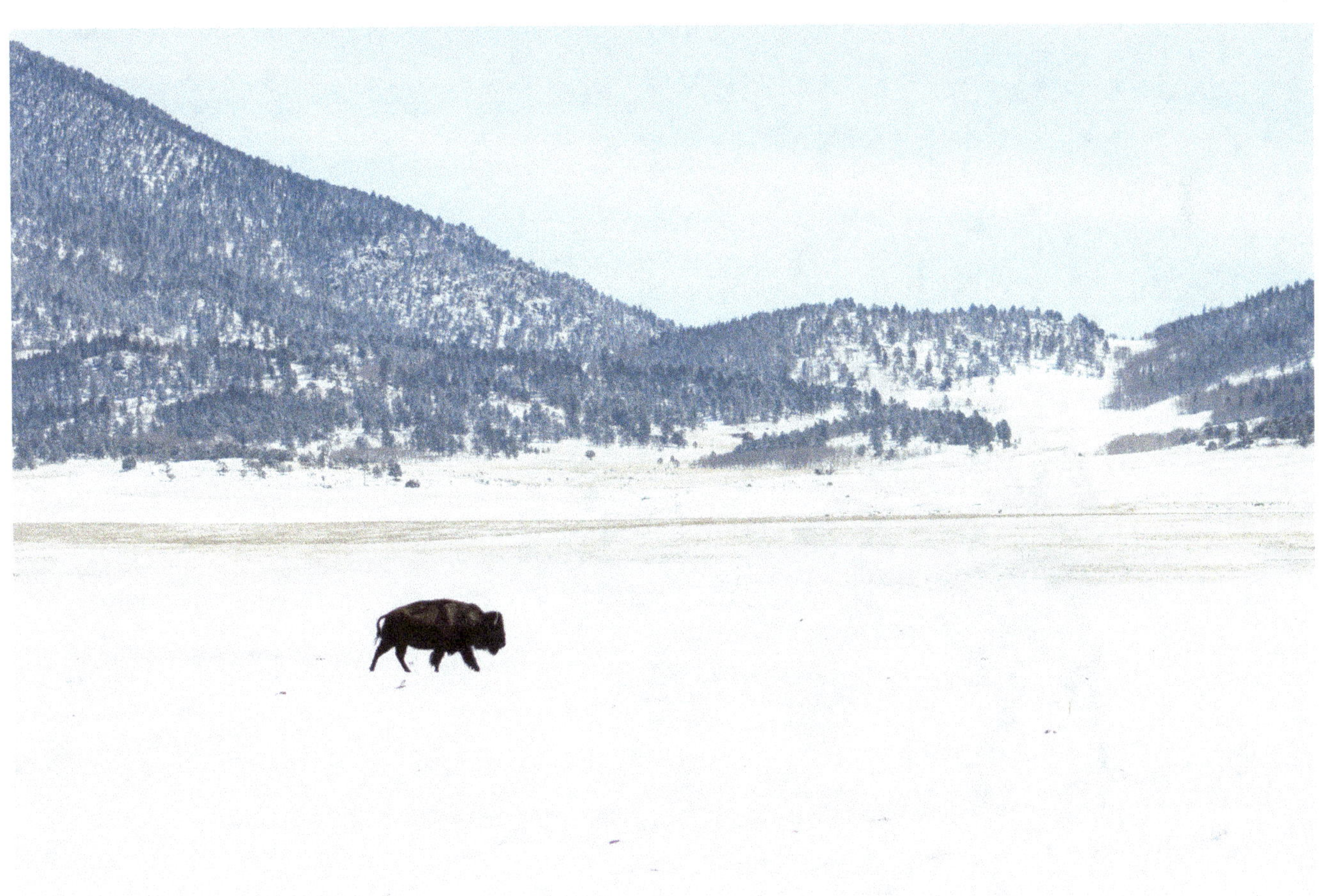

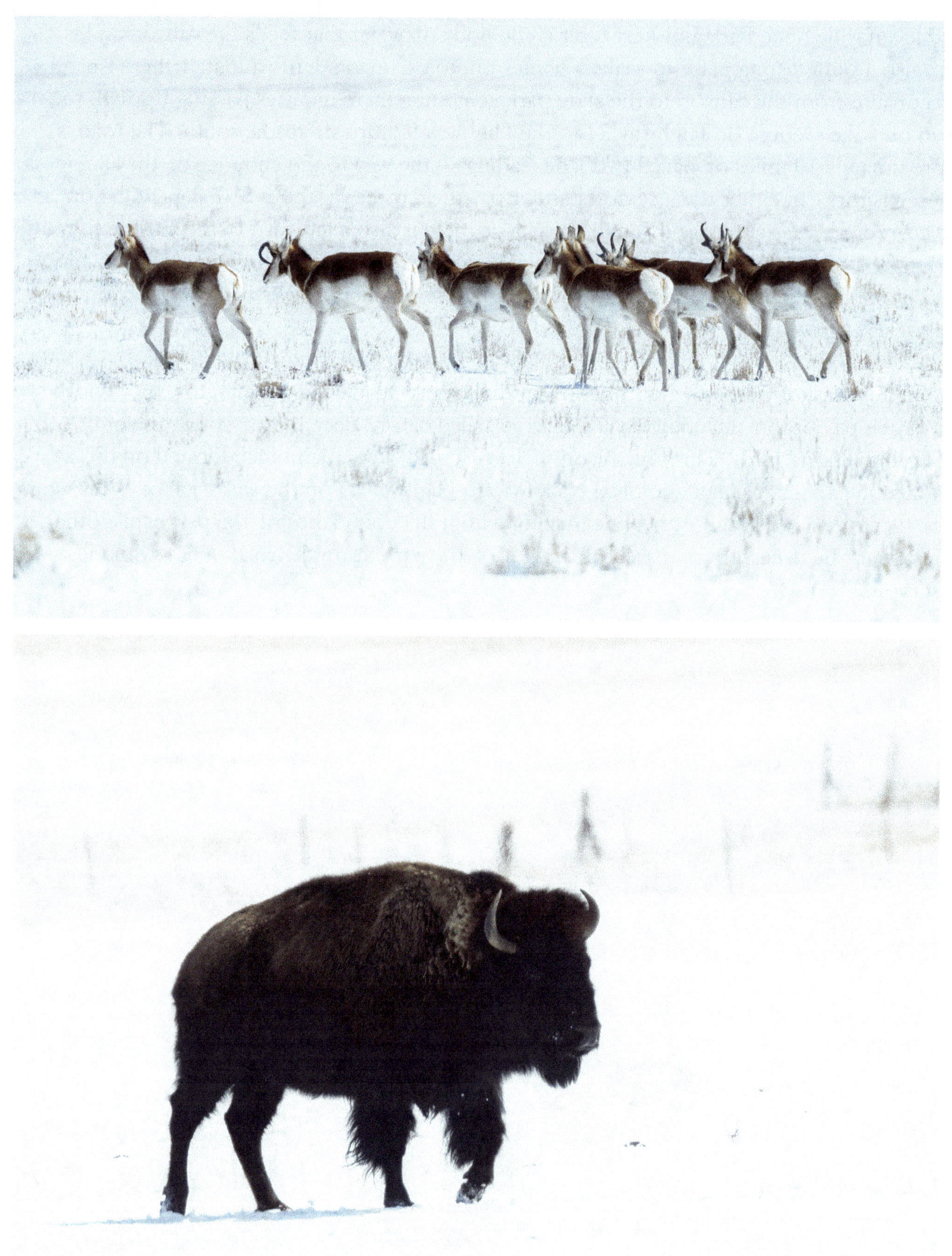

The Central Mountains

I had never considered undertaking a winter 14er before but when I got the call from my buddy Ralph mentioning that we should do a winter climb, I was thinking that all my snowshoe treks on Bald Mountain might just be enough training to accomplish such a feat! Most 14ers are inaccessible in winter without a full fledged winter camping trip, but a **Mount Elbert** summit expedition seemed feasible. It is Colorado's highest peak and a fairly long nine mile round trip, but the parking lot is accessible and it is Class 1 all the way to the summit. Class 1 is the least dangerous of all the ratings, and just a non technical walk to the top. Of course a nine mile walk at 11,000 feet plus in deep snow is still a significant undertaking! We checked the weather forecast and a nice day was on tap for that very week, plans were made and the trek was on! My plan was to travel light and conserve as much energy as possible, but going without a camera was unthinkable! For this journey I decided to pack only my light plastic 18-55 kit lens.

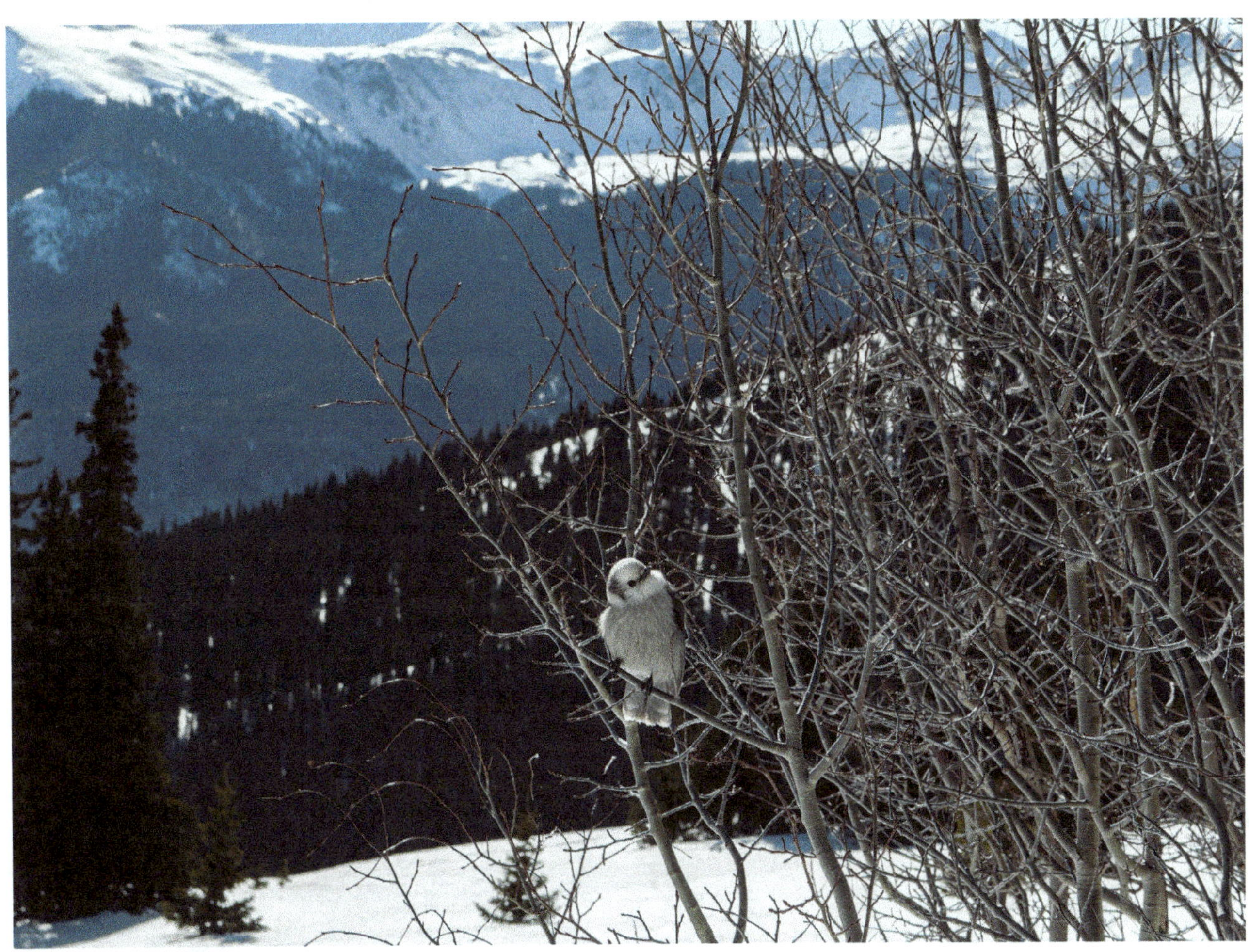

I consulted my 14ers.com account for trail conditions and the reports were favorable, including recent accounts indicating the snow wasn't deep and that a trail of microspikes would mark the way all the way to the summit! We arrived before first light and began the long hike in the dark in reasonably comfortable 15 degree temperatures. With spirits high and stomachs full of a good breakfast we were off. After a couple miles on a jeep road we made the turn onto the east ridge, our chosen route. As advertised the trail was well packed and easy to follow. The sun was soon beaming down and the day was warming nicely. We soon picked up an enthusiastic partner as a Canada jay followed us for a mile or two, jumping from bush to bush before eventually giving up and going back to his normal bird activities.

We were making steady progress until mid morning when we were confronted with the unexpected, overnight a light snow had drifted over a big meadow completely burying the trail under a sea of white. We had put our faith in the trail and weather reports and assumed that the microspikes were all that would be necessary. The snow in the meadow was several feet deep and without snowshoes we were ready to give up. But I could see faint prints leading in a direction and under those prints the trail was packed and suitable for microspikes. So we forged ahead, feeling out the trail with our ski poles and only occasionally falling into the deep snow. It took a little time but we eventually made it back into the trees and passable trail on the other side.

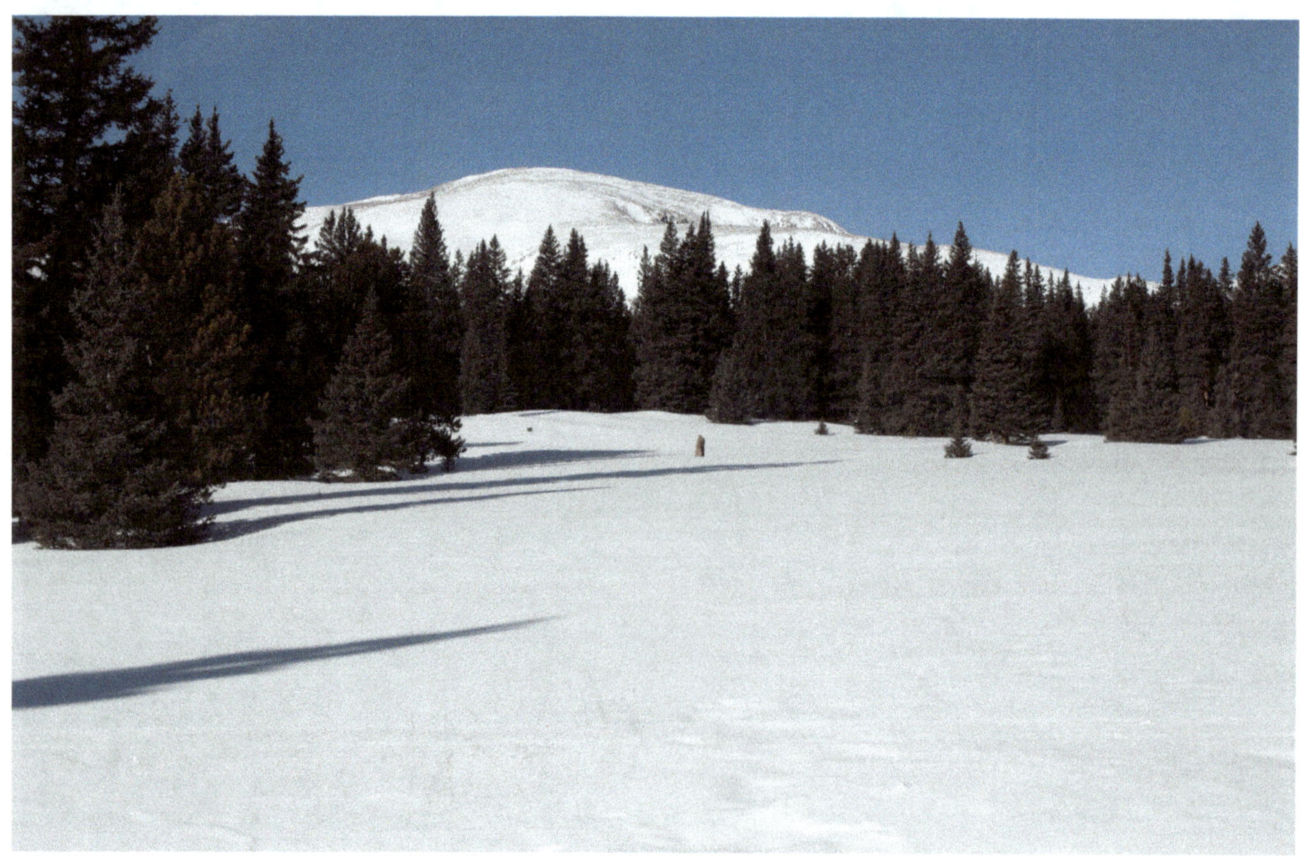

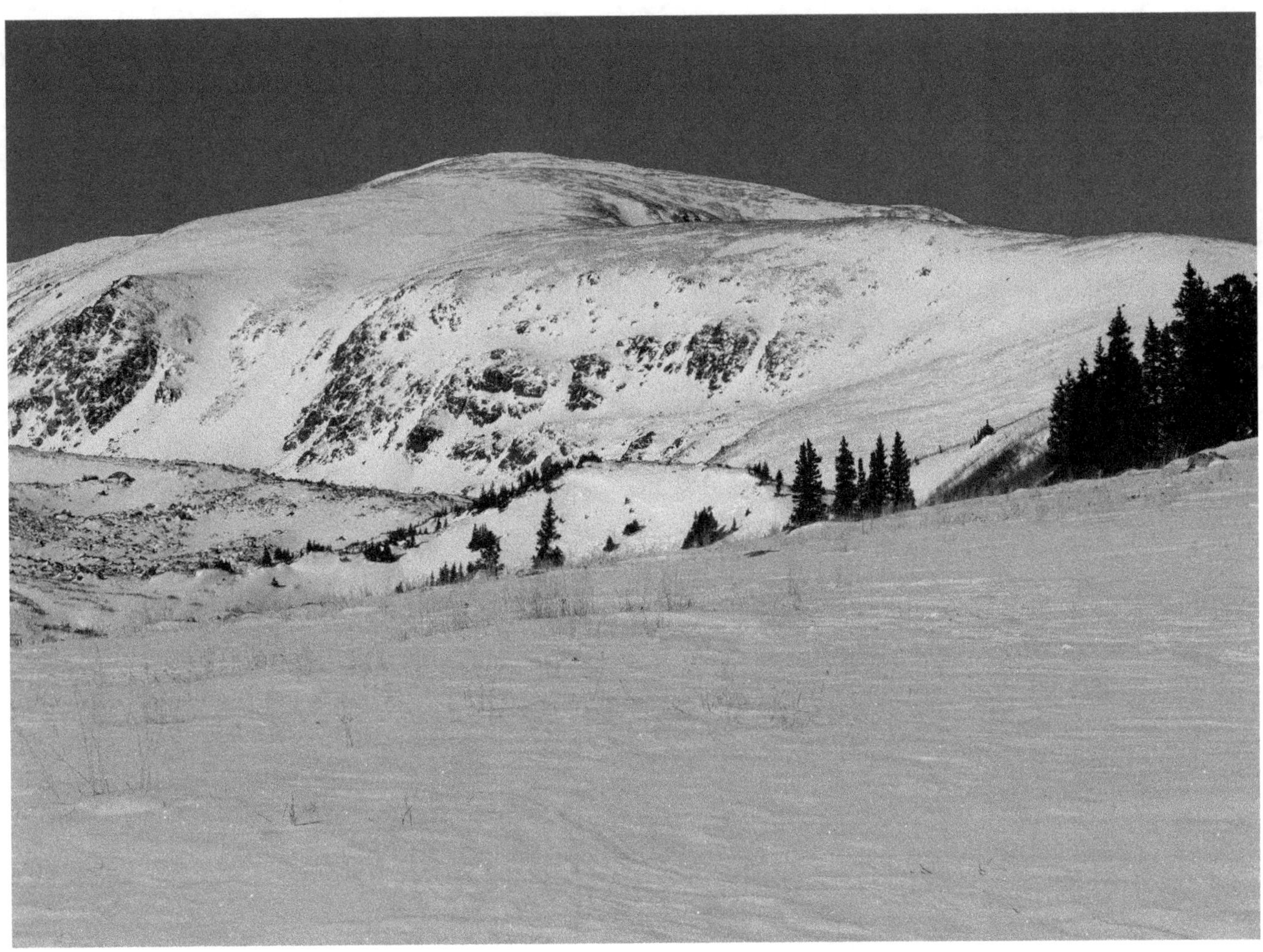

Eventually we cleared the tree line and the summit came into view. The beauty of the snow covered mountain at that elevation was staggering. Time was of the essence but I could not resist stopping often for pictures. The 18-55 isn't the greatest lens but a circular polarizer was a useful asset, keeping glare and chromatic aberration to a minimum even with an inexpensive lens.

The promised trail of microspikes on shallow snow finally became a reality and we trudged onward toward the summit, picking the easiest route as we went. The day was warming nicely as we discussed a quick summit by around noon and an easy hike down the mountain back to the trailhead. A large knoll eventually appeared before us, providing a nice windbreak from the ever increasing breeze that had been blowing in our faces all morning, and we decided to take advantage of the brief calm to take a leisurely lunch along with more picture taking. Ralph decided to take a short side hike to the top of the knoll to survey the trail and get a good look at our destination at the top of the mountain (next page).

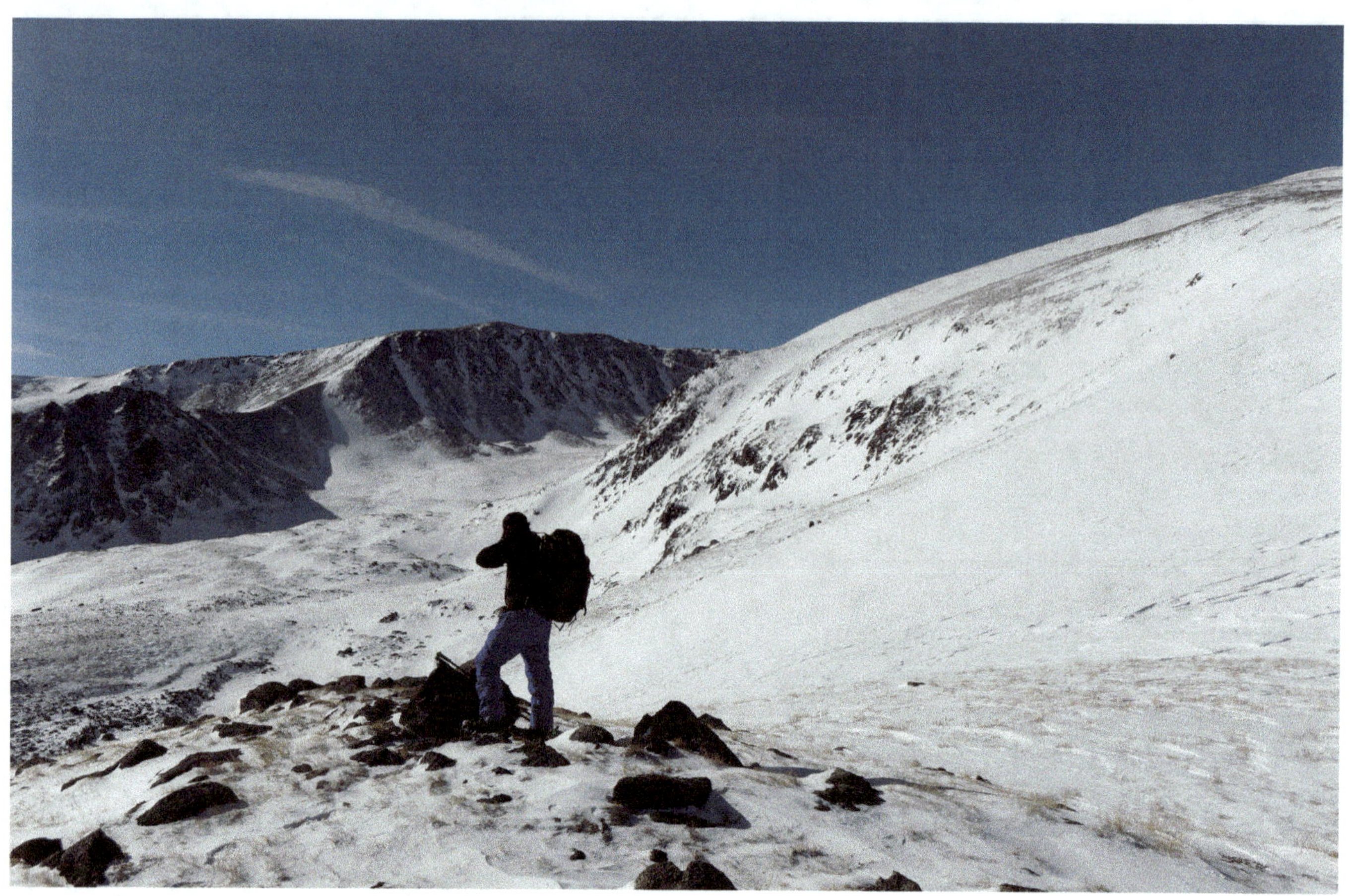

A summit by noon was looking ever more likely as we neared the top of Colorado's highest peak. To our chagrin however, arrival at that destination revealed the dreaded false summit. Our noon goal proved to be a mirage as we were forced to push back our arrival time an hour to 1:00 p.m. By then we had been hiking the relentless ascent for over six hours and the fun and excitement was beginning to fade. Fatigue and lack of oxygen were taking a toll and we were only able to hike a few yards at a time before stopping to recover.

The peak neared and our 1:00 p.m. summit was tantalizingly close. The view of the end of our march provided the necessary adrenaline to keep pushing, but soon came the sinking feeling that we had been fooled yet again by a second false summit. Already an hour past our original turnaround time, the summit was now in jeopardy and we decided upon a hard 2:00 p.m. deadline. The excitement of the adventure was now gone and a death march to the top of the mountain was all that remained. Our 2:00 p.m. hard limit approached and our progress was slowing as the air became thinner. Failure began to infiltrate our minds as 2:00 p.m. came and went. Our hard deadline was behind us but the summit looked so close. I couldn't bear the thought of getting so close without actually reaching Colorado's ceiling and we unwisely forged ahead.

Now almost a full hour past our most recent time goal, we were forced to contemplate failure and decided once and for all that we would not continue upward past 3:00 p.m. That would leave less than two hours until sunset for the four and a half mile descent, and with the mountain rising high behind us to the west we really had no idea when the light of day would abandon us.

And then suddenly with only ten minutes to spare we were at the top of Colorado, 14,433 feet above sea level with nothing but sky above us. There was an eerie calm, as if sound itself was struggling to survive the snow and thin air. The sky was so blue up there it was almost black and my camera didn't quite know what to do with the haze in the thin air, rendering strange bluish looking low contrast results on the LCD screen. Fortunately I had a camera along that could shoot images in raw mode, enabling wide latitude for white balance and contrast adjustments in post. I quickly shot images in every direction eager to capture such a momentous achievement, an official winter climb to the highest point in Colorado.

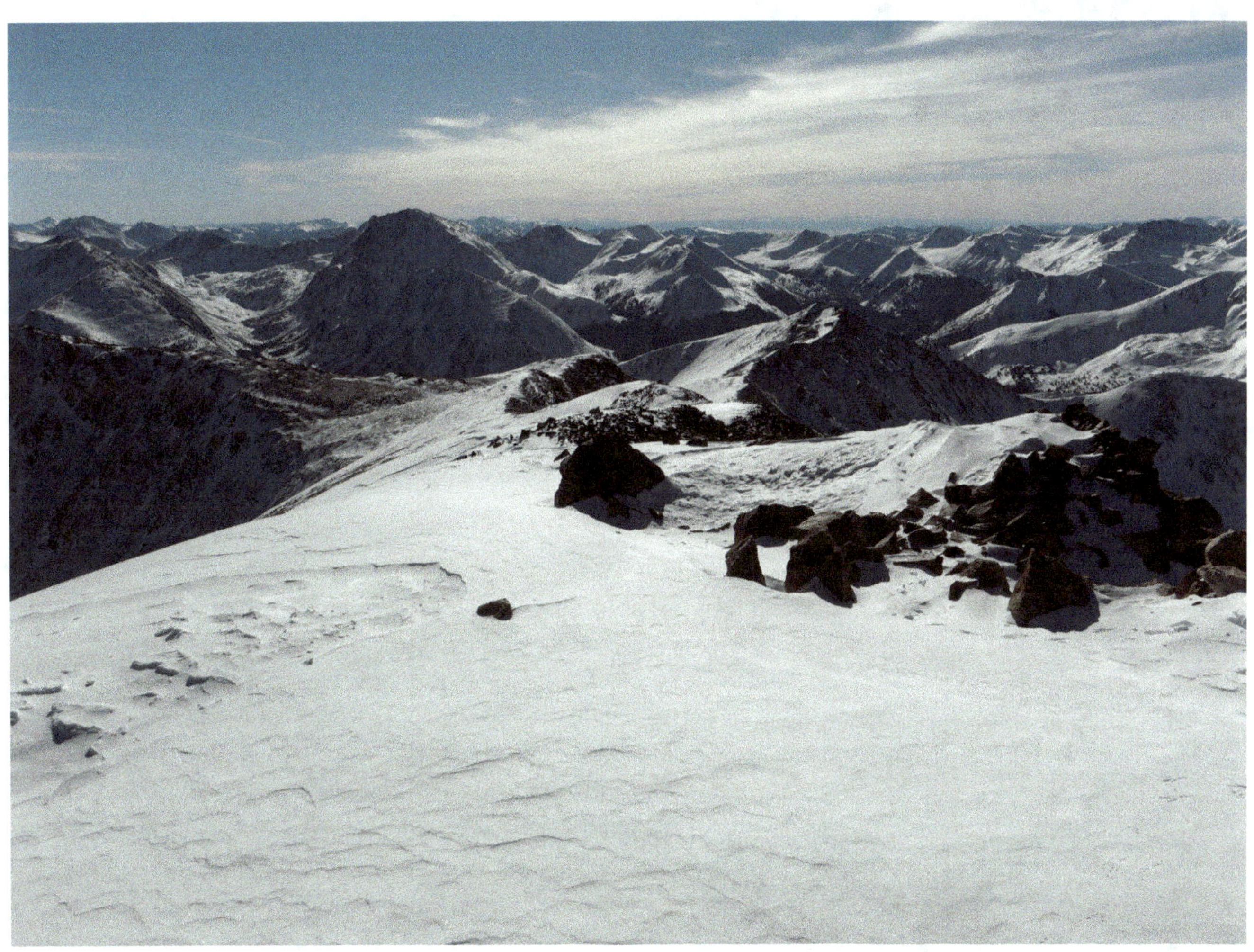

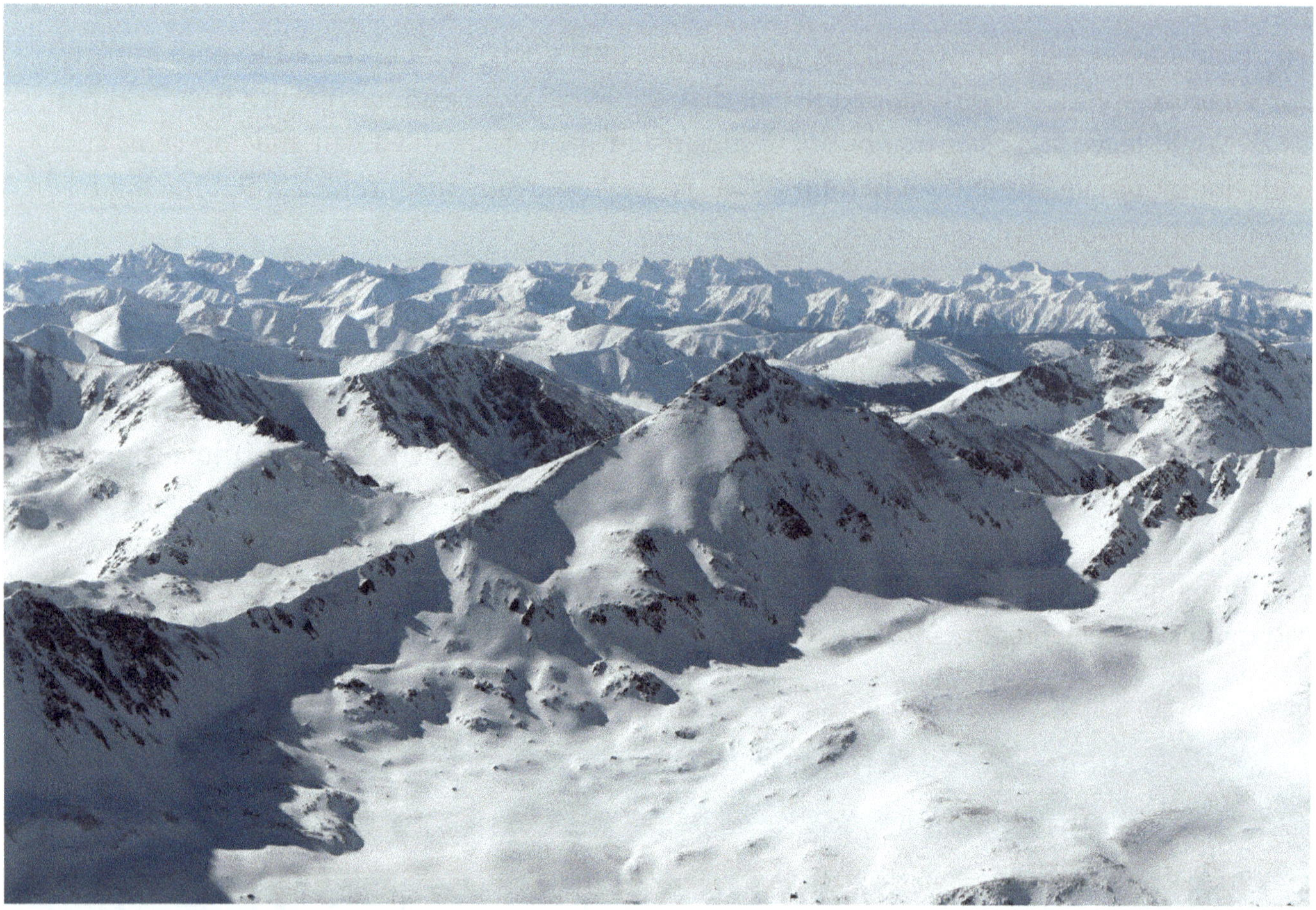

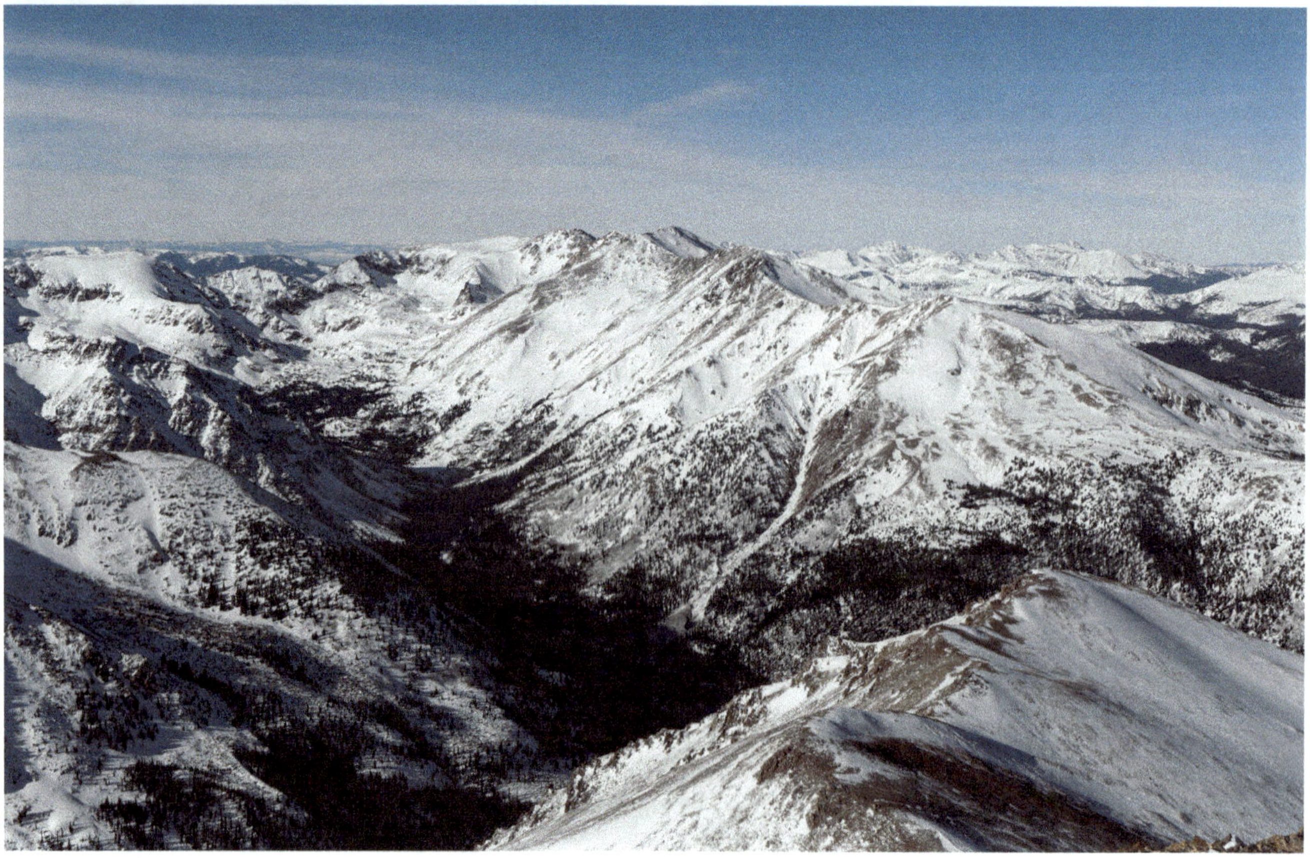

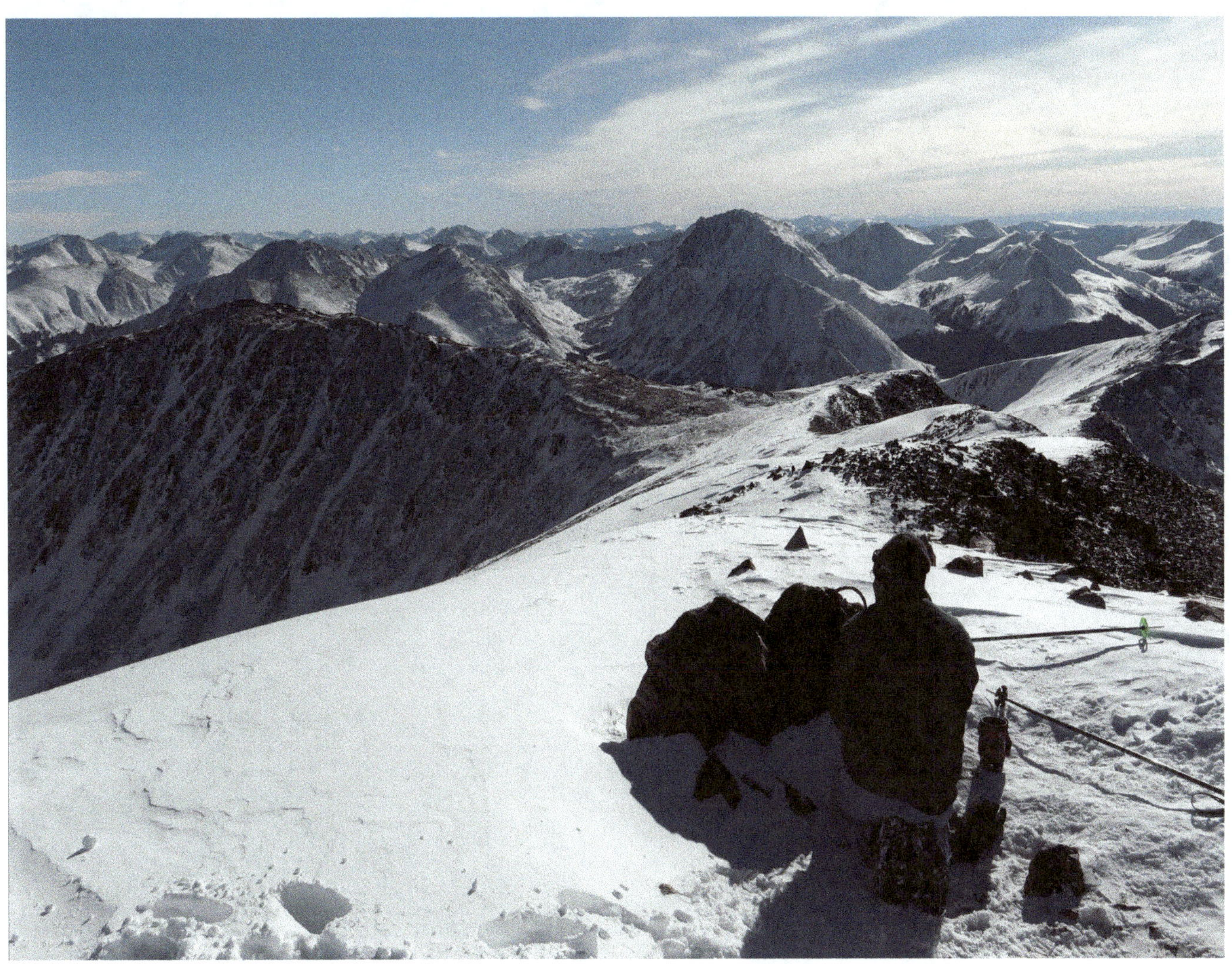

Even though it was an hour past our deadline and a full three hours past our original goal, it seemed fitting to take off the gloves and enjoy a few moments in such incredible magnificence. At that moment I felt like I was standing upon a place that no man had ever stood. There were no tracks in the windblown snow and no other people in sight in any direction. Ralph heated water on the Jetboil for a cup of coffee to warm us while I continued shooting every composition I could find.

However the warmest part of the day was behind us and as the excitement of summiting began to wane I noticed a whooshing sound as a stiff breeze began to build. My bare fingers began to burn as the temperature quickly dropped and the reality of the situation began to sink in. The sun was well on the backside of the day and we still had a long trek before us. Soon the gloves were back on and packs securely strapped to our backs. We hustled down the mountain and made it to the clearing that almost ended our adventure, just as the sun was beginning to fade. Fortunately we were on the jeep road by the time full darkness had obscured our world with only the miracle of battery power to light the way. It seemed like the truck would never come into view, but eventually our journey was complete and we were safely on our way home.

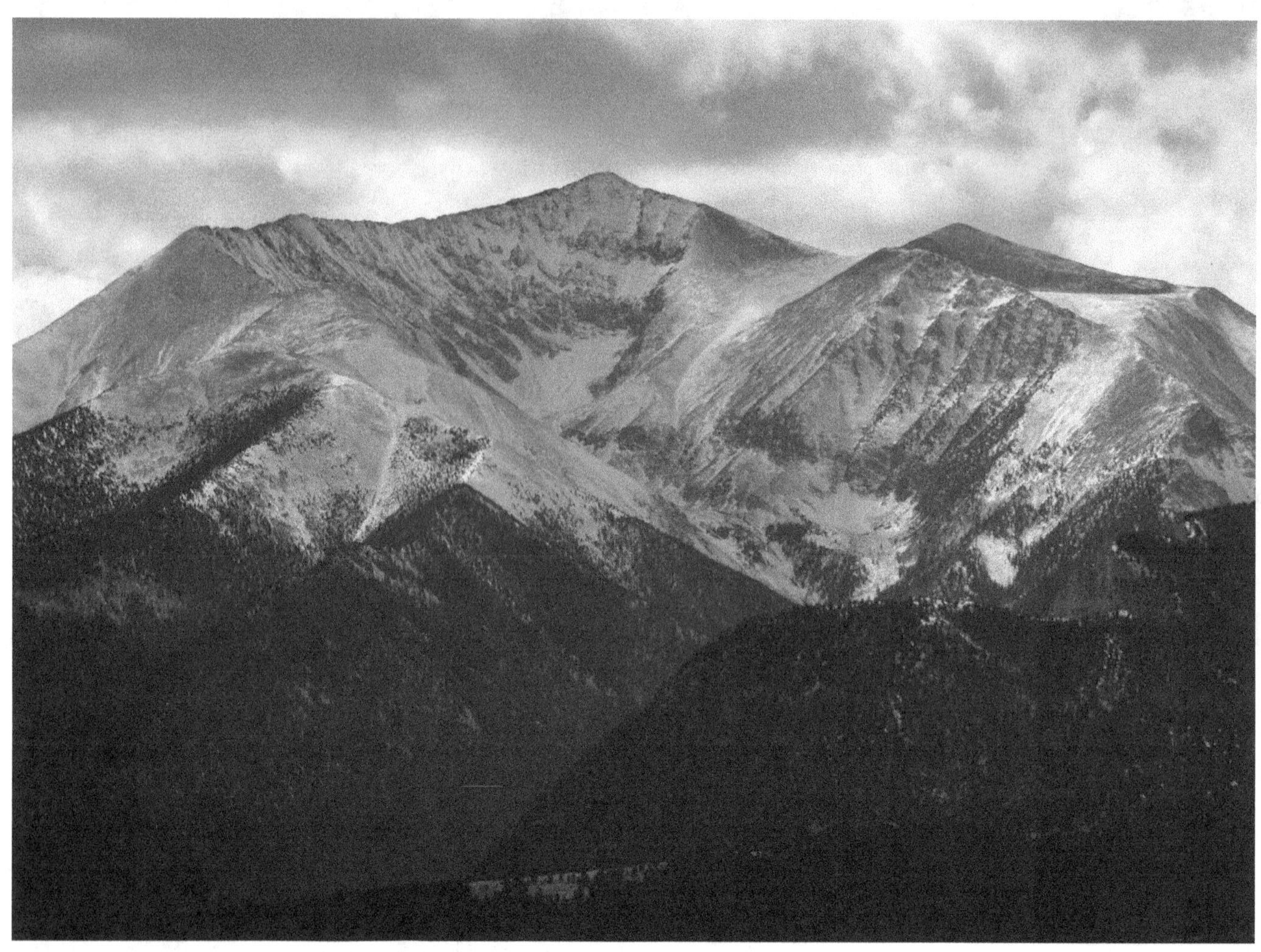

For pure majesty, the **Collegiate Peaks** of the **Sawatch Range** are hard to beat. Standing tall over the towns of Buena Vista and Leadville, these peaks are named after Ivy League colleges and are some of the tallest peaks in the state. Unfortunately the main arteries for actually getting into the interior of the range are closed for the winter, but there are plenty of fabulous vistas that can be photographed from Highway 24 between the towns of Leadville and Poncha Springs.

A network of trails on the east side of Buena Vista on the other side of the river is accessible in the winter providing some excellent views of the peaks if you can climb high enough. There is a nice parking lot with a pedestrian bridge providing access to the east side, so crossing the river is no problem.

Bring a wide angle lens or a zoom, there are plenty of compositions suitable for either type of photography. I've had good success with both my 24-105 and my 70-200mm lenses along that scenic stretch. Gigantic Mount Princeton (above) will definitely require a wide angle lens to take it all in!

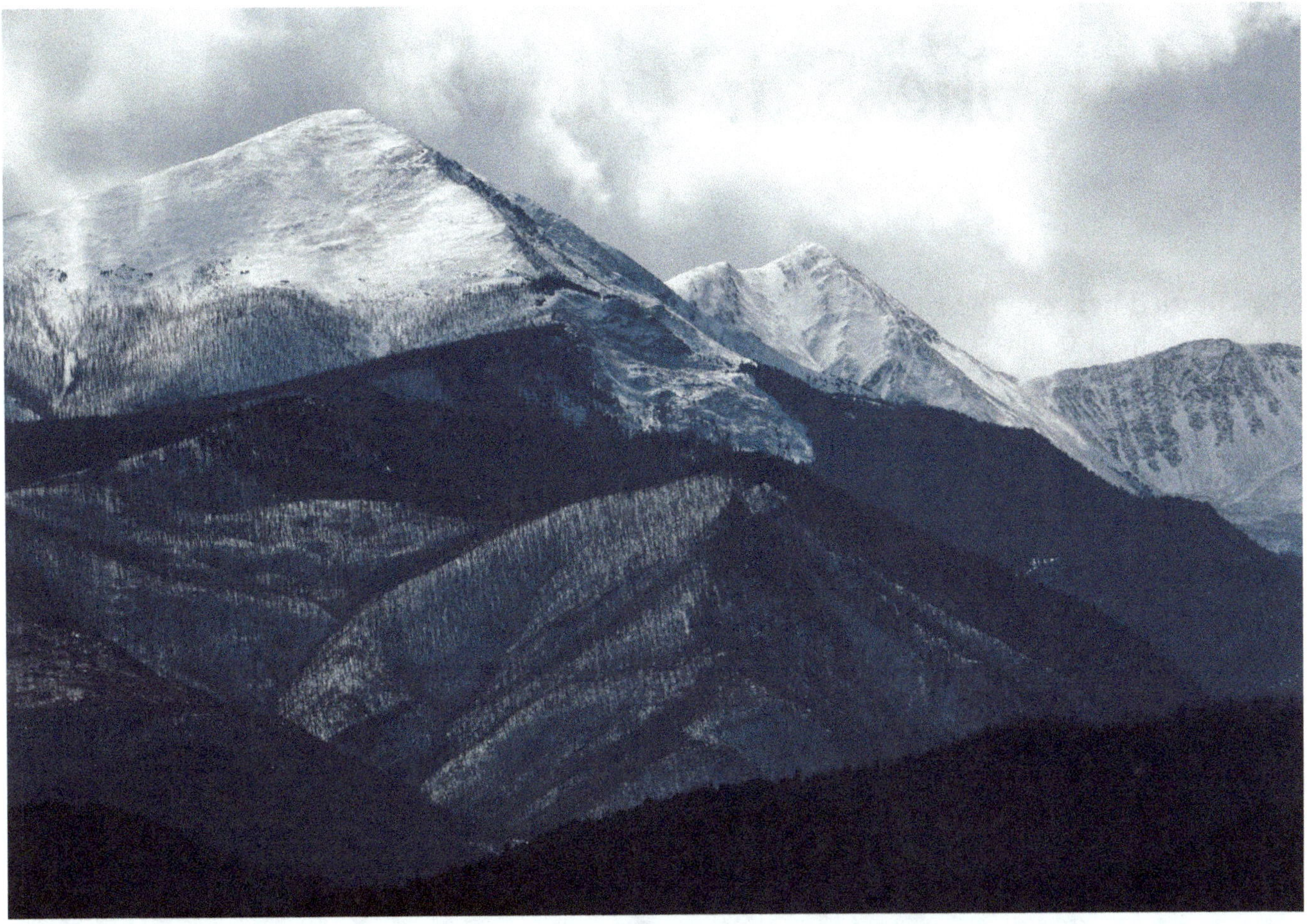

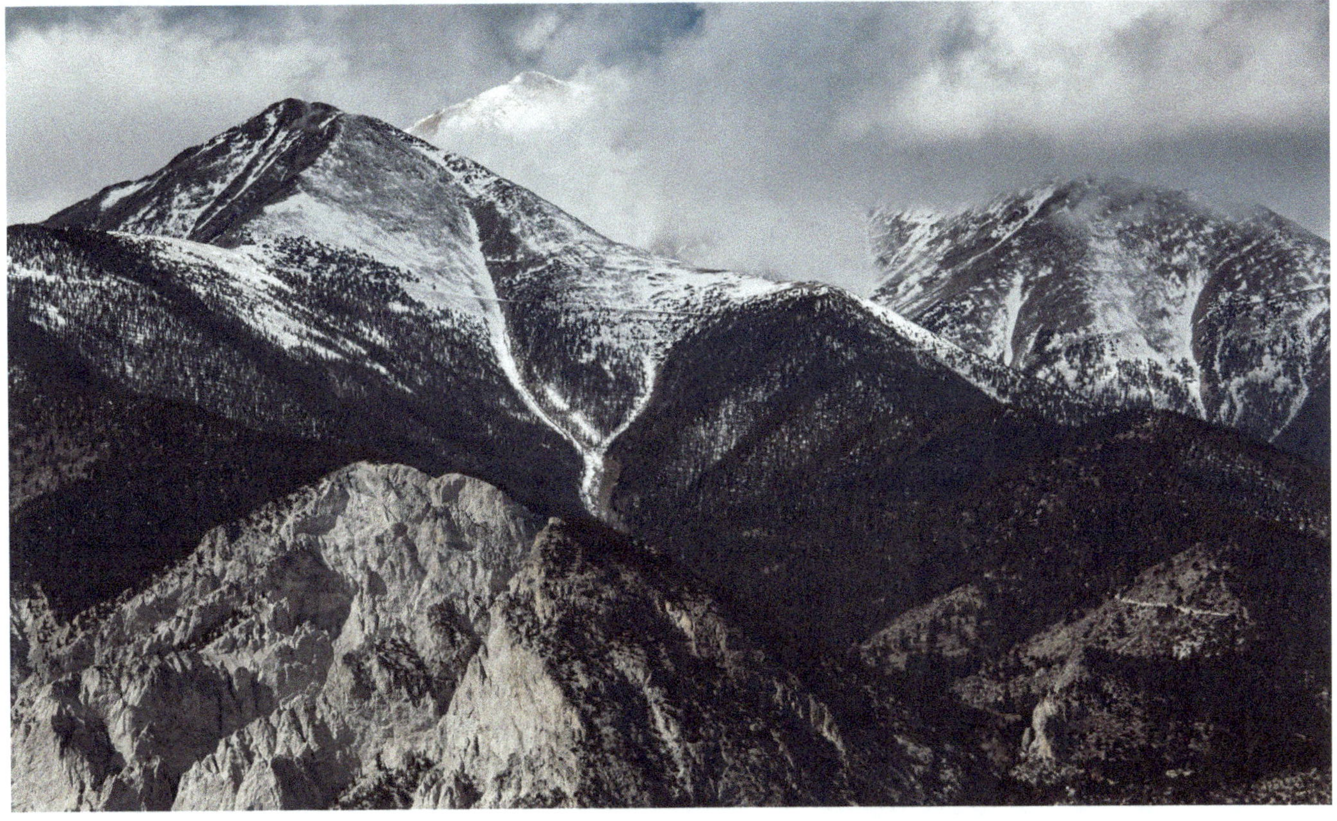

The San Luis Valley

Nestled between the rugged Sangre de Cristo and San Juan mountain ranges lies the San Juan Valley, home to the **Monte Vista and Alamosa National Wildlife Refuges**, the historic Rio Grand River and the stunningly beautiful **Great Sand Dunes National Park and Preserve**. The wildlife refuge is free to visit while your national parks pass or day pass purchased at the entrance will be needed to gain access to the dunes. Many prefer to visit the area in the summertime but there are a few good reasons why a photographer might want to visit in the winter months. First and foremost is of course the snow, the Colorado Rockies are simply more beautiful when covered in deep snow. The second is the amazing fall and spring sandhill crane migration. According to the **rove.me** website, approximately twenty thousand cranes stop over in the valley from October to late November and again in the spring from late February until sometime in March.

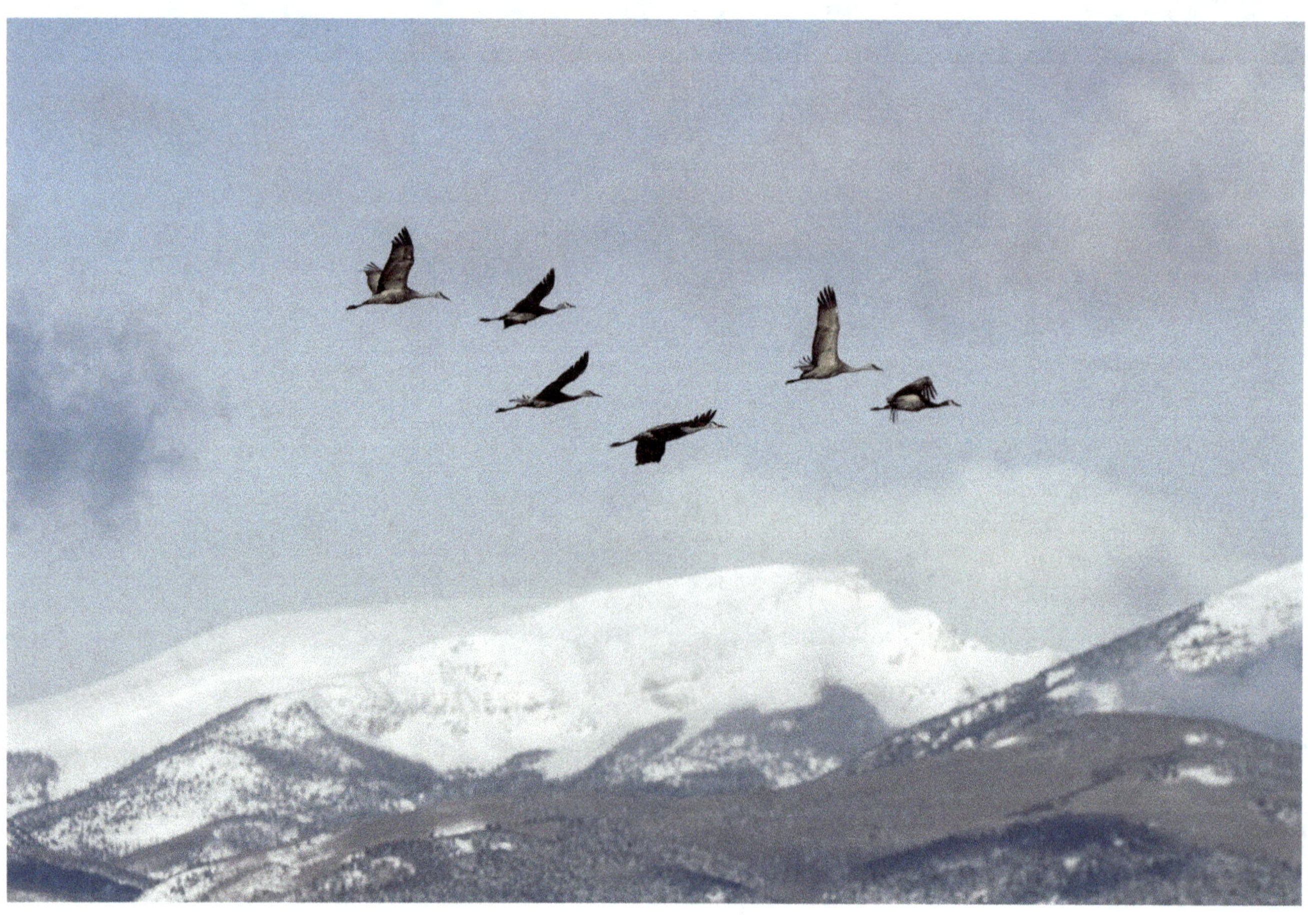

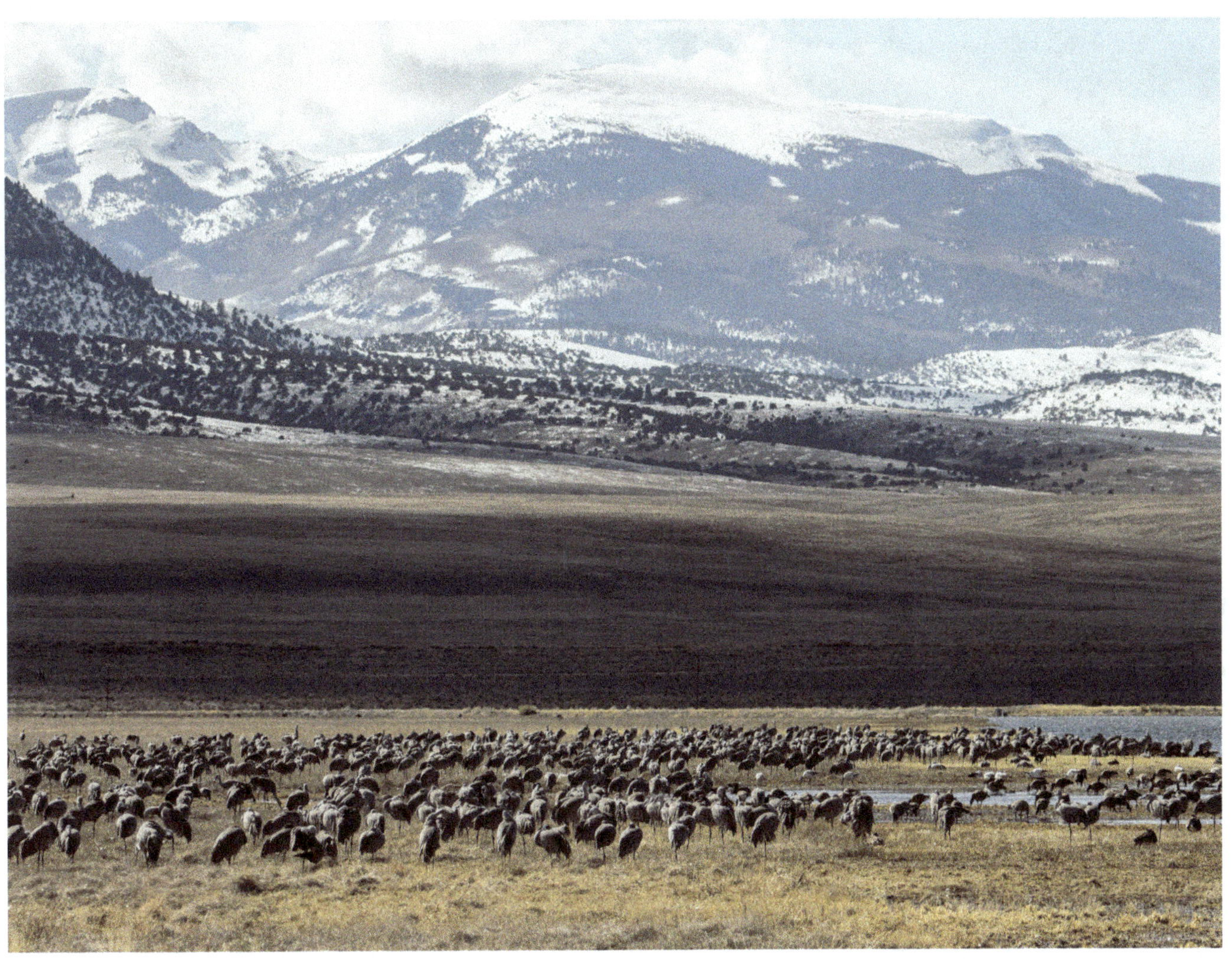

The best place to view the cranes is just south of the town of Monte Vista on Highway 15 at the wetlands area. Sunrise and sunset are when the cranes are most active in the wetlands with sunrise providing the best lighting on the San Juan mountains in the background and on the birds themselves as they strut around the surrounding fields. Late afternoon will most likely find the largest gathering of birds, albeit not in the best lighting conditions. As sunset nears, the flock will become more active as they prepare for flight en masse to head out into the grain fields in search of food and shelter.

During my visit in March, the birds began departing for the fields in groups rather than in one massive ascent. Rather than just focus on individual birds in the sky, I did my best to capture groups against the snowy San Juans in the background. Shutter priority with a speed of a 1600th of a second was my preferred shooting mode, however as the sun began to retreat I backed that off to a 1250th of a second to gain a stop of light commensurate with a lower ISO value. White snow and bright sky in the background adversely affects the camera meter, so it's important to keep checking exposure compensation to make sure the birds aren't just black blobs in the sky.

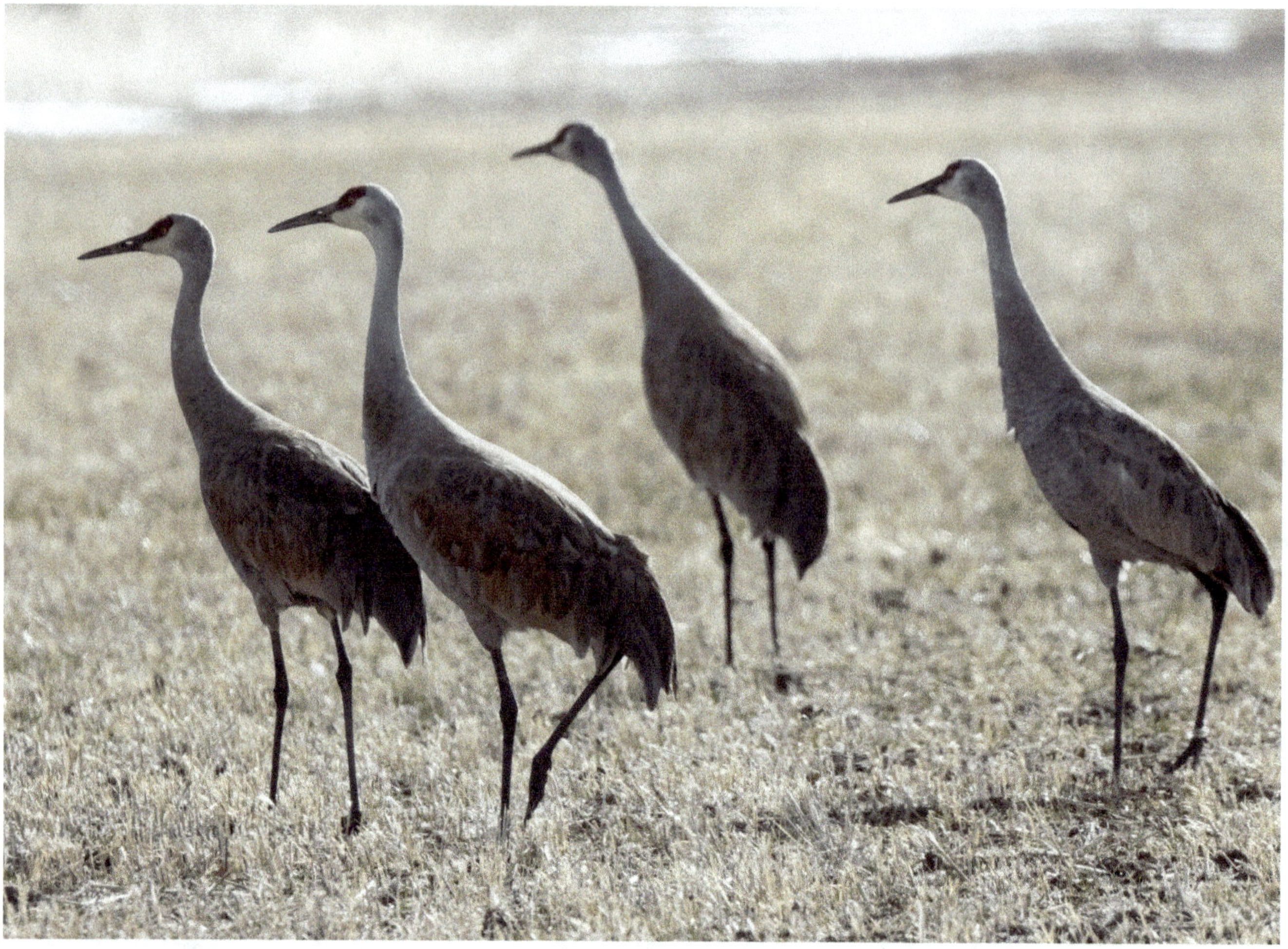

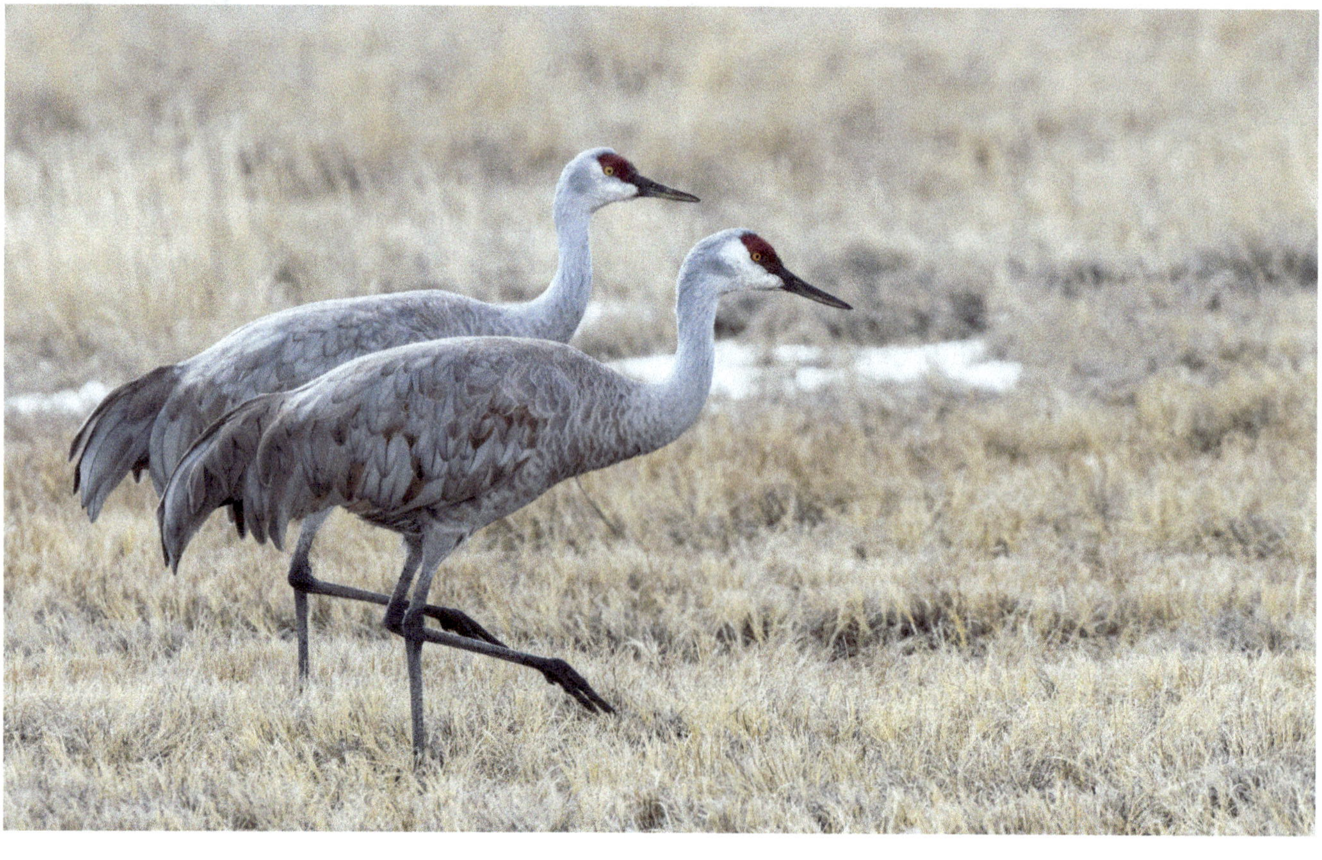

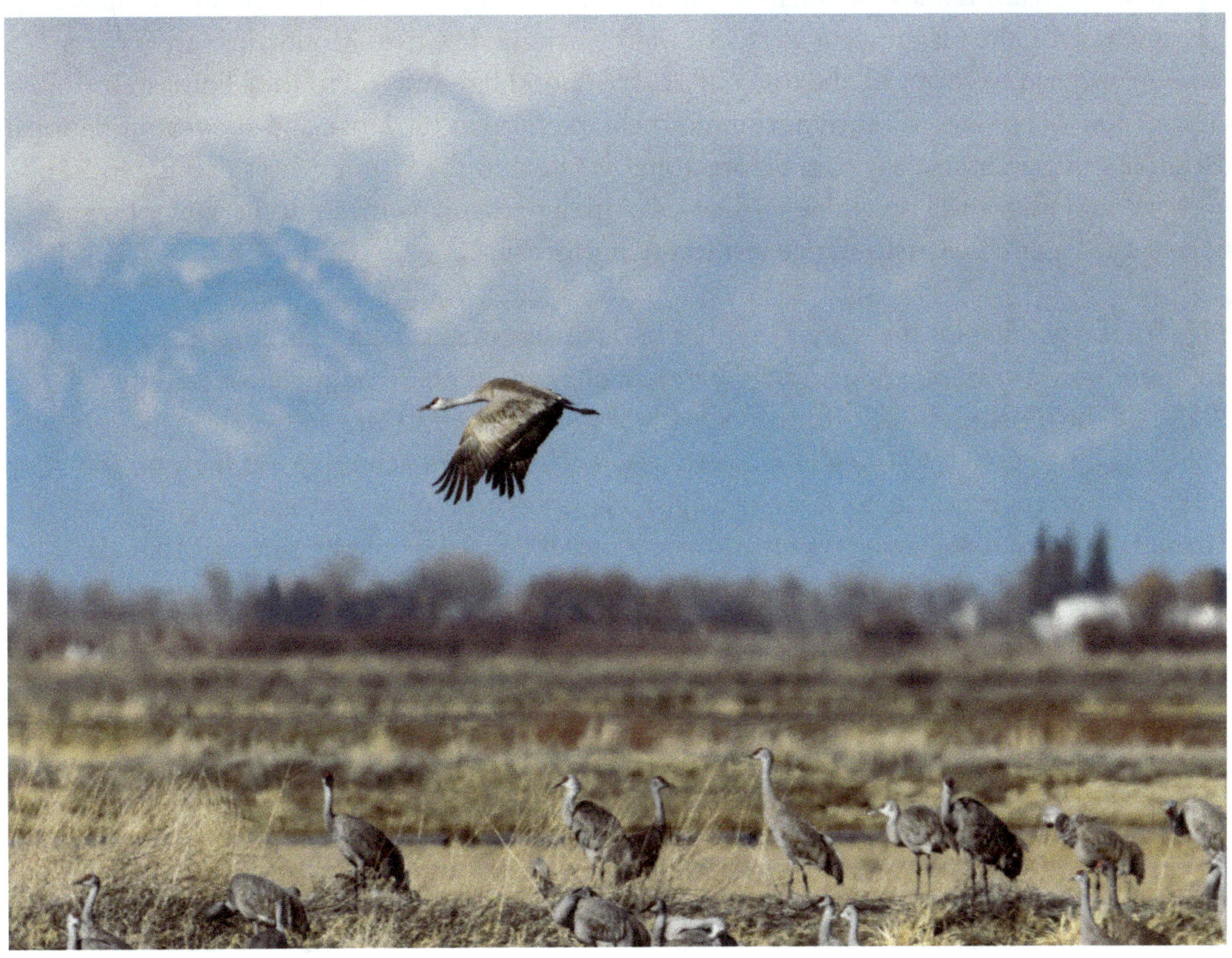

From a photographer's standpoint, the sandhill cranes are the perfect subject for birding as they are quite unafraid of people. There is a fence at the wetlands to keep people out of the staging area but the birds think nothing of strutting fearlessly right past tripods and big lenses. For this reason a long prime may not be the best choice, unless of course you don't mind constantly changing lenses. I found that my 100-400 zoom with a 1.4x tele-converter worked well at the refuge, giving me an effective range of 140-560mm of focal length to work with while switching back and forth between close and distant birds.

During the midday hours I left the wetlands and moved over to the Alamosa Wildlife area where I saw various hawks and a wonderful northern harrier which unfortunately I wasn't able to get close enough to for meaningful pictures. I was also excited to catch my first glimpse of the Rio Grande River, although it being another case where I wasn't able to find a compelling composition worthy of putting in a book.

The Great Sand Dunes National Monument lies just northeast of the wildlife refuges at the base of the magnificent west face of the Sangre de Cristo Mountains. To visit the sand dunes head west out of the town of Alamosa on Highway 160 to the Highway 150 intersection where you will turn north into the park. Stop at the kiosk and show your national parks pass or purchase a day pass before going forward to the visitor center parking lot. The massive sand dunes will be visible to the west with a particularly magnificent view of a section of the Sangre de Cristo Range just to the northeast.

From the parking lot there are a number of access points to walk out onto the sand where fantastic views of the dunes and the mountains can be photographed. I found my 24-105 to be the most useful lens for this situation, wide enough to take in the entire panorama while just long enough to bring in dramatic views of the approaching storm high on the peaks of the Sangre de Cristo. There was just a light breeze on this particular day so I wasn't worried about sand collecting on my camera, a mistake that I would be sure not to make if I were going to take a long hike or shoot on a windy day. Sand is constantly moving in the dunes and insidiously collecting all over my camera and lens. Even on a nice day I'd caution against bringing your best equipment, and even then covering it with a good rain cover for protection. If you require more than one lens for the journey I would recommend using two camera bodies, completely avoiding changing lenses and risking sand blowing into internal electronics and mechanisms..

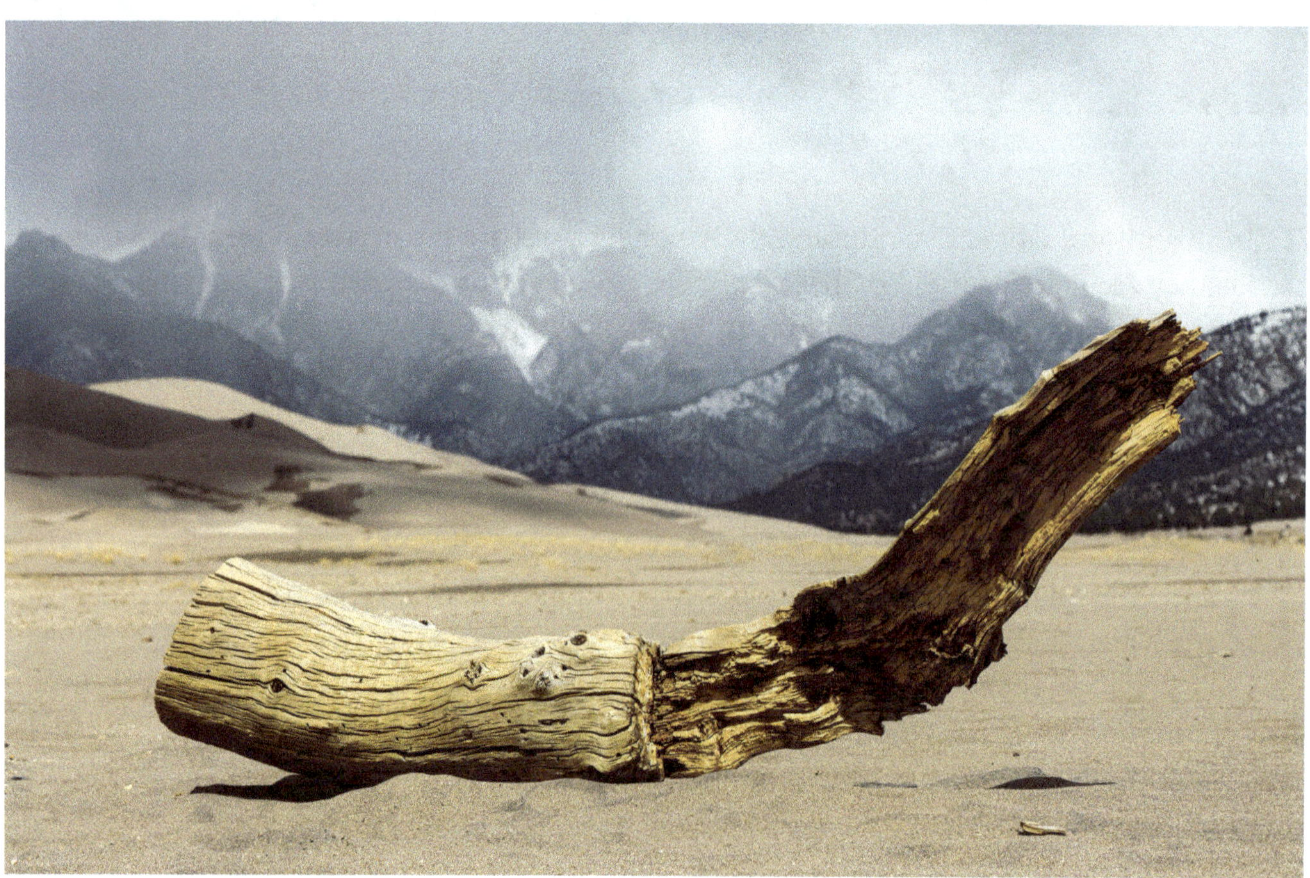

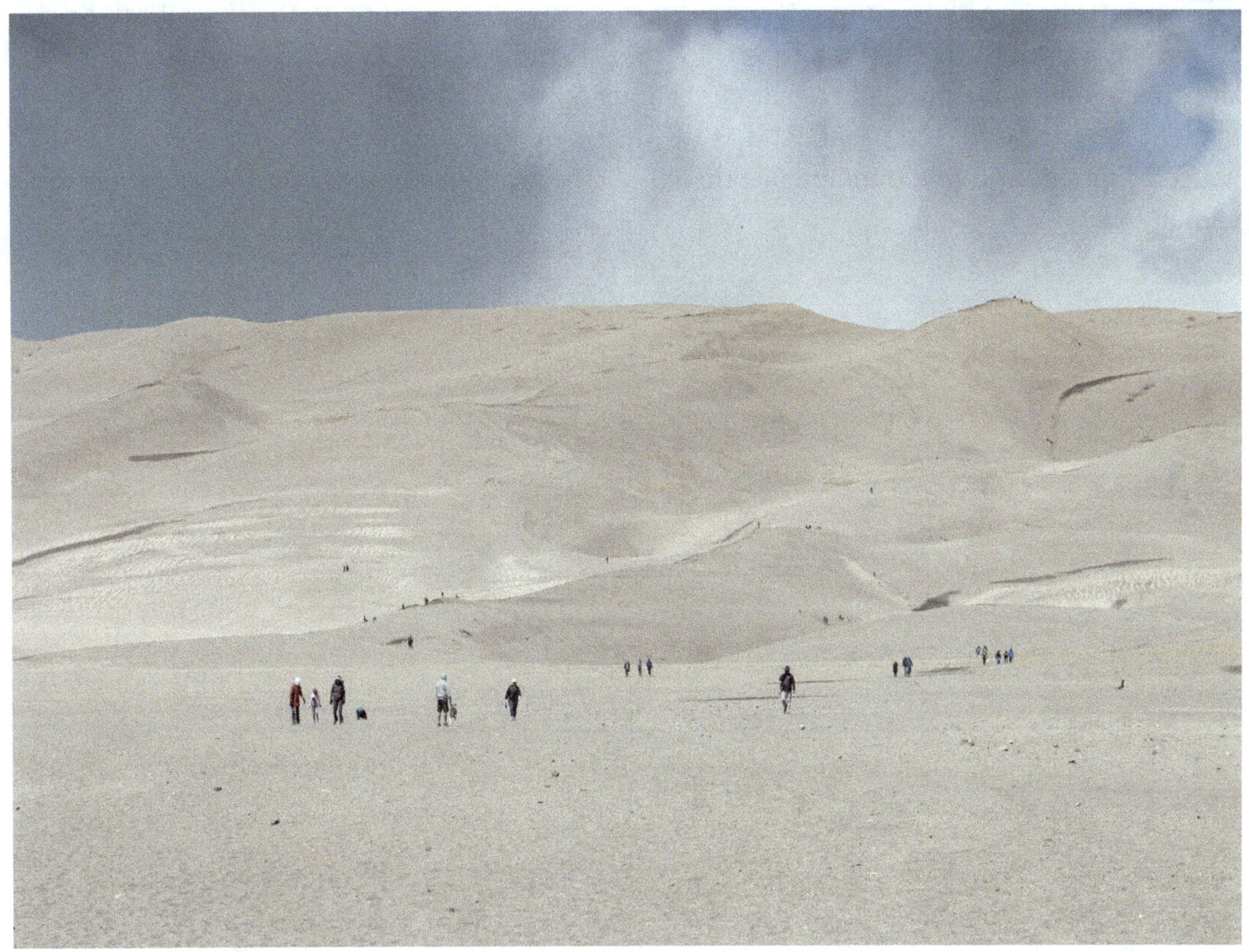

Be sure to pack snacks and water if you plan on hiking out onto the dunes, distances are deceptive there due to their massive size and lack of landmarks to offer perspective. The soft sand also makes for a slow tough slog, making the return trip more laborious and time consuming than one might imagine.

Manual mode with auto ISO is a good option for photographing the dunes. Aperture priority might also be a good choice as maintaining a fixed smaller opening will increase depth of field. My 24-105 is sharpest in the f/6.7 to f/8 range and I was pleased with the results, good detail in the foreground sand with acceptable sharpness in the distant dunes. Proper exposure is ensured by allowing the ISO to float. During the bright light of day it is unlikely that the ISO will exceed 400 and digital noise won't become a problem. Bring a tripod if you want to use a slow shutter speed to get creative with the blowing sand or clouds and be sure to switch to a static ISO to avoid the camera playing exposure tricks on your captures.

The **Sangre de Cristo Range** is beautiful from my usual location in the Pikes Peak Region, but the views from the west side are even more fantastic. Shoot the mountains in late afternoon for the best lighting and use a long lens of 200mm or greater to bring in dramatic views of the rugged peaks. And as the theme of this book suggests, there is no more magical time to capture the mountains than in the beautiful harshness of a Rocky Mountain winter.

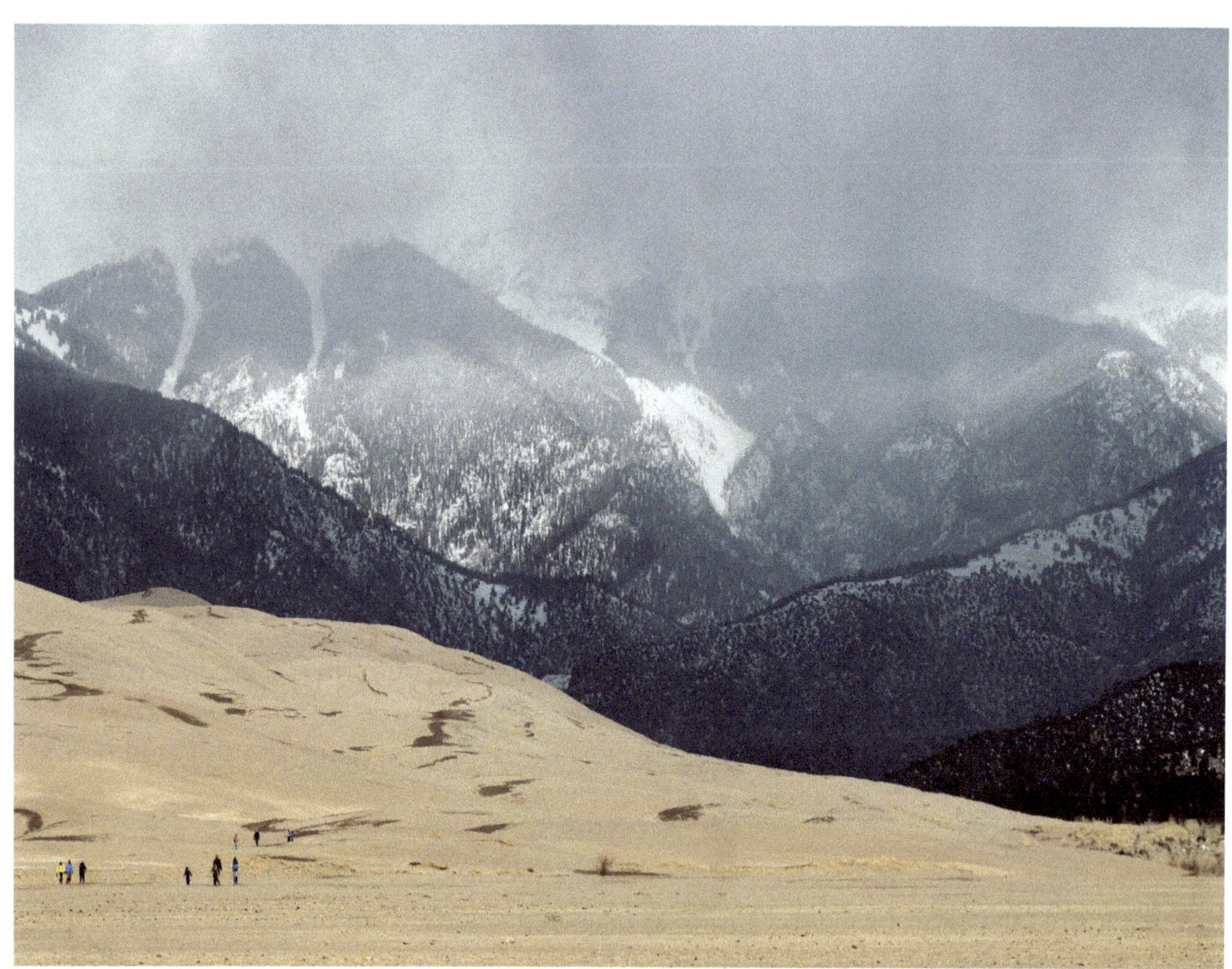

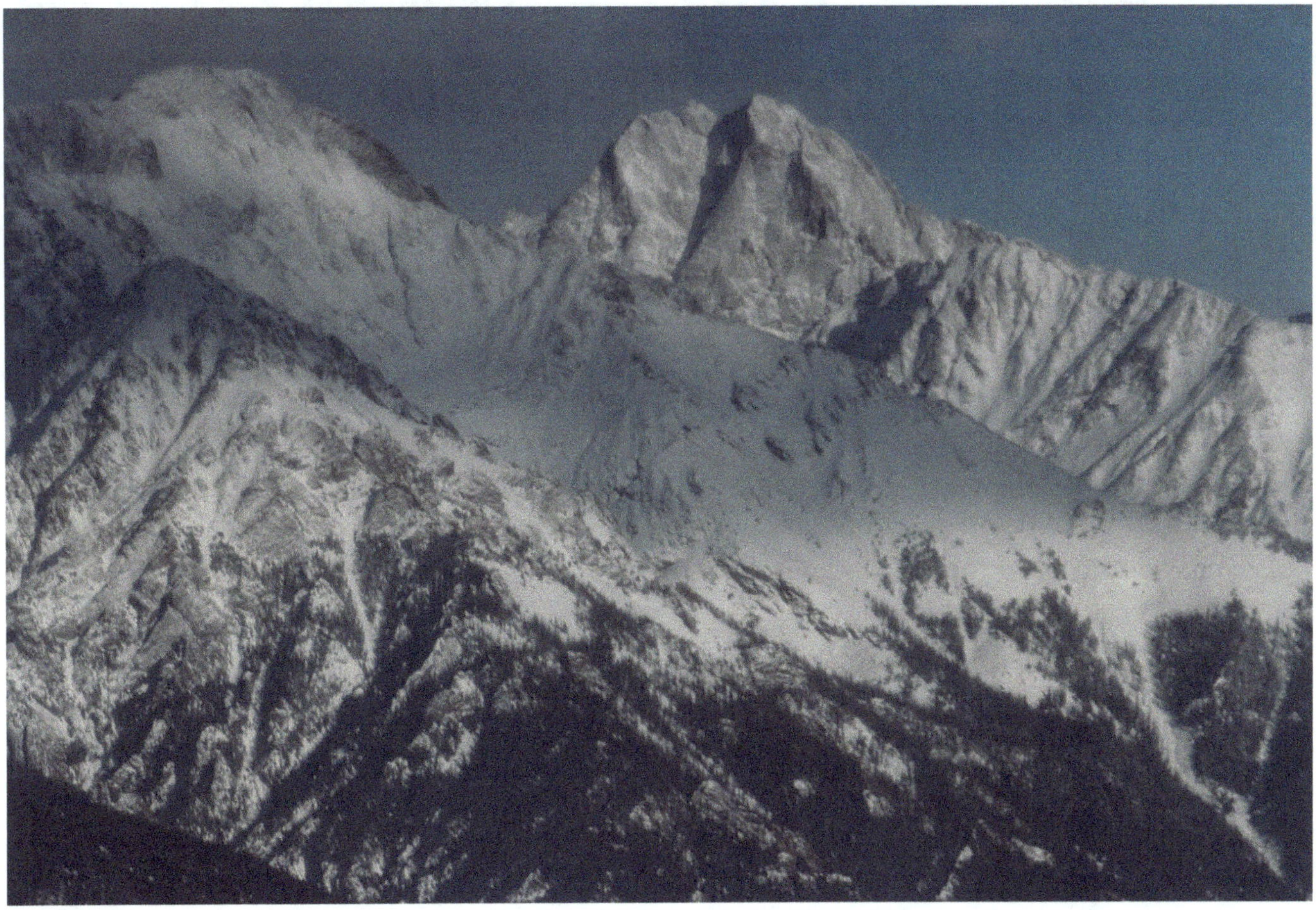

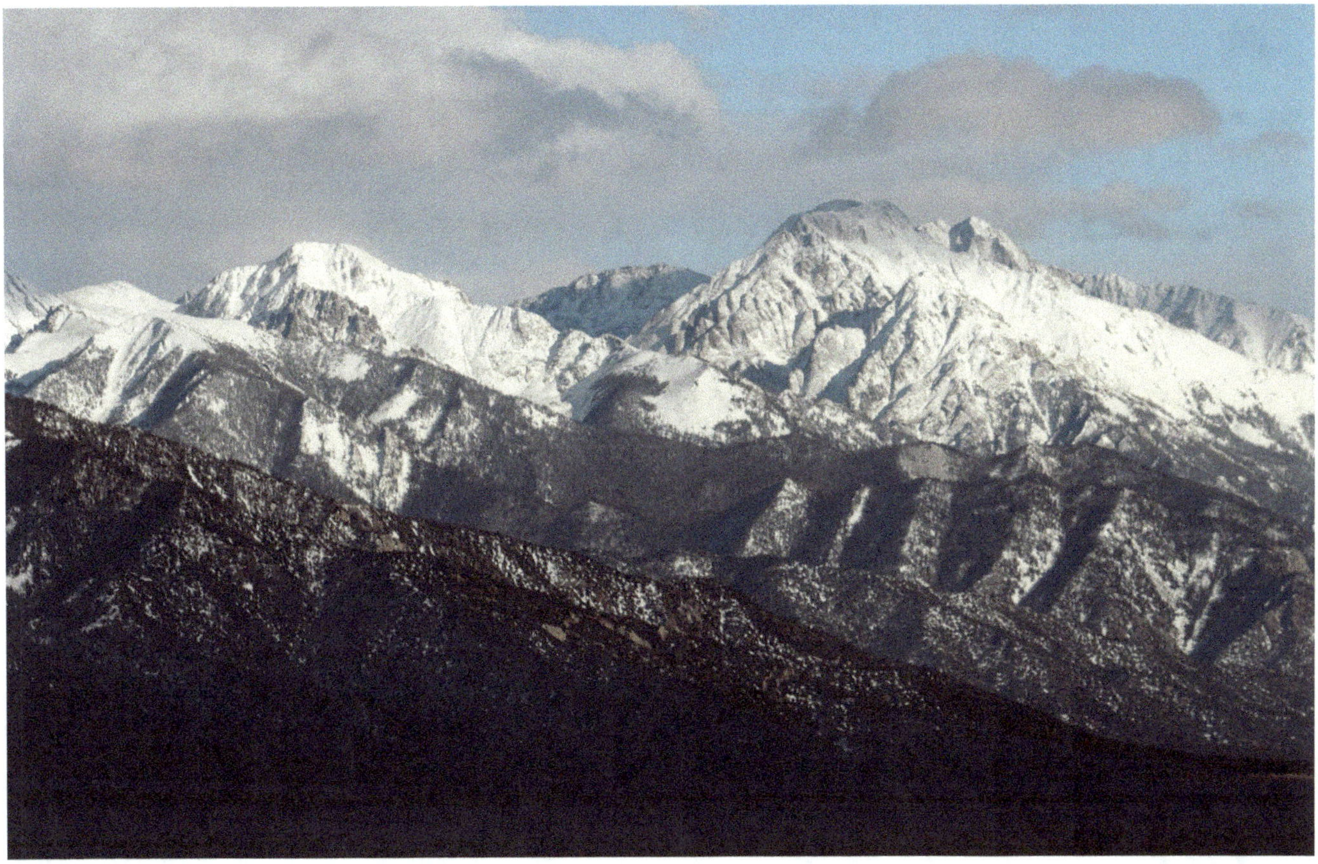

Final Thoughts

A couple things I didn't get around to mentioning, if you are going to be out in the cold for a long time it might be worth putting your extra batteries in a pocket next to your body. Extreme cold drains battery power quickly so it's beneficial to keep them as warm as possible.

I went into some detail describing how to protect your gear from the elements, but the danger doesn't end there. Condensation from warming your ice cold equipment too quickly can cause a lot of damage. It's best to put your cold camera inside it's cold case or pack before bringing it in. Leaving it in the pack for a while after it's indoors allows it to warm slowly and will help prevent condensation.

Also some advice for long treks, keep your water bottle in your pack as close to your body as possible. That little bit of extra warmth might keep it from freezing solid. Also sugar in your energy drink freezes at a lower temperature than plain water so keep that in mind when deciding what to put in your liquid bottles.

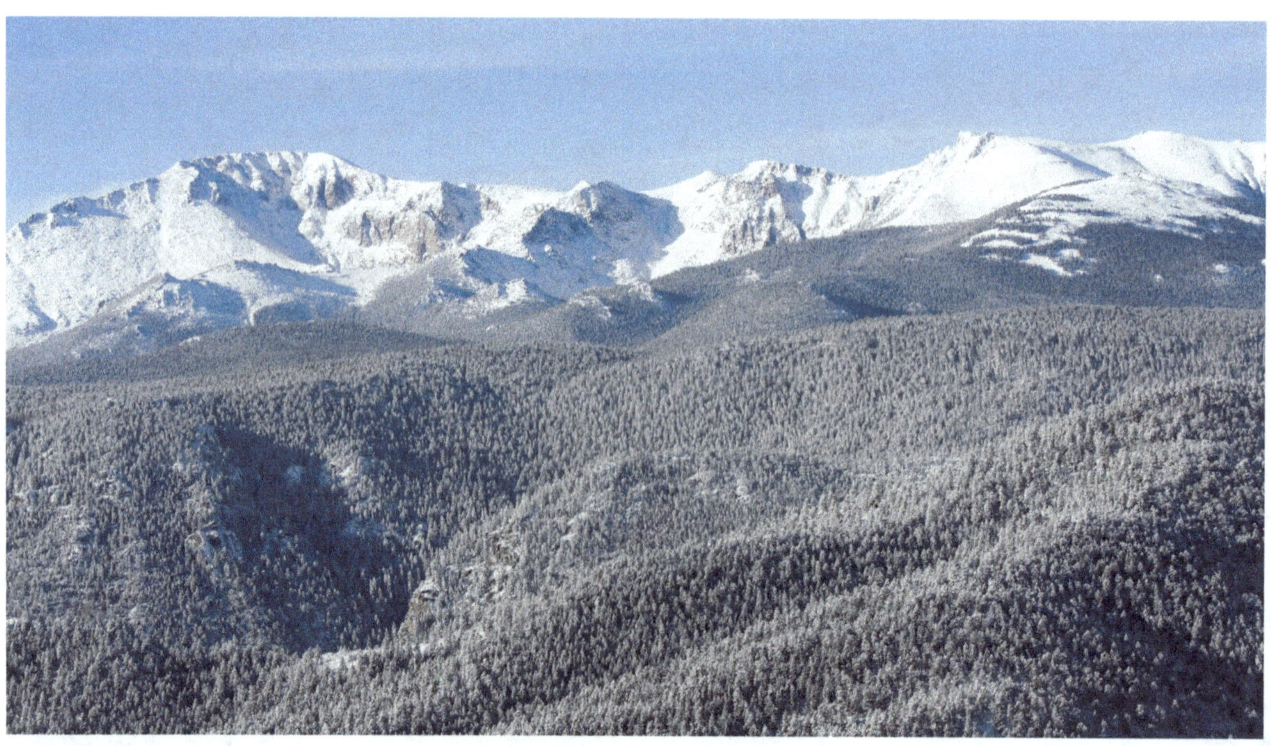

Epilogue

As another winter will soon be upon us I am getting excited about visiting the eagles in Eleven Mile Canyon and perhaps even further reaches of my beautiful state. Snowshoes and microspikes have been retrieved from summer storage and I'm eagerly anticipating the first measurable snow. I will continue to visit Little Grouse Mountain often, if only for the valuable exercise that the place affords.

However I don't want to just keep shooting the same scenes over and over so it's possible I won't be re-visiting any of the more northern sites described in this book anytime soon, choosing instead to stay local most of the time and writing in my blog while preparing for less frequent and more distant adventures.

Colorado voters have passed a resolution requiring Parks and Wildlife to reintroduce wolves to the western side of the state and it is my fervent hope to somehow be a part of that, if only as a photographer capturing the excitement of the development of the new pack. Wild horses are also on my mind as ranchers do their best to see them completely eliminated from public lands to make room for their livestock. Perhaps through my writing I can draw attention to their plight and help preserve such an important aspect of our western heritage.

Visiting Yellowstone in the winter is high on my priority list as is a visit to Glacier National Park perhaps resulting in enough material for a new book. In any case, I hope my readers find this publication useful and entertaining as I embark upon future adventures in unexplored regions of Colorado and the rest of the country!

Books by This Author

Wildlife Photography in the Colorado Rockies: Explore the great diversity of wildlife found in the Colorado Rocky Mountains. Learn where to find and how to photograph the birds and animals from the diminutive song sparrow to the mighty black bear.

Two Decades of Digital Photography: Twenty years of the author's favorite pictures and how they were made as camera technology has progressed through the years

Seasons of the Raptor: Four seasons of photography with Colorado's most beautiful raptors

The Blizzard and the Camera: Short story about photographing wildlife in severe weather

The Cinnamon Bears: Short story about photographing bears and the shot of a lifetime

Mountain Goats in the Sky: Short story about climbing a fourteener and photographing mountain goats

www.ingramcontent.com/pod-product-compliance
Lightning Source LLC
LaVergne TN
LVHW061248100826
845148LV00008B/1056

* 9 7 9 8 9 8 6 0 7 6 6 2 1 *